D1713662

Don Quixote and the
Poetics of the Novel

Also by Félix Martínez-Bonati:

*Fictive Discourse and the Structures of Literature:
A Phenomenological Approach*

Félix Martínez-Bonati

Don Quixote and the Poetics of the Novel

Translated by Dian Fox
in collaboration with the author

Cornell University Press

Ithaca and London

This book is published with the aid of a grant from the Program for Cultural Cooperation between Spain's Ministry of Culture and United States Universities.

First published 1992 by Cornell University Press.

International Standard Book Number 0-8014-2359-7
Library of Congress Catalog Card Number 92-5913
Printed in the United States of America
Librarians: Library of Congress cataloging information
appears on the last page of the book.

∞ The paper in this book meets the minimum requirements
of the American National Standard for Information Sciences—
Permanence of Paper for Printed Library Materials, ANSI Z39.48-1984.

Elisa Bonati Martini
(September 6, 1910–February 10, 1991)
In memoriam

Contents

Prologue

Proceed, strange inventor, proceed
with your subtle design . . .
> —*Mercury* (Hermes, the god of interpretation) to *Cervantes,*
> in Cervantes's *Journey to Parnassus* (1614)

Presumably it has always been realized that verbal utterances mean more than they plainly say, and that narratives contain significations that are not simply the events of the stories they tell. One finds reflections on the polysemy of discourse in classical, Jewish, and Christian hermeneutics of antiquity and systematically elaborated in medieval biblical studies. Renaissance and neoclassical poetics, as well as Romantic criticism, have their own concepts for the various types of meanings conveyed by literature, and twentieth-century thought has offered new views on the matter. Sigmund Freud, Carl Jung, Georg Lukács, and Claude Lévi-Strauss have inspired vast numbers of followers to explore the meanings of stories.

Northrop Frye suggests that the dimensions of literary meaning correspond, as Dante postulated, to the four levels of signification that medieval theologians found in the Scriptures.[1] I think that certain fundamental literary terms still widely used today indeed correlate with that fourfold system. Despite obvious differences, the literal, moral, allegorical, and anagogical meanings distinguished by Thomas Aquinas can be related to the mimetic, rhetorical, allegorical, and symbolic aspects of literary art.

Traditional hermeneutic concepts provide a preliminary ordering of the riddles of signification. Unless they are greatly transformed, however, they do not encompass the whole field of literary meaning. Besides, any of a work's dimensions of meaning can be ambiguous. Ambiguity and polysemy potentially inhere in the *objective* signification of a literary text. Furthermore, the historico-cultural and personal relativity of aesthetic reception must be added to the complexity of the realm we ordinarily designate as meaning in literature.

Novels have a mimetic dimension and therefore a referential significance, which usually rests on the typicality of their fictional events and characters. Also inherent in this literary genre is a rhetorical-didactic force. Occasionally novels have allegorical meaning, and they may even achieve symbolic splendor. They also possess more abstract, formal properties, including both generic and particular structures, such as plot lines and narratives techniques, styles, metafictional aspects, and intertextual relations. Finally, from an existential point of view, reading (and writing) a novel can be understood as a quest for an image of life that may be realistic or dreamlike, disquieting or comforting, a quest whose characteristics are determined by the horizon of a historical situation as well as by the condition of civilized existence in general.

Don Quixote cannot be rightly approached without a sense of these multiple dimensions. It is many things. It is the expression of a search for truth and redemption in an age of shaken religious faith, political pessimism, and renascent naturalistic thought. It is also a most complex work of literary art, rich in technical ingenuity, varied styles of imagination, metafictional and intertextual games, allegorical images, and enduring symbols. But it is not possible to study all of these aspects simultaneously. One has to choose a method if one is to obtain a reflective and conceptual knowledge of this novel.

In this book I attempt to describe the poetic design of *Don Quixote* against the historical background of prose fiction and its genres. I also propose an interpretation of its meanings. Design and interpretation are united by Cervantes in the lines that serve as an epigraph to this prologue. Descriptive discoveries with respect to design, as well as predescriptive perception of the aesthetic whole of the work, are the basis of interpretive argument. It is true that poetological description addresses only form, but design is signifying form. Poetic form is itself a signifier, the least obvious but the most decisive and, for interpretive endeavors, the most reliable of literary signifiers.

Here I can only begin to suggest why this is so. As the phenomenological school of criticism has assumed, the fundamental meaning of a work of fiction and art lies in the ideal consciousness that is shaped in it. A new frame of mind, an imaginary and artificial self, is adopted by the reader in the process of experiencing literature. It is through this medium of a consciousness transformed, however slightly, that a new image of the world can appear. Who do we become when we read

Don Quixote? What character does our sensibility, our intelligence, our notion of life around us assume? In this sense, description and interpretation seek out the "thought," or the world view, that the work conveys.

The forms highlighted by my study of the *Quixote* reveal themselves as the structure that sustains its vision. They shape a novelistic work that displays and at the same time questions, through various metafictional modes, the entire traditional literary culture of its time, and even questions literature as a universal element of civilized imagination. In doing so, it illuminates human experience in its deepest, transhistoric dimensions.

For reasons that have become widely accepted in the wake of psychoanalysis and structuralism, but that nevertheless I will consider more than once, the *Quixote*'s thought should not be taken to be the same as what Cervantes the man was capable of producing in either ordinary or unusual life situations outside of the act of creating the work. Clearly this assertion does not imply that there is no relation between his beliefs and his novelistic, theatrical, and lyrical writings. Common sense and experience tell us that works of the imagination are nourished by the conscious life and personal circumstances of their creators. But they are also nourished by other works of imagination, long-standing traditions, universal archetypes, and inscrutable oneiric sources.

Above all, poetic thought does not consist of one or more doctrines, endowed with definable concepts and systematic assertions, which the images of the work merely allegorize, even when the work does indeed have allegorical structures and meanings. As the Romantic tradition of aesthetics has shown, from Kant, Goethe, Schelling, the Schlegel brothers, Coleridge, Schopenhauer, Carlyle, Emerson, Baudelaire, and Nietzsche to Heidegger and many of our contemporaries, concepts never exhaust the wealth of significant traits and suggestions embodied in the artistic image. The image can be a symbol of limitless meaning. The major works give us images of life (selected, embellished, reduced, transformed) that place us in a situation that is new for us in terms of feeling and thinking. From this experience emerges the possibility of a vision of the world that is not our own, liberating us momentarily from our habitual certainties. Thus the recreative imagination can be an exercise in freedom. Readers of fiction are in that state of supreme paradox in which one becomes absorbed in the inwardness of one's own subjectivity by assuming another's mind and imaginings. But this paradox is also the creative experience of writers, who do not limit themselves to reproducing figures they already know. Rather, as Socrates explained to Ion, they subject themselves to forces whose logic they cannot control (although they can always accept or reject the results).

In a work of the magnitude of the *Quixote,* the revealing impulse of the imagination goes not only beyond views consistent with the theological and philosophical doctrines of the era but also beyond what Cervantes himself could have conceptualized. Consequently, it can be said, in a particular and precise sense, that the thought of the *Quixote* is not the thought of Cervantes. Accordingly, many keen interpretations of his work attribute to it truths that, being inconceivable in the sixteenth or the seventeenth century, seem anachronistic, implausible anticipations of recent ideas; Américo Castro, for instance, projects onto the figure of Don Quixote an anthropological conception akin to the existentialist and Orteguian view of personal identity.[2]

Certainly, one frequently finds inappropriate interpretations of the *Quixote,* which quickly diminish rather than enhance our experience of the work. The richness of this novelistic world allows ample room for arbitrary exegesis. Hence all the greater need for the interpreter to rely on careful descriptions.

These chapters on the *Quixote* develop two critical observations that I believe to be well supported by the evidence but that may have the ring of paradox to many ears. First, this novel never creates a realistic image of life, though from the beginning it explicitly and implicitly suggests the ideal of a truthful imagination, and though the intense and transcendent evocation of the sense of reality is one of its essential significations. The text simply does not permit a realistic construction of its figures and events.

Second, the style of Cervantes's imagination (in this even more than in his other works) is discontinuous, irregular, and almost always intrinsically adulterated, impure. In the *Quixote* we do not find a single, homogeneous fictitious world; we find a conglomeration of stories ruled by diverse and sometimes incompatible laws of stylization. The numerous actions of the work not only lack a unified plot that contains them all but reside in a variety of regions of the literary imagination; they embody diverse poetic cosmologies. Moreover, with only one exception, they are not consistently faithful to the laws of stylization on which they are based. Instead, they distort those laws.

The imaginary universe of the *Quixote* is also not completely "hermetic." I use Ortega's term. In this regard, however, I am contradicting what he says about the *Quixote* in his *Ideas sobre la novela*.[3] The illusion aimed at by writers and readers of romances and novels of the classic types, the reader's absorption in the imagined "reality," is shattered in several ways in the *Quixote*, especially by Cervantes's recurrent ironization of his characters and plots, which reminds the reader of their occasional inverisimilitude and the fact that they are merely literature.

An attempt to read the *Quixote* with expectations of a realistic imagination, a consistent, unifying style, and a hermetic closure will lead readers to find striking deficiencies in the work (which should move them to shift their interpretive tack). Traces of such disappointments abound in commentaries written at the turn of the twentieth century. They can even be found in current commentary. That kind of reading experience typically results in interpretations that try to reconcile the greatness of the work with its notorious "defects." Thus Cervantes is excused as an undisciplined genius, and the inconsistencies of the work are taken to be minor lapses or whims that do not diminish the truth of its characters.

The German Romantics, who offered many important insights into the *Quixote,* naturally faced the same textual elements, but they welcomed them with a spirit open to unrealistic imagination, irregularity of style and composition, and ironic gestures. Nevertheless, the Romantic interpretation also raises expectations that the text of the *Quixote* does not meet. Anyone who tries to find an image of heroic sublimity in the protagonist and unconditional validity in his chivalric mission adopts a course of reading that collides with the objective characteristics of the work. Understandably, the most outrageous and consistent representative of this interpretive school, Miguel de Unamuno, would alter and correct Cervantes's text.[4]

All the same, the *readings* given *Don Quixote* by this or that generation, and by all of us across the centuries, *as experiences of novelistic enjoyment,* probably do not vary much. In its essential traits, the text is sufficiently redundant (in information theory's sense of the term), and the figurations that it directs the reader to construct are superlatively clear and strong. The various elements in the text that hinder both a realistic reading and one that results in the romantic idealization of the protagonist cannot be overlooked. (At most they fade under the influence of selective attention and memory.)

It is an undeniable feature of the experience of art that creations of other ages are as capable as contemporary ones of eliciting our full imaginative and emotional response. Our certainty that we have understood the work is part of such a response; on those occasions, we believe that we are in possession of the experience offered by the author; we cannot doubt that communication has taken place. Thus, when we read the *Quixote* successfully, we feel that we are united with readers of other generations and with Cervantes in a community of imagination, thought, and sensibility. We take it for granted that the work we have read is a common and enduring property, an intersubjective and stable entity (not an unrepeatable confluence of historical, social, and personal circumstances that happen to be our own just at the moment and, mysteriously, happen to make sense together).

There are good reasons for postulating the objective truth of these unmeditated, habitual aesthetic assumptions. It is telling that today these reasons have to be reasserted. The current strength of skeptical relativism makes the repetition of certain elementary presumptions not entirely superfluous. The following ones are among the basic assumptions of this book.

Meaningful exchanges about a given work presume the objective identity of that work; that is, that the speakers are referring to the same thing. Literary conversation with contemporaries, agreement or dissent with critics of old would be impossible, or mere delusions, if our assumption of the existence of an object held in common by all subjects involved were not valid. The force of these analytical assertions is not diminished by reflections on the fragility, insubstantiality, and fleetingness of the aesthetic experience.

Certain motifs of Jacques Derrida's thought come to mind here. I will suggest a nonskeptical version of them. A literary work is experienced in a series of stretches of time. Therefore, it is never originally, directly present as a whole. When we are reading a passage, we remember the parts we read before, and we are continuously integrating the images of memory with those of the (somewhat extended) present instant into a growing totality. At the end of our reading, we possess the whole, but only as a recent and already evanescent memory that still vibrates in our sensibility. This is the way literature exists. The work, then, has a peculiar way of standing as a totality in our consciousness. Nonetheless, we share this entity with others who have gone through a similar experience. We can evoke the object in conversation by naming its title, and we can all assure ourselves of its identity by synthetic descriptions of the total experience of it. We may characterize the experience of the *Quixote* as, say, one of multifarious, even contradictory images of life and a humor that is fundamentally serene but that occasionally takes on a sarcastic or triumphant tone. For those who have read the book successfully, such vague references are quite meaningful. Any appropriate "impressionistic" characterization of the book revives the readers' memory of the complex whole of world, mind, and language that is given in the aesthetic experience. One could not judge such descriptions to be fitting or wrong if they did not point to an intersubjective referent, the common content of the readings. The aesthetically experienced whole is the necessary foundation and the basic common referent of all critical reflection, whether casual talk or scholarly commentary.

However, scholarly critical appraisals and interpretations of the *Quixote,* as of all works, are something other than aesthetic reception or impressionistic, synthetic characterization. To see commentaries and studies as direct and faithful manifestations of the critic's primary reading of the work seems to me theoretically wrong and methodologically misleading. Any interpretation that may be formulated will always be a doctrinal transformation of the experience of reading. The prejudices, unconscious assumptions, intellectual traditions, critical vogues, and ideological inclinations of the times all affect the image of the work much more in critical discourse than in reading for the sheer experience and joy of literature. The historical relativity of straightforward reading is truly minor in comparison with the epochal constraints of conceptualized criticism and interpretation. Critical expression necessarily takes into account only certain aspects of the totality experienced in the reading, those features that respond to the ideological or theoretical interest of the critic. The cost of theoretical reflection, intellectual distance, and conceptual command of the material is always loss of the integrity of the experienced work. A history of the documented interpretations of the work cannot, then, be the same as a history of its conjecturable receptions, customary modes of consumption, or readings. The relationship between commentary and primary reading is undeniable and basic but very complex. Thus, to postulate that successful, satisfying readings of the *Quixote* are always essentially the same is not inconsistent with acceptance of the personal and historical variety of its interpretations. To the extent that these interpretations are objectively valid, they can be seen as partial and complementary truths. What everyone experiences equally as a reader cannot be critically objectified in its totality. Each era, with its peculiar arsenal of aesthetic concepts, has its own possibilities of explication.

While reading, we always also perceive unthematically and vaguely things that only a corresponding theory can bring to light. I believe that today, armed with the teachings of phenomenology, stylistics, the New Criticism, and structuralism, and with the suggestions that derive from deconstructive practices, it is possible for us to give considerable precision to the description of some of the aspects of the *Quixote* that moved Friedrich Schlegel and others of his circle to declare it the supreme paradigm of the "ironic" and "Romantic" work. In this book I intend to show that if readers look closely, these properties of the novel have always been present in their readings, as they were in those of the Romantics, and no less so in the original design of Cervantes, as the text makes evident.

Nevertheless, many signs indicate that there are some personal and temporal variations in reading (and we even have direct evidence of that in our own rereadings of works that have left their traces on our memories), although they may be at times only minor inflections of attention and resonance. There is also the influence of explicit interpretations on new readings. If the reading is not flexible and open to the particular game of the text, and if criticism is insufficiently conscious of its own biases, we get readings that are not just individually nuanced but disoriented and infelicitous, and theoretical interpretations that are not only incomplete but erroneous. If readers meticulously follow the game proposed by the text, they give the work the greatest and most appropriate measure of freedom of play, and in doing so they learn to read it. Similarly, critics ought to search for the objective foundation of their interpretations in those deliberately and methodically partial, abstract observations that we call descriptions. The greater the work that goes into the description (of plot lines, typical forms, recurring motifs, generic structures, characteristics of style, etc.), the more solid the basis of summarizing interpretation and the more certainly mistaken prejudices can be discarded to permit a more auspicious rereading.

Obviously, messages first have to be understood in accordance with the codes chosen by their senders. Other "codes" or interpretive approaches can then be applied to the decoded message, and thus secondary interpretations are generated—interpretations responding to such questions as: What is behind the message? What are its tacit

presuppositions, its ideological implications? What are the uncon-
fessed intentions, what are the unconscious desires of its sender? What
general hypotheses does it confirm or suggest? What prospects of
action does it open up? In principle, even if we leave aside false,
aberrant interpretations, the potential series of derivative ones is endless. (They should be thought of, however, not as a chaotic collection
but as an extremely complex systematic construction.) But such supplementary approaches would have nothing to go on if the primary
meaning had not first been established. Analogously, although a poetic work is not strictly a message, a literary text is meaningful by virtue
of a particular language in a particular historical stage of its development. Besides, there are additional "codes" that contribute to the
basic meaning of a literary text, such as the common knowledge and
values of its intended public and the literary culture of the time, with
its own conventions and expectations. Thus the codes that are pertinent for the simple reading of a given literary text are established by
the cultural-historical circumstances of its original production. It has
been a leading hypothesis in literary studies (and a subconscious assumption of all readers of texts of the past and of cultures not their
own) that languages of other times and cultures can be reconstructed,
and that their texts can be understood as they were meant to be. The
difficulty of this task and the impossibility of doing it perfectly do not
make it less worthwhile and necessary. Literary works must be presumed to have a transhistoric identity. Indeed, that is the only identity
they can have.

When the assumptions that held at the time a given work was
produced (that is, the relevant linguistic, literary, and cultural codes)
and the totality of its text come together in a reading that makes fairly
complete sense, only then does that literary work actually exist. Since
the pertinent codes and the text itself are definitive, unvarying conditions, the result of their interplay, if it is at all meaningful, must be
definitive too, and the same whenever the work is read well. An
alternative concept postulates that a work may be brought into being
that is different from the one established by the original codes but that
still meaningfully encompasses the whole text. This is an illusory
speculation, however (as Borges's "Pierre Menard, autor del *Quijote*"
rightly suggests with the failure of its protagonist's lifelong interpretive enterprise).[5]

It follows that different secondary interpretations of a work cannot
be both true and incompatible with each other. I thus urge readers

who may inadvertently have surrendered to them to question the relativist and subjectivist positions so commonly found among critics.[6]

In this book I have tried to achieve an unencumbered description of *Don Quixote*, without excluding those characteristics of the work that one tends to disregard (because the admirer, under the influence of aesthetic ideals that are not relevant to this novel, sees them as detrimental to the formal perfection of art and to the truth of the literary representation of life). Among these characteristics are the inverisimilar aspects of the characters and the action, the irregularities of style and composition, and the infractions of novelistic closure. It seems necessary to me to view these things, like the other properties of the *Quixote*, in a positive light, as essential parts of an artistic design, a stylistic will, a poetic truth. From the description of its form an interpretation of its meanings follows, and above all a clearer intuition of the cognitive and ethical intent of the work, as well as a more precise circumscription of the conceptual space in which definitions of these symbolic dimensions can be attempted.

A careful description of the various aspects of the work shows what sensitive readers already intuit, although as critics they may still be unaware of it: the *Quixote* cannot be understood as the prototype of the modern realistic novel. The opinion that it is the first modern novel persists even today in much of the best Cervantes criticism, and it comes invested with great traditional authority: Menéndez y Pelayo, Ortega y Gasset, Dickens, Flaubert, and Tolstoy embrace it. It suffers from the doctrinal burden not only of realism and modernism but equally, despite its different poetology, of Romanticism.[7] The *Quixote* is a creature of another sort; its form is more complicated than the form of the modern novel. It is literally a work sui generis, whose structure therefore seems to me all the more worthy of admiration and study.

The stylistic incompatibility of its several imaginary regions and the violations of form in the work naturally lead to questions about its problematic unity and its genre. The frustration of the realistic impulse and of mimetic truth raises the question of its allegorical and symbolic truths. How, without a realistic image, can the work refer to the corruption and beauty of the real world? The first chapter of this book is devoted principally to a study of the discontinuities of the style of imagination in the *Quixote* and to a critique of the thesis of its alleged realism; the second, to the problem of its artistic unity; the third, to the question of its genre; the fourth, to that of its doctrine and truth. The fifth reviews the points made earlier and explores the relation between reality and literature with respect to this novel.

Since 1974 I have been presenting parts of this book in lectures and articles. The Introduction and Chapter 1 constitute a new version—greatly expanded and corrected—of "Cervantes y las regiones de la imaginación," a lecture I gave, at the invitation of Alberto J. Carlos, in March 1974 at the State University of New York, Albany, then published in *Dispositio*, 2, no. 4 (Winter 1977): 28–53, and in a French translation by Denyse Pouliot, Georges A. Parent, and Jean-Claude Simard, in *Études littéraires*, 8, nos. 2–3 (1975): 303–43. Chapter 2 has developed from "La unidad del *Quijote*," a lecture given at the Casa Hispánica of Columbia University in March 1976 and published in *Dispositio*, 2, nos. 5–6 (Summer–Autumn 1977): 118–38, and in an anthology edited by George Haley, *El Quijote* (Madrid, 1984), pp. 349–72. Chapters 3 and 4 are elaborations of ideas sketched in my essay "El *Quijote*: Juego y significación," *Dispositio*, 3, no. 9 (Autumn 1978): 315–36. I am grateful for the permission granted by the publishers of *Dispositio* to use these materials. These and other articles thematically and methodologically related to this book[8] resulted in dialogues with various Hispanists and Cervantists, whose kind attention has moved me to complete the project. Over many years my obligations of gratitude within the academic community have grown to considerable proportions. The largest is the one I owe to my late teachers of Spanish literature, Antonio Doddis and Juan Uribe-Echevarría. I also thank Francisco Ayala, Gonzalo Sobejano, Philip Silver, Francisco Rico, John J. Allen, Ruth El Saffar, Juan Bautista Avalle-Arce, Richard Bjornson, Antonio Gómez Moriana, George Haley, Alan Trueblood, Joseph Szertics, Mario J. Valdés, José María Pozuelo Yvancos, Leda Schiavo, Pedro Lastra, Patricia Grieve, Ignacio Soldevila, Graciela Reyes, and Diana de Armas Wilson for their interest in my work and their suggestions. Although a few of those suggestions were offered quite some time ago, I have not forgotten. I owe no less recognition to my colleagues of *Dispositio*, Cedomil Goic and Walter Mignolo; also to my colleagues and students at Columbia University, the University of Illinois at Chicago, and the University of Iowa, where I began these studies. Dian Fox, whose scholarly work with Golden Age texts I greatly admire, has generously undertaken the English translation of this book. Susan Fenwick has given me invaluable advice. Cornell University Press's Bernhard Kendler has been a patient and careful helper. I thank them most cordially. Finally, I am grateful to the Alexander von Humboldt Foundation for the support granted to me in a critical period of my work.

FÉLIX MARTÍNEZ-BONATI

New York City

Don Quixote and the
Poetics of the Novel

Questions and Points
of Confusion

Now, for the poet, he nothing affirms and therefore never lieth.
—Sir Philip Sidney,
An Apology for Poetry (1595)

Some Persistent Issues in Cervantes Studies

The Aims of Criticism and Don Quixote. The elementary and, in a
sense, natural aim of literary studies is to learn to read, and to help
others to read, selected texts in such a way that the works are accu-
rately and completely recreated and thus their significance is experienced. Without a measure of success in this task, our attempts to gain
any systematic or speculative knowledge of literature and its circumstances would lack their specific subject matter and foundation. The
classic philological and poetological disciplines, while they have their
own cognitive purposes that justify them independently as intellectual
enterprises, present us with information that can be used to establish
the identity not only of the text and its basic codes but also of that
more elusive entity, the poem, which paradoxically is imaginary and
at the same time objective and historical. It is plain that the felicitous
reading of the poem does not necessarily presuppose a formal reflexive
effort, still less a methodical study sustained by institutionalized disciplines. The life of art is nourished by a partly subconscious tradition
of contemplative habits, concrete models, diffuse knowledge, and enthusiastic conviviality. But when such traditions are multiple, as they
are in our civilization, which itself is pluralistic and open besides to
works of the past and to expressions of alien lifeworlds, access to the
aesthetic experience of works of art often requires something more
than spontaneous sensibility. The habitual intuitive disposition that,

in the process of entertaining ourselves, we have learned effortlessly since childhood often must seek support from attempts at conceptual formulation of the meanings of symbols, and above all from observations, ratiocinations, and hypotheses about the functional design of the poem whose being we want to actualize. Thus criticism serves reading. Philological and historical research recovers for the reader the referential meaning of words and allusions. Stylistic analysis sensitizes our perception of the verbal texture, the tones, and the semantic echoes of the words. Paraphrases explaining the nature of persons and actions refine our understanding of the fictional events. And structural schemes help us project the formal anticipations that our imagination must follow, as if without seeing them, to construct the characters, scenes, and landscapes of its interior replication of the world. Critical studies can provide guidelines (though no more than guidelines) for successful reading.[1]

Has the imposing tradition of critical studies on Cervantes (like those on Góngora's poetry, for example) yielded a basic consensus on how to read his work? Do we have a canonical "reading" or, put less equivocally, a standard interpretation of the *Quixote?*[2] Do we have a coherent ensemble of complementary studies that can provide a convincing and comprehensive view of this work? I think not. And not because of any scarcity of admirable studies of numerous aspects of the work, or of inspired elucidations of its meaning. The magnitude and complexity of the subject is generally considered to be the main reason that we still have no exegesis that is both comprehensive and capable of eliciting general assent. But another obstacle is the confusion that reigns over the ends and means of the study of literature.

Thanks to the historical-philological work that culminated in Francisco Rodríguez Marín's and Rodolfo Schevill and Adolfo Bonilla's editions of the *Quixote* in the first half of the twentieth century and that has continued to advance the critical establishment of the text, the clarification of its vocabulary, its grammar, and its allusions, we have a basic body of directions for its reading.[3] For stylistic aspects and the characterization of Cervantes's language, we have the contributions of Helmut Hatzfeld, Leo Spitzer, Enrique Moreno Báez, Dámaso Alonso, Angel Rosenblat, Howard Mancing, and others who have begun to reveal the various metamorphoses that the diction undergoes throughout the text and the multiple verbal texture of the work.[4] Also at our disposal are observations on its architecture (by Moreno Báez, Knud Togeby, Edmund de Chasca, Joaquín Casalduero, Edward Dudley,

J. B. Avalle-Arce, E. C. Riley, Cesare Segre, John J. Allen, Howard Mancing), although in general these works focus on limited aspects of the novel's composition.[5] And certainly more direct, sometimes un-sophisticated manifestations of criticism are not lacking: those that (justifiably to a point) deal with imaginary objects as exemplars of the corresponding classes of real objects, and consequently discuss the psychology of the persons, the geography of their travels, the so-ciology of their relationships, the historiography of their secular hori-zon, and the philosophical-moral evaluation of their actions.

But the variety of respectable interpretations of the literary form and the signification of this work is undeniably excessive, an indica-tion of a confusing disparity among fundamental approaches.[6] This disarray is immediately conspicuous when one considers the assorted positions assigned to Cervantes's work in the traditional scheme of the historical sequence of artistic and literary movements. Some writers (among them Ludwig Pfandl, Jean Cassou, and Stephen Gilman, the latter in his study of Cervantes and Avellaneda) situate it in the final, mature years of the Renaissance; many others, such as Casalduero and Hatzfeld, in the heart of the "Jesuit Baroque"; and there are those (such as Knud Togeby, and not without some justification, as I will indicate in due course) who see in the Second Part of the *Quixote* the inauguration of Classicism, after the Baroque of the First Part.[7] This is not a typical quarrel, like those in which a work is moved across one of the conventional historiographic boundaries. Therefore, it is not enough to indicate in this case that the venerable period concepts are imprecise, that "Renaissance" is not purely a stylistic notion, and that, following José Camón Aznar, we must consider Mannerist tenden-cies.[8] Here a more elemental uncertainty with respect to the charac-teristics and nature of the work to be classified seems to be added to the vagueness of the categories.[9]

The perplexity is still greater, as we know, in regard to what is usually called Cervantes's "thought." The disparity among conjectures concerning his religious, philosophical, political, and moral convic-tions, even his aesthetic ideals and critical principles, is extraordinary. Confining ourselves only to twentieth-century commentaries, we find the thesis, maintained by Hatzfeld, Casalduero, Moreno Báez, Cesare de Lollis, and Paul Descouzis, of a "Counterreformist" ("reactionary," says Lollis) Cervantes, entirely in accord with the spirit of Trent and Spain's struggle for Catholic hegemony.[10] On the other side, we have Américo Castro's first thesis, in *El pensamiento de Cervantes*, that of the "skillful hypocrite" Cervantes, inspired by the humanist and Neo-platonic philosophy of the Italian Renaissance and by Erasmism, and forced to dissimulate for fear of the Inquisition; and later the shifting of Castro's emphasis toward the circumstance of Hispanic castes and the supposed condition of the surgeon Rodrigo de Cervantes's family as "New Christians." Some critics conceive of Cervantes as a "utopian socialist"; others see him as a critic of the remnants of feudal ideology, and as a liberal and "progressive" spirit. These examples suffice to demonstrate the absence of agreement in conceptions of Cervantes's intellectual identity—quite striking in view of his longstanding eminence.

Aesthetic interpretations of Cervantes's masterwork, whose lack of a basic normative consensus I indicated, are equally at odds. The *Quixote* is praised for its realism and for its symbolism, as a comic parable and as a tragedy of idealism, as a picture of the society of the period and as an allegory of the human condition. Unamuno sees a heroic myth where Heine saw a satire against enthusiasm.[11] Is it the first modern novel or is it the sum and final manifestation of the prehistory of the novel?[12]

Moreover, Hispanic pride hampers critical efforts, for traditionally this work is seen as the highest expression of Spanish spiritual identity. That view leads to the association of the *Quixote* with supreme values, and naturally also with doctrinaire postures: Heroism, Idealism, and the Faith, the Homeland, Goodness, Justice, Truth, Liberty, and Progress. As a result, the work is praised for qualities it shares with many others, or possesses only to a small degree, or does not possess at all.[13]

The truth is not only that we do not have a canonical reading of the Cervantine texts. We lack an explicit system of hermeneutic principles that would permit it to be initiated and carried out. It is difficult to know where to begin, how to order the proliferation of interpretations and bring them to a less equivocal terrain of dialogue and verification.[14]

Realism, "True History," and Aristotle. To make way for my subjects, I must first consider some very generalized points of confusion that obstruct the correct understanding of the Cervantine text. They have to do with "realism," literary parody and satire, and the work's "philosophy."

What critical commonplace has been repeated more often than the assertion of the *Quixote*'s "stupendous realism"? It is true that many Cervantes studies question such a characterization. Distinctions have been drawn between the Golden Age's "verisimilitude" and the "realism" of the nineteenth and twentieth centuries. But the analysis of these concepts, which will prove useful for understanding the nature of the novelistic world of the *Quixote,* has been precarious. As a consequence, this novel is considered in relation to aesthetic ideals (such as the realism of the image of life) that are not its own, and that therefore wrongly make the work appear highly defective and hinder the reader's grasp of its most splendid games of irony. Certainly the *Quixote* is a very profound image of life, and for that reason it is rightly known as *true,* but its image of life is not a *realistic* one. (The analysis of this matter will occupy us to a considerable extent.)

This and other points of confusion about the mode and nature of the relationship of the Cervantine work to reality persist. The attacks voiced in the *Quixote* on the "lying histories" of the chivalric romances and the narrator's repeated assertion that this is a "true history" are taken literally as serious statements of Cervantes's. Américo Castro, following Giuseppe Toffanin, goes as far as to project into this expression ("true history") the Aristotelian concept of historical truth, the truth of the "particular," as opposed to the "universal" or ideal truth of poetry. Despite Angel Sánchez Rivero's early and clear refutation, Castro's judgment has continued to recur in Cervantes criticism.[15]

What Aristotle does in his *Poetics* is to contrast the nature of the historical work—that is, of historiography—with *every* kind of poetic creation, whether the people represented are superior, equal, or inferior to the audience, and whether or not the modality of its representation is idealizing (like that of painters who show men "better than they are"). A work such as the *Quixote* cannot be considered "historical" (that is, endowed with the "particular" truth of a record of real events) in the Aristotelian sense or in any other. The fact that in Cervantes's times a book like his is called an *historia* can be related, and indeed has been related, to a linguistic circumstance: that there was no word for what we today call *novela* (novel). The word *romance,* as the name of a literary genre in Spanish, ordinarily designated, and still designates, the traditional ballads, and *novela* designated a literary narration of limited length, as its cognates still do in Italian and various other European languages. The linguistic deficiency, however, does not signal a lack of conceptual discernment, and it would be unwarranted to suppose that the authors of that time (or of any time) did not know the difference between a work of fiction and an account of events that really happened. (What occasionally may not be known, as in the case of the living myths of a community, is whether a given text belongs to one category or the other, wholly or in part.) At one point the *Quixote*'s narrator himself calls his own an "imagined history" (I.22). The opposite term is also found in the *Quixote*—that is, "true history" as applied to the authentic historiographic narration—on the lips of the Priest (I.32) and of Don Quixote himself (II.58). As an example not extraneous to the subject matter, in the Prologue of the *Amadís de Gaula,* Garci Rodríguez de Montalvo confidently distinguishes the imaginary creation (a relation of "feigned things" or "hoaxes") from the historiographic narration (a "chronicle"). It can be noted also that a contemporary of Cervantes, Mateo Alemán, speaks of his own fictional work as a "poetic history," and, in the "Prologue to the Reader" of his Second Part, even condemns the inclusion of names of contemporary historic figures in "fabulous histories."[16]

In his neo-Aristotelian treatise Alonso López, el Pinciano, another contemporary of Cervantes, leaves no doubt about the essential opposition between historiography and "imitation." Nor do the numerous Italian theorists of the sixteenth century (among them Lodovico Castelvetro, Filippo Sassetti, Vincenzo Borghini, Orazio Ariosto, and Alessandro Piccolomini).[17]

Further sources of confusion are the traditional use of the word *historia* in Spanish to designate the content or object of all narrative forms, and especially the conventional literary play with the word and concept of *historia* as a pretended historiographic text, a play deriving from the basic literary fiction that what is set before the reader is a real and "true" narrative discourse. In the literary tradition in which Cervantes situates himself, this leads to the parodical posture of "historian" assumed by the fictional narrator. Already the chivalric romances pretend to be "histories" and "chronicles." Moreover, Lucian's *True History* was a well-known work in Cervantes's time.[18]

In Aristotle's *Poetics* we find fundamental distinctions for analyzing the notion of "realism," and also for determining the diversity of imaginative style that is exemplified in the opposition between the *Quixote* and books of chivalry.[19] But there we are dealing not at all with the distinction between the particular truth of history and the universal truth of poetry, but precisely with styles.

Toffanin, in support of his thesis, cites, among others, the passage in the *Quixote* (II.3) in which Don Quixote, Sancho, and Sansón Carrasco converse about the "history" of the pair's exploits already in print. Here Sansón reiterates the doctrine of the difference between history and poetry:

> ". . . some who have read your history say that they would have been glad if the author had omitted some of the countless drubbings that Don Quixote met with in his various encounters."
>
> "Ah! There's where the truth of the history comes in," rejoined Sancho.
>
> "Yet, they might in all fairness have kept quiet about them," said Don Quixote, "for there is no point in writing about actions that do not change or affect the truth of the history, if they tend to diminish the stature of the hero. Aeneas, I am sure, was not as pious as Virgil made him out to be, nor Ulysses as prudent as he is described in Homer."
>
> "That is true," replied Sansón, "but it is one thing to write as a poet, and another as an historian. The poet can tell or sing of things, not as they were, but as they should have been; and the historian must write them, not as they should have been but as they were, without adding to or subtracting from the truth."[20]

The Bachiller's remarks seem to indicate that the *Quixote* indulges in no poetic idealizations, and so is history.

This passage, however, is a superlatively ironic game, in which Cervantes, to all appearances deliberately, confuses diverse issues. Don Quixote's words imply that Homer and Virgil are historians, while Sansón supposes them to be poets. It is also worth observing that Don Quixote is not wrong, in that the historian too has some latitude in regard to the degree of stylization with which he presents persons and events, in the favorable or unfavorable aspects he chooses to emphasize. In denying this latitude, Sansón imparts a comically pedestrian sense to the formula of the veracity of History, with the result that the published history of Don Quixote is nonidealizing and antiheroic because it is true history, not invention. Are we going to accept this thesis to explain the genesis of the work's style?

Let us specify the meaning of Aristotle's assertion that the poet, not bound by the limitations of the historian and allowed to invent or transform the images of persons and actions, can give these images a universal or ideal character. We can distinguish three lines of argument in this complex notion. First, the poet can construct his figures and events in such a way that they are transparent incarnations of universal human types and laws of human action; that is, he can make them verisimilar *imitations* of (the essential forms of) nature, whence they assume some philosophical relevance (*Poetics*, IX). Second, he can select as the subject of the work either exclusively the good (in the sense of superior personal virtue) and exemplary (the characteristic subjects of the epic and tragic genres) or exclusively the ordinary and inferior (peculiar to comedy) (*Poetics*, II). Third, he can surpass the highest excellence of nature and depict beautiful beings that are partly unreal (in the epic and tragedy); or, in the other direction, accentuate ridiculous ugliness to the point of caricature (in comedy) (*Poetics*, XV.8, XXV.6). The historian, like the portrait painter, can do these things to some extent, but only within very narrow limits, because his essential aim of creditably telling the concrete truth of what has really happened obliges him to accept sequences of acts whose causes are not intelligible, as well as various personalities who occasionally lack a distinct and clear ethical profile and show attributes that are not edifying but also are not comic. He must, for example, faithfully recount "what Alcibiades did or suffered" (IX, 1451b); in the truth of these singular propositions consists "the *particular* truth of History."[21]

We can thus reformulate this Aristotelian conception: the imperative of "the particular truth" impedes the formation of images endowed with a definite *style*. (In this context I am referring to generic styles.) History therefore seems to constitute systematically a manner of representation that is devoid of style and displays the formless variety of ordinary experience. And, as a consequence, historiographic narration seems to present the paradigm of the realistic non-style, and thus to oppose, as a poetic *possibility*, the idealizing traditional forms. This is the root of the confusion of Toffanin and his followers. The essential character of the historical truth has been taken for one of its implications or consequences (namely, the lack of a definite and sustained idealization), which, as a form of the imagination, can take place outside the field of historiography, and without being at all subject to historiography's particular veracity. In the image of life that it gives, realistic fiction resembles History, but, unlike History, it can and generally does entirely lack particular truth.

Doubtless the historical development of drama and literary narrative, from the purity of the classical genres to the most inclusive realism, has drawn the character of the poetic image closer to that of historiography. But, leaving aside for now the fact that even modern realism stylizes and creates images essentially different from the historiographical ones, Cervantes finds himself far from abandoning marked and traditional stylizations. What he does is reform and adulterate them. He is not fully and consistently "realistic," and not because he fails in the attempt, but because his formal design takes him elsewhere.[22]

That the *Quixote* should be understood, in its style and in its relationship with reality, as a work that obeys the ideal of the particular truth of History is an error of which we can unburden Cervantes studies. What we find behind this misunderstanding is Cervantes's creation in the *Quixote* of a new region of the literary imagination, one of adulterated and ironic verisimilitude, which I will call "comic realism," despite the problematical implications of the term. I will explain these concepts in detail.

Having discarded this confusion, we can ask whether the *Quixote* is "realistic" (in the way that fictions are able to be realistic). To answer this question, we have to explore the concept of realism.

Included in the concept of realistic fiction is, to begin with, Aristotle's notion of *verisimilitude*—that is, analytical consistency with the possible, the probable, and the necessary, according to the notion that the spectator has of the world presented by the work. The Stagyrite considers this quality imperative for poetic validity. This verisimilitude is precisely the foundation of the kind of universal truth that inheres in poetry. Aristotelian verisimilitude, however, does not suffice to characterize what today we call *realism*, and it is obvious that we would not designate as "realistic" many works that Aristotle justifiably considers verisimilar. Beyond verisimilitude, the meaning of modern realism requires that this created world possess the features of the world of our ordinary experience. It is verisimilar, for example, for an angel or a goddess (once the existence of such beings is admitted in the spectator's vision of the world) to carry mortals in the air and instantly deposit them in a remote place. Our expectations of the necessary, possible, and probable depend on our beliefs, and Aristotle explicitly admits this relativism of verisimilitude. But a work in which supernatural beings intervene with exceptional actions, violating the hermetic transcendence of their silence and their distance, will not be considered "realistic" by modern readers, precisely because it would fall outside the sphere of their *experience* of life, although it may not exceed that of their beliefs. If verisimilitude, or correspondence with what is held to be necessary, possible, and probable, is one of the essential properties of realistic fiction, another is congruence with common experience; that is, the *familiarity* or *ordinariness* of the kinds of objects and actions represented.

Let us remember that the fundamentals of the Aristotelian division of the arts, and of the poetic genres, are the concepts of *object, medium,* and *manner* of the imitation. For our present analysis, we can leave aside the category of medium (which encompasses the materials of the imitation, and is reduced, in our case, to imaginary discourse), as well as the manner, which allows the distinction of the dramatic forms (enacted by speakers) and the epic (narrated by one primordial voice). On the other hand, the category of the object of the imitation (which is made explicit in the Aristotelian distinction of imitations of men superior, equal, or inferior to us) is central to our concern. Extending the Aristotelian concepts beyond their original application, we can say that a "realistic" imitation has as a defining feature (among others) its being an imitation of persons similar to us; that is, subjects that belong to the sphere of daily experience. This criterion is what I have called "familiarity" and designated as second to that of "verisimilitude" in the complex concept of realism.

But it is possible to draw from the *Poetics* still a third criterion for elucidating the problematic nature of notions such as realism, one already suggested at the start of these considerations, in respect to artists who paint people better than they are, those who paint them worse than they are, and those who present them just as they are (XV, 1454b). We can call this category the *character of the abstraction,* or the *principle of stylization.* We are talking here not about the kind of persons represented (heroic semigods; men like us; subhuman creatures) but about the direction in which the figurative abstraction that represents them operates: upward (the direction we can call "idealizing"), downward ("caricaturizing"), or on the same level as experience ("objective"). (Lucian, for example, does not paint the gods as Homer does.) The principle of *objective* stylization obviously corresponds to the concept of realism.

It is not necessary to emphasize that these Aristotelian triads (and our commentary) represent only a beginning in organizing the theme of generic styles, and in what follows we will be moving beyond this conceptual frame. But the concept of realism becomes more sharply drawn when we explicitly ascribe to it the defining features (deduced from the *Poetics* or suggested by it) that I have called "verisimilitude," "familiarity," and "objectivity."

Is the *Quixote* a realistic fiction, in this sense of the word "realistic"? It seems to me that we cannot maintain that it is. I would like to point out here that if the Cervantine imagination had been subjected to the realistic imperative, many fundamental aspects of the work that we know would not have taken form. The highly improbable, for example, is abundant in the accumulation of casual anagnorises and peripeties toward the end of the First Part. The episode of Marcela and Grisóstomo introduces the world of pastoral utopia, alien to daily experience. The expansion of the central characters throughout the work exceeds the bounds of verisimilitude, and the narrator himself winks at us to underline it (for example, in quoting the "translator" who declares the chapter in which Sancho assumes quixotic manners in his conversation with his wife [II.5] to be apocryphal or in remarking on the admiration and perplexity of those who hear Sancho speak so elegantly as governor [II.49]).[23] The objective stylization of some characters intertwines with the idealizing of others (such as the young beauties) and the caricaturizing of a Maritornes. Finally, in a fictional work that was thoroughly realistic, the temporal paradoxes would not fit. They not only go beyond the improbable and even the empirically impossible. They create a chronological framework that a priori is unworkable, a labyrinth of time that can make Robbe-Grillet blanche.

And regarding that repeated assertion that construes the *Quixote* as a complete picture of the Spanish society of its times, I think, as Erich Auerbach does, that it suffices to examine a historiographical vision of the sixteenth and seventeenth centuries in Spain to understand that the severe, somber, multiple face of that peninsular society is not *shown* in the *Quixote*.[24] It is a very different thing to admit that connections, inevitable in all works, can be traced and inferred between the novelesque creation and the real world of the author, as, for example, Américo Castro has done in relation to Hispanic castes and other subjects.[25] What leads to the (deceptive) impression of a complete social panorama is the pictorial variety of social types: high nobility, hidalgos, merchants, ecclesiastics, peasants, soldiers, students, vagabonds, criminals, and so on. But the characters who assume these conditions and offices are not there primarily to expound the framework of the social organization and its vital relationships by exemplifying its roles (as in the nineteenth-century novels that Wolfgang Kayser called works "of space").26 Fundamentally, the *Quixote*'s characters incarnate figures from the tradition of comedy: impostors, *milites gloriosi,* plain dealers, clowns, rustics, gallants, maidens, and so forth. The complete universe that the work offers us is not that of historical society. It is the archetypal universe of literature, whose relationship with real life is more indirect and abstract than that of a sociographic representation, or than that of realistic literature.27

A fourth feature of the modern notion of literary realism is related to the modern spirit of scientific investigation, the systematic search for information that broadens and changes the typologies of traditional knowledge. Let us call this feature "empirical revelation," or simply "empiricism," representing interest in the newness of unexplored or previously undescribed areas of daily human existence. Such an impulse leads the characters of realistic literature to distance themselves from literary archetypes and approach typological concepts of historiography, contemporary medicine, ethnography, and similar disciplines, and sometimes to move beyond them to eminent individuation. In Cervantes the "literary" vision still predominates, although he prodigiously reshapes its molds. Certainly there are characterological aspects to Cervantine figures, although they frequently do not go beyond traditional physiognomic and humoral characterology, within whose limits the protoempirical speculations of Huarte de San Juan also remain.28 These empirical elements do not constitute the substance of Cervantine characters. It is futile to look for complete psychological accuracy in them.29

Other properties of the realistic novel which the *Quixote* certainly lacks are related to the spatial, temporal, and personal focus of the modern narrator, the admission of "detail" and trivial matters as the sustained foreground of representation, and to the rather grave metaphysical temper that determines it. The fact that the Cervantine technique is so "scenic" (to use Percy Lubbock's term) leads to confusion, but in the *Quixote* we do not find the typical "scene" of the modern novel.30 Sometimes it evokes the scene of traditional comedy.

Legitimacy of the Concept of Literary Realism (a Parenthesis). But nowadays can one speak so confidently of "realism"? A number of critics have declared that realism does not deserve its name, or that it should not be understood as an artistic style that is closer to reality than others. For some of these critics this is so because there is no stable reality to serve as the referent of art, or because art never really intends to refer to it. Thus the difference between realism and other forms would simply consist in using different artistic conventions. The word "convention" here has the connotation of the arbitrary, or that which has historically evolved within the medium of ideology, that is, without a direct cognitive relation to reality. Realism would be the form of expression of certain cultural movements, but would have no objective, cognitive determination. Other critics of realism adopt a skeptical stance and dismiss it as unable "to depict reality as it is."

These positions are either metaphysical or beside the point. To depict reality as it is, such an infinitely vast theme, is not a task that artists can attempt or art's contemplators expect of them. At best one could hope for a glimpse of that immensity through some images (realistic or fantastic) that can have a revelatory power. Otherwise it is a task for a god. Now, confusion arises because the realistic novel's omniscient narrator is godlike, seeing through the private actions, the minds, and even the unconscious motivations of others. (So do most fictional narrators, whether the narratives are realistic or not.) However, neither writer nor reader takes this omniscience for anything but a device of fictional representation. Besides, this godlike translucidation of reality is applied in any novel to a very small, imaginary corner of the world. The realistic writer delivers *aspectually* impossible, modally fantastic images of events that are in themselves entirely possible and probable, according to the judgment of our sense of reality, in the sphere of ordinary experience. (In one sentence: fiction presents in the modality of perception what can be known only in the modality of inference. Moreover, all representative art exhibits the fantasy of an observation without any reaction on the part of those observed. Even the figure portrayed in the posture of looking at the spectator is not looking at or reacting to the real spectators. Fiction is an effort of imagination to *see* life as it is by itself—as it is when it is not being observed.) What happens in realistic novels is possible in our real world, but the mode of experiencing it is a fantasy of immediacy. It is precisely the search for the most direct representation of the forms of reality that has led to the progressive subjectivization of the image of life (the retraction of the represented objectivity back into the contingent process of individual consciousness) and to the development of techniques of focalization such as the free indirect style and the stream of consciousness. In the *Quixote* we find only elementary tools of this kind. Cervantes does not produce novelistic images of the dramatized immediacy of subjective experience. In comparison with realistic manners of presentation, his narrative mode is still classificatory and distant, and his dialogues appear stylized and generally devoid of contingent irrelevancies (which are not a mere conventional sign of "reality," or "reality effects," as they are ambiguously called, after Roland Barthes, but a factual feature of that immediate experience the modern novelist wants to represent).

That realist novels are indeed structured by certain typical forms of representation (the fantastic central consciousness, the alternation of summary and scene, the dramatization of the subjective immediacy of experience, details alien to the process of the story, and other more or less general and more or less exclusive features of the genre) results from the appropriateness of these compositional techniques for the goal of an imaginary vision of human experience. If they are "conventions," there is nothing arbitrary about them, and nothing that necessarily corrupts the sense of reality.

But are they not, as all artistic forms are, historical-ideological products, datable, used during a certain time and discarded by later writers? Do they not, like all generic styles, constrain the image of life, imposing on it lines of *sense* (individual growth and purification through experience, the destructive consequences of illusions, etc.) that do not belong to reality, but are remnants of myth? Whether such lines of sense are or are not valid models of real life's possibilities may be debatable. But this too is beside the point as far as the distinctive referential validity of realism is concerned. The pertinent question is: Are the events represented such that they are conceivable, for our sense of reality, as possible parts of the world of ordinary experience? Raskolnikov's deeds are; Superman's and Amadis's are not. And, despite having the opposite meaning in all respects, neither are Don Quixote's.

The Question of Cervantes's "Thought." Various objections to these assertions of mine are foreseeable. Do I mean to say that the work that satirized and supposedly destroyed the genre of fantastic and inverisimilar knightly adventures, precisely by opposing the fictional lie with daily reality, does not reflect this daily life? Does the symbolism of the falls and the blows that Don Quixote suffers time and again because of his romance-induced lunacy then mean nothing? Is not the collision between illusory ideal and hard reality the thematic core of the book? And how could Cervantes present such a collision if he did not display a true figuration of the world of ordinary experience as the book's basic imaginary level? Have I forgotten what Ortega says in the *Meditaciones del "Quijote"*? And what explanation can I give, on the other hand, for the reiteration of the theme of realism in the ironic references to pastoral novels, contrasted with the true existence of the goatherds, in the colloquy of Cipión and Berganza?

But (and here we begin to approach the issue of the novelist's thought or philosophy, and especially his poetological doctrine) if Cervantes really condemned the pastoral utopias, why does he include at least one in the *Quixote?* Why, until his death, does he keep up the project of completing *La Galatea?* If he wanted to inaugurate literary realism, why does he write the fantastic *Persiles* in his last years, and with such enthusiasm? And why, after all, does he place the thesis that condemns literary fantasies on the lips of two dogs who chat about literature? It seems to me that the whole of Cervantes's work obliges us to reject the supposition that criticism of unrealistic literature, as an explicit argument in his work, has been something other than a literary topic, even then traditional, that he repeats with that lesser degree of conviction with which the literature of his age often ritually reproduces venerable commonplaces. (This intertextual game is often a discipline of irony, which can attain the supreme cynicism of the Gongorine voice that offers, in the "First Solitude," generally held to be one of the most wonderfully contrived and studiously difficult poems of world literature, a eulogy—of simplicity!) When the Priest carries out the scrutiny of the hidalgo's books (for whatever allegorical value we may attribute to the passage), those that are judged to be well written are saved from burning, even if they are pastoral novels and books of chivalry. Can we believe that Cervantes did not understand that the pastoral genre, which he himself cultivated, was precisely at the service of the effort to concretize a utopian imagination, and that consequently it was preposterous to criticize it for not being realistic?

Leaving aside the criticisms in various parts of his work directed against the vulgarity and incongruity of artistically inferior productions, the meaning of the Cervantine literary satire (as well as, in general, the true spiritual attitudes of the author) is revealed not by what is *said* in his works, or even so much by what *happens* in his imaginary worlds, but substantially by what these works effectively *are,* as poetic creations. The form of the works is the sign that cannot deceive, the telling imprint of the fundamental, animating moves. The character of the gesture of the creator *qua* creator is "expressed" in the constitutive form of his creations; the form indicates to us the nature of the imaginative matrix, the origin of the laws that order the fictitious universe. (I intend to show and describe the design, in the main inexplicit and presumably semiconscious, of the crafting of *Don Quixote.*)

When Cervantes began to write the *Quixote,* moral and aesthetic condemnation of books of chivalry was already a traditional issue, and certainly of minor importance in comparison with other intellectual preoccupations. The immense popularity of the genre, like the peak of the attacks of orthodox and heterodox critics and moralists, had already passed.[31] Because the polemic against these books was, then, practically unnecessary and the condemnatory arguments were unoriginal (and since, as his career as an author shows, Cervantes's apparent conviction that it was necessary to cast out unrealistic forms of the imagination was not, in fact, authentic), the explicit theme of the evil of books of chivalry in the *Quixote* has to be understood as a superficial motif. Its justification and significance, as we will see, emanate from an incomparably more profound endeavor that confronts reality and literature in all its forms and questions every kind of institutionalized imagination.

Much is said about literature in the *Quixote* (as in others of Cervantes's works), but I think that, in comparison with what the writer actually produced, not much is said that is significant theory.[32] Commonplaces of Renaissance criticism are repeated, especially from its neo-Aristotelian-Tridentine phase; diverse critical principles are mixed together, sometimes incongruously, in the end delivering no more than a repertoire of poetological themes, which can indicate the direction and some of the sources of the Cervantine critical preoccupations, but nothing very telling with respect to his art, or to the creative dilemmas that he really confronted and resolved, or to the extraordinary literary venture he undertook and executed in the *Quixote.* All that is outside the scope of the literary theory of his time. Cervantes must have suffered from that lack of conceptual orientation, and there are indications in certain aspects of the construction of the First Part that make it seem that he did. He must have felt intensely the insufficiency of the literary theory at his disposal, in particular the inadequacy of the Aristotelian norm of the (dramatic) unity of action for the majority of epic or narrative forms. This is a norm that enjoyed supreme authority and prestige at the time, although it was not exempt from dissent. It is especially inappropriate for narratives *of character,* in Wolfgang Kayser's terminology. ("Epic of character" is a generic category that can be applied with advantage to the *Quixote* to illuminate its questions of unity and structure.) Cervantes's work can be seen as an eminent example of the divorce of literary practice from theory which René Wellek considers characteristic of some centuries of doctrinal dogmatization of Aristotelian and Horacian ideas.[33]

Because of all that, and because, as it can be conjectured, the intellectual vocation of Cervantes is from beginning to end the vocation of a poet, of a creator of literary fictions (someone for whom language is above all the instrument of the image, and not that of the formulation of conceptual thought), his use of theoretical discourse is ancillary, quite conventional, and, finally, contradictory. The theory introduced into the fictional world is suspended and remains ineffectual there, converted into urbane and educated conversation, and somewhat ritualistic. Within the Cervantine world, theory seems to be subordinated to the artistic imperative that Benedetto Croce emphasizes in his *Aesthetic:* to become a part of the created image, and to lose its relationship, not pertinent here, with the real world. In short, it would become "intranscendent," to use Ortega's term; it would not violate what Ortega has also called the "hermeticity" of the imaginary world.[34] None of the neo-Aristotelian themes is given a remarkable development in Cervantes's texts; rather, one gets the impression that he deliberately confuses them. The most important text in this respect, the conversation between the Priest, the Canon, and then Don Quixote beginning in Chapter 47 of the First Part, equivocally repeats echoes of Aristotle, Horace, and their Renaissance followers. The theoretical insufficiency of these discussions would seem to be appropriate, rather than irrelevant, on the artistic level of the imagined world, where they are conversations of itinerant clerics.[35]

I think it is necessary, however, to reconsider these last points. Have I not been led to a superficial interpretation by the authority of Croce and Ortega, and by the force of the modernist aesthetic ideal in their doctrines? Indeed, the paradigm of rigorous hermeticity of the novelistic world is not pertinent to the *Quixote,* whose design obeys a more

flexible law. Moreover, I believe that the partial openness of its fictional horizon is another of the manifestations of the generic difference
that separates the *Quixote* from the modern novel proper.[36] It also
seems undeniable to me that the more or less extensive "discourses" of
Don Quixote on the Golden Age, arms and letters, the principles of
government and justice (to Sancho), peace (to the battling brayers),
poetry (to Don Lorenzo de Miranda), and other minor speeches, far
from being consistent expressions of the personality of the one who
pronounces them, are almost like quoted pieces of a doctrinal nature,
and conceptually incompatible with one another; they are vaguely
reminiscent of pieces of a collage, and show something of the archaic
discontinuity that one finds in certain medieval works. It is a marvel of
the Cervantine art that we can accept them as manifestations of the
spirit of the mad hidalgo.

In any case, the Cervantine scheme of maintaining the character of
verisimilar conversation in the ecclesiastics' poetological exchange is
notable. The motivation of the theme could not be more convincing,
since it responds to the Canon's astonishment at Don Quixote's peculiar derangement, which, it is explained, is the effect of his many
chivalric readings. Then, between the conversation of the two clerics
and the one they carry on afterward with Don Quixote, there is a
markedly prosaic interval, which begins with the mention of very
minor details, quite rare in the book (in this case, instructions that the
Canon gives his servants for feeding the horses). Even immediately
before the Canon's appearance, there has also been a passage regarding options for comfortable travel (I.47), as if to frame the theoretical
colloquy in trivial irrelevancies ("reality effects").

Can I continue to maintain that Cervantes sacrifices the poetological consistency of these passages for the sake of a doctrinally
equivocal image, in which discursive knowledge becomes neutralized,
as though weightless? Studies by Edward Riley and Alban Forcione
have proposed syntheses of Cervantes's aesthetic conception, extracted
from the dispersed poetological expressions that are found in the
Cervantine corpus and confirmed by the examination of the critical
doctrines that were debated in the sixteenth century, whose echoes in
this corpus are unmistakable.[37] According to these authors, such the-
oretical-novelistic passages would constitute a judicious version, and
even a somewhat original one, of the aesthetic ideals of Cervantes's
time; more important, they would represent an appropriate concep-

tualization of at least certain aspects of the creative practices of the author.

I have some reservations on this score. First, I think it is right and necessary to insist on the purposeful superficiality and inconsistency with which Cervantes generally treats expressions of doctrine. Second, the description of the artistic design of the *Quixote* presented here makes it evident that Renaissance poetology (as much in its more orthodox neo-Aristotelian manifestations as in its pro-romancesque and even anti-Aristotelian alternatives) is fundamentally inadequate for the comprehension of this novel's form. This second assertion, naturally, stands or falls with the ideas developed throughout this book. With respect to the first statement, the following considerations may be worthwhile.

First of all, we must keep in mind (and here I am indebted to Riley and Forcione) that it is easy to err in interpreting the discourses of the Canon and the Curate if we do not properly consider the doctrinal background of the period. Some arguments that may appear to us to be incongruous were not in the understanding of Cervantes's age. Thus, at first it seems out of place for the Canon to deem instances not of lack of compositional unity but of extreme inverisimilitude to be censurable because they violate the principle of the "proportion of the parts to the whole, and of the whole to the parts" (I.47). With some plausibility, Forcione interprets this subsumption as reasonable, by virtue of a very broad concept of proportion, documentable in six-teenth-century criticism.[38] Another false impression of illogicality can be gotten, I think, from the relationship that the Curate establishes between the principle of verisimilitude and the unity of time—when he censures the theatrical practice of presenting a child in swaddling clothes in the first scene of a piece and in the second scene showing the same individual as a bearded man (I.48). Today we would not call this an infraction of verisimilitude, but in the neo-Aristotelian poetics of the time, as well as in the classicist tradition up to the end of the eighteenth century, the justification of the unity of time is not pri-marily one of formal aesthetics, but is a function of the ideal of mim-etic illusion. It was thought that the temporal discontinuities in the action represented destroyed the illusion of witnessing genuine life. (This concept can be found in such sixteenth-century authors as Vin-cenzo Maggi, Lodovico Castelvetro, Francesco Bonciani, Alessandro Piccolomini, and Francesco Buonamici, and later in the classicist poet-

ics of Pierre Corneille. In the second half of the eighteenth century, in
England, Samuel Johnson still believed it necessary to argue against
this dramaturgical dogma.[39] In Spain it still had some force at the
beginning of the nineteenth century, though certainly it had undergone some interruptions. As early as the seventeenth century, apolo-
gists for Lope de Vega argued, like the Italian "moderns" of the sixteenth century, against the unities.) Nor is the Curate's criticism of
changes in place from one act of a *comedia* to the next as a failure to
observe the unity of time illogical, since he refers to displacements
from one continent to another, which cannot help but imply major
temporal leaps.

There is an inconsistency that in my view cannot be dismissed,
however, in the double position the Canon assumes in his initial
speech. I do not refer to the fact that he begins by censuring the extant
books of chivalry and immediately goes on to praise the possibilities
of the genre. (There is no contradiction here, only a suggestion of
Cervantes's ambivalence in regard to unrealistic kinds of literature.)
The inconsistency lies rather in the fact that the Canon, in order to
condemn the books of chivalry, takes the point of view of the "an-
cients" of sixteenth-century polemics, urging rigorous unity of action
in the narrative work, strict verisimilitude, and moral exemplarity;
and then, in his praise of the possibilities of the genre, he assumes the
position of the "moderns" of that century, defenders of Ariosto and of
the *romanzo*, of multiple actions, variety of style, the fantastic imagination of the marvelous, and to some extent the justification of the
poetic work in the pleasure of the audience. Can it be doubted that
Cervantes would be well aware of the incompatibility of these points
of view? Can we, then, legitimately maintain that Cervantes deliberately confuses the poetological doctrines of his time? The more or less
subtle introduction of inconsistencies into his characters' critical discussions not only ensures the novelistic verisimilitude of the dialogue
and the subordination of theory to image but also underlines the
ironic distance of the narrator and, a fortiori, of the author.[40]

If we take philosophy to be an explicitly conceptual and abstract
expression of knowledge, the philosophy (including the literary theory) present in the Cervantine work is insignificant, and its sources
have already been well determined. Don Quixote's advice to Sancho
on governing, for example, is admirable, but certainly not for its
original philosophical value, since it represents a selection of known
ethical motifs (very widely held in those years, as Martín de Riquer

indicates).[41] What is admirable is that the fictional personality can deliver the advice with supreme naturalness and from the heart without destroying the imaginary unity of the character—the very same person we have seen attacking windmills while insisting they are giants and seeking to do battle with a lion and then proceeding to ask the witness to this insanity for written testimony to his valor.

Cervantes's spiritual adventure is not directed toward the ideas and abstractions of theoretical intelligence.[42] He handles them with ease and detachment, as minor materials of his imaginary exploration; he does not entrust to them anything of substance. Therefore, the task of determining what his "thought" was, in the sense of his theoretical convictions, not only is practically impossible, owing to the dearth of doctrinary expressions strictly on the author's part; in the end it is also of little relevance. What Cervantes has given us is not of that sort. That he knew the fundamental doctrines of his epoch has been shown by Marcelino Menéndez Pelayo, Marcel Bataillon, Américo Castro, Martín de Riquer, Jean-François Canavaggio, Enrique Moreno Báez, Edward Riley, Francisco Márquez Villanueva, Ciriaco Morón Arroyo, and others.[43] On the other hand, attempts to determine what his position was in relation to then-contemporary doctrines have failed to produce even the rudiments of a consensus. Unnecessary obstacles to interpretation are added, in my opinion, because of the insistence on understanding him as the subject of one consistent, systematic world view. This presupposition is explicit in Helmut Hatzfeld's assertion that a Cervantes with two ideologies is an "untenable conception."[44] But not only is it possible for a person to see life differently at different times; it is highly probable that a writer, in his creative effort, internalizes various ideas and values inimical to one another.[45] And even if we could identify one ideology as being that of Cervantes the man, those that take shape in his works could well be of a different stripe. The relationship between the real author and the implied author in the work, as we know, is not one of plain duplication.

The distinction I am making between Cervantes the man and the consciousness objectified in his work may seem to be a trendy disregard of the unity of the individual subject. Rather, it is an invitation to assume some consequences of the complexity of this entity. Even within the modest limits of our own spiritual experience we can find evidence of these scissions between our convictions and our image of the world. Do we not live most of the time according to principles of judgment and action that are conventional and traditional, some of them acquired through explicit indoctrination and others subconsciously internalized, and is it not true that our decisions are based only in small measure on genuine ethical discoveries resulting from our own meditations? And are not the ethical abysses that open up before our reflection completely different from the "provisional code of morals" that guides us, not just for a certain time, as Descartes presumed, but for our entire life? Every day we see scientists sustaining simplistic political and ethical principles with a lack of conceptual discrimination and study that would provoke their indignation if they found the same deficiency in their own discipline. And is the investigation of the novelist into the image of life so different that it cannot, in its turn, part from and contrast with his routine consciousness? The Socratic ideal of living *an examined life,* or the Cartesian one of suspending the totality of our convictions and entirely rebuilding our thought and our ethics, is a goal toward which we make very minor progress in a lifetime, and *therefore* our consciousness becomes and remains divided between the urgent "knowledge" that each day requires and the knowledge scarcely glimpsed in moments of high contemplative tension. A great novel, like a great work of philosophy, is the crystallization of such moments, and thus it is no wonder that its vision distances itself from the principles according to which its author, day after day, gets along decently with his fellows.

Highly contradictory opinions are held or suggested in various parts of Cervantes's work, at times within the same passage. As a result, and because no method of discrimination can be invoked, it is vain to look for places that express the thought one wants to attribute to the author. No hermeneutic principle makes it possible to determine which of the statements presented within the novelistic fiction are attributable to the author as an expression of his own convictions. And in the case of Cervantes, we have little from his own hand other than his works of creative imagination.

Let us take a relatively simple case. Was Cervantes, in his intimate feelings, opposed to the expulsion of the Moors? Castro thinks so. Bataillon does not. And there are passages in the Cervantine works that can (in a debate deprived of specific hermeneutic principles) be offered as proof positive for both hypotheses.[46] Helmut Hatzfeld documents echoes of the Tridentine texts in a catalog of passages from the *Quixote*, but this is flimsy proof of the author's orthodoxy if at the same time it has been established, as Hatzfeld has explicitly done, that irony dominates the entire work.[47] The fact that some of these doctrinal statements are made by a character defined by his madness and others by a character defined by his credulous ignorance does not strengthen the argument. It is surprising that even today some critics still try to establish Cervantes's ideology by describing the convictions of some of his characters. The same critics usually credit Cervantes with the invention of the ironic space of the modern novel, without noticing the contradiction between these two views.

Riley's more critical approach, of preferentially considering the words of those characters who seem to be surrounded by respect and endowed with spiritual authority, also seems insufficient to me. Are Cipión and Berganza among them? And what about the licentiate Vidriera? Does not the inextricable combination of wisdom and folly belong to the substance of Don Quixote himself? What makes Riley's study on Cervantes's theory of literature convincing is that he reinterprets the poetological commonplaces that the author has put on the lips of his characters in the light of his actual novelistic practice—that is, according to what he really does in his works. With this approach Riley gives those theoretical generalities a specific sense that is to some extent well suited to the creation. But even so, as I intend to show, this theory of the novel remains very far from reflecting the complexity and the scope of the work's artistic design.

The procedure formulated and used by Américo Castro in *El pensamiento de Cervantes* does not work well either. Castro tries to ascertain what Cervantes "thought" not by means of what is said but in the light of what occurs in his works, as if Cervantes had willed an immanent justice to prevail in his imaginary worlds. To give the most important example, does Don Quixote's return to sanity and his renunciation of knight errantry mean that Cervantes wants to suggest that there was nothing but derangement in the chivalric mission, and that all wisdom resided in the domestic convictions of his home town?[48]

Understandably, the topic of ambiguity in Cervantes (which Angel del Río and Manuel Durán in particular have analyzed) has become prominent.[49] And it must be noted that this issue has at least two sides. On the one hand, ambiguity is understood as "perspectivism" (an equivocal word about which I will have more to say later) or, more precisely, as the objectivity with which diverse political, religious, ethical, and literary attitudes are represented in the world of his fiction. It seems that not a hint of the author's preferences is found in the image he delivers. Neither marked sympathies nor total antipathies are elicited. The narrator's voice is detached or ironic, and he rarely judges unequivocally. On the other hand, there is Cervantes's direct ambiguity in the rare declarations that can be taken as his own, the dedications and (only partially) the prologues. It is plain that he tends to fictionalize even these parts (although, as Alberto Porqueras Mayo sees it, this may correspond to the general Mannerist inclination of the era).[50] But when their tone is serious, the self-contradictions, in the brief space of a few lines, become disconcerting. It is as if the author did not wish to speak, as if he fled from the primary and direct use of language, the commitment of a real discourse that would represent his position, that would be *his* words. He goes so far as to patch together sentences taken word for word from Fernando de Herrera's dedication in his edition of Garcilaso to form his own brief dedication of the First Part of the *Quixote*. It is as if the author thought that nothing significant could be *said,* that only the *image* could convey to us what is substantial about life. (Perhaps the licentiate Vidriera is, in part, the satiric image of the pretensions and vanities of theoretical discourse.) It thus appears that we find ourselves before an exclusively poetic vocation, literary in the narrow sense of the word. The poet, as poet, is he who keeps silent, so that imaginary voices expressing interior worlds may be heard. He keeps silent because he has nothing to say to us, because what he has to communicate is not of the nature of what can be said. Therefore, if the task of seeking the "thought" of an author within his fictional work is always, in a sense, a methodological impossibility, then in the case of Cervantes, because of the exclusivity of his spiritual vocation, it is not only methodically blind but deprived of an object, because there is no such "thought" of Cervantes.[51] The well-known study by Américo Castro does not contradict this assertion. Castro shows the illustrious humanistic sources that have nourished the author's spirit, thus casting aside the notion of a Cervantes "the lay genious," but he does not go so far as to reconstruct a Cervantine conception that is coherently delineated. The thought of the poet Cervantes is not a discernible system, exclusive of others. It is a conglomerate of irreconcilable conceptions that are articulated not in the space of a logic that is impossible here but in that of an image that overwhelms and consumes conceptual constructions. His work displays the multiple doctrinal schizophrenia of supreme forms of art. (Possibly the erroneous interpretation of the artistic function of the philosophical passages in the dialogues of Cervantes's works led the way to taking the idea of the "ingenious layman" seriously.)

We shall reconsider these assertions. Am I suggesting that Cervantes had no convictions, neither religious faith of a particular bent nor a skeptic's lack of belief, neither principles of ascetic morality nor the prudence of ethical Epicureanism, neither a Platonic vision of the natural order nor an attitude of pragmatic empiricism, or any position along these lines? Is it possible to live without beliefs and notions of the universe, without ideals and preferences? Certainly not. Although the tribulations of his life must have taken the presumed bloom from his youthful convictions, it does not seem reasonable to doubt that the mature Cervantes would have had a great and articulate wisdom, with its pertinent beliefs and values. But the Cervantes objectified in his work is the spirit that is brought to life in the poetic fiction, a new and essentially different mind. And what the *Quixote* makes reality is not a "thought" but a poetic vision. It is the irruption of a liberating growth in the history of the imagination.

When one speaks of Cervantes's "thought," if one refers to a coherent set of doctrines or ideological convictions, formulable in terms of the philosophy, theology, and literary criticism of his time, and considers these doctrines as the principles of a vision that is expressed through the work—that is, as a matrix that determines the content and form of Cervantes's creations—then, I repeat, there is no such thing as Cervantes's thought. That a work like this would be artistically sustained by the world view common to the Tridentine theologians, or by that of Spaniards of superior intellect who came from families of *conversos*, or by the tradition of inner Christianity inspired by Erasmism, or by any plausible mixture of these and other "historical dwellings" (in Castro's felicitous term) or ideologies, is one of those ideas that come apart as soon as we turn our attention to them. Taking my thesis to its most extreme expression: the hypothesis (certainly subject to debate) of a sincerely Counterreformist Cervantes, a convinced supporter of the Catholic-Tridentine dogmatics, is not at all incongruent with the fact that Cervantes, as the creator of the ironic space of the modern novel (not of the definitive genre, but indeed of one of its basic formal structures), inaugurates a form of imagination of human life that explodes all dogmatic unanimity. Wolfgang Kayser has pointed to the Cervantine creation of distance between the narrator's vision of the world and that of the characters.[52] Let me add that the narrator himself is subjected to the ironic suspension of his ways of seeing and appreciating. The intellectual space loses its hierarchical organization, and the burden of judgment falls on the reader (to whom Cervantes the prologuist of the First Part says, ". . . you have your soul in your own body and as much free will as anyone, and you are as at home in your own house and master thereof as the king is over his taxes, and you know the old saying: 'Under my cloak a fig for the king.'"). Therefore, I say that Cervantes creates an artistic form that dissolves unanimity and constitutes what has been called his "perspectivism," as well as narrative "irony" or "objectivity."

The Meaning of Form

Stories of Undermined and Equivocal Exemplarity. In recent years Francisco Márquez Villanueva has renewed some of Américo Castro's theses on the thought of Cervantes. I do not question Márquez Villanueva's reconstruction of the political and spiritual circumstances of the period.[53] Rather, I am inclined heuristically to accept his descriptions of the historical context as valid. I only ponder the effect that such information produces when it is projected, as supposition and allusion, on the reading of the *Quixote*. I try out these possible clues on the body of the work to see whether or not they bring it to life.

Márquez believes that a fairly well-defined intellectual profile of the writer is perceptible, and further that one can see how Cervantes's literary work emanates from those "intellectual roots" (p. 175). His conclusions on this subject lead him to take a position similar to Castro's on various controversial issues, especially in regard to Cervantes's attitude toward the expulsion of the Moors and toward Erasmian ideas of a Christian Epicureanism. I have some reservations about these points of view. The first, indicated above, is that the plausibility of a thesis about a political and ideological posture taken by Cervantes the man does not imply that this posture is his sole and permanent conception of the subject, or that it informs the meaning of his work. At the very most, some indications of heuristic value for the interpretation of Cervantes's novels may arise from biographical conjecture (which, in any event, is based largely on a selective use of the Cervantine literary corpus). The ultimate test of an interpretive hypothesis is the experience of trying to read the texts in accordance with the suggested interpretation. In the case of the *Quixote*, this is the only plausible test, since the biographical data are poor and the work offers itself to us in all its vast textual integrity, written in a Spanish that is not very different from that of the present and within a culture that in many respects is still our own. Thus the hypotheses of spiritual biography ought to be accepted or not, in the final analysis, according to the value of the interpretation they suggest of particular passages of the work of fiction. (In this context, the characters and stories of Ricote and Don Diego de Miranda are central.) This is one of the typically circular ways that, according to Schleiermacher and Dilthey, are inherent in all hermeneutics: the plenitude and coherence of meaning that such literary interpretation can offer are forceful arguments in favor of the validity of the historical-biographical suppositions on which the interpretation is founded. In the end, then, it is our pondering of the possible readings and their respective coherence, richness, and depth that can permit a well-founded decision about the preferred meaning, which is the one that, *eo ipso,* we will attribute to the creative intention of the author. This "creative intention" is equivalent, more or less, to "the author as such," the one objectified in the work. It includes levels of meaning that probably were not explicit and deliberately conscious, since large volumes of unperceived connotations, habitual meanings that are no longer heeded, neglected implications of the traditional generic forms that are used, and similar subliminal company (not to mention the repressed meanings of symbols only half elucidated) pass like shadows through the slender shaft of the pen. All of which strengthens still more the supposition that the objectified spirit of the work will never entirely correspond to the ordinary convictions of the person who is about to put the pen to the blank page.

But the reading of the passages that are pertinent here, as of so many others of Cervantes that seem very simple at first sight, involves us in numerous doubts and possible ambivalences that have little to do with the historical context. The Cervantine text is, and has been in these debates, the main field of the battle of interpretations, and Márquez Villanueva does read it with great acuity. Nevertheless, I believe that some aspects of the literary configuration of these episodes do not favor his interpretation. I will mention them presently.

Another point that must be considered is that there are few arguments about facts in these disputes. More than anything else it is the particular shape that scholars impose on the same materials that everyone handles that determines their positions. And these positions frequently consist in attributing to Cervantes an ideology akin to the critic's. Castro wanted a liberal and tolerant Cervantes, Christian in his own way, and distanced from the official society and majority beliefs of his time. Others have wanted him to be an orthodox and militant Catholic and an enthusiastic upholder of imperial policies. But the persistence of the debate among honest and erudite scholars ought to make us consider the possibility that Cervantes's work is the positive concretization of a superior form of indifference before these alternatives, an indifference to whose level it is necessary to raise the interpretations.

The so-called ambiguity of Cervantes is frequently the serene objectivity of his images of life, which remain open to plural interpretations because he has given us no sign of doctrinal or conceptualizable orientation. His stories and characters allow the reader's particular view of the world to be projected upon them, as it could be projected upon a collection of data in no definite order. They do not resist it; they contain it without difficulty, but neither do they fully confirm it, and, after a more attentive reading, they somehow leave it drifting in uncertainty. According to Helena Percas de Ponseti, who I believe refers to this same phenomenon, readers see themselves reflected in the Cervantine work "as in a mirror."[54] Perhaps all supreme works of literary art, those that truly present life, have this effect. Each person's experience of life, in its immensity, is capable of validating, apparently and subjectively, the most disparate and even crazy ideologies (a truth that is obviously part of the polysemic parable of the *Quixote*). I concede that to take this position is tantamount to attributing a nihilistic element to the Cervantine vision, and that such a thesis smacks of anachronism. More will be said on this issue.

In any case, it seems to be a fundamental task of the critic of a work such as this to pick out the points that can be documented as objectively given, before the reader's ethical inclinations are projected on them. And the exceptional difficulties that the *Quixote* presents in this respect, in addition to those I have just indicated, reside in the functional inconsistencies of design and the formal ruptures of an ironic work that dismantles the direct image. A large part of this book deals with such peculiarities.

Márquez Villanueva draws from the episode of the encounter with Don Diego de Miranda very definite conclusions in regard to the Cervantine axiology. Cervantes would more or less subtly ridicule the figure of Don Diego (who has seemed exemplary to many critics, and whom Oscar Mandel even postulated as an emblem of the ethical standard of the work)[55] as an embodiment of the limitations of Christian Epicureanism and its circumspect wisdom. Conversely, Don Quixote's temerity in challenging the king's lion to fight would be truly exemplary. The critic, influenced here, I think, by what seems to be a supreme playing out of the ideal of a resolute and risk-taking life, and opposed to a prudence that he terms "bourgeois," opts for one side of a dilemma that, to my judgment, Cervantes merely presents. And he presents it here somewhat obliquely: Don Diego is not a perfect incarnation of Christian humanism (although considerate and refined, he is depicted from the beginning as conceited and extremely naive), and Don Quixote's adventure with the lion (one of his several exploits that clearly have no superior moral content) is not an example of heroic grandeur. Thus both ideals appear ironically estranged. The ethical dilemma of heroic activism and Epicurean introversion that momentarily sparkles in this encounter with the man in the green cloak underlies the whole work and is, *as a dilemma,* one of its major significations, symbolized in full scale by the contrast between Don Quixote and Alonso Quijano the Good.[56]

Ortega insists that the thought created by Cervantes's novel is profound and enigmatic. "In no other book is the power of symbolic allusions to the universal sense of life so great, yet in no other book do we find fewer guideposts, fewer clues to its own interpretation. For that reason, in comparison with Cervantes, Shakespeare seems to be an ideologue." But on another page he suggests, I think without contradiction, what the nature of the Cervantine vision is (and my interpretation agrees with Ortega's): "Some, with charming foresight, caution us not to be Quixotes; and others, following the most recent fashion, invite us to an absurd existence, full of feverish gestures. For both groups, apparently, Cervantes has not existed. It was to raise our minds above that dualism that Cervantes came upon the earth."[57] There is no contradiction here, because we are dealing, as I will try to show, with two different planes of meaning. The fundamental plane of this poetic thought is a negation, the negation of the supposed doctrinal truths. Above this plane of intellectual emptiness and openness arise inexplicit affirmations that the reader intuits but that cannot be formulated.

Behind the Ricote episode Márquez Villanueva finds a Cervantes akin to his own sense of humanity and of political responsibility. His argument is complex; I cannot do it justice in a few words. I will only indicate two aspects of the literary form of the passage (two of the fundamental discontinuities of style that I study in this book) which I believe require us to doubt that Cervantes expresses himself here as that subject of "moderate" political thought, that "instinctive liberal,"

Christian humanist, anti-Machiavellian, and man of warm optimism in regard to human nature that the critic sees in him. Márquez Villanueva concedes this point indirectly, for when he claims that Cervantes was not being sincere when he had Ricote, a Moor, commend the royal policy of expelling the Moors (II.65), he implicitly accepts that the meaning of the literary work on this point differs from the hypothetical thought of Cervantes the man. A literary work, as such, is incapable of this kind of insincerity.

Ricote's applause for his enemies' policy, particularly in his last speech in II.65, at first seems strangely inconsistent and lacking in verisimilitude; it seems to invite us to conjecture that Cervantes was dissimulating. It agrees fairly well, however, with the devices Cervantes uses elsewhere, which are a regular part of the ironic modality of the work. Thus the reader's perplexity before Ricote's declarations dissipates if the appropriate key for reading is used. If one reads them "normally," they are certainly anomalous. They are difficult to accept as stemming from the convictions of the man who pronounces them, since he condemns himself along with all other Moors; and his words are so emphatic and eloquent that they can only justify the evils inflicted upon him and his family. As interpreters in persistent search for psychological verisimilitude, we cannot understand Ricote's words as involuntary lapses, still less as ironic witticisms. A more recondite psychological probability can be construed if we think of Ricote as extremely truthful and candid, or conversely, as the shrewd tactician of a self-deprecatory *captatio benevolentiae,* or possibly both at once. But such a psychological conjecture is not a compelling reading; it does not transform the narrative image. And this lack of distinct verisimilitude deprives the character of pathetic force and radically reduces any humanitarian and compassionate effect. If Cervantes had intended such an effect, that would not be a good strategy. But it is not enough to say that Ricote's words lack genuine verisimilitude, and that this kind of ungrammaticality may be the author's sign for us to perceive the critical sense of the episode. This is one of the numerous passages in the book (and in Cervantes's work in general) where we find the phenomenon of the transitory and abrupt usurpation of a character's voice by an extraneous, impersonal discourse, thoroughly inappropriate to his psychology and circumstances. In the following chapters I will provide quite a few examples of such dislocations. For now, I will only indicate that a passage somewhat different in content but identical in form is found in *The Little Gypsy Girl,* where the old gypsy man offers a defense of his people in a speech that suddenly becomes a declaration of professional criminality, thus startlingly ironizing and invalidating what has seemed to be a cogent utopian self-celebration. In this passage, too, there is no room for an interpretive construction that would salvage its psychological verisimilitude. The possible effect of sympathy for the gypsy is left suspended in an atmosphere of sarcasm. There is something of a collage of ideological discursive fragments in this Cervantine procedure. In regard to the (minimal) literary personalities of Ricote and the old gypsy, their speeches are neither sincere nor insincere; they fall outside of the characters who deliver them. The literary effect of these discursive strategies is to distance the thematic complex in question and for a decisive instant to undermine the characters' illusory humanity and neutralize their pathetic appeal. In a quasi-Aristotelian way, readers are excused from sustained compassion; they are liberated so that they may serenely reflect on the moral dilemma.[58]

Within the basic comic realism of the *Quixote*, then, Ricote is reduced to a neutralizing inverisimilitude, and thus is deprived of genuine poignancy.[59] And what happens, in the metafictional sphere that I am examining, with Ricote's beautiful daughter? Is she at least an unequivocal object of our compassion? Indeed, she is less so than her father, since Ana Félix does not even completely enter into the stylistic region of comic realism. On the contrary, Cervantes places her within a framework of an ironized romancesque and Byzantine genre, of disguises, journeys, dangers, and peripeteias. Although readers will not be given the full resolution of this story, when they see her within that framework they are led to believe that she is completely out of danger *by the sole force of the generic form* in which she navigates and wanders.

The novelist's vision includes but overwhelms all immediate humanitarian feeling and also the opposite, the harshness of a long-term raison d'état. Cervantes shows both in effigy, with lights and shadows, uniting in his strange serene pessimism the ethical projections of a Christian humanism and of a Machiavellian reason.[60] There is something here of that vision which, according to Hegel, manifests itself preeminently in classical tragedy, and which otherwise is an integral trait of his dialectical comprehension of universal history: the most terrible thing to see is not the ("merely") moving event of the suffering of an injustice but the fatality of a conflict in which both sides are right.

This and several, if not all, of the stories in the *Quixote* (those of Marcela and Grisóstomo, Dorotea and company, the Captive, the encounter with the Knight of the Green Cloak, Camacho's wedding, and even the main one, that of the madness of Don Quixote himself) are ambiguous. Exemplary behavior, excess, and a fall go hand in hand, and happy endings are never unequivocally so. The values incarnated in the characters become doubtful: Marcela's liberty, the matrimonial bliss of Dorotea and Luscinda, Zoraida's religiosity, Don Diego's Christian Epicureanism, the moral character of the lovers who deceive Camacho, and—the sum total of all the Cervantine ambiguities—the knight errantry of Don Quixote.

Two Kinds of Rhetoric. I concede that the distinctions that I have just made and the preferences they entail are familiar. But we are not merely recalling the insights of the New Criticism, of the critical formalism of this century, of nineteenth-century aestheticism, or even merely the tradition of idealistic and Romantic thought in general (although it was there, in the work of Kant, Goethe, Schiller, the Schlegels, Schelling, and their successors, that the old intuition of the autonomy of art, as a realm not subordinated to systematic thought, ethical doctrines, and established values, found an appropriate conceptualization). These distinctions are part of a persistent concern, thematically complex and profound, of aesthetics and of philosophic thought in general; a concern that, though in contradictory fashion, is manifest in Plato's attacks on rhetoric, Locke's on eloquence, and Kant's on oratory.

Resistance to the use of imaginative or rhetorical means for doctrinal persuasion is not limited to defense of the autonomy of art. It has been noted since antiquity that subjecting thought to the passionate suggestions of an imaginative language runs counter to the sound discourse of reason. Conversely, a Romantic tenet, that subjecting imagination to explicit doctrines inhibits its peculiar powers, has become a widespread antirationalistic notion. Both of these concepts are alive in our intellectual tradition. Kant, like many other philosophers, sees in persuasive art a means to deceive and obfuscate one's fellows' faculty of knowing, an emotional violence (by seduction or intimidation) that disrupts the workings of the intelligence, and an infraction, contrary to ethical mandates, of the addressee's freedom to reason and choose in tranquility (*Critique of Judgment,* bk. 1, LIII). And in his aesthetics he severs beauty and the sublime from all cognitive or ethical content (though not from relationships of great significance to cognition and ethics). When Plato condemns poetry, he accuses it of stimulating the passions—that is, of irrationality—so that he groups it together with rhetoric as an enemy of knowledge, though he admits that there are kinds of art that are akin to rationality and prepare the way for it. Aristotle clarifies the relation of superior art to the passions in his theory of catharsis. The passions are a fundamental part of the artistic experience, but the effect of this experience is to neutralize them, to purify the soul of their oppression. The ultimate distance of the spectator from emotive forces, postulated by Aristotle, vaguely resembles the notion of Romantic irony, and expresses the common aesthetic experience of serenity, elevation, and freedom of mind. (Such terms have always been used to describe the effect of the contemplation of art.) Theorists of the sublime up to Kant, Schiller, and Schopenhauer insist on the liberating force of contemplation. This aesthetic quality characterizes a vast and exemplary class of artistic creations, among which the *Quixote* certainly will be found.

Today, as we know, a rejection of the distinction I have briefly outlined is drawn from Nietzsche's work. The inevitability and universality of rhetoric as an instrument and form of the will to power is affirmed, and it is thus vindicated against the classical attacks. Paul de Man, for example, points out the eloquence of Locke's condemnation of eloquence, and also the fact that Locke's philosophical discourse, like Kant's, includes fundamental metaphors to support the arguments.[61] And who would deny that Plato frequently resorts to the enchantments of literary imagination to persuade us of the truth of his thought (even if he indicates that this would not be the truly *divine* mode of treating his themes)?

But these factual contradictions do not mean that the thesis against rhetoric is necessarily invalid. Possibly they indicate only that it is human to lapse into passion against passion, or to use counterdeceptions against deceivers. De Man's objections do not establish that it is impossible to offer an argument altogether objectively (in a soft voice, say, and without persuasive intonation), an argument that can convince only if it is rational. Certainly, the use of metaphors and images in philosophic discourse presents extremely difficult questions about the cognitive possibilities intrinsic in language, but it does not imply that the discourse in which these figures appear is substantially of a persuasive-rhetorical nature, and not argumentative-rational. As Josef König used to say, philosophers can successfully handle images with exact descriptive intent.

But is not all communication necessarily persuasive, "conative"? Is there not, as Bertrand Russell maintains, an imperative bracketed within the coldest of scientific assertions, the imperative "Know that . . ." or "Observe this demonstration which I believe is valid . . ."?[62] We can concede this by redefining the traditional distinction between rhetorical and theoretical discourses as one of degree or kind rather than more radically of essence. But such a conceptual readjustment does not diminish the importance and reality of the distinction. The fact that we always have a vested interest in our relationships with our fellows does not permit us to ignore the difference between a relationship respectful of the greatest possible freedom of the other and one of domination and subjugation, in which a person is degraded into a mere instrument of someone else's will.[63]

If I convince you to be free, to become aware of your freedom, to take charge of your choices and decisions responsibly and rationally, perhaps my discourse ought to be called rhetorical; perhaps it expresses my desire for power, if not over you, then over the ways of the world. It may even be that, knowing you to be free of prejudices and passion, I shall expect you eventually to take a position similar to mine, because I trust human reason when it operates undisturbed. But I cannot force you in any doctrinal direction, since that would pervert and nullify my whole aim, which is oriented by the regulative ideal of a rational unanimity. In such a case, then, my discourse can be called rhetorical, and it ought to be called didactic, but in a sense *toto coelo* different from the prerational inculcation of normative views. The postulate of rationality is that in the ideal educated community we are united not by doctrines but only by a dialogue in which each person keeps an open mind regarding the unemotional essence of the other's argument. The traditional distinction of "convincing" by argument and "persuading" by emotional force points to the substance of what we have been examining.

(I am aware that in contemporary thought—in the work of Emmanuel Lévinas, for example—phenomenology, as a method of achieving objectivity, and logic itself have been considered forms of violence, and that a way of relating to one's fellows has been sought that avoids the possessive and dominating limitation of these cognitive acts. In such a search, perhaps the utopian appeal of an impossible encounter is at work. But the ethical impulse that leads to an attempt to overcome the theoretical attitude is the same one that begins by rejecting persuasion as well as dogmatic intimidation in the name of free rational criticism and objectivity. This is not a subject to be pursued here. I shall only point out that a will persists that seeks, in the forms of intellectual life and its communication, the maximum *respect* for the addressee's freedom, and the ideal of a truth that imposes itself without force, without emphasis, and even without formulation, arising from the pure activation of the image of the world that lies dormant in the depths of each individual's experience.)

It is thus possible, as I am doing, to draw a fruitful analogy between the relationship of the discourse of reason with that of persuasion, on the one hand, and the relationship of an imaginative and symbolic art with a didactic and allegorical art, on the other. Imagination can proceed autonomously, with no set preconceptions, following the spontaneity of the image with its own unforeseeable logic, creator of alternative worlds. Symbols are thus generated whose meaning will never be entirely encompassed by conceptual formulas. The symbol will animate thought, but it cannot moor it; rather, it will leave thought in relative liberty, especially if the symbol is ambiguous or if the work contains plural and contradictory symbols. This didacticism of an imagination free of doctrine is, then, similar to that of purely rational argumentation, in that it does not emotionally constrain the recipients but, on the contrary, activates in them the spontaneity of the mind.

The *Quixote* can be seen as a vast and subtle rhetorical-didactic operation, in the second of the senses of these terms that I have delineated. It begins by seducing readers with the joys of the comical and its devices, or with conventionally romancesque appearances that conceal a problematic depth, in order to carry them along toward growing uncertainties, to perplexities of ethical judgment, and to symbols of inexhaustible meaning. These complications will temporarily suspend the force of readers' convictions, and at the same time will activate their sensibility and their intelligence.

It is obvious that entertaining oneself by reading fiction is, in any event, a deferment of all mundane activities. Meditation and reflection have the same effect. But the forms of intellectual and imaginative experience that I am referring to go beyond the momentary suspension of action, because they induce a suspension of the *principles* of judgment. The philosophical tradition ever since Socrates, and including, among many others, Descartes and Husserl, has seen in this suspension the founding act of reliable knowledge and wisdom. The corresponding aesthetic operation is that temporary disengagement from real life and its convictions, in the secluded, absolute space of "play," in which the material of passions, doctrines, and ideals is neutralized, and, as Friedrich Schiller says, annihilated by the artistic form.[64]

Leading to this conception, Kant separated the aesthetic domain from both the positively cognitive and the ethical. He defines the aesthetic experience as one without determined concepts of the object and without purpose. Nevertheless, as becomes evident in the course of the considerations I have been developing, the conception that derives from Kant offers us no doctrine of "aestheticism" or intranscendent "formalism." Art *is* intranscendent, but in the sense in which Ortega uses the word. Art can live only in an absolute, hermetic space. But the spectator, in the end, leaves this space, and leaves it a different person. Aesthetic transport is an escape with a return, a productive alienation. Thus, already in Kant's aesthetics, beauty as well as the sublime is an experience that opens a path to a superior perception of the ontic dignity and the moral responsibility of the human subject. The absorbed contemplators sense their supernatural condition, and with it their rationality and freedom. A glimpse of metaphysical and religious transcendence is thus granted, according to the *Critique of Judgment,* on the horizon of aesthetic experience, but not in a conceptual way. For Schiller, the projection of this experience is worldly, educational and political, but no less alien to all doctrine. It is a form of sensitization and transformation of the contemplating subject that impels human beings toward their liberty and perfectibility. Also Rilke's well-known sonnet on the archaic torso of Apollo states that art urges us to change our life, without telling us what life we ought then to follow.

The discourse of reason and the free artistic imagination are radically diverse undertakings that can prosper only separately, but nonetheless they are twin resources provided by our culture, and among their uses is precisely spiritual liberation from dogmatic oppression, inveterate prejudice, and the biased influences of the power of others.

I believe that I have made clear the difference that must be recognized between two *toto coelo* diverse types of "rhetoric" and "didactics," and I have suggested the way a tradition that extends from antiquity to the present has understood the place of superior forms of art in this respect. Superior art is an education for those who contemplate it, of their intellectual and moral sensibility—that is, of the *sources* of knowledge and ethics. Art is an experience that should be defined as preethical, and, with respect to a conceptual knowledge, as precognitive as well as metaconceptual.

The concept of intuition in Bergson's and Croce's philosophies; the notions of clearing, uncovering, and the like in Heidegger's; in the field of criticism, the subversive dialoguism in Bakhtin's thought, the "estrangement" in the theory of the formalists, the critical objectivation of axiological presuppositions in Wolfgang Iser's theory of reception—whatever the point of view, all ultimately refer to a form of our spiritual life. In the *Quixote,* this form reaches a pinnacle of complexity, wealth, and boldness.

Method. I have maintained that we cannot define the spirit manifested in Cervantes's work by any expressions of a doctrinal nature in it, or by the exemplarity of its stories, but only be determining what this work is. Formulated differently, Cervantes does not tell us anything in his work; he *makes* it for us. Are we to understand what Cervantes communicates to us in his work, what gifts he bestows on us there? Let us see what he does and what we recreate in it. If we are to understand the work's signification, then, the essential task is above all to describe it as a poetic work—that is, to explain the nature of its component parts and the organization that unites them. I thus indicate my methodology. The only certain and unreservedly reliable expression of the essence of an author's poetic *inspiration,* of the basic inclination of his spirit as a writer, is the constitutive form of his work, the radical outline of his images, his "style"—in a sense that does not refer merely to the linguistic peculiarities of his diction but rather defines the distinctive character of his whole imagination, the stylizing tendency of his fictionalizing view of the world. What we are given in the *Quixote* is an imagined vision whose intimations of meaning are multiple and cannot be objectified in a system of thought. They can be focused and revealed by a description of the constitutive form (the matrix of the design) of that vision, so that they may be apprehended intuitively. In other words, only the observation of the complex *poetics* of the *Quixote* permits us a certain measure of reflection on the meaning that we experience in its reading.

The degree of certainty and clarity attainable in critical reflection is optimal on its primary descriptive level, where generalizations can be verified more or less immediately with reference to the text. Less precision is possible in the case of interpretive conceptualizations that simplify and summarize the meaning envisioned in the description of the form. Exactitude must continue to diminish as we proceed to generalize about the Cervantine work as a whole, and it is reduced still further when we link the poetic vision to the conjecturable personal experience of Cervantes the man. It is not at all unjustified to relate work and author. But it is necessary to keep the limitations of such an intellectual operation in mind. What we attempt to see clearly here is the vision of the author of the *Quixote*, strictly and only as it is presented in this work. This vision has, one must suppose, a natural link with the person and the life of Cervantes. But it is the product of the alienation of his lived experience by the forms of literary tradition in *one* among the various constellations of styles that he tried in an effort to redeem his life in enduring and joyful images.

Having clarified the confusing theme of Cervantes's "thought" in some measure, and having made the requisite distinctions between the quotidian convictions of the person and the spirit brought to life in the work, we seem to be back with the traditional themes: Cervantes, creator of the mythical figures of Don Quixote and Sancho; Cervantes, creator of the modern novel; and Cervantes, realist and ironist of the idealizing and romancesque imagination.[65] It is commonly thought that this, together with the creation of his characters and their singular world, is the specifically literary historical achievement of the man who lost the use of a hand at Lepanto: to inaugurate the major literary genre of the modern era and to establish realistic vision in fiction at the same time that he comically destroys the empire of romancesque fantasy. As we know, there is no lack of authority behind these ideas, well proclaimed by Menéndez Pelayo in his lectures commemorating the first publication of the *Quixote*.[66] Nevertheless, we have now begun to see that the Cervantine work is not subjected to a strictly realistic design, and that it not only does not destroy the idealizing and unrealistic modes of fantasy but rather uses and reforms them. Certainly the *Quixote* presented structural innovations that can be easily misunderstood as the invention of the generic form of the modern novel. Also, it is apparent that this work employs literary satire to move in the direction of realism. But we will see that these impulses emanate from a more profound and fundamental action, a spiritual reform that consists of the simultaneous and all-embracing ironization and incarnation of the literary institution. Its fundamental import is the Cervantine discovery of what I will call the system of the regions of the imagination.

Chapter 1

Cervantes and the Regions of the Imagination

We need not wonder to find Hector quoting Aristotle, when we see the loves of Theseus and Hippolyta combined with the gothic mythology of fairies. Shakespeare, indeed, was not the only violator of chronology, for in the same age Sidney, who wanted not the advantages of learning, has, in his *Arcadia,* confounded the pastoral with the feudal times, the days of innocence, quiet, and security, with those of turbulence, violence, and adventure.
— Samuel Johnson, Preface to his edition of Shakespeare (1765)

The subject of this poetry is the affairs and works of shepherds, principally their loves; but simple and harmless, not baneful with the rage of jealousy, not marred by adulteries, rather competitions of rivals, but without death and blood. . . . The customs represent the Golden Age.
— Fernando de Herrera, *Anotaciones a Garcilaso* (1580)

The Discontinuities of the Novelistic World

The Work's Stylistic Design. The fundamental motif of the *Quixote* is that of a mad hidalgo who (and this is his madness) believes that the world of his daily experience and the world represented in books of chivalry are one and the same real world. He does perceive a difference between these realms, however. For him the chivalric deeds really took place in another era, a better one. His mission derives from these two suppositions: The present world is an extension and a corruption of its own heroic past. From there it follows that, because he is dealing with two phases of the same reality, it has to be possible to restore justice, or at least the lost heroism. Precisely because he assumes that the fundamental continuity of the world unites his daily experience with the sphere of romancesque adventures, Don Quixote interprets and falsifies his perceptions in terms of the world of books of chivalry. That sets the stage for the satirical and comic device that consists in the conflict between the idealizing and fantastic imagination and the reality of daily experience.

The *satiric* lesson thus seems to be that there is no such continuity between the world of fantastic idealizations and the real world. And this lesson seems to be made possible by the adoption of a *realistic* imagination as the basic level of the work, in contrast to the fantastic imagination of the protagonist. Cervantine "realism" would then be the foundation of the immediate satire of Don Quixote's foolish credulity, and, in a more general sense, of the simplicity of readers who seek in literature, and then in reality, a heroic and romantic dream, beyond life's possibilities. (Such a doctrine could ultimately be linked to the tradition of ascetic rejection of the literary imagination, whose sources are found in Plato, Tertullian, Saint Augustine, and Boethius. But it is clear that Cervantes's entire work is in fact opposed to this repressive ethics of spiritual conduct. To put Cervantes's satire in the same category as the attacks of sixteenth-century moralists against the romancesque imagination is ill advised on the face of it and, as we will see, largely wrong.)

It seems to me undeniable that this motif, the discontinuity between the spheres of daily experience and the chivalric world, is present in the work and is fundamental. Nevertheless, I am going to maintain that the work reaches beyond the scope of this satirical structure, defuses its definitive air, and shows its limitations. If the *Quixote* were simply a realistic satire of romancesque idealization—that is, the counterposition of two types of imagination (fantastic-ideal and realistic)—there would be no way to explain or to read most of the work. One would have to declare that the pastoral chapters (at least those dealing with Grisóstomo and Marcela) constitute a grave error of inconsequence. The stories of Dorotea, Cardenio, Luscinda, and Don Fernando (especially in their resolution) would constitute appalling deviations from the realistic design. The inverisimilar transformations that the principal characters undergo throughout the novel, or the fascinating temporal paradoxes of the work, would be author's lapses that deprive his creation of artistic consistency. The description of Camacho's wedding would be a censurable excess; the encounters and anagnorises at the inn, concessions to novelesque or conventional Byzantine tastes.

We would then find ourselves maintaining the hypothesis, which several of the contemporary critics I have cited have opposed, of a Cervantes who writes carelessly, without discipline or artistic consciousness, endowed only with the power of his talent.[1] We have learned from the phenomenological and structuralist criticism of our century, however, as well as from the great critics of all times, beginning with Aristotle, that a good part of the power of artistic genius is precisely the strictest discipline of the imagination. A correct reading of the *Quixote* shows that the Cervantine fantasy is supremely rigorous, and the occasional authentic mistakes in detail that we find in this very extensive work, such as the presence/absence of Sancho's donkey in some passages of the First Part, corroborate its artistic consequence, for they arise from the gravitation of fundamental lines of its architecture (in this case, the aesthetic bond that unites the central characters with their mounts).[2]

Cervantes's radical intent hides beneath the surface of the satire of idealizing stylization. So far as this dimension of the work is concerned, I believe his design is to make manifest the discontinuity of the various archetypal forms of fiction, thereby exposing the relativity of literature's institutionalized imagination. The key for understanding the style of the Cervantine imagination in the *Quixote* is this: To satirize romancesque stylization (or any other style of imagination), the space in which the satirized form is introduced need not be realistic. If suffices that another law operates there, that the principle of stylization is different.

Within the spectrum of the regions of the imagination, the basic plane of the *Quixote*—the domestic world of Don Quixote and Sancho Panza—is doubtless much closer to the strictly realistic extreme than to the world of books of chivalry. And that is what leads to the impression, strengthened by the contrast, that we are entirely in realistic terrain. That is not the case. Let me add that Cervantes's *humorism,* as distinct from the satirical dimension of his creation, is sustained not by the projection of the fantastic idealization into the climate of realism but, quite the contrary, by the projection of the everyday world into the more ideal sphere of comedy. This can be seen very clearly in *Rinconete and Cortadillo,* where the somber ambience of delinquency and the picaresque is transmuted into forms of ironized rhetorical elevation and grand theatrical gesture, and resolved (apparently) in the harmless and funny. This comic method operates also in the *Quixote.* It consists not in making the idealization laughable by placing it in the ordinariness of everyday life but in making mundane misery laughable by placing it in the purified atmosphere of the happy world of comedy, where nothing serious happens, and at the end all is well. (Let us recall in passing Aristotle's observation that the properly comical effect is brought about by a nongrievous ugliness, which does not involve serious damage [*Poetics,* 1449a].) After all, the multiple beatings that Don Quixote and Sancho suffer never break their bones or hurt them seriously. The loss of half an ear, which the Basque cuts off Don Quixote, does not modify the way his face looks, for no one seems to note its absence. In the adventure of the herds of sheep, his teeth shattered and cleanly carried away by stones hurled at him make up a stylized comic catastrophe. Besides, this calamity does not seem to have consequences that would be natural (though it is at least mentioned later, and Sancho names it as one of the causes of Don Quixote's sad visage [I.19]). And so that our heroes may ride at their pleasure and sleep outdoors if night overtakes them in the wilderness, the stable summer extending from the first sally in July to the final adventures in August lasts several months, if not years, judging from Sancho's letter to Teresa Panza, dated 1614. (True, there is an *ad hoc* rain, so that the second barber will have a reason to cover his head with the basin that Don Quixote will take to be Mambrino's helmet [I.21].)

The ironization of literature itself, in its totality, which Cervantes displays in the *Quixote,* falls first of all on the comic stylization of reality. (By virtue of this basic trait of intention, the work's mimetic mode is continuously and in the most radical sense self-reflective, metafictional.) Author and reader alike smile before the noninjurious levity that the blows of life acquire in its sphere. And therefore the Cervantine smile is always a little melancholy, for the ironization of the forms and the spirit of comedy is accompanied by the sober understanding that reality is much, much worse.

We see, then, that far from a simple counterposition of idealization and realism (or of "romantic lie and novelistic truth," in René Girard's terms),[3] Cervantes operates from the beginning with a complex system of diverse spheres of stylization, moving among the initial evocation of a semirealism based on daily and domestic elements, romancesque fantasy (projected by Don Quixote in his imaginations and discourses), and the happy abstraction of comedy. These are the three fundamental regions. From them the work takes us to others. The task of describing them with their specific characteristics and in their reciprocal and hierarchical relationships is that of elucidating the "transcendental" structure of the *Quixote*.[4] A large part of this study is devoted to that task. Let us briefly survey its most important points.

The *Quixote* is structured not by unitary action in the Aristotelian sense but by a plurality of actions, which, according to the Italian critics of the sixteenth century, is peculiar to the *romanzesca* form. The variety of actions does not itself imply a multiplicity of imaginary regions, it only makes it possible for the work to display them. It can be said that the actions of the *Quixote* are ordered as follows. There is one principal action, Don Quixote's sally in search of fame. It is articulated in the generally discrete and independent "adventures." These adventures and encounters lead frequently to episodes not connected to Don Quixote's and Sancho's actions, episodes that at times constitute substantial stories of other protagonists, whose destiny is not influenced at all by the book's two main characters. Don Quixote's adventures are normally kept in the comic-realistic sphere, which permits occasional near-fusions with the picaresque region (for example, in the adventure of the galley slaves). Only when rapt in a dream or daydream does Don Quixote penetrate a romancesquely idealized world, and even then comic-realistic and grotesque notes corrupt the sphere of the marvelous (as in the Cave of Montesinos and in the quixotic evocations of typical scenes from books of chivalry).[5] On the other hand, the stories in which Don Quixote and Sancho take only minor parts (those of Dorotea and company, of Camacho's wedding, of Roque Guinart, etc.) or are merely incidental spectators (those of Marcela, the Captive, Claudia Jerónima, Ana Félix) or are absent altogether (the events of the *novella*, "The Man of Ill-Advised Curiosity") depart from comic realism and display other worlds of the literary imagination, including the pastoral utopia, courtly intrigue, Byzantine peripeteias, the Moorish novel, and the rationalist tragedy. In one way or another, the entire system of the institutional imagination of literature is embodied in the book. But with only one exception (the story of ill-advised curiosity, whose revealing singularity we will examine in Chapter 5), all the regions of the literary tradition appear adulterated in the *Quixote*. They are not merely ironized by being juxtaposed but are adulterated by foreign elements that deprive them of stylistic purity.

Here I want to suggest a historical correspondence that may at first seem to be an extemporaneous association, but that can help us to understand the complex phenomenon of the discrete spheres of the imagination. I have just implicitly indicated that the historical position of Cervantes's work is, in one of its dimensions, *prerealistic*. The sphere against which heroic idealization and romancesque fantasy are counterposed, and thus ironized, approaches realistic vision by way of its elements of daily life, but does not completely reach it, because of its comic stylization.[6] In this imaginative operation, which constitutes only one of the twists of the Cervantine vision, our author is genealogically linked with Lodovico Ariosto and with Joanot Martorell (partial affinities that Cervantes himself explicitly suggests), and also with Lucian, as Menéndez y Pelayo remarks.[7] Here the "realistic" elements are the instrument of ironization (distancing, suspension) of the kind of imagination that was then traditional. This operation is repeated, symetrically inverted, in *postrealistic* literature of our century. Realistic imagination (which is now the traditional one) is ironized by writers such as Kafka and by those who follow the call of "magic realism" when they introduce elements of the fantastic into the sphere of the mundane. Between the black humor of these writers of our time and the luminous humor of earlier times lies the gray seriousness of the realist region.

That Cervantes is conscious, conceptually as well as intuitively, of the phenomenon we are examining is demonstrated by some passages in his work. The Curate says of *Tirante el Blanco,* in his well-known judgment from the sixth chapter of the First Part, "that by virtue of its style, this is the best book in the world: here knights eat, and sleep, and die in their beds, and they make wills before their deaths, with other things which all the rest of the books of this genre lack." It is worth remarking that "style" here does not mean the singularity or the character of the *diction,* as it usually does today, but rather denotes what I have called the "principle or law of stylization." An equivalent use of the word "style" is found at a significant point in the *Persiles* (at the end of chap. 15 of bk. 3). There, as in other parts of this extraordinary novel, which also displays and contrasts regions of the imagination (albeit with less depth, and somewhat hurriedly, and in terrains that are not only geographically more exotic), the narration passes from one sphere to another, from the tragic and marvelous to the sordid and mundane, and from there to the bizarre and romancesque. In that transit the narrator says that what happened later to his characters "requires a new style and a new chapter." Don Quixote, too, sometimes uses the word "style" to indicate the form of the imaginary world (II.29).

It is significant that the central characters in the *Quixote,* as we will see, cannot enter imaginary spheres other than the comic-realistic, which is Don Quixote's and Sancho's own sphere. To the world of the pastoral stories (in particular, that of Marcela and Grisóstomo) and to the world of the courtly stories (that of Dorotea and company), the protagonists of the book appear as only occasional spectators. On the other hand, the protagonists of the *Persiles* travel through the center of all or nearly all of that novel's imaginary regions (not generically institutionalized). They can do so because they are much less individuated characters than Don Quixote and Sancho. The abstract substance of the Byzantine heroes does not in and of itself generate dense surroundings; if it did, such an ambience would have to be defined stylistically, and would encapsulate them, thus impeding their migration, not through geographical regions but indeed through imaginary ones.

I will note incidentally that the collection of the *Exemplary Novels* assumes particular interest when it is contemplated in terms of the transparent variety of the imaginative spectrum.[8]

For the most part, the *Quixote* presents its protagonists on the road, moving from adventure to adventure (and from conversation to conversation), time and again changing locales. Some types of places appear repeatedly: Don Quixote's home, the highway, the inn, the forest, the residences of hidalgos and nobles. The simple change of place (from one point on the highway to another, for example) does not, in general, indicate a more profound change of imaginary climate. But the frequency with which the changes from one place to another of a different kind coincide with a mutation of the principle of stylization seems to me too great to be considered incidental. At such moments we can intuit that we are passing not only from one point to another on Don Quixote's and Sancho's itinerary but also from one sphere of literary fantasy to another. The Cervantine imagination at times signals the articulations of style with transitions of setting.

The first and most notable of these profound displacements occurs in Chapters 10 through 14 of the First Part. Until then, the novel has unfolded in its basic sphere, which I have called *comic realism*. After the fight with the Basque in the middle of the highway, master and squire leave the site of the battle and at dusk encounter (in a setting vaguely depicted, but characterized by vegetation and rusticity) a group of goatherds who are preparing their meal; they are received with primitive but cordial hospitality. We are still in the comic-realistic sphere (although the landscape has already changed a little). These goatherds are simple people; literature plays little part in their lives, and they do not understand a word of the sonorous speech with which Don Quixote regales them after supper. Although they could be called "shepherds" (*pastores*), they are called "goatherds" (*cabreros*).

The discourse with which Don Quixote has favored them is in praise of the Golden Age. It evokes the great thematic complex of the utopia of country life (of Greco-Latin lineage, and among the most prominent of the Renaissance). In the Renaissance and beyond, this utopian theme has its own poetic genre: pastoral literature. And it is obvious that in the literary context of the time, the topic of the Golden Age—expressed, moreover, in redundant pastoral epithets—sounds a note of bucolic idealization. One of the goatherds has already sung to entertain the group—his verses are appropriately unsophisticated—when another arrives with the news of Grisóstomo's death and the story of his unfortunate love. Although it retains a weak link with the sphere of comic realism (Grisóstomo is a student and Marcela is the heir of well-to-do country folk), this story already decidedly belongs to the utopian unrealism of the pastoral genre. In this world, other laws operate. Delicate maidens can live alone peacefully in the wilderness, singing most of the day, and possessing a Ciceronian rhetorical power when the occasion requires it. The heroes, if they are disdained by the objects of their love, are destined to die from it, for their lives have no meaning beyond the yearning for the beloved beauty. The victim of unfortunate love is buried with literary ceremonies and without a trace of Christian rites, and no one is scandalized by this radical paganism.

Obviously we are in another region of the imagination. And the place where Don Quixote and Sancho attend the funerary rites of the shepherd poet is of another sort, too; it is a mountain valley at the side of a great rock.

Another moment in the transition from the comic-realistic region to Marcela's and Grisóstomo's pastoral one is the following. Before the novel's course takes it all the way into the pastoral region, Pedro the Goatherd, in telling the story of the pair (I.12), says that the town "abbots" object to the burial the shepherd poet wanted because it has aspects that "ring of heathen." But Pedro adds that the dead poet's friends want to carry out his wishes to the letter. This they do, and in the sphere that the characters have reached at that point, the rite's paganism no longer provokes scandal. Another sign of stylistic displacement is the numerous linguistic corrections with which Don

Quixote interrupts the goatherd's narration. Here the difference between vulgar and cultivated speech is an anticipatory emblem of the confrontation of the two styles of vision.[9] The dialogue between Don Quixote and the gentleman Vivaldo on the way to the burial (I.13) also belongs to the apparatus of this transition, since it touches upon the subject of idolatrous love (common to the chivalric and pastoral spheres) and evokes the romancesque knightly sphere, which thus serves to support the bucolic idealization, just as later, when Cardenio's story is about to be introduced, the pastoral in turn serves to support the novelesque courtly sphere (I.23). Sometimes the mention of an otherwise uncharacterized father who is a peasant *of means* functions as pivotal for these changes of region, the attribute of wealth seeming to be a bridge between comic realism, the pastoral, and the courtly sphere. (It is not only Marcela's father who is a rich peasant; so are Dorotea's and Leandra's.)

In the Second Book of *The Galatea* there is a remarkable displacement in the opposite direction. With the hermit Silerio's narration of the story of Timbrio and Silerio we leave the utopian pagan Hispania, with Latin toponyms and without Christian names, rites, and attitudes, and move into the courtly world of an Italian *novella*. The shift from the strictly pastoral imaginary region is also marked here by a geographical displacement, from the inland meadows to the port of Barcelona. There for the first time appear clerics carrying a crucifix in a procession, justice incarnated in fallible and impersonal institutions, the big city, and other elements of the broad region of cape and sword ("capa y espada": let us call it that, and give this traditional Spanish term for a theatrical genre a broader sense than usual).

The laws of one stylization are incompatible with those of the other. The regions of the imaginary are not continuous. It is true that Cervantes seems at times to make Don Quixote and Sancho pass from their own sphere to these foreign regions. But there they are only spectators, and the pertinent stories are, in the Aristotelian sense, episodes, not part of the plot's logos. It is more accurate to say that the central characters arrive at the borders of foreign regions. It should be observed that when Marcela's episode ends and she retires into the forest, Don Quixote follows her almost immediately, but he cannot find her. This impossibility, rather than representing a physical obstacle, translates the absolute and necessary frontier of style.

The eminent emblem of these interregional impossibilities is the search for Dulcinea, a search necessarily unfruitful in a double sense.

On the objective plane, the plane of what is represented in the work, the impossibility is, so to speak, material: Don Quixote wants to find a princess who exists only in his mad imagination (and *he does not want* to find Aldonza Lorenzo). On the metanarrative plane, the plane of the work as a poetic representation, the impossibility is the confabulation of a character of the romancesque marvelous realm with one of comic realism. Thus the three feigned or inauthentic appearances of Dulcinea (as one of the three peasant women from Toboso, as a figure of Don Quixote's vision in the Cave of Montesinos, and as a disguised servant in the Duke's elaborate practical joke) have a plural significance. On the objective plane, they give a pensive turn to Don Quixote's insanity, which then seems to become a purely psychic agony. (At such moments his madness is pathetic and, for some Romantics, sublime.) On a less obvious plane, the pseudotransfigurations insistently evoke the theme of the force of the law of stylization. Aldonza Lorenzo is the transregional alter ego of Dulcinea, and her (also false) appearance in Sancho's lying account to Don Quixote (I.31) remains in the comic-realistic region.

Cervantes marks transitions between imaginary worlds with a series of thematic and tonal anticipations, or with violent contrasts. We have seen the gradually marked transition with which the story of Marcela and Grisóstomo is introduced. At the episode's end, on the other hand, we have a grotesque contrast to return us to the comic realistic world. Here the adventure of the Yanguesans (in which Rocinante makes advances to their mares, and ends up as throttled as his master) immediately follows the story of the Platonic adoration of ideal beauty incarnated in a woman. The fact that the chapter on the Yanguesans (I.15) begins with faint eclogue-type echoes in the form of the *locus amoenus* accentuates the humor of this transition.

In Chapter 19 of the Second Part, Don Quixote and Sancho are on the road, in the company of two students, devotees of fencing, who at a certain moment test their skill to settle a point in the doctrine of swordplay. The Bachiller Corchuelo is defeated, and in exasperation he flings away his sword. He tosses it so far ("three-quarters of a league") that they decide to send a servant to look for it, and to continue on the road without waiting for him, because they judge that he will take a long time. The image of this incident surprises us by its exaggeration, which deviates from the preceding forms. But it is precisely in its hyperbolic character that an anticipatory signal is given with which Cervantes, again, is preparing a transition to another imaginative sphere.[10] For in the next chapter comes the description of the culinary circumstances of Camacho's wedding: the pots are so large that they hold whole sheep, "without their reaching the surface of the broth, as if they were young pigeons"; the plucked chickens are too numerous to count; the stuffed birds are "infinite"; and the cheeses, stacked like bricks in crisscross tiers, form a wall. Once again we are in another imaginative region; and we can say that this region is a country of ancient folkloric lineage, the land of Cockaigne ("Cucania" or "Cucaña"), a comical variation, incontinent and plebeian, of the Golden Age.[11]

It is true that our author does not consistently maintain this law of stylization throughout the wedding episode (which would readily become cumbersome), and soon gives a (hardly genuine) pastoral turn to the sphere he has created. This ought to indicate to us again that he does not necessarily intend his structural design to project *pure* regions or forms of the literary imagination. Cervantes formally constructs a considerable part of his narrative works by superimposing diverse principles of stylization, by mixing archetypes that are opposite and sometimes dissonant. The same can be said of the internal structure of the characters, whose richness can be traced partly to the conjunction of contrary and even contradictory archetypes within the character's identity. (I examine the structure of Cervantes's characters in Chapters 2 and 3.)

Another aesthetic climate can be perceived in the story of the Captive. Here the imaginary region is crossed by the winds of history. In this tale there are chronicle-like fragments with references to great events of the time, sober heroism, a serious though ambiguous religious theme, and an autobiographical tone (the actual provenance of the subject from the author's life is, of course, something else, not relevant for an appraisal of artistic form). The narration has no comic aspects; dignity is sustained and understated. Although it is not realistic in the modern sense, for its elements of the marvelous are foreign to ordinary experience, it does present a picture of authentic heroism without excessive idealization. This part of the *Quixote* also has well-prepared transitions, which mediate between the region of the novelesque comedy of Dorotea, Cardenio, and company and the serious region of the Captive. The first is the Moorish woman's "No, not Zoraida: María, María!" Its meaning is not fully explained at first, but the tone is unequivocal. Then comes Don Quixote's very empirical praise of arms, strewn with allusions to contemporary history.

Certainly I cannot set out in detail the complete design of the transcendental structure of the *Quixote*. I can only finish demonstrating
its existence by pointing out a few other parts of its architecture of
imaginary regions. Cervantes's lucid artistic consciousness and the
strict discipline of his imagination are thus evident in their formal
results.

In a few passages (I.21, I.50, II.22) Don Quixote evokes the world
of the chivalric imagination beautifully and succintly. The purity of the
form evoked is almost total. Almost, because Cervantes does not
refrain from sprinkling it with traces of irony, which connect the
chivalric vision with the hidalgo's madness and with basic comic
realism. This can be observed, for example, when the hero depicted by
Don Quixote, after the wonderful reception and dinner at the castle in
the company of the most beautiful and elegantly attired maidens, is
left alone at the banquet table, "reclining in the seat and perhaps
picking his teeth, as is the custom" (I.50). This matter of picking the
teeth after a meal is just the sort of trivial detail of daily life that does
not belong in the idealizing region of the imagination. It is a thing of
another "style."

Upon finishing the romancesque evocation of Chapter 21 of the
First Part, Don Quixote says that "this knight is the son of a worthy
king of I don't know what kingdom, because I believe that it must not
be on the map." This is not only a humorous deflation of the hidalgo's
inspired fantasy; it is a deliberate inconsistency in the artistic manipulation of the character, for the voice that can make such a comment is
not his but the voice of reason, the author's and the reader's. We
should not confuse this phenomenon with the semirealistic game in
which Don Quixote's psyche is always fundamentally divided between
madness and good sense, in which he is "a man mad at intervals."
This is something else. Here Cervantes shatters not just the romancesque illusion but also the "realistic" or verisimilar one. Not only
that; he causes a fissure to open in the cloak of fiction itself, alerting us
for an instant to true reality, our own. Usurpation of a character's
voice by the point of view of reason and the sense of reality is not rare
in the *Quixote*.[12] We will soon see other instances of it. They demonstrate quite clearly how distant the design of the work is from realistic
hermeticity.

In addition to these foreign elements that he allows into the knightly
region, however, Cervantes has already proceeded to construct a
global contrast of imaginative spheres in Chapters 21 and 22 of the

First Part. Immediately after the ideal and fantastic image of Chapter 21, he introduces the picaresque world of the galley slaves, the satire of the miserable human condition, transposed and thus lightened to the humoristic key of comedy.

After the ultimately comic-realistic adventure of the galley slaves, our heroes leave the highway and strike off into the forest. The change of place here is a significant change of landscape and a prelude to the change of aesthetic region that Cardenio and Dorotea bring with them. Both appear for the first time in the natural and seemingly stylistically neutral environment of the hills and forest. The region of Cardenio, Dorotea, Luscinda, and Don Fernando is the world of novelesque intrigue, where love is entangled with honor and deception. It is a sphere of *partial idealization:* the gallants are handsome and the maidens of superlative beauty, but their moral character is defective. Here we are far from the absolutes of the pastoral (or of the Byzantine) sphere. Nevertheless, the formal idealization of this novelesque region is seen in the tendency to sketch each character as a single dominant quality. Thus, as Salvador de Madariaga has indicated, Dorotea is cleverness, Cardenio cowardice.[13] We can add that Don Fernando is prideful amorality and Luscinda confusion.[14] The most general principle that governs in this sphere is also a principle of comedy: chance, through marvelous coincidences, resolves injustices and leads to a happy ending of multiple marriages. The characters seem to have been cleansed of a part of their considerable moral defects through unexplained mysterious transmutations, and brought closer to flat and transparent images of extreme gallantry and beauty.

Let us note briefly that all the aesthetic regions seem to have some weak point in their structure, something rather like the place where the violence of stylization, the transcendental hubris of *the form,* is revealed. Stories belonging to the regions in which the law of the maiden's superlative beauty governs (as in the pastoral and the novelesque-courtly regions) tend to run into difficulties when they have more than one heroine, especially when two or more supreme beauties meet in the same scene. Cervantes, who often finds himself in this conflict, resolves it in good humor, suspending the admiring bystanders in the perplexity of not knowing whom to consider more beautiful. Alternatively, a hierarchy is maintained in favor of the principal heroine, leading the marveling gentlemen or shepherds to the reflection that if they had not seen that one, the other would have seemed to them the most beautiful woman in the world. The ironization of literary conventions is evident in such passages. But in the context of Cervantes's work, the implications of this irony are exceptionally profound, since it is linked to and part of the exposition of the principles of literary imagination as a whole.

As the paradoxes that flow from an axiomatic system reveal its hidden imperfection, so in each of the imaginary regions there necessarily emerge inconsistencies of the stylistic architecture which fracture the image, producing a disillusioning and involuntarily—or better, mechanically—ironic effect. In view of these complications, what difficulties Cervantes has faced in his endeavor to articulate the heterogeneous whole of all the imaginary regions in a single design! The points where heterogeneous regions interface with each other expose the work to the destructive force of the amorphous, in which the image dissolves without a dominant line, like the profile of a body misshapen by unarticulated bones. Precisely at such tangential points we sense the touch of Cervantes's virtuosity. I have already indicated the variety and subtlety of the transitions from region to region, the play of progressive anticipations and violent contrasts. And there is the extreme audacity of placing characters from different aesthetic universes in a common situation. At times (such as at the burial of Grisóstomo, the encounter with Roque Guinart, and the presence of the protagonists at the peripeteia of Ana Félix) Don Quixote and Sancho's approach to foreign regions (of the pastoral, of romancesque chivalric banditry, and of the Byzantine) encapsulates and alienates them. There foreign airs reduce our wanderers to the marginal passivity of the background; they are quiet and they watch. But elsewhere Cervantes extracts from the collision of different regions the highest intensities of meaning. Recall the encounter, in the natural neutrality of the mountains, between Don Quixote, the mad hidalgo of comic realism, and Cardenio, the mad gallant of idealized love-and-honor intrigues. The impulsiveness with which they embrace and the lengthy exchange of astonished looks that silently pass between them (with which the chapter [I.23] ends) constitute a moment charged with humor, multiple irony, and profound meaning. In the foreground we have spontaneous sympathy between two persons who have decided to follow the road of extravagance and who recognize in the other their own passion and madness, with which they ironize themselves; underneath we have the encounter of two literary regions, of two different worlds. It is an exchange of looks, of derangements, and of universes. The melancholy suggestion of insuperable solitude, and at the same time of the essential unity of what is human, beyond particular insanities and beyond particular imaginative worlds, emanates from this metapoetic confrontation.

The sparks from these tangential meetings of noncommunicating worlds are possible in the *Quixote* because, notwithstanding the multiple ironic game, Cervantes firmly maintains the diverse identities of the regions. We saw that it is a formal necessity for Don Quixote to be unable to reach Marcela, though he follows her almost immediately when she retires from the scene of the burial. It is not the density of the vegetation but the laws of style that separate these inhabitants of two globes constructed differently, two noncommunicating spheres. The divergence of the anthropologies projected in the different imaginary regions shows with maximum clarity when they can be compared in respect to some particular point that they have in common, as when they meet in the allusion to the same real circumstance of Spain's geography (thus dually fictionalized). Marcela, such a beauty that men die of love for her, lives peacefully and without fear of attack in the Sierra of her pastoral utopia, while Dorotea, likewise a supreme beauty, but from another world, that of courtly intrigue, having just arrived at the same geographical region, is the victim of two attempted rapes, one by her "faithful" servant and the other by a local "cattle rancher" (I.28).

It is worth noting the exactitude with which Cervantes discriminates and distributes words that are conceptually almost synonymous, but stylistically different, in relation to the regional aesthetic variations. We already saw that he distinguishes "goatherds" (*cabreros*, of comic realism) from "shepherds" (*pastores*, of bucolic idealization). Now, in the region of courtly intrigue, he calls them "cattle ranchers" (*ganaderos*). The stylistics of the vocabulary confirms the styles of the imagination.

The most complex and extensive case of interregional imbrications is, without a doubt, the entrance of Dorotea, Cardenio, and company into the comic-realistic world. This imaginative adventure of Cervantes's is rich in admirable metapoetic articulations. The prelude to the encounter anticipates with enigmatic symbolism the complications that follow. Fleeing from possible pursuit by the Holy Brotherhood, for having freed the galley slaves, Don Quixote and Sancho enter the Sierra Morena (I.23).[15] Shortly afterward they find Cardenio's satchel—that is, a sign of his existence that indicates an elevated lifestyle, as much in wealth as in culture. Here for the first time the novelesque intrigue creeps in through the papers of the gallant which Don Quixote reads. Then Cardenio himself fleetingly passes before their eyes, but reduced to an aspect that is diminished and rustic. The signs of style, then, are already here ambiguous, regionally mixed. Almost immediately they hear a whistle like that of a "shepherd," and then a "goatherd" appears. This denominative duplicity, which is maintained throughout the episode, is most exact, since the group that this goatherd-shepherd represents has something of pastoral idealization without completely attaining it. They are figures of an intermediate, neutral, semi-idealized realm, which serve as a bridge between the characters of comic realism and those of the courtly novel. The first thing the goatherd does is to ask them "who had brought them to this place," rarely visited by human beings. Thus the note is sounded of transitional and neutral space, foreign to Don Quixote and Sancho's natural habitat in a double sense, geographical and metapoetic. Then the goatherd insists on the inaccessibility of the terrain in which they find themselves, "because if you penetrate half a league farther in, perhaps you will not know how to make your way out; and I am amazed that you have even gotten this far, since there is no road or path that leads to this place." Can literature more discreetly emblematize the process of quasi-impossible imaginative transition that we witness in this chapter? This passage, like many others in the work, requires a double reading, one naive, so to speak, attentive to the narrated and described world, and the other reflexive, obliquely observing the forms of literary representation, rich in artifice.

The introduction of figures of novelesque idealization into the comic-realistic realm, which in Dorotea's case as in Cardenio's occurs through the nonurban, asocial filter of the forest, is facilitated by the fact that on the primary plane of narrative mimesis the two are escapees. Both have fled from society to the wilderness, and at the same time, on the plane of stylization, from the courtly sphere to a stylistically indefinite space. After telling her story to the Curate and his companions, and when she begins to *act* in their world, Dorotea *disguises* herself and *pretends* to be the Princess Micomicona of the deception prepared to ensnare Don Quixote. She does not have to show herself as she really is, and thus her interaction with Don Quixote and his fellows is facilitated. Dorotea's carefree and uninhibited conduct while she is pretending to be Micomicona, despite her own tribulations and most unfortunate condition, is psychologically inverisimilar, but it is aesthetically justified as a consequence of the change in imaginative region, for in these passages she inhabits the comic-realistic interlude of her courtly peripeteia. (Here, as at many other points, it is evident that the controlling principle of Cervantes's writing is not always verisimilitude—and hardly ever realism.) As for Cardenio, he has gone mad—that is, he has lost his personal identity—and his madness opens up a field of legitimate inconsistency of conduct for his character and makes him transregionally adaptable. These figures recover their own being when they are among their own kind at the inn. At the end, when the story of novelesque intrigue has concluded, Cervantes once again humorizes the metapoetic encounter by making Sancho the witness to the kisses that Dorotea and Fernando surreptitiously exchange. These two, then, finally descend to the comic-realistic sphere, newly transfigured (and only in this coda to their already concluded story), as though Cervantes were extending them metapoetic if not poetic justice.[16]

All in all, despite or because of the subtlety of these transits, the heterogeneity of the imaginary regions that overlap here is never suspended. The idealized figures of courtly intrigue persist for the duration of their story—with the exception of the codas that follow the denouement—as beings alien to comic-realistic subjects. When Sancho sees Dorotea for the first time, he is supremely impressed, "since it seemed to him (and it was indeed so) that in all the days of his life he had never seen such a beautiful creature" (I.29). When the group arrives at the inn, "everyone [there] was astonished at Dorotea's beauty, and even at the handsome figure cut by the youth Cardenio" (I.32). These passages too require a double reading: intra- and metapoetic. Admiration for the extreme beauty of a being from our world coincides here with admiration before the visible ideal of a being from another world.

Revealing Detail and Intuited Totality: A Methodological Reflection. Permit me a brief methodological excursus at this point to justify these interpretive steps.

Borges, whose work is permeated by the desire to give an adventuresome and even heroic touch to an existence turned inward and irremediably bookish, has adorned the novelesque figure of the detective with attributes of the scholar and philologist, and at the same time has tried to make a detective activity out of reading. His own stories are constructed around minimal clues, designed for the attention of one who distrusts appearances and searches for the revealing detail that can invert the entire apparent meaning of the text in an instant. His critical essays and commentaries on great and minor works are often also configured in this way. Indirectly, this propensity is representative of one of the intellectual currents of the century, that of mistrust, of the search for what is behind the facade and is presumably the true meaning of statements and attitudes. It is the tradition of Freud, as well as that of the criticism of ideologies, of the deconstruction of works by means of the marginal sign, of the reconstruction of an epoch through its minor documents, and the like. Positively stated, it is the belief that one lives in false consciousness, and that the truth emerges from blindness as an oblique glimmer, filtering through minimal openings. This attitude easily degenerates into an arbitrary criticism that seeks the effect of paradox and founds aberrant interpretations upon one detail chosen ad hoc, overloaded with a supposedly final signification, which lacks any other textual basis. Such readings are too close to the text, out of focus.

The opposite line of thinking in our century (frequently found together with the first in the same subject and even in a single work) is the phenomenological approach, confidence in the lived, conscious experience and in a sense in appearances, when they are erected and maintained in the face of critical attention. The criticism that flows from this second intellectual attitude rejects the preeminence of the isolated detail or of the marginal trait, requires the validation of the interpretive hypothesis through the broadest description, and, ideally, the inclusion of all the elements of the work in the design of an organized whole. But above all this criticism looks for the appropriateness of the interpretive formulas to the intuitive experience of the "naive" or plain reading, the one not predetermined by explicit theory. The "significative" detail can do no more than confirm an understanding that is founded on all of them and not on any one in particular.

The classical stylistics of Karl Vossler, Leo Spitzer, and Amado Alonso was based on observation of the minor striking detail (ungrammaticalities, extraordinarily frequent words, anomalies in proper names—in sum, the "peculiarities" of a text) to arrive at an understanding of a poem in the totality of its meaning. The search for singular details had a heuristic function, and thus only the satisfactory intuition of the whole work validated the chosen detail as well as the procedure. Despite biographical and psychologistic inconsistencies, then, the phenomenological component of this method was essential.

No attempt was made to force the acceptance of a counterintuitive description, an ideological prejudice, or a sensational, whimsical new "reading" based on the merits of minor observations as the work's reality.

My methodological intention here is to progress toward a descriptive interpretation in which corroborating textual detail is always justified by reflection on the major lines of the work in its totality, as it reveals itself to the attentive intuition of an "idle" reader.

Nonetheless, the use I have made of minor details of Cervantes's text can give rise to doubts that I do not want to disregard. Can we suppose that Cervantes consciously meant that these and other minor details should be double signs, marginal symbols of the broader lines of his poetic design? No simple answer can be offered, because there are many degrees and modalities of consciousness and intent. According to the diffuse commonplace psychology of literary creation, Cervantes may have been either totally or only subliminally conscious of the allegorical and metanarrative function of these passages. But what is relevant here is that these minor elements are very secondary on the literal plane of narration and do little to advance the story line, but in their allegorical modality do emphasize what must have been Cervantes's conscious intent when he wrote these discontinuous transitions of imaginative style. Indeed, he must have been intensely aware of the difficulty of these transitions, which have the quality of an oxymoron. I think we may suppose that in the process of writing, the great design of the narrative image generates and carries with it the multiple elements that constitute it, and fixes their minor particularities to its own advantage. The marginal detail (which occasionally can escape the dominant significative intent and hint at a hidden and subversive meaning, thus providing a basis for psychoanalytic diagnostics or "deconstruction") does not normally oppose the operative conception, but serves it; it is a part of the constructive design. The old hypothesis advanced by Aristotle—and by Schelling, Coleridge, and many other Romantics—of the organicity of the work of art, the functional solidarity of its parts, is still valid. Hence the isolated detail may, as Spitzer thought, lead to an understanding of the ultimate sense of the work. It is more probable, however, that it is the intuitive understanding of the totality of the work that, going back to its entire textual basis, illuminates the polysemy of incidental details and finds a kind of objective verification in them. The quotation of passages of a text in support of an interpretive thesis has no other force than the intuitive one of the thesis facing the tribunal of the enlightened reader's experience.

Layers of Meaning: Mimetic and Metafictional. In regard to this second sojourn at the inn, when so many things that occur are of other worlds, it is only metapoetically explicable that Don Quixote then does what he almost never does: he sleeps for a long time. His participation in such stories is prevented by the power of style. In general, passivity is a rare attitude in Don Quixote, and it occurs only when another law of imagination dominates the scene (during the encounter with Roque Guinart, for example, in a romancesque-ironic world).

If one is not prepared to read simultaneously on these two levels, the direct and the metapoetic, and attends only to the supposedly verisimilar or realistic actions, the work, as I indicated earlier, often seems defective. Thus the reader who seeks verisimilar consistency is led to create superfluous interpretive constructions of the implicit background. E. C. Riley supplies us with two significant examples of the one-dimensional reading I regard as mistaken. Riley wonders why, at the inn, Don Quixote remains detached from the stories of the Captive, Dorotea and company, and Don Luis and Doña Clara. And he answers: "The inference is that he is too absorbed in his own inner world; he is too mad to notice."[17] Can we imagine within a verisimilar frame that this individual who generally notices everything (though he misinterprets it), who gives full attention to the world about him so that it can provide him with adventures, is going to ignore the great torrent of extraordinary events that rains upon the inn? Don Quixote's conduct in these passages cannot be more inverisimilar and contrary to the premise of his character. In fact, there is no convincing psychological explanation for it. It seems, on the direct plane of the events, gratuitously casual, underdetermined, if not contradictory. But there is a perfect ironic explanation for the neutralization of the figure of Don Quixote during the major part of these chapters, and it is that it would not be possible to introduce him into the literary spheres of life of those other characters, spheres that are radically different in their stylization from Don Quixote's, and in which his vigorous figure would disintegrate (as to some extent it does when he enters Roque Guinart's orbit). The logic of these passages is that of style, not that of a quasi-realistic psychology.

Riley's other observation that is pertinent here refers to Sancho's tumble into a pit, after his governorship, on the road to the residence of the Duke and Duchess, and his too-providential reencounter with Don Quixote. The latter has gone out into the field to practice in preparation for his battle to preserve the honor of Doña Rodríguez's daughter. When Rocinante breaks into a gallop, horseman and mount nearly plunge into a hole in the ground. There the amazed Don Quixote hears a voice coming from the depths, which he soon recognizes as Sancho's. For Riley, this passage is literarily very weak, a serious "lapse from realism."[18] But Sancho not only has fallen from his dreams of grandeur into sober disenchantment, and from the road into the pit, but at the same time from his transfiguration into a wise judge and legislator and an authoritarian governor back into his original and proper figure of a clownish rustic. Sancho's metamorphosis in his role as governor is one of the most audacious metapoetic operations of the book. When the humble squire errant returns to his proper self, who could welcome him if not his master, who is his counter-figure and complement? Instead of elaborating a verisimilar peripeteia, Cervantes, with an openly humoristic gesture and beautiful irony, declares the metapoetic logic of this encounter when he makes it, on the literal plane, the purest coincidence. This willful stroke of a creator who reveals himself to be free of mimetic domination, and who crosses the line of verisimilitude when his design requires it, seems to me one of the most admirable passages in the book.

The *Quixote* does not lack for emblematic images of the theme of the inexplicit background of all representation, especially literary representation, and of how one can err by excess, particularly by excess in the search for realism, in the interpretive construction of this background. Thus in a dialogue between the first innkeeper and Don Quixote (I.3):

> He asked him if he brought money; Don Quixote responded that he did not bring a cent, because he had never read in the stories of knights errant that any of them had done so. To this the innkeeper said that he was mistaken; that, although it wasn't written in the stories, since it had seemed to the authors that it wasn't necessary to write about a thing so evident and so necessary as bringing along money and clean shirts; just because of that, one should not believe that they didn't bring them. . . .

The innkeeper continues to provide details of the presumed tacit implications, like an interpreter who would like to project *à outrance* a realistic image onto the books of chivalry. Elsewhere (I.13) Don

Quixote responds to Vivaldo's affirmation that there have been knights errant without ladies, such as Don Galaor:

> Sir, one swallow does not make a summer. Moreover, I know that secretly this knight was very much in love; indeed, his habit of paying court to all the damsels who attracted him was a natural inclination that he was unable to keep in check. But, in any event, it is very well determined that he had just one whom he had made mistress of his will, to whom he commended himself often and very secretly, because he prided himself on being a secretive knight.

There are other places in which this point of the limits of the interpretive imagination imposed upon the act of reading is humorously allegorized.

Other Regions of Traditional Imagination. Various other regions of the imagination appear on the horizon of the *Quixote*. I will mention briefly the sharp foreshortening of the universe of the *Byzantine* novel that we find in the episode of Ana Félix in the Bay of Barcelona. This is a world of lovers separated by pirates and shipwrecks, in which the heroine constantly fears for her threatened virginity (unlike a *pastoral* heroine, who does not lose her maidenhood unless she wants to, as Don Quixote says in his speech on the Golden Age) and frequently disguises her sex with a man's clothes. (Cervantes boldly ironizes this style by making it the virginity of a *man* that is threatened in this instance, that of Don Gaspar Gregorio. Ana Félix is concerned about him, she explains, "considering the danger that Don Gregorio ran, for among those barbarian Turks a boy or youth is held more valuable and esteemed than a woman, however beautiful she may be" [II.63]. So she tells the Turkish king that Don Gregorio is really a woman dressed like a man, and she proceeds to dress him like a woman to protect him from the potentate's carnal desires. The role-switching here clearly shows Cervantes's design of fracturing the inherited form that he evokes, at the same time that, as always, he uses it with pleasure and to advantage.)[19] But the Byzantine heroine is also unlike the heroine of the *courtly* novel, for at least since Heliodorus she has been impervious to seduction, and is prepared, as she says insistently, to take her own life rather than lose her "honor." The Byzantine universe has improbable reunions and anagnorises in common with the courtly novel, but whereas the reunion in the courtly novel is definitive and there is only one change of fortune, the anagnorises and peripeteias are repeated time and again in the exotic adventures of travels and navigations that follow in the footsteps of Heliodorus's *Aethiopian History*.[20]

One caricaturesque and comic version of the pastoral universe (which in its genuine form is nothing if not serious and highminded) is inserted toward the end of the First Part: the story of Leandra, the "goatherd" Eugenio, and the *miles gloriosus* Vicente de la Roca. If the delinquent Ginés de Pasamonte is part of a picaresque comedy, the great bandit Roque Guinart is part of an ironized romancesque and semiheroic idealization. The sphere of popular epic also appears in the storyteller's rhapsody in Maese Pedro's puppet show, as the learned epic is parodied in Don Quixote's description of the soldiers-sheep in the splendid Chapter 18 of the First Part.[21] And (finally?) of course, the quiet solitudes that lyric verse projects are not absent from the work. (Such forms as proverbs and didactic oratory, which also appear in the world of the *Quixote,* are literary "genres," but they do not represent spheres of the imagination.)[22]

It is appropriate to wonder whether the episodes of the Cave of Montesinos and the Isle of Barataria constitute stylistic regions that differ from basic comic realism. It seems to me that the first of the two episodes does not, but perhaps the second does. The quixotic vision inside the cave, I believe, constitutes not an independent stylistic region but one that is a subordinate part of comic realism, as dreams are a subordinate part of experience as a whole, which is defined substantially by wakefulness. What Don Quixote's vision has of grotesque and absurd fantasy obeys not a fantastic stylistic law but a law of common oneiric imagination. What could have been a realistic fiction of a dream is not one, however, for it also suffers the comic idealization of everything having to do with Don Quixote. The events of this dream hold the same relationship of stylization with respect to real dreams as Don Quixote's ordinary actions do with respect to real actions.

The Isle of Barataria, although inserted in basic comic realism, nevertheless suggests a diverse imaginative region. Several critics have indicated that the inverted world of Carnival prevails there.[23] So it does, but not consistently. There is something very peculiar in this episode: we do not know whether everything that happens to Sancho there is the handiwork of the Duke and his servants. Some things seem "truly" to happen. While the elaborate jokes belong to comic realism, the "true" acts of Sancho as governor belong to a world of fable. In making Sancho intermittently an efficient and wise governor, and proclaiming *truly* that he instituted such good laws "that to this day they are observed there, and they are called *The Constitutions of the Great Governor Sancho Panza*" (II.51), Cervantes with affectionate irony lifts one angle of the episode (the part that connotes the wisdom, moral perfection, and leadership ability of the common and humble man) to a utopian picture of human hope. There is a moment of the ironic-sublime in this warm and melancholy affirmation of an illusion that is known to be one. And something unique in the *Quixote* occurs in this space. One of the central characters, Sancho, is radically transformed by the ambiguous and variable law of the foreign region he has entered. His figure as expert leader, sometimes scornful and always sure of himself, alternates with that of the poor rustic transposed to an inappropriate position and victimized by his deceivers.

A Most Contrasting Style: The "Impertinent" One. In light of this architecture of contrasting aesthetic universes, it certainly does not seem accidental that just when the comedy of the courtly novel heads toward its appropriately improbable and happy resolution at the inn, the tragic novella *The Man of Ill-Advised Curiosity,* which follows the strict law of Aristotelian verisimilitude and whose action, far from all chance and improbability, has the iron unity of the necessary or probable consequences of the tragic error, is discovered and read there. In *The Man of Ill-Advised Curiosity* we have an extremely abstract world, with almost no explicit characterization of its protagonists beyond their sex, age, and condition. All speak the same rhetorical and rational language, including the narrator of the story, who obviously observes the blindness of its characters from an ironic distance but whose conception of the world seems to be no different from theirs. This novella is a quasi-deduction of exemplary steps, a dialectic of fundamental motifs of the human condition based on the tacit assumptions of a pessimistic anthropology. (Certainly we have no justification for blithely attributing these anthropological hypotheses to Miguel de Cervantes, since his other stories, though admittedly subjected to less severe tests of verisimilitude, often exhibit just the opposite conceptions.) Furthermore, it is perhaps the only Cervantes novella that can unqualifiedly be called "exemplary" (as distinct from those in his *Exemplary Novels*), for the story consists in a deliberate ethical-anthropological experiment, a "test" under controlled conditions, that has something of the protoscientific air of the times. A thematic justification for the inclusion of this novel in the *Quixote* has been much sought after. I believe that the reason for its presence there stems less from vague similarities of content than from the nature of its form, from the function of architectonic counterbalance that it fulfills in the Cervantine edifice of literary regions. *The Man of Ill-Advised Curiosity* is exceptional here for its stylistic purity. It is the only story in the *Quixote* without breaks of style or mixtures of archetypes, without the ironization of its imaginative genre. Here Cervantes executes with perfect mastery the ideal of the severest neo-Aristotelian classicists of his time, and in so doing exposes by contrast the formal corruption of his various other configurations. With full structural justification, then, this is a story that does not belong to the same fictional level as the others, and appears as a fiction within a fiction, as a text that is at the same time inside and outside of the work. The intentional fashioning of this design is tangible in the spirit of the novella, in its position in relation to the other stories, and in the explicit underlining of the classical character of its form. It is stated in the narration itself that the events of the story form a chain, that Anselmo "went on adding link by link to the chain with which his dishonor was binding and fastening itself." Classical peripeteia and anabasis are alluded to: "after a few months Fortune turned her wheel." And, at the conclusion, the unitary and causal linearity of the dramatic development is formulated: "This was the end for all of them, the offspring of such an insane beginning." These indications of the essence of the design are in themselves inconclusive, but if they are considered within the totality of the constitutive form that we perceive reflexively, they have verifying force. (These ideas about *The Man of Ill-Advised Curiosity* are developed further in Chapter 5.)

Julián Marías also offers a nonthematic artistic and formal justification for the inclusion of this story: Cervantes used a fiction within the fiction to reinforce by contrast the effect of the "reality" of Don Quixote's world. (In interpreting this story's function from the point of view of artistic composition, this observation of Marías coincides with the views of Raymond Willis, Bruce Wardropper, and Richard Predmore about the function of the various presumed narrators and texts of Don Quixote's story: this multiplicity of texts is a way of suggesting the autonomous objectivity of the character and his world.)[24] Marías's explanation is not incompatible with mine, but it is less specific, because the effect of "reality" of Don Quixote's world also derives from many other sources of contrast. I have already mentioned its fundamental juxtaposition to more fantastic and idealized kinds of literature. Other examples of fiction within a fiction are the episodes of Maese Pedro's puppet show, Clavileño, and, in a way, the Cave of Montesinos. In another sense, so are the practical jokes of the Duke and Duchess, Altisidora's histrionics, and, in general, the multitude of deceptions of which Don Quixote is the victim. In this order of things, the basic contrast is, naturally, between Don Quixote's chivalric imagination and what occurs to him in his adventures.[25]

A Design Alien to the Modern Novel. It has been said many times that the *Quixote* is the sum of the literary genres of its epoch, the conjunction of the forms and themes of books of chivalry as well as of pastoral novels, of the learned epic as well as of the picaresque narrative, of Lope de Rueda's comedy as well as of the Italian *novella.* This sum, however, is not the homogeneous product of a crucible that melts various materials into one, but a heterogeneous combination of the domains of the poetic spirit, whose regions are kept separate by incompatible organic laws. Therefore, I believe that the question whether the *Quixote* is the first modern novel, the prototype of the genre, cannot be answered in the affirmative.[26] One of the essential attributes of the modern novel, despite all its variety, is its internal homogeneity. For each there is one law, and one law alone, which determines its imaginary universe. In the period when the form reached its maturity there is a very explicit consciousness of this fundamental trait; it is seen in the critical texts of Henry James, for example, and in the following assertion of Emile Zola, where the aesthetic ideal of stylistic homogeneity is clearly perceptible: "If one has the right ear in matters of this kind, the first page sets the tone for all the rest, a harmonious totality is established that it is not permitted to transcend without incurring the most abominable of discordant notes. One has chosen the ordinary mediocrity of life, and it is imperative to remain there."[27] The modern novel in its totality, on the other hand, is, if not one single region of the imagination (the "realistic" region), at least a domain of kindred regions, incomparably less varied and multiple than the domains frequented by Cervantes. He was still in a spiritual situation that allowed forms inherited from the entire past of the literary imagination to be collected and revived.

But could it not be said, at least, that comic realism, the basic region of the *Quixote,* is the origin of the modern novel? I think not, because this sphere is also the object of the ironization that all literature, all fictional representation of life, undergoes in the *Quixote.* In the modern novel (essentially that of the eighteenth and nineteenth centuries, say from Daniel Defoe to Henry James) reigns a serious illusion of immediate reality, the gravity of modern realism. In the *Quixote,* that illusion is ironized and shattered at every step. In the *Exemplary Novels* one can find some elements of the modern novel that are absent from Cervantes's long narratives.[28]

Don Quixote and Sancho traverse the imaginary replicas of the roads and places of Spain. As we follow them, we are at the same time traveling through the provinces of literary fantasy. We pass through the forms of daily and domestic experience, comic idealization of ordinary life, romancesque-heroic stylizing, pastoral utopia, picaresque comedy, baroque hyperbole, courtly intrigue, and Byzantine peripeteias. Taken together, these regions constitute a system of aesthetic principles that share some common features, and that in other respects are also diametrically opposed. (In Chapter 4 I sketch the structural system of the imaginary regions.) The *Persiles* unfolds in a similar way, though with another order of regions. Anyone who reads in this strange journey only a succession of varied adventures in changing settings (in the manner of the traditional Byzantine novel that it superficially imitates), without perceiving the transcendental changes of imaginative atmosphere behind the geographical mutations, fails to grasp the plenitude of the work that subdued Cervantes's final efforts. The loss is comparable to that of a painting reproduced in black and white—but deeper, for the regions of the imagination are primarily transparent forms, not objective ones. Endowing them with a perceptible presence is an exceptional metapoetical achievement of the Cervantine creation.

The *energy* and the *discontinuity* of the style, or principle of stylization, produce the distancing of literature itself and the forms that constitute it. The structuring medium, through which we see the objects represented in the work, changes time and again in character, in coloration, and thus loses its innocent transparency and becomes a semiobject. With this objectification of the fundamental forms of the literary imagination Cervantes's ironic effort attains its peak. The literary forms become part of the subject matter of the work. The essence of literature as phenomenon is objectified; the system of the poetic faculty is subjected to irony. Cervantes does not tell us but shows us that each poetic institution has specific powers and limits, that there is no definitive and absolute imagination.

This profound design of exposition of the poetic faculty itself determines and limits the sense of explicit parody and literary satire in Cervantes's work. The particular weight of the mocking of certain literary modes (here the chivalric) is small when all of them are being subjected to irony. The recurrent theme of literature and the poetological conversations appear under an oblique light when we observe the disproportion of their conventionality and simplicity as compared to the supremely original artistic task of which they form a minor part. The ostensible audacities of the Cervantine imagination (the labyrinthine game with time, the introduction of the First Part into the world of the Second Part, the stretching of Sancho beyond his verisimilar limits in passages occasionally said to be apocryphal by the narrator, the mediation of a second narrator, the introduction of Avellaneda's book and of one of his characters into the world of the Second Part) are revealed as almost natural consequences of the fundamental ironization of the imaginary world.

We can, then, affirm that Cervantes has made visible the transcendental foundations or forms of the interior experience of the world. By exposing the conditions and limits of the imaginative experience in this way, he has tacitly realized a kind of critique of poetic reason. One of the great liberating virtues of his work is the discovery that there is no absolute mode of the human imagination, that to well up with life it has to submit itself to the limitations of a configuring abstraction, of a "style." Thus we are offered an escape from one of the subtlest modalities of interior slavery: the ingenuous acceptance of the forms in which we imagine the world and its processes, the tyranny of myth over our experience.

I have examined here only a formal aspect of the work, but we should not think that the creative deed it implies is merely formal; for the celestial bow of the regions of the imagination is like Ulysses's bow: to extend it, it is not enough simply to have it at hand. As Schelling would say, the energy of infinite life is needed. Cervantes also shows us this: that irony directed in the work against the very same work is not necessarily an obstacle to the richness and vitality of the created world, a fact neglected by those critics who unilaterally emphasize the metafictional, self-ironic aspects of the *Quixote*.[29] His example can further suggest that in all works, in all significative experiences, the deconstructive moment is always only transitional. It shakes petrified tradition and opens the way for its reconstruction.

Forms of Literary Reflexivity

Literary Thematizations of Literature, Metanarrativity, and Metafictionality. The description and interpretation of the literary regions in the *Quixote* (which, as we have seen, constitute a fundamental form of its poetic universe and a complex literary signifier) can be related to a topic much discussed in recent years, that of the (auto)reflexivity of literature and especially of the novel.[30] This phenomenon is defined as the appearance of signs that indicate the fictional character of the story, interrupt the mimetic illusion, expose the "literariness" of the text, indicate the artificiality of its forms, or seem to comment emblematically, or reproduce metaphorically, the themes of the work. The field of these phenomena of reflexivity of literary discourse is vast, and I do not think it has been sufficiently clarified. For our purposes we have to make some distinctions. First of all, we must differentiate the reflexivity of the work from what we may call its thematization of literature, for not all thematization of literature generates an effect of metaliterary reflexivity (that is, of "disillusioned" consciousness, which keeps in view and does not "forget" the fictionality of the game in which it finds itself). We must also distinguish expressions that are merely metanarrative from metafictional expressions. In general, the metadiscursive or reflexive expression is not a sign of literariness or fictionality; it may be found in all kinds of discourse, both oral and written. At every moment, discourse may include references to itself. (*This sentence is an example of self-reference of discourse.*) Reflexivity is an essential possibility of human language. Finally, we ought to distinguish explicit metafictional signs from inexplicit or indirect ones.

In the first place, there is a *primary* thematization of literature in the *Quixote* insofar as literature is an essential part of the fable because it is the cause of the hero's madness and the source of the motifs of his quest. The entire work displays *within* the fictional world the conflict between literature and reality (and between "false" heroic idealism and reasonable morality) in the form of the conflict between romancesque and comic-realistic imagination.[31] In this world, literature and its forms are spoken of (by Don Quixote, the Curate, the Housekeeper, the Niece, the Barber, Ginés de Pasamonte, the Canon, the Knight of the Green Cloak, his son, etc.). Manuscripts are sought and quoted. Grisóstomo, Ginés, Don Lorenzo, Cardenio, the Canon, Cervantes (the fictionalized writer character, friend of the Curate and transcient lodger at the inn, who leaves behind some of his books and works) write literature. The storyteller of the puppet show recites it. The players of the troupe of "the Court of Death" act it, as do the maidens of the "feigned Arcadia." The Innkeeper and his companions listen as it is read; the Curate reads it to his circle at the inn. The Duke and Duchess have read the story of Don Quixote. Others have already read the apocryphal continuation. All this is thematization of literature but not at all reflexivity of the work upon its own character as literature, because it is all plainly an integral part of the represented world.

On the other hand, a first glimpse of metafictionality is offered when those who speak of literature indirectly thematize the phenomenon of the diverse styles of the imagination that the work displays. In the first chapter we are told that Don Quixote "was not very satisfied with the injuries which Don Belianís gave and received, because he imagined that, as great as the doctors may have been who had cured him, he should still have his face and his body all covered with scars and welts." In the third chapter Don Quixote and the Innkeeper dispute whether knights errant packed along money and clean shirts, and how to interpret the fact that nothing is said about that sort of thing in books of chivalry. Then the Curate praises *Tirante el Blanco* "for its style." More than once Don Quixote analyzes the problem of the things that are not mentioned in the books, considering alternatively that they are taken for granted or they are not part of the life of a knight errant (like having ordinary meals [I.10], negotiating a salary with a squire [I.20, II.7], paying for services [I.45], etc.).

Also indirectly thematized is the ambiguous being of the imaginary or fictional entity. In the Sierra (I.25) Don Quixote explains to Sancho that Dulcinea and Aldonza are two configurations of the same person. And to the Duchess: "God knows whether Dulcinea exists on earth or not, or whether she is fantastical or not; and these are not matters where verifications should be pursued to the full" (II.32). In short, passages of this kind are numerous.

The most profound thematization of literature in the *Quixote* (that which effectively exposes the limits of the institutional imagination) is also indirect. It is realized in the juxtaposition, marginal or incidental intermingling, corruption, and ironization of the regions of the imagination. Such thematization does indicate the literary, fictitious character of actions and persons. This indirect thematization is a metafictional reflexive sign, as is, more or less markedly, all perceptible generic or traditional style, all forms recognizable as poetic (as verse normally is in compositions that use it). We have here, then, a form of fiction's inexplicit reflexivity.

Internal signs of fictionality and forms of inexplicit reflexivity are also the inconsistencies of the *Quixote*'s narrative frame, especially the temporal paradoxes in the various texts mentioned: Cide Hamete's "old papers"; Cervantes's contemporaneity (as "friend" of the Curate) with Don Quixote; the writing, publication, and ample distribution of the First Part in two or three weeks; and so on. Thus the text indicates the ironization of the book's character as "true history," an ironization that is fairly obvious as early as the Prologue, if not the title.

The most interesting of these forms of inexplicit fictional reflexivity are the numerous passages of double reference, which require reading at two levels, the ingenuous, mimetic level and the formal, reflexive one. I have already pointed out some of them: the encounter of Don Quixote and Cardenio, the fruitless search for Marcela, and other events that have a metapoetic dimension. In such cases we are generally dealing with narrative passages or with characters' speeches that in one respect simply represent a fact of the fictional world and in another respect symbolize a trait of the novel as novel, denoting its fictional and literary-formal attributes allegorically. Don Antonio says to Sansón Carrasco (II.65): "May God forgive you for the wrong you have done the world in wanting to return to sanity the most diverting madman who was ever seen!" And ". . . were it not uncharitable, I would express the hope that he may never recover, for by his cure we would lose not only the knight's good company, but also the drollery of his squire, Sancho Panza. . . ." Rodríguez Marín reproaches Don Antonio for "egoism" and "hardness of heart" because of these words, and he alludes to similar reactions by others.[32] Such judgments reflect a reading that is not attentive to the metapoetic dimension of the book, for this is one of the many cases in the *Quixote* in which the implied author-reader usurps the voice of the character.[33] The health of Don Quixote's fictitious *person* (which is discussed *within* the world of the fiction) is the death of the *character* (which can be talked about only from outside of that world). It is undeniable, I believe, that such passages play with this inherent duplicity of literary representation.

An analogous duplicity distinguishes, for example, the passage where Sancho renounces his governorship. On the mimetic level, the reasons for his return to his ordinary condition are various: the distress of annoying deprivations, the acknowledgment of his own limitations, and his disillusion with respect to the fortunes and vanities of this world. But on the artistic level there is a stronger reason. The character cannot be maintained for long in an alien archetypal role. Cervantes has done violence to its figural base of rustic and clown by extending it and partially transfiguring it into a cunning Solomonic judge of folkloric descent. (This is indeed an act of literary violence, despite the fact that the two characterizations share a link, the common popular element, which makes it possible for this transitory transfiguration to take place at all.) Sancho, the imaginary *person,* sees himself overstrained and out of place in that social position because of who he is, intellectually and temperamentally. The *character* Sancho is also overstrained and outside itself. This fictional event, then, is a part of the novelistic world and at the same time the emblem of an audacious formal operation that cannot be sustained for long without damage to the frame of minimal mimetic verisimilitude and consistency of character.

In other semiotic duplicities some statements made by characters are situated simultaneously on two discursive levels: the intra- and the metanarrative. I refer to the various judgments that Don Quixote and Don Fernando pass about stories that someone has just told in their presence. The peculiar thing about this phenomenon is that Don Quixote and Don Fernando are responding to accounts that tell them about serious and moving events that have happened very recently. For all his commentary, Don Quixote says (I.12) to the goatherd who has just finished telling about the pathetic life and death of Grisóstomo: ". . . I am grateful to you for the pleasure which you have given me with the narration of such a charming story." A short time before, he had asked him to go on, "for the story is very good, and you, good Peter, tell it with much grace" ("con buena gracia"). Pedro had responded (and here the keenness of Cervantes's multiple ironic game will be noted): "I pray that I don't lack the Lord's [grace], *because that is the one that should be invoked in this case.*"[34] The polysemy of the word "grace" denotes with astonishing precision the double reference of these statements: first, the comparatively frivolous one of literary entertainment, and second, the very serious one of human suffering.

Once the intrigue of Dorotea, Don Fernando, Luscinda, and Cardenio is resolved, with swelling rhetoric, copious general weeping, recognitions, and changes of fortune, Don Fernando wants Dorotea to tell him how she has happened to arrive at the inn. "She, in a few well-chosen words, told the story she had related to Cardenio, and it so pleased Don Fernando and his company that they wished it had lasted longer, such was the charm with which Dorotea described her sad experiences" (I, 36). With these duplicities of a metapoetic dimension, Cervantes makes sure that the appropriate ironic attitude is assumed by the reader, who otherwise could resent the extreme improbability of the action in this part of the work. Don Fernando's perplexing comment when the Captive concludes the account of his penuries and miraculous salvation is of the same order. Don Fernando congratulates him for the literary value of his story:

Indeed, captain, the way in which you have told your strange adventure has been as fascinating as the remarkable strangeness and novelty of the events themselves. The story is an unusual one and full of astonishing incidents that hold the listener in suspense; in fact, we have enjoyed it so much that we should be glad if we could hear it all over again, even if this meant listening till tomorrow. (I.42)[35]

While these discourses are primarily internal events of the story (which connote a not entirely verisimilar attitude of a person who is wholly indifferent to others' travails), they are also external, meta-poetic commentaries, belonging rather to the reader and to the author of the work. They are, then, forms of reflexivity that are simul-taneously inexplicit (for being events of double meaning, one of them emblematic of the literary realm) and semi-explicit (for what they say can almost be read flatly as a critical, metapoetic judgment). I will add that in two of the cases cited, we are dealing with transregional speech acts: they cross over from comic realism to the semipastoral world, and from courtly intrigue to the Morisco-military story.[36]

When we consider this pervasive duality of meaning (one of its dimensions directly mimetic, the other reflective, metafictional), an aspect of the burial of Grisóstomo becomes apparent which is not obvious at first. While natural curiosity about the destinies of their fellows has led the travelers to become witnesses of the ceremony, they are also comic-realistic contemplators of a spectacle that must be radically strange to them. Ironic distance from pastoral stylization is thus deployed within the fiction, and readers are invited to extend this game of reflectivity to all their reading. There are numerous instances of distanced contemplation *within* this fictional world. Among them are the "critical" judgments of Don Fernando and Don Quixote that I just mentioned. The encounter of comic realism with other imaginary regions generally contains an element of reflexive contemplation, perplexity, or amazement inserted in the minds of the characters. Their "natural reactions" are at the same time indirect representations of the effects of the laws of style.

As we see, the thematization of literariness or the (auto)reflexivity of fiction is multiple in the *Quixote*. This objectification of what normally is transparent (the constitutive forms of the image) occasionally goes so far as to make the discourse itself opaque. The most notable moment of this materialization and near-autonomy of language is the parody of epic discourse on the lips of Don Quixote, in Chapter 18 of the First Part.[37]

Region and Genre. It is not difficult to admit the relevance of such observations for establishing the critical standard to which I alluded in the Introduction. Numerous traces of readings that we should consider partially erroneous are found in older as well as recent commentaries and exegetical notes to Cervantes's texts. They include interpretations that diminish the work through disregard of the complexity of its artistic dimensions. Some critics censure features that would indeed be aesthetic inconsistencies if the law governing the work were that of realism or even consistently that of verisimilitude. The grandiose equilibrium of the multilayered Cervantine edifice is thus reduced to a simple counterposition of good domestic-realistic sense and romancesque madness (an understanding that still has its scholarly defenders). It is not necessary to emphasize that even from this narrow perspective the work offers a great vision. But it is also evident that the optimal reading of the work is the regulative idea of criticism.

Finally, I would like to add some quick observations of a general nature. The fact that in the world of a given work there is more than one locale or ambience (for example, that the country and urban settings alternate in it) does not imply, naturally, a plurality of regions of the imagination. One and the same image of the human condition can be maintained in diverse environments. In the Homeric world of the *Iliad,* there is the space of the heroes and the space of the gods, but the image of the life of heroes and gods undergoes no transformations.

We can say that both spaces are provinces of the same imaginative region. The Byzantine world of Teagenes and Cariclea (as distinct from that of Persiles and Sigismunda) is notably homogeneous, despite the many changes of scenery. In Longus's *Daphnis and Chloe,* the bucolic continuity is interrupted by a pirate attack, a Byzantine-style incident that is enough to suggest the diversity of imaginative regions, and that gives a clear signal of the pastoral region's intense need for stylistic counterweights. The idealization and reduction of the human condition in the Renaissance utopia of rustic life, much more extreme than in Longus's idyll, apparently turns out to be too tenuous to provide substance for a long narrative, and requires a more sanguine ballast. This unpeaceful counterpart to the pagan idyll can take the form not only of the Byzantine region but also of courtly intrigue, that Renaissance form which is usually called "novelesque." In Jorge de Montemayor's *Diana enamorada,* which (if we set aside the interpolation of the story of the Abencerraje) presents an admirable equilibrium and harmony of *un*ironized imaginative regions and provinces, the region of amorous courtly intrigue constitutes the fundamental complement of the pastoral. Let us also remember that, as this chapter's epigraph from Samuel Johnson indicates, conjunctions of the world of chivalric books with that of pastoral novels are not unusual.

As we can see, the concept of imaginary region is not equivalent to that of literary genre. A work can include more than one aesthetic region; on the other hand, it would be illogical to say that it can belong to more than one genre (in the traditional Aristotelian sense of the term). There are genres, such as the pastoral novel, that are essentially pluriregional, and others, such as the modern realistic novel, that are essentially uniregional.

Critical Concepts in Regard to Pluriregionality. The phenomenon of the pluriregionality of some works had been perceived before the emergence of Romantic criticism. If the discontinuity of style is the latter's desideratum, it constitutes a *vitandum* for classicist sensibility. We have seen that Samuel Johnson conceptualized these distinctions when he criticized Sidney for mixing the pastoral and feudal "times" in his *Arcadia.*

What I have called the imaginative pluriregionality of the *Quixote* has been partially observed from various critical perspectives. Earlier I alluded to the enlightening studies by Francisco Ayala. E. C. Riley reduced the diversity of regions to the opposition of the novel (a form characterized by the probability of the events, the general historical authenticity of the world represented, human rather than superhuman protagonists, etc.) and the romance (a narrative form characterized by superlative protagonists, fortuitous coincidences, poetic justice, etc.).[38] But in the *Quixote* we do not find a "novel" in the modern sense, and the varieties of "romance" involved are very dissimilar. Later Riley developed ideas more akin to my own.[39] Joaquín Casal-duero sees the variety of imaginative forms as a result of Cervantes's confrontation with the past (the Gothic, represented by the books of chivalry, and the Renaissance, represented by the pastoral novels) from the affirmation of a Baroque present.[40] This view suggests that for Cervantes the comic-realistic space is absolutely cast as the valid form of the present, whereas in fact he ironically undermines this sphere, too.

The reduction of the complex Cervantine architecture to only two planes (idealistic-fantastic and realistic) is the traditional position, and it still predominates today. Ortega y Gasset is not the only one to reaffirm it. It is found (to give another celebrated example) in Georg Lukács's *Theory of the Novel*. On the other hand, A. W. Schlegel and the German Romantics in general (and, in their wake, Hegel) emphasize the values proper to the flowering of the *Quixote*'s marginal stories.[41]

Naturally, the *Quixote* can be counted among the works belonging to what Rosalie Colie calls Renaissance "inclusionism": "books of books," reductions of various genres, such as Rabelais's *Gargantua and Pantagruel* and Robert Burton's *Anatomy of Melancholy*.[42] (Let me note in passing, in relation to what I indicated in the Introduction, that Colie's concept of the Renaissance includes, among other stylistic movements, mannerism and the baroque, "from Petrarch to Swift.") It can be said that the literary context of the time has its own systematic order of generic forms, among which the inclusive forms must be counted (perhaps in a remote analogy with the paradoxes of set theory). This structure of the literature of a historical moment seems to be reproduced, if not totally and identically, and reorganized in the internal structure of the inclusive works of the same period. This could be the suggestion that derives from the comparison of the structure of regions of the *Quixote* and the generic system of the Renaissance.[43]

The phenomenon of the variety of regions of the imagination is different from "intertextuality" (also present, of course, in the *Quixo-*

te), if we give the word the strict sense of a relationship of two or more particular texts. There is intertextuality in a strict sense when the text of the work evokes another text (cites it, paraphrases it, parodies it, alludes to it). Such an evocation supposes that the diversity and the parallelism of the two discourses, this one and the one evoked, are persistently shown; they do not disappear. The stylistic contrast or, alternatively, the antagonism of meaning beneath the stylistic similarity of the two discourses is frequently played with. Thus, for example, the *Quixote* includes lines of well-known ballads and, according to Arturo Marasso, situations found in the *Aeneid*.[44]

Changes in region are something else. The text assumes the character of the region evoked; it becomes an expression of it and its style; it metamorphoses. The duality of the intertextual game does not persist here. We could call this poetic operation "interregionality," "mimetism of stylization," and even a "transcendental pastiche." Gérard Genette's very inclusive concept of intertextuality more or less embraces all of these forms.[45]

It is clear that the *Quixote,* insofar as it is a parody, has an important dimension of intertextuality. But it is not quite accurate to speak of the *Quixote* as of a *parody* of books of chivalry (though it can always be called a *satire* of them). The Cervantine discourse (except in occasional speeches by Don Quixote) is never like the chivalric, not even when it introduces familiar motifs from books of chivalry. And the world of Don Quixote differs radically from their world. Cervantes never gives shape to the chivalric region on the basic plane of his narrations. (He does extensively shape the pastoral, the courtly, the picaresque, and the Byzantine, though he deforms them.) We can understand, then, why Vladimir Nabokov terms it a *picaresque* novel(!).[46] The Russian novelist's classification cannot be said to be terribly exact, but it illustrates the distance between the basic region and style of the *Quixote* and those of books of chivalry.

Cervantes did not invent narrative pluriregionality. He objectified the whole system of literary regions, then ironized and subverted it. In doing so he exposed the traditional and natural limits of the human imagination. At the same time, having thus diminished the authority of forms of *marked* stylization (including the picaresque), he cleared the way for the realistic and uniregional sphere of imagination of the modern novel, without actually creating it.

Chapter 2

The Unity of the *Quixote*

> The unity of anything is its essence, because its being consists in its indivisibility and in its division from any other thing, and from this it follows that since everything seeks to preserve its own being, so also it seeks to preserve its unity, because disunity tends toward corruption and disintegration.
>
> —Giovambattista Strozzi, *Dell' unità della favola* (1599)

> It is by virtue of unity that beings are beings. This is true as much with respect to things whose existence is primordial as with respect to any that, to whatever degree, should be counted as beings. What thing could exist if not as *one* thing? Deprived of unity, a thing ceases to be that to which its name is given: there is no army unless it is a unity; a chorus, a flock have to be *one* thing. Also a house or a ship requires unity: *one* house, *one* ship; nothing remains if the unity is lost.
>
> —Plotinus, *The Enneads*, VI, ix, I (ca. 260)

The Concept of Unity

The question of what constitutes the unity of an object of any sort (a door, a theater season, a political constitution, a voluntary act, a human life, a celebration, whatever) takes a special turn when the object in question is a literary work (or any other work of art). One frequently finds truly astonishing assessments of the unity of literary works, so that the concept acquires a sense that apparently does not apply to other classes of objects. It is often said, for example, that a certain work *has no unity,* or that its unity is *weak.* These judgments normally entail a negative evaluation, since the fact that a work has unity seems to be, if not valuable in itself, at least the necessary condition for superior artistic qualities. A principal aspect of the aesthetic phenomenon is manifest in such judgments, as witnessed by the antiquity and persistence of this classic theme in literary theory, whose most influential formulations we owe to Aristotle. As we will see, there are good reasons to suppose that the question of unity, so much debated in the poetics of the sixteenth century, intensely engaged Cervantes's critical reflection.

The complex concept of poetic unity involves *three* notions. First, unity is a *numerical* notion. One is what two, three, four, and so on are not. The classical (or rather Renaissance and neoclassical) dramatic unities of *action* and *place* correspond to this numerical notion of unity. Second, a thing is one and has unity if it is or seems *entire*, complete, and is not a half or a fragment but a whole. Finally, a thing has unity, in an intense sense, if its parts are all necessary and strongly connected to each other, so that the loss of any one part would destroy the whole, and any addition would weaken it. In this third aspect of unity (which can be called internal cohesion), we are dealing as much with the intelligible coherence of the causal logic of the story represented as with the consistency of tone or character of the work in its entirety. The classical unity of *time* (which ultimately refers to the *continuity* of the time represented) is especially related to the notions of completeness and cohesion. These latter two formal imperatives apply equally to unity of action. Moreover, in Aristotle's *Poetics*, unity of action is placed more insistently under the norms of completeness and cohesion than under the idea of the number one. To summarize, numerical unity, integrity (completeness), and (logical and stylistic) cohesion or necessity of the parts are the three fundamental notes of the concept of the unity of the individual poetic work. The three appear clearly, although they are not explicitly established, in the Aristotelian arguments on the unity of action.

Unity is, if not a structure inherent in the transcendent being of things, at least one category, in the Kantian sense, a necessary condition for the possibility of the full existence and presence of any object of experience. Thus it is understandable that this category assumes exceptional importance with respect to the artistic work, for the object, in this case, is imaginary. This implies that its consistency is by its nature precarious, its presence unstable. Composition and style are cohesive forces that make possible and intensify the presence of the object. They are not contingent additional attributes or qualitative superdeterminations that would respond to the exigencies of artistic taste; rather, they are necessary conditions for the aesthetic experience itself. The subject of the aesthetic experience (each one of us as reader) wants to find an object in it. The traditional, largely subconscious norms for reading poetic works are oriented toward the production of an imaginary object, in which our experience of life and the world is particularized, condensed, and sharpened. It can be said that such an object, being imaginary, is "interior," and only its latent horizon, the real world, is truly transcendent. That means that the objectivity of this object is limited and, as I said, precarious. But it does not mean that the literary experience is nothing more than a fragment of an immanent and incessant movement of consciousness and the unconscious (or of "language," of "discourse") in which it would not be appropriate to distinguish delimited units, with a beginning, a middle, and an end. Those current tendencies of philosophy and literary criticism that are inspired by Freud, structuralism, and the sociology of knowledge declare the concept of the human subject, especially the conscious subject, to be metaphysical, and dissolve the identity of imaginary objects in a hypothetical infinity of interconnected and continuous texts. This linguistic continuum would contain within itself the semi-illusory subject and object, consciousness and world, reader and work. In this emphasis on the substantiality of this semiotic network (which ultimately is the substantiality of the human body, as Freud indicated in his late *Abriss der Psychoanalyse*),[1] the central phenomenon here is hidden: that human activities such as literature constitute the institutionalization, the perpetuation of the effort to produce both object and subject, to constitute the world in the imagination and constitute ourselves as individual interiorities. Reading is part of our repeated (utopian?) attempts to see and to be. This is such a radical effort that it postulates an absolute, definitive vision in every work read, a consummation of our knowing and existing. After we have returned to the much less differentiated continuity of our daily existence, we understand that the work we read does not succeed in summing up the world or in giving our individuality an enduring being, but that does not alter the reality of the utopian effort or the institutionally determined character of the poetic experience. Its significance is to extricate us, in an operation of imagining reminiscent of Münchhausen, from the changing continuity of life, gathering up the dispersed parts of our being and projecting a vision that at that instant is unquestionable. To correspond to the postulates of this effort by the reader, the work, in its design and execution, must submit to an intense differentiation, capable of distinguishing it from any casually proximate images, of giving it closure and separating it, and of preserving its individuality and its meaning. That is, the work must be constructed cohesively, must preserve its integrity and uniqueness. The work is subjected to the imperatives of identity and unity.[2]

The Disintegrating Forces

The unity of the *Quixote*, according to the prevailing conception, is founded upon the central characters. Wolfgang Kayser therefore declares it to be a novel "of character."[3] But what provides the foundation for the unity of the characters themselves (also imaginary entities)? And what other principles of unity operate in this work?

To determine which forces give unity to the *Quixote*, it is useful first to consider the opposite forces that operate in it—multiplicity, disintegration, and inconsistency.

Action. The novel presents many stories and actions, not just one. There are the (in a strict sense) intercalated stories, such as those of the Captive, "The Man of Ill-Advised Curiosity," and other lesser ones. And there are semi-episodes, more intimately linked to the central story line of the book by the marginal participation of the protagonists, such as those of Marcela and Grisóstomo, Cardenio, Dorotea, Camacho's wedding, Claudia Jerónima, and Ricote and Ana Félix. Finally, we have the "adventures" of the protagonists themselves, which can be considered as the episodes of a fundamental action of departure, search, and return. This is not strictly a single story itself, for it is repeated in each of Don Quixote's three "sallies." Undoubtedly the *Quixote*'s action does not obey the rule of numeric unity. The actions do not occur in a single place, either.

The multiplicity of the actions is, naturally, one factor of disintegration. Above all, it is important that the protagonists' adventures, as in books of chivalry and the picaresque novel, tend toward fragmentation. There is no link of necessity or of probability between one of Don Quixote's adventures and the next; they are linked only by possibility. It is possible (on the mimetic plane, that of the represented deeds), but not necessary or probable, that after the adventure of the flocks of sheep, for example, that of the dead body follows. Because the cohesion of the actions from episode to episode is weak, the good reader of the *Quixote* normally does not remember the order of the adventures exactly. When they are seen as a whole, however, their sequence acquires a sense, for the character of the adventures slowly changes in accordance with the changes in the personalities of the protagonists, and this (as I will show) gives a certain relevant order to the succession of the parts. But this order is not causal, it has no strong logic, nor can it be discerned in each of the adventures. The *Quixote* does not have unity of action in the intense, Aristotelian sense of the term. From the point of view of the logic of the action, parts of the work could be removed without causing the remaining narrative to lose intelligibility.

Time. Other factors of disintegration add up to the (successive) multiplicity of the actions. To consider the function of *time,* as much in the *Quixote*'s unity as among the forces of disintegration that operate in it, we must distinguish at least four "times": (*a*) The real time or duration of reading, corresponding to the length of the work; (*b*) the imaginary time inherent in the story that is being told (from the beginnings of Don Quixote's insanity, say, till his death); this is the time that we suppose to be continuous, unilinear, unidirectional, irreversible, unrepeatable, regular, like the real time that we measure with calendars and clocks; (*c*) the imaginary time of the act of narrating (or writing) the story (the act of the narrator or implied author, not the creative act of the real author, which is not recorded in the work and is not part of it); (*d*) finally, the aesthetic-phenomenal time with which the story as well as the act of narrating are actualized in our reading: the *durations* presented and lived in the experience of the poetic world. In literary narratives, this aesthetic time is usually discontinuous and has multiple parallel lines; it is almost always unidirectional but reversible, repeatable and almost always irregular. One hour of time inherent in the story's events can occupy more phenomenal time than many years of them. Story time can be presented more than once, in reiterations; it also can be presented in anticipations with respect to the primary course of the actions, or running parallel to other stretches of time. There seems to be no limit to the ways aesthetic-phenomenal time can be manipulated. Cervantes makes a most audacious, incomparable use of the possibilities implicit in the imaginary time of the poetic narration.[4]

About the first and simplest, the real time of the reading, it is useful to make the apparently trivial observation that the *Quixote* is a very long work that cannot be read at one sitting. Obviously the integrity of works of this size already suffers during their immediate actualization, in the reading, by the inevitable process of forgetting. Moreover, the predominantly episodic character of this work precludes a dramatic tension opposed to fragmentation, which could fortify the thread of memory across distant hours.

The imaginary time of the story, for its part, presents other difficulties for the unification of the work. True, the facts of the central story exhibit continuity and relative brevity, obvious factors in cohesion. One summer Don Quixote decides to go out as a knight errant, and in the course of that summer he makes his three sallies and dies. There are no voids in this story, no gaps determined by events outside the process of madness, chivalry, and death. But what there is, more marginally, is a great deal of time that does not fit into this unitary frame and that breaks it irreparably. If we count the days of Don Quixote's life that Cervantes presents to us without narrative ellipsis, though with certain imprecisions (one day in this place, three on the road to somewhere else, some weeks at home between the second and third sallies, etc.), we will add up a total number of days that, with some indulgence in the count, can fit into an extended summer. Don Quixote leaves for the first time, however, on one "of the hot days of the month of July" (I.2), and toward the end of the third sally he arrives at the beach in Barcelona "on St. John's Eve at night" (II.61). Since it seems absurd to leave in July and after weeks of coming and going to find oneself in the month before one left, Rodríguez Marín, following Hartzenbusch, understands that the day referred to is the one that marks St. John's decapitation, August 29, and not the saint's day June 24.[5] This solution would avert the chronological absurdity but not the incongruence, since the weeks presented in the narrative do not fit between the beginning of July and the end of August. If we consider other determinations given in the work, the perplexing temporal paradox seems as appropriate as the chronologically more acceptable interpretation. Indeed, more appropriate. Then what about the temporal position of the narrator? At first he declares that "not much time" has passed since Don Quixote lived, then sinks him deep in the past of the archives of La Mancha and of old manuscripts. He leaves Don Quixote interred at the end of the First Part, yet makes the writer Cervantes a friend of the Curate, so that Don Quixote becomes a contemporary of the narrator. Then, shortly after Don Quixote's second return home, the narrator makes him learn about the publication and translation of his "history," which assumes that he belongs to the past. A few weeks after the beginning of his chivalric wanderings (which would have to be considered to be before 1605), the expulsion of the Moors, in 1609 and 1611, is a consummated fact, and Sancho's letter to Teresa Panza bears the date 1614. The past (the life of Don Quixote) ends up as the future, since he lives after the end of the book (the 1605 First Part). The future (the expulsion of the Moors, etc.) ends up in the past, for it has taken place within a few weeks of a summer day before 1605. (Adding to these paradoxes, as Luis Andrés Murillo notes, is the fact that in Chapter 4 of the Second Part, it is said that in a few days the festival of St. George, which falls in April, will be celebrated; and that in Chapter 11 of the same part an allusion is made to the Corpus Christi festival, which falls in May or June.[6]

This labyrinthian chronology does not contribute to unitary organization of the work's architecture. As we see, the time of the act of narration is no less paradoxical than the time represented in the story; and the relative distance between them, which is implied by the use of the narrative preterite tense, is inverted and confounded.

Ontic Coherence and Inconsistencies of Design. The logical inconsistency in the *Quixote* is not limited to temporal paradoxes. I am not referring to the "slips" and "oversights" for which Cervantes's nineteenth-century commentators and even his contemporaries took him to task. The majority of these supposed lapses are nothing but the misunderstood consequences of his unrealistic stylization and of his audacious metapoetic game. I do not mean errors when I speak of the disintegrating forces in the *Quixote,* but rather a design, a creative intention that includes impulses of dissolution as part of the artistic form. Many readers have thought, for example, that Cervantes altered the names or epithets of certain characters out of forgetfulness. Today, however, this seems less probable than Leo Spitzer's hypothesis that behind such variations is a will to perspectivism. Even in the most striking case of this kind, that of the name of Sancho's wife, Maurice Molho has offered a subtle and convincing interpretation.[7]

An authentic and obvious error, or rather an artistic defect, in the final text of the First Part is recognized by Cervantes in the Second Part. Sancho appears riding on his ass when the animal must be far away, in the hands of Ginés de Pasamonte. Here we have a defect, precisely because this kind of inconsistency is not part of the design. The thematic world of the objects and the actions is coherent in the *Quixote.* The barber's basin, to mention a debated example, is always a barber's basin, and the construct of the "basinhelmet" is a conciliatory flash of wit from Sancho's characteristic simplicity-cleverness.

Maintaining that the object in question is a helmet is an amusing joke shared by all the reasonable persons there.[8]

But the error of the absent-present ass is instructive, for it becomes understandable and significant when it is considered in relation to the structural frame of the work.[9] As we saw, the causal links between one adventure and the next are very weak. Each adventure, with its internal causal tension, is constructed on the permanent basis of the relationship between the two central characters. The principle of the solidarity and sustained counterposition of the two figures, to whose concretization the two mounts belong, is much stronger than that of the continuity between diverse adventures. Hence the psychological-attentional probability of this lapse. But, I insist, we are dealing with an error here, because the elementary principle of the ontic coherence of the natural and objective world is more fundamental in the work than the artistic structure of the counterfigure Quixote-Sancho. Ideally, Sancho should have found himself temporarily but consistently without a mount, and the beast's structural function should have been made up for in some way, even if only by a consistent complaint about the ass's absence.

The Contradictory Internal Constitution of the Characters. Just as the temporal paradoxes must be considered not as mistakes but as part of the design of the work, other positive inconsistences in the *Quixote* are obviously desired or accepted by the author. An example is the physical and spiritual transformations of the two central characters, which go beyond a verisimilar evolution. Don Quixote is presented initially as a man around fifty years of age, "of a sturdy constitution, but wizened and gaunt-featured, an early riser and a devotee of the chase." In sum, his is a physique that in Ernst Kretschmer's well-known terminology would be called athletic leptosome. Sancho is introduced as a big-bellied man with long legs ("Sancho Zancas," I.9), that is, an overgrown pyknic or (now in William H. Sheldon's term) an endomorph.[10] Within a few weeks, though, Don Quixote impresses those who meet him with his extreme thinness and his pale, yellow face, and Sancho displays the laughable figure of the very small and round governor. (It is worth noting that the changes are kept within the margins of variability that Kretschmer assigns to the corresponding typical constitutions, but it is clear that this does not make them all possible in the same individual.) These changes reflect a general development toward a greater comic stylization and a lesser realistic concretization. (The "insignificant" details—those not pertinent to the stylizing idea that governs the design—progressively diminish. Thus Don Quixote's errand boy disappears forever, mentioned only in the first chapter and never again.[11]

As for the intellect, what a great distance there is between the foolish Don Quixote, admirer of Feliciano de Silva, and the wise reader of Garcilaso and counsellor of Sancho on government! And no less between the simple rustic "with very little salt in his noggin" (I.7) who allows himself to be swayed by the fool and the ingenious governor and amusing conversationalist who follows his master out of affection and pleasure at seeing the world.[12] These transformations do not fit within the verisimilar frame of the eighteenth- or nineteenth-century *Bildungsroman,* although, as Menéndez y Pelayo says, there is a hint of that novelistic development in this Cervantine creation.[13]

The fact that the inverisimilar alterations of the central characters still become convincing to the reader has deep roots. The physical alteration is supported by a process of increasing stylization that, as I suggested, affects the entire imaginary world of the work and that accentuates the transformation of the "realistic" sphere into that of comic idealization. The modifications of the spiritual personality are based on a dual artistic structure of the character. Two fundamental characterological principles operate in both protagonists. The *madman* is *enlightened;* the *simpleton* is *realistic.* Thus both can surprise us, convincingly, with wisdom or good sense in the midst of their follies. (That is why what would be a negative artistic inconsistency in a unitary character—and even more so in a "flat" one, to use E. M. Forster's term[14]—is in Don Quixote and Sancho a preprogrammed twist that activates the other internal pole of the character.) In the chapters devoted to Don Quixote's penitence, in which he wants deliberately to "perform mad acts" and discusses insanity, good sense, and pretense with Sancho (I.25), as well as in the chapters on the encounter with Don Diego de Miranda (II.16–19), Cervantes pushes this game of Don Quixote's double personality to its limit. Don Diego, disconcerted and appropriately cautious in his judgment, does not know whether to consider Don Quixote the greatest lunatic in the world or a most discreet, ingenious individual. There Don Lorenzo, the son, describes him as an "intermittent madman, full of lucid intervals."

Cervantes's consciousness of this game becomes explicit in Don Quixote's declaration (II.32) that "at times [Sancho] is so wittily foolish that it is no small entertainment to guess whether he is simple or cunning."[15] In the internal process of the whole work, emphasis is shifted from one of the poles of the person to the other. Don Quixote is progressively wiser and less insane, Sancho sharper and less simple. This is the structural basis of what has been seen (not with complete precision, in my opinion) as a process of "sanchification" of Don Quixote and "quixotization" of Sancho.[16]

The internal duality of the character is expressed in several ways. Alternating in Don Quixote, and at times mixed together, are his fantastic deliriums and a sober consciousness of real conditions. He accepts as an excellent visor the one that he has put back together with wire and cardboard, but he does not test its solidity again. He invokes Dulcinea as a high princess, but he admits to Sancho that she is a country girl from a neighboring town. He proclaims and takes himself for a knight errant, imitator and follower of Amadís, but he knows, more or less vaguely, that there is something of pretense in his emulation, something of an inauthentic role. (With a somewhat different emphasis Mark van Doren has treated this point lucidly.)[17] Therefore, when, after much wandering, Don Quixote's dream of being what he wants to be seems fulfilled, because he sees himself received as a famous hero by the Duke and Duchess, the narrator tells us: "and that was the first day ever that he felt thoroughly convinced that he was a knight-errant in fact and not in his imagination, for he saw himself treated in the same way as he had read that such knights were treated in past ages" (II.31).

In these dualities we also see the reconfiguration and combination of archetypes which are such an essential part of Cervantes's writing, and which I discussed in Chapter 1 in relation to imaginary regions. Here we could speak of *bricolage,* in the sense, more terminological than metaphorical, that Claude Lévi-Strauss gives the word when he characterizes the fabric of myths as being combinations of fragmentary remains of other myths. They are not, according to the eminent anthropologist, narrations of a single piece, but aggregates of ready-made parts, whose diverse origins and lack of syntactic-narrative coherence are noticeable.[18] But the Cervantine *bricolage* to which I refer is not (as is, say, *The Book of Good Love* by Juan Ruiz, archpriest of Hita) a juxtaposition of heterogeneous *texts,* of narrative fragments.[19] What is going in the *Quixote* is an operation more profound than the redistribution of preformed materials. What Cervantes intermixes are *matrix forms of the imagination.*[20]

We have a very neat instance of such intermixtures in the exemplary novel *The Jealous Extremaduran*. There the archetypal form of the tragic myth and the archetypal form of the comic myth are united in the same story, so that each of its characters carries within itself two prototypical figures that are more than contradictory, for they belong to different aesthetic worlds.[21] Thus the effect and the meaning of the work are profoundly ambiguous, perturbing our tranquil repose in the univocal forms of the literary imagination. *The Jealous Extremaduran* is a tragedy of the powerful, rich old man's transgression against natural affinities and cosmic order. It is also a comedy of the ingenious struggle of the young couple against the prohibition of the paternal impostor and the consummation of their union.[22]

Don Quixote encompasses the diametrically opposed archetypes of the *miles gloriosus,* in which the blusterer's lie has become the delirium of insanity, and the wise and prudent old man, who judges sententiously. Sometimes he is even a Christ figure, the innocent victim of mockery. As for Sancho, he mingles the rustic, simple and stupid, with the buffoon or jester (*gracioso*), witty and resourceful. These are certainly not the only hybridizations of literary matrices that we find in the *Quixote,* but they suggest the dissonances of supreme creative freedom with which Cervantes questions and overwhelms the most radical unity of the literary work: that of type and genre of the imagination.

As I have indicated, there is more to Sancho's interarchetypal game. Upon becoming governor, he shifts between the astute and expeditious authoritarian and the confused, ridiculous timid soul. Another transformation is seen when he assumes gentlemanly and Quixotic airs before his wife, in an openly ironic and playful chapter. In case there are doubts, Cervantes explains it: "The translator of this history, when he reaches the fifth chapter, declares that he considers it apocryphal because here Sancho talks in a style that is far superior to what one would expect from one of so limited an understanding, and he makes such subtle comments that they seem beyond the range of his intelligence" (II.5).

These transformations cannot be read as part of a verisimilar representation of an individual, much less a realistic one. But they can be seen as a kind of discreetly hyperbolic allegory of the complexity and relative inconsistency of the human subject.[23]

If they are not verisimilar, where do the plausibility, the artistic logic and necessity of these transformations come from? We are dealing, I believe, with transitions based on commonplaces of our culture: the servant who before his wife wants to give himself the airs of the master, and so imitates his own; the common man who surprisingly will stand up to exceptional challenges; the cleverness hidden by the habit of humility, which reveals itself when the opportunity arises. These ordinary notions about what is possible in the world serve to connect the various figures within the character, and help to maintain a formal identity of the subject that inverisimilarly moves from one to another.

Thus also the Curate and the Barber exhibit a contradictory psychic constitution, irreducible to a verisimilar psychology. On the one hand, they are affectionate and well-intentioned friends of Don Quixote; on the other, mockers, at times insensitive and even cruel to him. This inverisimilar discrepancy truthfully allegorizes human imperfection. If we tried to interpret these characters' conduct as realistic and consistent, we would have to conclude that they are unfeeling, idle hypocrites, and somewhat perverse. But that would go against the strong impression of good sense and bonhomie that at least the Priest makes in so many passages, and against his global function in the economy of the story. Nevertheless, Howard Mancing, in his meticulous and illuminating study, concludes that, in effect, the Priest is a perverse personality.[24] This conclusion follows from the assumption, which Mancing does not question, that it is appropriate and necessary to construct the world of the work according to a verisimilar or realistic law, and that the appearances of a character should be composed in such a way that they are reducible to a coherent personality. But this assumption is out of place here, and it forces the elements of the text toward a design that is not Cervantes's.

The Narrative Frame. The fictional source of the act of narrating is also inconsistent. In the prologue to the First Part, Cervantes presents himself as Don Quixote's father, and then as his stepfather. The narration is begun as if it were the original source. (This immediacy of the narrator's relation to the story is already clearly implicit in the phrase "whose name I do not want to remember.") Soon, however, he mentions "the authors who write about this case" (I.1). In Chapter 8, for the first time *one* author is mentioned, different from the narrator, so that the narrator becomes a "second author." Then we find an Arabic manuscript, by one Cide Hamete Benengeli, who is not necessarily the same as the (first) author mentioned before, but who assumes that position in what follows. Added to this Arabic manuscript is its Spanish rendering, made by a translator commissioned by the initial narrator. Furthermore, the initial narrator and second author is the image of the author and writer of the prologue. After Chapter 8 of the First Part, this initial narrator and prologuist becomes definitively the "second author," whom we should understand to be a paraphraser of the translation of Cide Hamete's text. Nevertheless, he proceeds in the same tone and in the same manner as at the beginning, narrating as if he were the original narrator, like a knowledgeable, direct observer of the events, and from the point of view of an invisible and clairvoyant witness, a point of view that, naturally, conflicts with the pretended multiple transmission of the story.[25] Throughout the two parts of the *Quixote* there are frequent references to the presumed text of Cide Hamete, and some brief literal quotations of its translation. These are stylistically ironized by their serious and even solemn tone, suggesting that the Arabic sage and his text are of a very different sort from the text we read. All the same, at the end of the book Cide Hamete seems to reclaim exclusive ownership of the character. This final passage, however, notably summarizes the game of the narratorial personas: the narrator, quoting verbatim, introduces Cide Hamete's words spoken to his pen; next come words proposed by Cide Hamete in the grammatical keys of the same personified pen; and, with no stated transition, Cide Hamete ends speaking in the tone and manner of the author-prologuist.

How, on the other hand, can the supposed Arabic original be reconciled with the Spanish linguistic games in the speeches of the characters (and even in those of the narrator), Don Quixote's archaisms, the Basque's ineptitude in Castilian Spanish, the pastoral inflections of the epithets in certain passages, and so on? It is obvious that the Cervantine game of multiple written sources is playful and is inconsistent by design.

Added to this suggested multiplicity of versions of the primary story is the manuscript of "The Man of Ill-Advised Curiosity," inserted into the book as a novella being read by the Curate to other characters. This device contributes to Cervantes's general ironization of the *book* as a conventional institution of his time, already begun in the burlesque parody of the prologue and the prefatory poems. All of this tends to rupture the formal frame of the work, a frame that normally is a natural support for unity.

Although not inconsistent, the dominant narrative situation is complex, for several of the stories included in the work are told mostly by the characters (the goatherd Pedro's account of Marcela and Grisóstomo, for example, and the tales of Cardenio, Dorotea, and the Captive), but they end before our eyes, that is, presented scenically by the voice of the basic narrator. In addition, within the fiction of the work there are feigned stories, of various logical statuses, such as the literary one of "Ill-Advised Curiosity," the invented narration of the invented Countess Trifaldi, the folkloric-anecdotic one of the madman from Seville, the narration-commentary *ad oculos* of the chanter in Maese Pedro's puppet show. This multiplicity of narrative frames fractures the presentative scale in the world of the *Quixote,* and it makes us see it as if through a pane of glass of highly variable transparency and different optical ratios. In this sense, we can indeed properly speak of a "perspectivism" (an objectivist one) in the *Quixote*.[26]

Usurpations of Voice. Adding to the complexity of the narrative situation is the phenomenon, not uncommon in Cervantes's works, of usurpations of voice, which I have already mentioned. In the discourse of a character, concepts and points of view emerge that are foreign to the character, thus rupturing the consistency and verisimilitude of the figure and its speech. This occurs when the goatherd-shepherd in the sierra tells Cardenio's story, and says, for example: "Although those of us who listened were rustics, his gentility was so great that rusticity itself could perceive it" (I.23). Already the first innkeeper (I.2) recommends his establishment with a denigrating characterization, a discourse that leaves room for a double reading. On the one hand, it characterizes the speaker as an impudent and humorous crook; on the other, we perceive the satirical intrusion of the author, who forces the truth (if somewhat comically exaggerated) onto the lips that would least wish to declare it. In the same way, the author's joking and satirical spirit at times takes over Doña Rodríguez's speeches, in order to make her ridiculous through her directly degrading self-references (II.37). The voices of Don Quixote and Sancho are often possessed by the lucidity of the narrator, whose thought and style creep into the characters' autonomy. Cervantes occasionally indicates the intentionality of these games of mental transfusion, as when Don Quixote observes to Sancho that one of his utterances does not properly belong to him. "That question and answer are not your own, Sancho: you have taken them from somebody else." And to Sancho's reply he insists, "You have said more, Sancho, than you possibly know"

(II.22). What makes our heads spin here is that, at the same time that Don Quixote is indicating that Sancho's voice has been taken over by an alien spirit, it is the critical-humoristic spirit of the author-reader that is speaking through Don Quixote's own voice. This doubling underlines the inverisimilitude of these deliberate transgressions.27

Akin to these transfusions are those arbitrary restrictions on the narrator's knowledge imposed by his assumption of a character's point of view. This technique, only occasionally seen in the *Quixote*, later became canonical in the modern novel. The facts are presented from Don Quixote's perspective, for example, at the beginning of Altisidora's prank, in the home of the Duke and Duchess (II.44). In some rare passages of the *Quixote* there are even manifestations of the indirect free style, which was not systematically used in novels until the beginning of the nineteenth century. Here is the example cited by E. C. Riley:28 ". . . and [Don Quixote] could not convince himself that such a history could exist, for the blood of the enemies he had slain was hardly dry on the blade of his sword, yet they were saying that his high deeds of chivalry were already in print" (II.3).

Now, in the light of what has just been discussed, we can define the indirect free style as the usurpation of the narrator's voice by the character's consciousness, which is exactly the opposite of what is more frequently done in the *Quixote*. And it is not insignificant that, while the usurpation of the character's voice by the implicit author's views is recurrent and "normal" in this work, the reverse operation is exceptional and not systematic. The intermittent inverisimilitude of the characters fits within the Cervantine poetics, but not within that of the modern realistic novel. On the other hand, the inverisimilitude of the narrator (of his point of view, omniscience, epistemic privileges) is a fundamental trait of the modern novel, a trait that, although essentially anticipated in the *Quixote*, does not yet reach its greatest development in Cervantes's novelistic art. On this important structural transformation of the narrative genre I will have something further to say in the final chapter of this book.29

Ruptures of Novelistic Hermeticity. Contributing to the unity of a novel is that quality of a closed, homogeneous, absolute world, in which Henry James, as we read in his prologues and critical essays, saw the artistic perfection of the narrative object. Ortega y Gasset, in his *Notes on the Novel*, calls this quality the hermeticity and intranscendence of the imaginary space. For both authors, it is imperative to make the imaginary presence of the authorial narrator disappear, because such an intrusive entity punctures the apparent self-sufficiency of the novelistic sphere, interposing the heterogeneous authorial reality. Moreover, it is necessary, Ortega says, to avoid allusions to the real, historical circumstance of the reader, since they would destroy his imaginary journey with urgent preoccupations and the presence of his daily reality. They would pluck him from his captivating and beneficial immersion in another life.

In the *Quixote*, hermeticity suffers considerable disruptions. The narrator, who from the prologue on seems almost identified with the (fictionalized) writer Cervantes, does not cease to be tenuously present, linked to the reader, an accomplice in the ironic game of self-distancing from the protagonists. By means of either declared or unmarked literary allusions, which evoke the cultural atmosphere of the time, the narrator points toward the reality of the historical present. Many other references to contemporary political, social, religious, and literary conditions also serve to include the historical horizon within the fictional world of the novel, that is, to dissolve the borders of the imaginary space. Recall, for example, the wars of Africa in the tale of the Captive; the expulsion of the Moors and the religious conflicts within Christianity in the story of Ricote and Ana Félix; contemporary literature and aesthetic discussions in the scrutiny of the hidalgo's library, in the conversations between the Curate and the Canon, and in some of Don Quixote's pronouncements; the brief sociology of the professions of soldier and scholar incorporated in Don Quixote's discourse, to some extent conventional, on arms and letters; the explicit references to the writer and soldier Miguel de Cervantes. On top of all of this, Cervantes makes the First Part of the book, as well as Avellaneda's continuation (both real entities in the real historical world) elements of the fictitious world of the Second Part. One character from Avellaneda's imaginary space (Don Álvaro de Tarfe) even appears in that of Cervantes. Far from being hermetically sealed, the imaginary world of the *Quixote* is mingled with historical reality and with other imaginary worlds.

Stylistic Disunity. The most profound and significant inconsistency of the *Quixote*, that of the generic matrices, is manifested essentially as a discontinuity of *style*. I refer less to the style of the diction than to the principles of stylization that operate in the imaginary world. In the stories and episodes, the *Quixote* presents a multiple variation of the world view. From this angle, the work, as we saw, seems like a collage of the diverse regions of the traditional literary imagination. The pastoral world is joined to the picaresque, the heroic-fantastic world of chivalry to comedy; erotic court-country intrigue is linked, if not to Byzantine wanderings and shipwrecks, then at least to military autobiography and Moorish romance. These heterogeneous worlds are not only juxtaposed but contaminated by each other. The *miles gloriosus* of comedy (in the story of Leandra), for example, and baroque hyperbole and picaresque industry (in Camacho's wedding) contaminate the pastoral ideal.

This discontinuity of style is reflected, certainly, in the varieties of diction, which go from the elevated oratory of Marcela, Dorotea, and even Cardenio to the semilanguage of the Basque; from Don Quixote's initial archaisms to a few words of Italian at the printing house in Barcelona; from Sancho's malapropisms and strings of proverbs to the picaresque lowlife jargon of the galley slaves; the rhapsodic discourse of the chanter in Maese Pedro's puppet show; the rhetorical affectation of the parodied books of chivalry; the epithet, placed before the noun and redundant, of the passages of ironized pastoral evocation on the lips of the narrator and of Don Quixote; and, not to prolong this list, the standard cultivated language of the Curate, the fundamental narrator, and, for the most part, Don Quixote. The verisimilitude of the images is not always affected by these changes in diction. It is not inverisimilar, for example (and not at all artistically censurable), that Don Quixote starts out by telling the "*fermosas*" of his "*fazañas*" and then gives up this phonetic archaism. But certainly such changes affect the continuity of tone and style and therefore somewhat reduce their contribution to the unity of the work.

Thematic Plurality. The *Quixote* does not have a thematic unity of clear conceptual univocality, as would be found in a didactic allegory. The effort to define "the idea" or "the philosophy" of the work has led, as we already have noted, to a bizarre variety of interpretations, and each of them is incongruent with the complexity of the epic vision of the book. If there is a formulable "message" in the *Quixote*, it is supremely contradictory, alien to the logical coherence of the concept. We cannot unite the various parts of the work as diverse illustrations of one and the same idea (for example, Schelling's thesis that it represents the eternal conflict of the ideal and the real).

Discontinuities between the Two Parts. The most obvious of the dualities of the *Quixote* is its division into two parts, separated not by the ten years that pass between the publication of one part and the other, for that does not imply artistic discontinuity between the parts of the finished work, but by external and internal formal differences. Among the external ones we have a new dedication and prologue in the Second Part, and the abandonment of the division into parts (the 1605 work was originally divided into four parts with an unequal number of chapters). Concerning the character and the internal structure, the changes are so considerable that they induce Knud Togeby to assert that there is a radical difference in the style of the composition, the First Part being "baroque," the Second "classical." Joaquín Casalduero treats them to some extent as two distinct works ("the 1605 *Quixote*" and "the 1615 *Quixote*").[30]

The intercalated or semiepisodic stories in the Second Part do not have the autonomous growth that they have in the first, nor are they interwoven in parallel developments. They are brief and are told in the presence of Don Quixote and Sancho, who almost always observe their resolution. In the Second Part, the protagonists are present almost continuously in the foreground of the scene. I have already suggested the changes that take place through the two parts in the central characters' physical aspect, personality, and conduct. In the Second Part there is a clear accentuation of Don Quixote's cultivated spirituality and of Sancho's proverbs and importunate, comical loquacity; also Don Quixote's aggressiveness and hallucinations diminish, and self-deception gives way to deception through the artifice of others. Don Quixote's false interpretations of plain reality are followed by his candid perceptions of a world disguised to fool him. Whereas in the First Part he suffers primarily physical battering, in the Second his torment is mental. Also we find a growing predominance of conversations over adventures, of the urban environment over the rural, of the residences of hidalgos and nobles over inns along the road. The atmosphere of the Second Part has changed. In a sense, it is freer, since the weight of irony on the ridiculous inferiority of the protagonists lightens and almost disappears. On the other hand, the tone is less comic and more pathetic. The search for heroic adventures is transformed into one for Dulcinea and her disenchantment, and into a meditation by Don Quixote, in part explicit, in part silent, before the spectacle of the world, which he now beings to see with the eyes of the enlightened.

Added to all this is the fact that the First Part is an object of reference in the world of the Second, as is Avellaneda's sequel. Don Quixote and Sancho are now celebrities, not the unknown strangers they once were. There are, then, substantial differences between the two texts (as Cervantes criticism has always recognized), and the question, perhaps too subtle but not meaningless, remains whether they are formally two halves of one work or two works that are intimately linked.

The Unifying Forces

The effect of breaking molds and surpassing limits, eroding laws of configuration, and ironizing the forms of literary imagination and even the traditional institution of the book as a product of one responsible author are essential in the literary experience of the *Quixote*. Nevertheless, the identity of the work is overwhelming, its presence unforgettable, its meaning no less intense for being inexhaustible. How, then, is the unity of the *Quixote* constructed?

A unitary principle seems to counterbalance each factor of disintegration in the work. Let us examine these compositional forces.

Paradigmatic (and Symbolic) Unity. The length of the work, as we said, forces the experience of reading to be fragmented, and makes it probable that as we read we will begin to forget many previous details and minor parts. For a work organized longitudinally by continuity of the actions, such erosion of memory tends to impede the progressive and enriching agglutination of the imaginary object's elements. In works such as the *Amadís,* the confusion arises quickly, and the growing difficulty in reconstructing the course and sequence of the hero's adventures in one's memory leads to indifference to the totality of the work, and causes the reader to look for limited enjoyment of the separate incidents, whose repetitive features thus become a factor that contributes to lack of interest. The *Quixote,* on the other hand, is not organized longitudinally on the continuity of the actions, but instead positively assumes fragmentation as a structural principle. The work is subdivided into semiautonomous units, each endowed with a relatively complete meaning, which largely proceed to repeat one type of action, and thus reinforce the symbolic permanence of an ambiguously exemplary movement. The loss of concrete details through involuntary forgetting is thereby used positively to emphasize the recurring lines of the archetype or paradigm. This is the *quijotada,* if we give this common Spanish expression a deeper and more complete sense than it currently has (the noble gesture destined for failure). Each of Don Quixote's "adventures," in effect, proceeds to repeat an essentially identical experience of spiritual and practical incongruence (with variations, some of them relevant for another structural line, as we will see later). Thus the inevitable fragmentation of the reading of the long book is not aesthetically detrimental, for the fragments have an independent meaning. At the same time, their serial nature leads to a cumulative growth through the reiteration, ever more enriched, of the fundamental symbol of the work: the equivocal fortune of Don Quixote's idealizing vision and conduct.

We can formalize this observation by way of known structuralist concepts, stating that the foundation of the *Quixote*'s unity is not syntagmatic but paradigmatic (or "associative," as Ferdinand de Saussure used the term).[31] Let me say at once, however, that on this paradigmatic unity a more tenuous but very significant syntagmatic, linear unity is constructed.

The lack of dramatic, Aristotelian unity of action, especially the weakness of the connection between one of Don Quixote's adventures and the next, is assumed, then, in a positive sense, by the paradigmatic structuring. Each Quixotic adventure displays the same inextinguishable symbol. Thus each one is saturated with meaning and does not need causal links with the surrounding ones to be imbued with tension. At the same time, each is strongly linked to the others as a new manifestation of the same signification. On the other hand, each adventure has an intense internal dramatic unity of action, which separates it even more from the preceding and the following ones. (The paradigm is internally constituted by a syntagm; it is the repeatable schema of syntagms.) It is apparent that a strong link with the immediately preceding and following actions would deprive each adventure of the distinct independence that the display of the symbol requires.

The Unity of the System of Stylistic-Generic Matrices. The disuniting variety of the stories in which the protagonists do not figure (whether they be intercalated, like those of the Captive and "The Man of Ill-Advised Curiosity," or semiepisodic, that is, minimally linked to the actions of the central characters, such as those of Cardenio and

Dorotea) is resolved in a more complex architecture. These stories not only lack a causal link among themselves and with the adventures of the protagonists, but they emerge, as we saw, by virtue of diverse and irreconcilable principles of stylization (comic-realistic, chivalric, pastoral, picaresque, Byzantine, and so on). In some cases, their detachment from the central body of the book already seemed excessive to Cervantes's contemporaries, particularly the interpolation of "The Man of Ill-Advised Curiosity," which even today is excised from some editions of the *Quixote*. This display of heterogeneous regions of the imagination bases its unity on the fact that these various styles of poetic vision represent *all* of existing styles, all of those that existed in the tradition of Cervantes's times. That is, they constitute and exhaust the universal system of the known literature. The difference and the reciprocal opposition, founded in basic common properties, of these principles of stylization, unite them in one structure. The unity of the *Quixote,* in this respect, is that of the universality of the matrix system of literature.

Unity of Time. The disjointedness that results from the chronological labyrinth is resisted with various forms of temporal order and regularity. The most simple one, but still a strong sign of the constructive tension of the work, is the fact that the story is told according to its natural or inherent order and (if we consider that its beginning is the hidalgo's turning insane) *ab ovo*. The aesthetic-phenomenal time in which the story of Don Quixote's going mad, his sallies, and his death unfolds has the same direction and the same order as the story itself. The presentation is chronological and it is linear. (Only a few chapters are exceptions, such as those that tell of Don Quixote's penitence in the First Part and Sancho's governance in the Second, because when the protagonists are separated, phenomenal time is bifurcated and parallel developments are revealed sequentially, so that one stretch of time is repeated.) In the secondary stories, on the other hand, Cervantes preferred (to use again Horatian terms) to begin *in medias res*.

Naturally, phenomenal time in the *Quixote* does not have the regularity of the quasi-real time that is inherent in the story. Days are summed up in one panoramic sentence, while conversations of a few minutes go on for pages. Nevertheless, this (later traditional) alternation of brief narrative-descriptive passages with long scenes in the *Quixote* generates a fairly regular rhythm of scenic diastole and pan-

oramic systole. The predominance of the scene as a novelistic technique in the *Quixote* and its regular coincidence with the paradigmatic unit of the adventure (and the protagonists' conversations
before and after it) create a relative temporal homogeneity. During the
development of each scene, the inherent time of the action, the phenomenal time of its imaginary actualization, and the time of reading
are homologically superimposed (this, of course, is part of the technique, and is not a peculiarity of Cervantes's). The sequence of the
adventures and conversations is reinforced in its paradigmatic unity
by the isochrony that derives from their common scenic presentation.
The continuous exposition of the long Quixotic summer articulates its
unity in the regular rhythm of adventures and conversations. Let us
not forget, however, that this fundamental rhythm is broken on various occasions by stories not connected with the protagonists, which
are presented in a predominantly narrative form, without greater scenic display (in this, too, they differ from the central adventures).

Also notable, in that it is a demarcation of limits, making it a
unifying temporal form, is the rigorous silence that is maintained in
the work with respect to Don Quixote's *past*. Lacking too are references to the *future* of the characters of his sphere, beyond the day of
the hidalgo's death. All that we know of him and the others is what
has occurred in these few months of his insanity. There are no recollec-
tions or narrative anticipations that go beyond this circumscription.
(In Gérard Genette's narratological jargon, we would say that the
Quixote lacks external analepses and prolepses.)[32] The exceptions to
this norm, although minor, stand out and even surprise us, thereby
confirming this design of almost chronicle-like closure. The first of
these exceptions is the reference to the fact that the hidalgo, before
going crazy, "was at one time in love" with a girl from a place neighboring his own, who never became aware of his love (I.1). But this fact
of the past is qualified as uncertain ("as far as what is believed" and
"according to what is understood"). And it is not the basic narrator
but Don Quixote who remembers that "for the twelve years that I
have loved her more than the light of these eyes that one day must
consume the earth, I have not seen her four times" (I.25). On another
occasion he declares his goodwill toward the comedy troupe, "because
ever since I was a boy I was a fan of the stage, and in my youth I
looked with longing on theater people" (II.11). Also in the modality of
uncertainty, the narrator says that "it is the opinion that for many
years he was sick in the kidneys" (II.18). In Chapter 31 of the Second

Part, Sancho makes a reference, not confirmed by the narrator, to an incident in Don Quixote's past. He also makes its certainty relative ("from what I understand"). A glimpse into the future, such as the statement that the Clavileño prank "gave the Duke and Duchess something to laugh about, not only at the time but for all their lives" (II.41), is extremely rare. The playful metafantasy that Sancho's laws continue to be observed in the town of his governorship "still today" (II.51) is another minimal example. In Chapter 58 of the Second Part, Don Quixote says, "From this sin [ingratitude], as much as I have been able, I have tried to flee since the moment that I came to the use of my reason." Finally, in the last chapter of the book, Don Quixote declares, "I am no longer Don Quixote de la Mancha, but Alonso Quijano, whose way of life brought him fame as 'the *Good.*'" I do not believe that there are many other instances that transcend the temporal frame of the story, and certainly there is none of significant length.

The chronological labyrinth is, then, marginal. The central temporality is coherent enough, articulately continuous, rhythmic, and endowed with an extraordinarily sharp beginning and end, which delimit the narrated time in a nearly absolute manner.

Orders of the Imaginary Population. If we understand as *character* the aesthetic-literary entity of all living beings mentioned in the novel, the characters of the *Quixote* are a most varied lot, so numerous that a unitary perception of the work becomes difficult. But they are ordered hierarchically, although in a very complex way that I can only suggest here. The principles of this ordering of the *Quixote*'s imaginary population are the following: (*a*) Belonging or not belonging to Don Quixote's intimate or personal circle. Clearly Sancho, the Curate, the Barber, the Housekeeper, the Niece, Sansón Carrasco, and, if we wish to include them, Rocinante and Sancho's Dapple belong to it. (*b*) Belonging or not belonging to the sphere of Don Quixote's possible action. The characters of "The Man of Ill-Advised Curiosity," for example, do not belong to it. (*c*) Being or not being the subject of a scenic passage; that is, appearing or not appearing "before the eyes" of the reader, in what Ortega calls the novelistic method of "autopsy," in an etymological sense of the word.[33] Marcela is a scenic subject, Grisóstomo not completely, for it is only as a corpse that he submits to Orteguian autopsy, that he enters the scene. (*d*) Being or not being the subject of a trustworthy narration. Don Clavijo and Princess Antonomasia, in the story of the feigned Dueña Dolorida, among others, are not. (*e*) Being the subject of a greater or lesser number of narrative or descriptive sentences. There are characters who dangle from a single sentence, or even from a subordinate clause, like the "errand boy, who saddled the nag and could use a pruning knife" (I.1). (*f*) Appearing in one or more sections of the work (a criterion that in general distinguishes the characters of the comic-realistic sphere from the inhabitants of episodic worlds). (*g*) Having a proper name or only a generic designation, or both.[34] Cervantes leans toward the common denomination ("the Housekeeper," "the Barber"), and he prefers it even if he has already conferred a proper name on the character ("the Curate"). This is certainly a wise technique, given the great number of figures (whose names would be difficult or impossible to remember) and the economy of characterization implicit in the descriptive terms. A natural complement of this technique is the use of proper names of descriptive connotation (Caraculiambro and others), a device of the transhistoric properties of the literary art.

The relationship among these principles is difficult to determine and at times paradoxical. The Housekeeper—a figure of some importance, after all—does not have a proper name, whereas Pedro Alonso, for example, a neighbor of whom we are barely aware, does (I.5). The Curate, the Barber, the Housekeeper, and the Niece, together with Don Quixote and Sancho, are the permanent characters, but almost without exception they are referred to by the appellative of their occupation or condition, not the proper name. Beings like the giant Pandafilando of the Malignant Eye, who is mentioned in the feigned Princess Micomicona's fabricated story, receive the minimum of presence under the principle of trustworthy narration, but the proper name of descriptive connotation and the few sentences that are dedicated to him confer on him an instant of doubly phantasmal being. Don Quixote, naturally, reaches the highest degree of imaginary being, and while he attains the maximum intensity and richness of presence, throughout the entire work he bears a false name!

Dulcinea is a particularly anomalous case because, although she is constantly mentioned throughout the novel, she is a semifiction within the fiction. She is the replica, imaginarily transmuted, of a character, Aldonza Lorenzo, who belongs to the personal circle and, *eo ipso*, to the sphere of Don Quixote's possible action, but who never appears. She is not an authentic subject of any scenic passage, although she is the subject of three made-up or self-deluding stories of the central characters (Sancho's accounts of the delivery of the letter [I.31] and his encounter with her in El Toboso [II.10], and Don Quixote's of his vision in the Cave of Montesinos [II.23]). She also makes two inauthentic scenic appearances (that of the three country girls on the outskirts of El Toboso [II.10] and that of the Duke and Duchess's practical joke [II.35]).

Indeed, the task of making a precise ontology of these imaginary entities is a notable challenge for that faculty of the philosophical intelligence which engages in the clarification of the *forms* of human thought.

The dispersive force of the multitude of characters is counteracted by the focus of the Cervantine presentation, centered on a fully illuminated foreground, where generally only two interlocutors carry on a dialogue. Presumed or mentioned bystanders disappear into a merely virtual background. Typical of this concentration are the scenes in Don Diego de Miranda's home. In those dialogues the focus is narrower than the limits of the presumed scene, and it leaves the mistress of the household outside the range of vision. (With no explanation, it even excludes Sancho.) But fundamental in this regard is the circumscription of the two protagonists in their solitary dialogues, dialogues that always have been considered, with good reason, as the heart of the work. Here the manner of presentation excludes all but the mere words of the two, except for very brief indications of position and gesture. The landscape is always imprecise, defined mainly by a note of remoteness and rusticity. At the core of the book, the scenic perspective becomes purely auditory in its imagery. The variety of the world and the profusion of actions retire to the shadows, so that only the souls and the language remain in the scene.[35]

This space of Don Quixote and Sancho's solitude is absolute; it is hermetic. For us readers the presence of both becomes stronger than our own presence.[36] Thus a central hermetic zone compensates for the dissolution of the imaginary borders of the work. But it remains evident, I believe, that the *Quixote* as a whole does not represent the ideal of a closed aesthetic microcosm.

The Continuity of the Narrative Situation. We have seen that the scriptural and narrative frame of the *Quixote* is complicated and inconsistent. Against this instability and even the apparent uncertainty of the sources of the imaginary discourse stands a dominant narrative situation, the one already created by the vocatives of the prologue to the First Part ("idle reader," "gentle reader," etc.) and maintained throughout the work, despite the discontinuities produced by the narrations of speakers or writers other than the basic one. Here we have a fundamental voice, which we tend to think is that of the narrator Cervantes. Of course, we know that this is only one among other possible objectifications of his spirit, intrinsic to this work and separated from its producer by the artifices of literary creation. This voice invites us to an ironic and friendly complicity. The bond between the intrinsic narrator and the reader through humor and intelligence is nurtured by the narrator's jesting or benevolent presentation of the protagonists' follies and misadventures. This narrative mode is most successful where no expression by the narrator is necessary at all to connote this benevolent and smiling condescension. I refer to the passages of *silent irony* in the face of sublime folly and moving simplicity (of which there is a good example in I.21). Part of this link of tacit understanding are the literary quotations and allusions that the narrator does not identify and with which he elicits a context of knowledge common to him and his readers. Certainly we find also rhetorically and primarily ironic expressions ("our knight," "Don Quixote"(!), the titles of the chapters, etc.) feeding the communion of narrator and reader, but they are not very frequent or their irony is soon spent. Also present are occasional phantasmal objectifications of the narrator, which embody his ubiquity and freedom: "But let us leave him here, for someone will help him, or if not, let him who dares to do more than his strength allows him suffer and be quiet, and let us go back fifty paces, to see what was. . ." (I.44). This basic narrator comes to possess a personal presence, sustained by a sensible distance between his vision of things and the characters' vision, so that their comprehension of the circumstances frequently becomes invalidated in fact, and in any case is already relativized in principle. This is the way the ironic space that characterizes the modern novel and makes it possible is created.[37]

The formally absurd frame of the *Quixote*'s narrative discourse, which would be ruinous for the credibility of a historical narrative, does not impair the mimetic force of the narrator's assertions or the solidity of the world they establish. Stylistically and aesthetically there is just one basic narrator in the *Quixote,* and his point of view is that of the original reporter, carrying with it all the privileges of fictional narrative. (This narrator is in no perceptible respect "an Arabic historian," and there is not even a formal reason to call him Cide Hamete, since he quotes Cide Hamete's words as those of another person.) The law of fiction is also in this respect different from the law of history. Therefore, one should not exaggerate the significance of the narrative paradoxes of the *Quixote.* One has to maintain the appropriate distance from the work, as Horace suggests with his *"ut pictura poesis."*

The Identity of the Characters. We see that the work is organized around the paradigmatic unit of adventure and conversation, with the two protagonists in the foreground, candidly discussing the motives for and effects of their behavior, subjected to ironic distancing by narrator and reader. The principal question about the unity of the *Quixote* is therefore that of the form of Don Quixote's adventures and of his and Sancho's conversations. But this question in turn poses another, the ultimate question of the unity of the characters themselves. If, as we have seen, Don Quixote and Sancho change considerably and inverisimilarly in physical aspect and in personality during the course of the work, how is their aesthetic identity maintained against these forces of dissolution?

I will not be able to answer this question exhaustively. But it is possible to show some of the artistic principles that have an identifying force and that imprint sustained individuality upon the very process of changing. Foremost is the universal literary principle of *repetition.* Without the most varied artistic forms of repetition used in literature, whether internal or contextual (meter, rhythm, parallelism, motif, topos, archetype, genre, etc.), the imaginary discourse and its situation, also imaginary, would be much less consistent. The identity of Don Quixote and Sancho is sustained by a system of repetitions.

The most obvious is the repetition of their names. Apart from additional designations and appellations, they are called regularly "Don Quixote" and "Sancho." Hundreds of times we hear these identifying signs, amply compensating for the marginal onomastic inconsistency to which Leo Spitzer gives perhaps disproportionate significance.[38]

But much more important than the proper names is the system of attitudes and gestures (physical and verbal) that provides the supporting framework for the aesthetic personality of the two protagonists. Here we are dealing with characterizing motifs of the two figures' uniqueness, motifs that at the same time are rigorously counterposed in a quasi-mechanism of great variability. Using several formulas, Don Quixote reiterates throughout the book that his actions are motivated by his chivalric mission, to serve the ideals of justice in the world and personal fame, and to offer homage in the form of toil and chastity to his distant lady.[39] To this ideological self-justification is opposed Sancho's candid expectation, also explicitly reiterated, that he will rise in social status and in wealth, united to the note of responsibility for his family. Opposed to Sancho's complaint about the harshness of the itinerant life they are leading is Don Quixote's stoic bearing; to Sancho's avid eating and sleeping, the knight's vigil and sobriety; to Don Quixote's aggressiveness and determination, Sancho's passivity and diffuse will; to a false, hallucinating perception of reality, realistic ingenuousness; to elevated madness, pedestrian good sense; to the social and intellectual authority of the lettered master, the subordination of the illiterate servant; to the calm gravity of the one, the light wit of the other; to certainty, doubt; to the projection of oneself beyond one's own body, the involution in animal warmth; to the spirit, vegetative denseness; to the literary reference, the anonymous proverb.

Syntagmatic Unity. This system suffers important modifications that correspond to changes in the basic paradigm of the work (the adventure that has its prologue and epilogue in Don Quixote and Sancho's conversation). These modifications are ordered in a progressive development. The series originated by the repetition of the paradigm thus acquires an order and a direction, although with some regressive lapses. Over the unconnected actions of the successive adventures a linear development, a syntagmatic structure, is being built. With it phenomenal-aesthetic time acquires, in great measure, the irreversibility of the story's time. That is, each of the units of adventure-conversation acquires a stamp of anteriority or posteriority with respect to the others. They are not always interchangeable in the order of their occurrence, despite the fact that, as I have indicated, there is no necessary or probable causal connection between them. A quite important example of such changes, which I mentioned earlier, is seen when the opposition of Don Quixote's fantastic hallucination to Sancho's realistic vision gives way to Don Quixote's correct perception of reality, which is undone by occasional deception on Sancho's part and continuous deceptions by others (the Curate and Dorotea, Sansón Carrasco, the Duke and Duchess, the Catalonian gentlemen), deceptions of which Sancho is also a victim. Both protagonists thus find themselves ever more markedly united, confronting malicious hosts and gradually divining the reality of the world. The "theoretical" conversations between Don Quixote and Sancho unite them at the beginning in a community of foolishness (one's madness is the other's simplicity). Their theme is Don Quixote's reinterpretation of reality in terms of books of chivalry, an interpretation to which Sancho submits, full of doubts, out of respect for the spiritual and social superiority of his master. These conversations lead increasingly to superior ethical reflections, accompanied by loose chains of proverbs and various witticisms. Sancho's initiation by Don Quixote into the world of chivalry becomes a general pedagogy, and even, to a small degree, a reciprocal one.

Also decisive is the alteration of the system constituted by Sancho's insistence on his having been promised an island and Don Quixote's reiteration of the promise. When, as guest and butt of the jokes of the Duke and Duchess, Sancho finally becomes the governor of an "island" and undergoes the crucial experience of disillusionment, the possibility of the repeated play of motifs between Sancho's demand and Don Quixote's promise disappears. Simultaneously Cervantes introduces the deception of both heroes about the possible disenchantment of Dulcinea by means of the lashes that Sancho is supposed to suffer from his own hand. Sancho is now the one who has the key to the desired good, and Don Quixote becomes the one who has to ask for his fortune. From this moment on, the game is reversed. Don Quixote demands and Sancho promises. This inversion of one of the basic paradigm's systems marks a fundamental change in the work. The stay at the residence of the Duke and Duchess, with the deluded fulfillment of Don Quixote's dreams of fame and Sancho's of power, represents the decisive crisis in the story, the internal crisis of the protagonists. After that, Don Quixote's discouragement grows ever deeper, and Sancho's insubordinations reflect the anarchy of a journey that now is without a goal.

Don Quixote's emotional suffering, his thoughtfulness, and his maturity of judgment become prominent in the Second Part. I believe that only beginning in Chapter 11 of the Second Part (where, faced with the actors of the wagon of the Court of Death, "he began to think how he would attack them with less danger to his person") does Don Quixote show signs of reasonable fear and prudence. Two chapters earlier there are suggestions of a lack of heart. The knight takes the sounds of Toboso at night "as a bad omen" (II.9). Then, after Dulcinea's "enchantment," Don Quixote declares himself "an exemplar of the unfortunate" and "the most unfortunate of men" (II.10). Don

Quixote's sadness and "profound melancholy" (II.16) become a recurrent motif. In the braying adventure (II.27), overcome by fear, he flees
on Rocinante at a full gallop. After the misadventure of the enchanted
boat (II.29), he pronounces the often-quoted "I can do no more." In
the Second Part the profoundly pathetic thread is interwoven with that
of heroic dauntlessness, which continues to surface until the end.

When Don Quixote leaves the residence of the Duke and Duchess
and comes across some bearers of saints' images (II.58), he expresses
for the first and only time, although ambiguously, the desire to find
something better for himself than knight errantry: "If my luck im-
proves and my judgment recovers, my steps could take me on a better
road than the one I travel now." The picture of St. Paul falling from the
horse, about whose conversion Don Quixote instructs Sancho, is the
suggestive emblem of this transformation of the Quixotic symbol and
its meaning. The search for adventures and fame, position and wealth,
is transformed into an indefinite, open, disoriented quest that invites
thoughts of the abysmal lack of sense the world is taking on. Don
Quixote's will has consumed itself and is now inert (in comparison
with Roque Guinart's dynamism, for example, it has no force). The
hidalgo is now emotionally weak and vulnerable, while Sancho maintains a plebeian health, immune to metaphysical depths. It is the
experience of a whole life, from youth's ardors and illusions to the
resigned undeception of old age, that is verified in the course of these
few weeks of a fifty-year-old hidalgo.[40] This incommensurability of
the external process of Don Quixote's wanderings and the spiritual
process of his vision of the world constitutes the most profound temporal paradox of the work.

Here the syntagmatic unity is not that of action, in the proper,
Aristotelian, sense, but that of an interior process, in the spirit of the
protagonist. We can see, however, that somewhat looser concepts of
peripeteia and anagnorisis are indeed applicable to this process, by
which they become ambiguous.

Though the repetition of the unit of adventure and conversation
gives the work a paradigmatic (associative) and symbolic cohesion,
this cohesion only unites the members of a series that in principle has
no end. One *quijotada* is joined by another, and another, but no
organic conclusion springs from this repetitive unit; it does not create
the sense of a totality determined from within. Such a series cannot
end definitively all by itself. A work whose unity is founded only in a
paradigmatic series never appears to be whole and complete. Thus the

epitaphs on Don Quixote's tomb at the end of the 1605 book do not impede the continuation of the series, neither for Cervantes nor for Avellaneda. And that is because the purely paradigmatic unity is weak. It juxtaposes and condenses, but it does not close. Books of chivalry are constructed according to this principle of open form, also evident in the sequels and second parts in the picaresque genre.[41] Not even the hero's death suffices to close a series where verisimilitude is not strict; it is permissible to declare afterward that the presumed death was only apparent. Given these considerations, it is not difficult to understand why Aristotle classifies episodic plots as inferior, and maintains the artistic superiority of actions that intrinsically have a beginning, middle, and end. Certainly not only the authority of Aristotle's *Poetics* (if not uncontested, predominant in Cervantes's time) but the artist's vision and reflection must have moved him to a profound preoccupation with the architecture of the *Quixote* and its proclivity for the imperfection of the interminable series.[42] Among other poetological themes, his characters speak of artistic unity at more than one point.[43] But the most impressive indication of his effort to give his work a superior unity is found in the very construction of the First Part, that is, the 1605 *Quixote*.

The 1605 work develops as a series of adventures, unlimited in principle, and it is obvious that the end given the series, when the Curate and the Barber reduce Don Quixote to passivity and return him to his hometown, is an external cutoff, not an organic conclusion. Whether Cervantes was planning a sequel or still did not fully appreciate the seeds of internal totality and conclusiveness present in the First Part, he did not give it an intrinsic line of closure. Exuberantly he constructed what could be called a symphonic ending through indirect suggestion, or through metonymic displacement. When the Curate and the Barber, with Dorotea's help, engineer Don Quixote's return home, and the end of his adventures nears—that is, the end of the book, which threatens to be inconclusive—something new begins to happen: a reunion with characters from the past adventures. Although we had not perceived them as such earlier, here loose ends from past actions emerge, and they are tied up and finished off, one after another, in rapid succession. Ginés de Pasamonte and Sancho's dapple, Andrés (Juan Haldudo's servant), and the barber whose basin was taken for Mambrino's helmet reappear; and the consequences of the freeing of the galley slaves are made manifest in the officers of the Holy Brotherhood. Don Quixote and company return to the same inn (the second one), where we again find the innkeeper and his family, and Maritornes (the latter, indeed, a little changed in character). It is as if the threads of the various adventures needed finally to be tied up together, to lend them a community of action. But, sensibly, the conjunction of the loose ends is purely external and inverisimilarly casual.

To this most superficial link of Don Quixote's various adventures Cervantes then adds a surprising accumulation of parallel stories. Their simultaneity contrasts with the previous course of the book, which up to this point is predominantly linear. Two of these stories are interwoven and have been introduced before: those of Cardenio and Dorotea. To them are added the one told by the Captive, which has a coda played out at the inn; the one read as "The Man of Ill-Advised Curiosity"; and the one, partly presented scenically, of Doña Clara and Don Luis. All of these stories have a dramatic structure, either comic or tragic, and all are resolved almost at once in the most conclusive way, through the Aristotelian conjunction of anagnorisis and peripeteia. Various recognitions, sudden good fortune or abrupt collapse and death, general reconciliations, multiple weddings—all of this has the character of a grand finale, densely interwoven and knotted, in this part of the 1605 *Quixote*. Nevertheless, the simple fact that this ending performed with full orchestra derives not from Don Quixote's melody but rather from the motifs of other characters' destinies makes it inconclusive for the work, despite all the accumulated suggestion of a resolution. Thus, with the stories of others finished, we see Don Quixote and those close to him take to the road again and take over the series of incidents and adventures, still lacking an intrinsic ending, for several chapters yet. Hence it appears as one of the finest ironies of the self-ironist Cervantes that it is precisely in these last chapters of the First Part that the Curate and the Canon carry on a discussion about literature, and in a quasi-Aristotelian mode criticize the lack of unity and perfection of the literary works of their time. Significantly, however, at the same time the extemporaneous aesthetes ponder the possibilities of books of the romancesque type, mentioning the breadth of the imaginary field, the variety and multiplicity of the forms and elements, the encyclopedic universality. The theme of the possibly disintegrating wealth of the novelistic creation is brought up here together with the perfect architecture of the classical ideal. The arguments of the clerics are conventional and inconsistent, but their themes coincide so perfectly with the location of their talk at this point in the work that this colloquium abstractly emblematizes the artistic dilemma of the Cervantine novel, a dilemma that becomes most acute precisely in these final chapters.

The First Part of the *Quixote* has a very marked beginning, the alienation of the protagonist, but it does not have an internal ending. Only the Second Part reveals the seed of the parabolic curve that lies in the First, and brings it to full fruition, thus providing a syntagmatic unity to the entire work. This line of coherent and complete development is not, I repeat, that of action. It is the progression of changes in the essence of the paradigmatic unity, whose center is Don Quixote's transformation. We are dealing with transformations that escape a concrete verisimilitude of the image, for they condense personal and historical ages of the mind into weeks, and present metonymic displacements in the semantic-symbolic field, which have a purely formal plausibility, as if they were the hero's psychic changes. What I have in mind here is the systematic connection of kindred notions, which Cervantes uses as a subterranean conduit to make Don Quixote's metamorphosis convincing. In this case, I am referring to the following series of cultural symbols and ideals: letters, the book, knowledge, spirituality, lucid moral consciousness, full humanity. Likewise, he uses the archetypal notion that deprivation and suffering are a source of spiritual purification and elevation. Thus Don Quixote begins as a devotee of bad books of chivalry, pretending to have both a social rank ("Don") that he lacks and a nonexistent past of great deeds, and as a hallucinating and aggressive madman. The hallucinations disappear almost completely in the Second Part; the aggressiveness diminishes, and on the road to Barcelona it is already gone. The addict of specifically chivalric books comes to be seen as the assiduous generic reader (an aspect of his past which is increasingly actualized through his erudite speeches). From a well-read and cultivated man one arrives finally at the enlightened and wise personality (yet all this while Don Quixote remains noticeably a madman until the end, thanks to the marvelous way Cervantes handles such archetypal displacements and crossovers). From insensitive pride he has reached mature dignity. From an aggressor has emerged a man who suffers. From a comic figure, distanced from the narrator and reader, he has become a symbol of human experience entering the intimacy of the contemplator. This transformation is, as I said, neither psychologically nor logically consistent. Its coherence is founded in the above-mentioned contiguities of the symbolic field of our traditional culture. Another aspect of this same artifice of contiguity and displacement is the character's diction. Once we have a subject who, although he says crazy things, speaks with well-turned and even rhetorically elegant phrases, he can be made to say (if not realistically, at least verisimilarly) things that are perspicacious and wise.

It is therefore convincing and "natural" that at the end of this search for himself and for the truth about life, Don Quixote recovers his reason and returns to his senses as Alonso Quijano the Good, who now is not only good but wise. His wisdom is to see through the vanities of the world, what Juan Luis Vives called appraising each thing according to its real value. Therefore, it is also easily admissible that having reached this goal of knowledge through purifying suffering, he dies. And this hero's death is not one of those that can be suspended so that sequels may be added. The entire parabola of the book has become the unmovable gravestone of that death. Cide Hamete's final exclamation underlines this obvious structural determination of the concluded work.

This configuration, which I have called the syntagmatic unity of the *Quixote,* has the value of a literary signifier (as does the transcendental form of the multiple and impure imaginary regions described in the previous chapter). The syntagmatic development constitutes a parable that illustrates the human experience. We can see that here the overall syntagm (the interior process of the subject of the three sallies) coincides, in a certain part of its features and meaning, with the repeated paradigmatic unity of the work: that of the adventure or *quijotada.* Both lines exemplify the real destiny of the doctrinaire and systematic imagination, but both are, in the end, ambivalent, for they contrast the febrile and clearly drawn elevation of the madman with the stray and pedestrian demeanor of the sane, and thus they do not force us to decide in favor of one of these ways of behavior or the other; rather they force us to face the ethical disjunctive as a problem.[44] We are not shown simply that deluded people learn by suffering blows, that disillusionment about the world is wisdom, and that the truth has always awaited us in the parental spirit and common beliefs. For our madman has become likable to us, and even admirable, *before* his recovery of normal health. Chivalry has shown him (and has shown us) values and goals that *cannot be attained in that manner,* but are not false. The return to sanity is not, then, as we see in the final chapters, pure joy and resolution, but also loss, melancholy, resignation. It is true that such ambivalence is not perceptible in each adventure (especially not in the first ones, which do not seem to exemplify positive traits), but it is undeniable when we contemplate the story as a whole.

The Ambivalence of the Quixotic Symbol. The existence of this essential syntagmatic line of the architecture of the *Quixote* has been established (definitively, in my view) by John J. Allen. In his *Don Quixote: Hero or Fool?* Allen shows how, as much by virtue of the presentative technique as in response to the character's transfiguration, the reader passes from a reaction of laughter and mockery at a subject that is seen from a markedly ironic distance to an attitude of sympathy and proximity. Howard Mancing has developed this line of interpretation with a careful lexical and stylistic study, which permits him to determine with great precision the evolutionary stages of the figure of Don Quixote and the decline of his aggressiveness and chivalric posture.[45] Donald W. Bleznick and Morgan Desmond illustrate other aspects of this subject.[46] Riley also examines it in Chapter 5 of his *"Don Quixote."* The collection of evidence about these changes in the personality and value of the central character is the basis for surmounting the disjunction of the "hard" and "soft" interpretations of the work. Allen himself regards it in this way.[47] For my part, in this book I try to present other arguments for this critical advance.

Nevertheless, it is important not only to remember that the force of the irreversible syntagmatic line is limited by the constant reiteration of the paradigmatic unit; we should also consider that Don Quixote's evolution is far from being consistent and would not satisfy the requirements of a *Bildungsroman*. There are retrogressions (which seem incongruent if we forget their paradigmatic and repetitive function), such as the adventure of the enchanted boat and Don Quixote's mad certainties with respect to Dulcinea, which persist to the end of the work. On the other hand, the paradigm contains *in nuce* the trajectory of the syntagm. The *quijotada* has the elements of a learning experience (although Don Quixote usually frustrates this possibility by explaining his failures as the work of enchanters). The adventures of the fulling mills and of the dead body, for example, end in enlightenment accompanied by embarrassment. And a section such as Chapter 18 in Part One, with the flocks of sheep, prodigiously synthesizes the circumnavigation of the whole book. It goes from the most extreme madness (which transforms the encounter with some sheep and shepherds in dusty solitude into the archetypal battle of universal history) to Christian compassion for the pain of one's neighbor, and the sensible and realistic assertion that "one tooth should be valued far above a diamond." Toward the end of this chapter, with his teeth broken and covered with vomit, Don Quixote approaches Sancho to comfort him with a lasting truth: "Know, Sancho, that a man can be no more than others if he does no more than others." Is this not an image of moving ridicule and at the same time of sublimity? We have here an emblem of the signification of the entire work, and of its ironic and ambivalent union of ("hard") satiric comicality and ("soft") elegiac evocation of the heroic. (As the work progresses it becomes increasingly apparent that the spirit of satire allows itself to be penetrated by that of elegy, if we give these words the sense of fundamental modes of literature which Schiller gives them.)

Equivalent to this episode (but within the coordinates peculiar to the Second Part, in which the ridiculous springs not from Don Quixote's error but from others' pranks) is the scene of the hero's farewell to the ducal court (II.57). He is stopped and grotesquely accused of stealing garters, with the Duke taking the jest to the point of formulating a challenge to Don Quixote. The latter responds with a sentence of insuperable dignity and gentlemanliness, without fear or arrogance, with perfect serenity, showing restraint and reconciling the (from his point of view) proper gratitude with the firm rejection of offensive and base suggestions: " 'May God forbid,' answered Don Quixote, 'that I unsheath my sword against your illustrious person, from whom I have received so many favors. . . .' " May God forbid . . . for if honor demands it, he, Don Quixote, will not be able to avoid it. With great consideration toward what he believes to be the Duke's momentary blindness, Don Quixote indicates elegantly, *only by implication,* that if the Duke persists in his obtuseness, the challenge will be accepted. We could search in vain through heroic literature (or, indeed, any other kind) for a comparable example of intelligent circumspection, fortitude confident of itself, moral sensibility, and opportune eloquence. What a ridiculous position, and what an admirable attitude!

Correspondence of Story and Style. There is a correspondence between the ambivalence of the *Quixote*'s syntagmatic line and the ambivalence of the work's use of the traditional forms of stylization discussed in Chapter 1. The ironic exposure of the forms of stylization constitutes a critique of systematic and institutionalized literary imagination. At the same time, the work represents a superlative celebration of these forms. Thus syntagmatic line and stylistic heterogeneity

are two great signifiers of the work that are related, but their signification (in both cases ambiguous) is not completely identical. They are
vectors in a most complex movement of the mind.[48]

The summary description of the paradigmatic and syntagmatic unities of the action of the *Quixote* already suggests an explanation of the
traditional critical alternative of "hard" and "soft" interpretations.
Those who pay more attention to the work's paradigmatic unity will
be inclined to read it as essentially a comic satire on the chivalric ideal.
Those who are more attentive to the syntagmatic evolution will find a
kind of elegy of that same ideal. As I have indicated, both readings are
one-sided and inadequate. Going beyond the rationalist-romantic disjunction in the interpretation of the *Quixote* is an inevitable consequence, I believe, of studies such as those I cited earlier.

The Symbol as Thematic Unity. The *thematic* unity of the *Quixote*
does not reside in an "idea," a philosophical postulate, or a conceptual truth. It resides in a complex symbol that is built around the
transformation of the protagonist. Like all symbols, as Goethe, Schelling, and the Romantic tradition understood, this one, instead of
expressing a thought, initiates an endless process of thinking. The
Baroque and Christian idea of enlightenment (*desengaño*) about the
world, although essential in the *Quixote,* does not cover the whole
range of reflection that this book opens up to us. It is true that in
Cervantes's novel we find a radical suspension of the value of human
action, as well as of the literary tradition, the institution of the book,
and the forms of imagination and knowledge. In his life and work,
however, this critical and skeptical transgression of the truth of his
historical circumstance is united with an affirmation of existence that
is at once melancholy and joyful, and with a complete and supreme
reliance on that same literary tradition, those same imaginative forms,
and the institution of the book.

It is the paradox of a happy disillusionment. Therefore, if, following
Benedetto Croce's conception of art, we had to find in the depths of
the work an ultimately lyrical unity, a feeling, as the source of this
intuitive vision, we would find ourselves immersed in a feeling not
only strong but complex and indefinable, the root of the essential
Cervantine expression: a smile that could never be portrayed.

This brief analysis makes us see the complexity and importance of
the question of the unity of a work such as *Don Quixote*. From the

perspective of this theoretical concept, we get a partial glimpse of the great constructive enterprise of Cervantes's imagination. The unity of this work is unparalleled, and far from the simple completeness of the univocal generic structures. The multiple critical and dissolving forces, both liberating and destructive, and the centrifugal expansion toward the encyclopedic totality of the world and of literature are counterweighted by the repeated and growing central symbol. Likewise, on another plane, the feeling of disillusionment is held in check by a breath of hope that is at once ironic and primitive.

Finally, as a methodological note, let us not overlook the fact that we have availed ourselves, as is the custom in literary criticism, of such metaphors as "dissolving forces," "functions," "organization," "counterweight," and "construction" (a typical mixture of organic and mechanical notions) to designate the unnamed forms and relationships of the imaginary realm. Metaphors show and reveal those forms, but not without falsifying them, for they impose alien categories on the new phenomenon. We still have a great deal to learn about the laws that govern this imaginary objectivity, which differs from the psychic reality on which it is undeniably founded. We cannot know how far metaphors that originate in the political, moral, and technical spheres—"laws," "norms," "foundation," "rules," and the like—distort the comprehension of art. A vast ontological field is open to critical investigation.

Chapter 3

The *Quixote:* Its Game, Its Genre, and Its Characters

The spirit of poetry, like all other living powers, must of necessity circumscribe itself by rules, were it only to unite power with beauty.
—Samuel Taylor Coleridge, "Shakespeare's Judgment Equal to His Genius" (ca. 1808)

What Kind of Game Is the Plain Reading of the *Quixote?*

The Reality of Genre and Kinds of Literary Games. The genre of a work is not merely an objective structure, hidden in the unique presence of the work. It is also a kind of game, one kind of activity (among others, intuitively different) in which readers are engaged as they enjoy their reading. We can postulate that when the reading is done well, the receptive activity is congruent with the objective structure. My considerations, which are not meant to touch upon more than a few aspects of the generic structure of this most complex work, will be situated between the active-receptive movement of the reading subject and the forms of the work that objectively determine it.

The concept of *game* which guides us here does not connote immaturity or frivolity, or the playful imitation of a serious activity, although it does not exclude the possibility of taking on those traits. Here "game" simply means a self-sufficient, absolute activity that has no particular relationship with any fact of our life outside the game. Games have a definite beginning and end and characteristic rules. They "circumscribe" themselves by rules. Thus understood, the concept covers much more ground than the word as it is ordinarily used. Rites, sports, intellectual disciplines, all appear as diverse kinds of games. Likewise, art and literature can be seen as systems that include collections of various games, genres of absolute actions. In what type of activity are we absorbed when we enjoy reading the *Quixote?*[1]

When we speak of the literary genre to which the *Quixote* belongs, it is plain that we are trying to visualize a more specific and significant form than the very general notion of *novel*, that is, of a fictional prose narrative that is relatively extensive (and which we do not necessarily intend to consume at one sitting). Knowing that a literary work belongs to this broad category (in which so many diverse types of imaginative games are possible) does not tell us a great deal about it. However, there is something singularly disconcerting about the enterprise of determining the relevant generic form of the *Quixote.* On the one hand, its structure is so complex, inclusive, and varied that it becomes all but impossible to describe it completely. We must limit ourselves to conspicuous aspects of the multifaceted design. On the other hand, this same complexity of the generic structure created by Cervantes in the *Quixote* makes it unexploitable for subsequent novelistic creations. The reading game, with its combination of diverse imaginary regions and various forms of stories, its hybridization of archetypes, its shifting narrative perspective, and its protean symbols, does not lend itself to satisfactory reproduction with other elements and materials. We are speaking, then, of a genre with just one constituent, a work rigorously sui generis. Although the *Quixote* has created a generic structure that in principle is abstractable and generalizable, it has not established a historical genre—let alone the modern novel. (With respect to this uniqueness the *Quixote* can be compared with Dante's *Divine Comedy.*) The fact that this or that aspect of the *Quixote* has been imitated, and that in many ways it has influenced the development of novelistic forms, is a separate issue.[2]

Let us reflect on some aspects of the aesthetic phenomenon of genre. It frequently happens that the reality of genre becomes very conspicuous to us, as if it had been freed from its subordination to the unique presence of the work. Thus there are days in which we are not in the mood for a serious spectacle; in others, comedy would be too light for us. Our mood sometimes leans toward one particular type of contemplative exercise; often it is inflexibly weak, and must be forced in the direction of the kind of spiritual activity and pleasure appropriate to the work that we happen to hold before us. Literary reading is an activity that assumes highly varied dispositions, although naturally related and classifiable. Two mystery novels by the same author will incite the same vibrations. The subsequent reading of a pastoral novel will arouse such a weak response that we realize that many atrophied chords lie neglected in the soul's past, and that the game in which our being can participate with the bucolic genre is very different from the detectivesque imagination. There are, then, recognizable *classes* of literary games. On the other hand, it is a fact that each superior work imposes an intense *particularization* of the contemplative movement. The task of poetics is to describe the major generic structures of typical literary games. Part of the task of interpreting the particular work is to determine which unique discipline it offers us. These pages are devoted to interpreting the *Quixote,* as a particular work, through the poetics of the nonproliferating genre created in it.

In order to approach this subject, let us take the most trivial and generalized of contemplative games as a point of departure, that of imaginary "identification" with a hero. In this case, the protagonist of the story that we read has virtues we would like to have ourselves. His vitality and spirit seem inexhaustible; his days are filled with struggles and triumphs; the best of everything (supreme beauties, social power, peace of mind, variety and wealth of the experience of the world, the gaze of collective admiration) sooner or later are bestowed upon him. Inside his skin, our feeling of life expands. (This magnification of our imaginary being, of course, can take on primitive or superior forms. We can ride with Amadís, but we can also follow the interior path of the hero of the Proustian "quest" of memory.)

In its most elemental versions, the hero's life is displayed as unequivocally oriented. What he desires is identifiable, and it is desirable in a superlative and unambiguous way. The adversary, for his part, is the incarnation of a purely destructive principle. Love and hatred (although it may be only the hatred of Satan or the destructiveness of time) can grow without the inhibition that comes from doubt, and fill the universe with their black and white flowers. The child experiences in imagination not only the vertigo of impetuous action, but also the marvel of strange spaces, of enchanted worlds. These games of action and space are continued beyond the romantic adventure, toward increasingly ironized forms, in which the reading subject seems to split into a young, alienated soul and a self-aware, smiling observer. The game of *knowing* possible worlds through the imagination acquires greater weight in more mature literary experiences. Also, interest in the particular personality that we would *not* wish to be will rarely be an early pleasure.

To what kind of game does Cervantes invite us in the *Quixote?* Here we are presented with a "hero" who believes himself to have unequivocal goals and definite enemies, but we are not directed toward an identification with him. His goals are exposed as unreal, his adversaries as nonexistent or products of his misunderstandings. His most salient attribute, madness, is not attractive, nor are his reiterated failures and the ridicule that he suffers. Instead of submerging and dissolving ourselves in his being, we withdraw in order to observe him from a distance. We ironize the hero. This posture is easy for us, for we have an eminent accomplice: the narrator. Even before we see the character in action, we have been won over by the narrator. His self-ironic, cheerful tone; the fact that with light humor he introduces us into a community of implications, tacit allusions, ambiguities that are a bit enigmatic—from the beginning his personality gains our sympathy. We are ready, then, to laugh or smile with him at "our" hero. We make an object out of the protagonist. Initially the subject of the work is our ironic gaze.

This initial articulation of the game of the *Quixote* will become more and more differentiated as the hero proceeds confusedly to distance himself from his own endeavor and from his projected personal identity, thus internalizing the ironic dimension. In the wake of this process, we move closer to him, and the presence of the person who narrates pales. But the essential game of the *Quixote* never becomes one of identification with the protagonist (as Unamuno would have it). Basically, it is an amused, amazed look at what is happening to him in his foreseeable *collisions* with the world that surrounds him. The discrepancy between his mad vision and the semirealistic determinations that define the basic worldly plane of the work induces the comic expectation of the clash, as much intellectual as physical. This sometimes coarse comic quality is an indispensable part of Cervantes's creation, and the *Quixote* shares this device with works as minor as the "Entremés de los romances."[3]

But Cervantes gives the comic motif of collision a refinement and depth that transpose it in multiple ways and extend it to many different dimensions of the work. The category at the core of this game of clashes is that of the *encounter,* the juxtaposition of the diverse and the heterogeneous, and of the incongruous.[4] There is not only the encounter of Don Quixote's fantasies with hard "realities," but also the encounter of the multitude of beings, conditions, offices, and destinies on the plane of fiction and, metapoetically, the contiguity and interweaving of styles of diction, figural archetypes, imaginary regions, and views of the world.

Among other projections, this radical universalization of the encounter has the effect of juxtaposing and equalizing varied delusions. The accumulation of artificial systems of "reality," one after the other, reveals the hubris of the constructed conceptions of the world. In Cervantes's vision, this plurality of creations of human mythomania (both the generic institutions of literature and rationalizing doctrines) is a varied and vain flora spread over the real ground on which one stands. This real ground is not the "realistic" plane of the world of the work (which obviously obeys a comic stylization and therefore is the result of an imaginative codification) but the real plane of the author and reader, the world in which we really exist, which is not organized stylistically or subjected to a formulable code. (We will return to this important theme later.)

The very figure of Don Quixote establishes the irreconcilable juxtaposition of the protagonist's age and his youthful model. This discordance, like so many others, is maintained through the work and is never resolved. Also juxtaposed are the protagonist's archaic gesture of free heroic individualism and the civil circumstance of institutionalized justice in the fictionally evoked historical present; likewise, the romancesque world view of books of chivalry and the comic idealization of daily life. We are confronted with insuperable counterpositions, and our task as readers is not to overcome them but, on the contrary, to contemplate their irreducible diversity. With the introduction of Sancho, the picture of such balanced antagonisms is enriched. Don Quixote and Sancho's journeying and conversing proceed to reiterate the disparate pair's encounter, bringing to light new facets of their personalities. Although, as we saw, there is a crisis in the two characters' personalities (especially in Don Quixote's), a crisis that is linked to their stay at the home of the Duke and Duchess, the greater part of the work consists in the encounter of their immutable identities, which only continue to exhibit their inexhaustible static richness. There is no "quixotization" of Sancho or "sanchification" of Don Quixote: such a possibility seems to me remote from Cervantes's design. (By contrast, one may think of the evolution of the personalities of figures in the modern novel, or the interactions and reciprocal transformations of the characters in dramatic structures.)[5]

Nor do the diverse regions of the imagination that the work displays tend to meld (as we saw in Chapter 1). Their intersections (or rather, tangential contacts) ironically underscore their heterogeneity. The work invites us to admire the diversity of the diverse, and to admire the contrasting richness of each static being. The movement is not within the figures but in the shifting aspects of themselves that they show us. Our gaze is what moves from one phenomenon to another, verifying their reciprocal reflections. The greatest dynamism of the *Quixote* is that of the reading mind implicit in the work. Hence one of the fundamental features of the book consists of putting Don Quixote and Sancho in a great variety of circumstances, so that the diverse situations draw new manifestations from them. On the other hand, as I have just suggested, there is no process of interior metamorphosis that *dramatically* unites the series of situations (except to a limited degree, which we considered in Chapter 2 as a syntagmatic transformation of the central paradigm of the work). We do not feel the pull of a directional psychological or dramatic dynamic. The suspense or tension of "what will happen next" is almost completely absent. That is not the game of the reading of this work. It is not the dynamism of Don Quixote's adventures that captivates us, it is the encounters they bring about: Don Quixote and the uncouth world of inns, Don Quixote and the burghers on the highway, Don Quixote and the rustic peace of the goatherds, Don Quixote and pastoral ideality, Don Quixote and the captive criminals, the cultivated hidalgos, the nobles, the maidens who seem to be in love with him, and so on. Sancho, too, proceeds to play out his possibilities as a character in the varied situations of that directionless journey. The simple, shy servant develops as an authoritarian head of the family before his wife, a rustic clown in the palace, a wise governor on the "island." One and the other vibrate in a new tone when they are put in the big city, or (a delicious moment) upon the shore, contemplating the sea, "which until then they had never seen" (II.61). We are always anticipating the collision between the imaginations of both of them and the various circumstances that they meet. And the variety of these circumstances brings to light new versions of their foolishness, promotes the inexhaustible creativity of their crazy explanations, in which (in yet another encounter) plausible reasoning and deranged fantasies are juxtaposed.

There is a playful pleasure in seeing these conjunctions of the disparate in really impossible but artistically successful congruities. In a subtle collage, a rare imagination superimposes not the pieces but the usual molds of our fantasies of the world. "Strange inventor" is the way Cervantes styles himself in the *Journey to Parnassus.* (The passage is quoted as the epigraph to my Prologue.)

On a less superficial level, the rationalization of the crazed imagination, *the encounter between reason and insanity,* is a principal figure of the *Quixote*'s game. There is special humor in the fact that the collisions of the Quixotic imagination with the surrounding world do not shatter the hidalgo's stubborn obfuscation, despite his discursive rationality and (when lucid) his honest subordination to the truth. There is only a minimum of mechanical repetition in this tenacious delusion, for the fact that the madman's vision of the world remains intact becomes *verisimilar* through a series of apparent confirmations. He is reassured in his views by his hallucinations and his erroneous interpretations of real signs (at times by fortuitous but not improbable coincidences, such as the swineherd's horn that sounds next to the inn when the trumpets of the castle would have sounded [I.2]). He is also confirmed in his insanity by the fitting deceptions that others carry out, and by the credulity of the simple individuals who treat him like a knight errant: Sancho, the "cousin," and to some extent Don Diego, the Knight of the Green Cloak. For Don Quixote, the incongruence of his own behavior often remains hidden under the appearance of the most natural appropriateness. And so the aberrant behavior seems to establish itself definitively and legitimately, with full rights, elbow to elbow with the common-sense travelers of the wide world.

Moreover, the hypothesis of enchanters and malicious genii with supernatural powers permits Don Quixote to account for his perceptual and semiotic world with impeccable logic.[6] (Rare exceptions to the coherence of the discourses are Sancho's random proverbs and occasional utterances by Don Quixote, as when he discusses the broken puppets with Maese Pedro.) Cervantes thus plays, and makes us play, with the arbitrariness and the variety of theories with which we can explain life's phenomena. The juxtaposition of the assumptions of common sense on the one hand and those of a fantastic vision on the other within a nearly permanent discursive coherence constitutes the encounter of two cosmological codes, antagonistic and irreducible, which prolong their precarious equilibrium throughout the work. The result is the humoristic (that is, not serious) ironization of our ordinary vision of things. As if with a smile, it is suggested that madness is only another form of rationality. But, I insist, the suggestion is not serious. This game is openly humoristic, for not only is the validity of traditional common sense not questioned by the *Quixote,* but it is posited as a foundation for all of the ironic construction. It is not the daily reality of the real author and reader or the common sense that units them that Cervantes upsets and relativizes, but the artificial forms (first and foremost the artistic ones) of the imagination and the theoretical constructions of the mind. It could be said that his is a limited skepticism, rather a manifestation of the absolute feeling of being on the ground of truth, a truth shared by people of good sense.

The fictitious world of the *Quixote,* then, is erected on a most solid *sense of reality,* common to the author and his readers, that is evoked in the work from the beginning. In the nonfictitious background of the book, the reality of life functions as a matter of firm and unquestioned consensus. By virtue of that common consciousness of a shared and present reality, the ironic and unrealistic constructions of the *Quixote* assume a playful air, joyful or melancholy, but without metaphysical transcendence. They are not anxious games of an autonomized imagination or a reason without firm ground under its feet. These encounters of irreconcilable systems of interpreting experience produce a relativization not of the sense of reality but of the conceptual and artistic codes, of the forms with which we want to articulate the consciousness of reality, at times discursively, at times in images.

An example of the purely humoristic suggestion of the lack of validity of our common sense, and at the same time the exposition of the fragility of the semantic fields, is the game with the very notion of madness. Nobody can be farther from being mad or closer to the ground of reality than the ordinary people of the work's world: the Curate, the Barber, the Housekeeper, the Niece, the harriers, innkeepers, and so on. These characters seem to embody in elementary form the good sense through whose medium the smiling author and ideal reader communicate with each other. But Sancho is more than once called "mad," and he deserves to be, if we apply the term to the foolish simplicity that is half of his personality. Upon this first-degree madness of Sancho's is superimposed the more advanced (and qualitatively different) derangement of Don Quixote. But Don Quixote is not so mad that his madness cannot be surpassed. Within his habitual madness, Don Quixote decides in the Sierra Morena that he will do penance in imitation of Amadís and execute "follies"—not "furious" ones, like Roldán's (Orlando's), but "melancholy" ones, like Amadís's (I.25). There Don Quixote very logically reflects that Roldán lost his mind because he had cause to do so, after Angelica's treachery with the Moor, but that he, Don Quixote, cannot "imitate him in the follies," cannot commit follies of that sort, for he has no comparable cause (I.26). If these follies that Don Quixote will feign—third-degree follies, say—do not move Dulcinea to respond suitably, he will go "truly mad" with disappointment and sorrow (I.25); presumably this will be fourth-degree madness. But there in the Sierra Don Quixote and Sancho have found Cardenio, and after seeing his actions, they feel pity for him and consider him "an unfortunate madman" (I.23)— fifth-degree insanity. And at the inn (I.32) this very Cardenio, upon hearing the innkeeper maintain that the stories in books of chivalry are true, judges him mad. With this sixth-degree madness that is attributed to the innkeeper we are back, as if in one of Escher's buildings, on the ground floor of those who personify common sense. What seemed like a ladder turns out to be a circle. (To top it off, the Curate then reads the story of Anselmo's tragic madness.) It is unquestionable that with this cycle of encounters with insanities, the conceptual field with which we try to articulate human alienation becomes riddled with irony. Nevertheless, this ironic game does not shake the certainty of the distinction that common sense makes between sanity and madness, a distinction belonging to a much more fundamental plane of the *Quixote.* Without the certainty and clarity of this "natural" distinction, neither the figure nor the destiny of the protagonist would be possible, nor one of the obvious allegorical meanings of the work.

In the encounters between the various normalities and insanities operates another essential principle of the game of the *Quixote:* that of the *duplications* and *transferences* of planes and functions. What appears as madness in relation to a preceding plane of reasonableness becomes reasonableness for a higher degree of madness. The shift is very subtle. When he prepares to throw himself into the metamadness of imitating the insanities of Amadís or Roldán, Don Quixote's basic madness assumes a hue of relative good sense. Precisely at this point, as he talks with Sancho, Don Quixote recognizes that Dulcinea is his fiction.

The plane that is being sustained assumes the qualities of the one that sustains it as it becomes in turn the sustainer of another. The most inclusive duplication is that of the text of the story. Presumably there are three texts: Cide Hamete's Arabic one; the version by the anonymous translator of Toledo (not a totally faithful one, as is indicated in II.18 and II.44); and finally the paraphrasing of the translation, presented by the narrator-author. The privileges of the original narration are transferred to the one we have before us. It is as immediate to the narrated events as Cide Hamete's could be (and, if we want to prolong the game, presumably even more so, since Hamete is a "historian,"

and as such should not permit himself the privileges of invisible witness with unlimited access to the minds of others and to other unexplained sources of information).

Another duplication that suggests an interplay of mirrors toward
the infinite is created by the literary fictions read or told by the characters of the Cervantine fiction, especially the inclusion of the First Part
as an object within the Second Part.[7] Also duplicated, like trans-
migrating phantasms, are the abstract figures of the characters.
Sancho and Teresa are stylistically transfigured into Don Quixote and
Sancho in their scene together in Chapter 5 of the Second Part.[8] It can
also be said that Roque Guinart (II.60) assumes the figure of Don
Quixote, his chivalric and authoritarian countenance, and temporarily deprives the protagonist of his personal substance; the mad
hidalgo here stands inert and off on the sidelines (and, in the metapoetic logic of the literary character, fatally wounded).

If the introduction of (second-degree) fictions within the basic plane
of the fiction lends the latter an aura of reality, Cervantes also occasionally plays in the opposite direction, introducing realities into the
fiction to point up the fictional nature of his characters and his story.
Mentioning the writer Cervantes as a friend of the Curate, or as "one
de Saavedra" in the Captive's story, together with incidental references
to historical individuals and events, undermines the fiction's basic
plane and makes way for the presence of the reader's real horizon.
Thus the planes of the real are reduplicated in the imaginary, transfer-
ring the attribute of true authenticity from one to the other.

Other variations in a different key are such stories as that of the
madman from Seville which the Barber tells, in reference to Don
Quixote's only apparent sanity, and those of Grisóstomo and Marcela, of Leandra and company, and of the feigned Arcadia, insofar as
they echo Don Quixote's imitation of literary models. As Francisco
Márquez Villanueva indicates, the tale of Princess Micomicona, invented by Dorotea to beguile Don Quixote, transposes her own story
to another stylistic key.[9] The stylistic echoes in the diction, on the
other hand, emphasize the duplicating design that we are examining.
The narrative voice, for example, at times adopts the manner of speaking of other narrators and characters. In I.29 the narrator gives an
account, in indirect style, of Sancho's reproduction of one of Don
Quixote's discourses, with the knight's characteristic phonetic archaisms. In II.10 Sancho speaks like Don Quixote. In II.28 it is the
narrator who parodies the hidalgo's diction. In II.52, as a late echo,

the narrator briefly adopts the rhapsodic style of Maese Pedro's chanter ("Here you see appearing . . .").

A notable duplication of planes that recalls Shakespearean comedy occurs in the tale of "The Man of Ill-Advised Curiosity." It relates to the act of pretending. To satisfy Anselmo, Lotario is supposed to pretend to Camila that he loves and desires her. When the pretended passion has become real, he must pretend to Anselmo that he is pretending to Camila. In the knife scene, Lotario pretends to Anselmo that he is pretending to Camila what he is really pretending in complicity with Camila. To continue deceiving Anselmo, Camila has alerted Lotario that he ought to react as if her behavior were authentic. Camila pretends so well that Lotario comes to doubt whether she is pretending at all, and for a moment the whole house of cards trembles. In this story as in all of the *Quixote,* the unstable and uncertain are the worlds of the mad imagination and of the wandering discourse of those who go beyond the limits of a serene sense of reality. The novella of "Ill-Advised Curiosity" (which I will dare to call an essential piece of the *Quixote*) shows us emphatically and tragically the solid reality of nature and the world.

A Special "Novel of Character." Up to this point my observations on some aspects of the *Quixote*'s genre can be criticized as narrowly subjected to the systematic and paradigmatic preferences of structuralism. I have paid scant attention to the more syntagmatic orientation of traditional literary vision; in sum, I have neglected to expand our historical horizon toward the forms of experience of Cervantes's times.[10]

Although I am not sure that such an objection is valid, it does not seem irrelevant. It is true that some contemporary methodological (and even literary) tendencies sensitize us especially to analogical relationships; it can seem inevitable that the corresponding deformations and blindnesses of the current intellectual epoch will occur. But I believe that there is descriptive, objective, evidence (which I have tried to present in Chapter 2) to support the thesis that the syntagmatic dimension of the *Quixote* is much weaker than the paradigmatic one. I will add the following argument. It cannot be denied that the idea of *madness* is central in the work. Well, then, madness is a phenomenon of an intrinsically and essentially systematic sphere: it is the disruption of the mental order taken for rational and sane, the invasion of an alien code of thinking and conduct. We cannot conceive madness (certainly not Quixotic madness) without conceiving the parallelism of two systems whose paradigmatic relations are in conflict. Such madness is a dissonant encounter of two codes, a forced conjunction of the irreconcilable.

The initial motif of the work, that we become interested in a bizarre individual and laugh at his madness laced with good judgment, establishes the nature of the reading game. We should enjoy the comicality of his departures from sensibility. The mad action, which is itself a deviation from the given occasion's pertinent code, becomes liberating when, as in the inoffensive field of fiction, it obviously lacks consequences for our own life. In a burst of laughter we enjoy an escape from the iron circle of natural and institutional reality, that is, from the continuous and tyrannical density of the norms of good sense.[11] Laughing at Don Quixote, we enjoy our superiority as reasonable persons, and at the same time the freedom of absurdity without suffering its painful consequences.

It is the marvel of this sustained collision between irreconcilable systems (delusion, assuming stability and consistency, united to the comic idealization of the postulates of common sense) that, by holding steady in precarious equilibrium, unleashes the movement of the reader's mind. The juxtaposition of the unassimilable systems, which can interact only marginally and subtly, makes us subliminally grasp their implications and connotations; that is, it gives rise to an incipient vision of the great orders of imagination and thought. Certainly, while all this is going on, our conscious minds continue to focus on the singular figures of the characters and their actions. (A Cartesian or Husserlian model of the subject cannot explain the operation of reading.)

I see no contradiction between these considerations and Wolfgang Kayser's thesis that the *Quixote* is a novel "of character."[12] Although "novel of character" is a more specific concept than simply "the novel," and we learn something more about the work through such a description (for example, that the episodic structure of the action is appropriate there in principle, and that it is irrelevant whether it may lack the Aristotelian unity of action proper of dramatic forms), this determination continues to be too general and of little significance for an understanding of the specific game of the *Quixote*. What I am proposing is a greater differentiation of a type of the novel of character. In this type, the central character is a conveyer of an ostensible, anomalous code of vision and conduct; hence the protagonist enters the scene from the beginning as the incarnation of a *systematic* conflict. But instead of giving this premise room for tragic development (in the Hegelian sense of tragedy, as the necessary and surpassable dialectical antagonism of the two principles), involving a single collision with a relatively quick resolution in the protagonist's fall, this central character prolongs the systematic conflict in a virtually interminable series of encounters. (That the series can be brought to a conclusion at the end is due, as we saw in Chapter 2, to the subtle transformation of the character and its barely perceptible departure from the code of conflict. Thus the final conversion is only a modulation of the basic, unifying paradigm of the work, which is maintained as a systematic repetition of the conflict of codes.) As the center of the work's architecture, Don Quixote represents the permanent figure to which the varied embodiments of comic realism and of other systems of the imagination are juxtaposed.

At this point it is worth observing that the indefinite prolongation of the systematic conflict between the protagonist and his world is possible only in the climate of comedy, that is, in that of a very attenuated "realism," idealized in the direction of survival and good fortune. In its own way, comedy weakens the laws of reality, and thus permits the conciliation of the work's basic pseudorealistic laws with an incongruous vision and conduct. The inexorability of the code of reality in the climate of tragedy, or in modern realism, would not permit Don Quixote to have many adventures. That alone is evidence of the structural necessity of avoiding realism as the *Quixote*'s basic plane, and adopting instead an ambiguous imaginative matrix.[13] In order to elicit the systematic conflict, the alienated system of the madman must be placed in confrontation with that of realistic good sense, but if the confrontation is to be maintained, the realistic system must be attenuated and idealized comically.

Cervantes awakens in the reader a sense of immediate and daily reality, while at the same time submitting the images to a subtle unrealistic transformation. Therefore, historical reality slips into the world of the *Quixote*, but very marginally and weakly, so as not to hinder the comic idealization of its fictionalization.

The first sentence of the book already exhibits this double movement: "In a place of La Mancha . . . ," that is, in our real and familiar world; "whose name I do not wish to remember," that is, in an underdetermined part of the real world, veiled by the vagueness of the unreachable, and thus whisked away from realistic control. (The archetypal initial imprecisions of the fairy tale still faintly resonate here.) Don Quixote's contemporaneity, introduced by "not long ago there lived . . ." and accentuated by later references to events of the period, is at the same time contradicted by recurrent mention of the sources and chroniclers of his history, and by some passages that suggest that the past in which he existed is distant. The contemporaneous typicality of "an hidalgo of the kind that . . ." is immediately attenuated by the characterization of his "strange" madness (in truth, inverisimilar, and patently a literary invention). Cervantes opens his book toward the horizon of historical reality, but at the same time he circumscribes it into a comic semihermeticity. Thus we can say that the basic plane of the *Quixote* interweaves three visions of the world: that of Don Quixote's insanity; that of the tradition of comic literature (which is one of the institutionalized dementias of the human imagination); and that of good sense, of daily living, open to the historical horizon of the real author and reader. The principle of comic idealization of daily experience clearly predominates in the imaginary space of this novel. But the common sense of reality remains as the infranarrative basis of the whole game of the *Quixote.* For that reason, it is possible for Cervantes to ironize the work's basic imaginary plane itself, that of comic realism, and with it all of the literary imagination. Also for that reason, the comicality of the *Quixote* has a melancholy profundity: the happy comedy is only imagination, while life is serious. Ironizing the literary image as such is like disturbing the quiet surface of water, awakening to the reality that what we see is merely a reflection, and that we have been back here, in our own life's unobjectifiable medium, all along.

The Double Movement of Style and Truth. Would it not be possible to maintain that in the *Quixote* there is also a movement of imagination that is the opposite of what I have just described? Is there not, together with the stylistic transition from the sense of reality to the happy illusion of comedy, also a reverse subterranean course of return to the crude truth? This less obvious change of tone and quality of the world view is not manifested in the immediate images of persons and events, but rather indirectly and conceptually. I think that such a movement, partly hidden, can be found in the story of Dorotea, Don Fernando, Luscinda, and Cardenio. If we may judge by what we know about Don Fernando's and Cardenio's personalities, the two marriages exemplifying the happy ending characteristic of comedy will be radically unhappy. Earlier I invoked Schiller's dictum that the artistic form annihilates, or consumes and neutralizes, the material incorporated in the work, including the explicit ideologies.[14] The statement that the novelistic form ironizes all doctrinal discourse expounded in the novel is only a specification of that principle. Now we see that the opposite principle also has validity. The subject matter of Cervantes's double story of Cardenio and Dorotea (in particular, the personality of the male protagonists) ironizes and invalidates its form (the "happy ending" of comedy's convention). An empirical element suspends the ideology inherent in the genre.

Likewise, the splendor of the ducal court (costumes, adornments, and settings) and its rejoicing are undermined by a great number of fleeting hints of mundane misery: the Duke's debts, his insensitivity and frivolity, the poverty of Don Quixote's dress, the manifestations of the toll that age takes on the human body (including Doña Rodríguez's bad teeth and the Duchess's suppurating legs), and others. Throughout the *Quixote* there are signs, not quite harmlessly and happily comical, of the vulnerability of the body (beatings, injuries, blood, deformity, ugliness). Perhaps these signs seem more intense precisely in the luxury of the ducal residence. Here we have various symbols of life's autonomous, recalcitrant materiality, besides those I have just mentioned: Sancho's "delicate" buttocks now become a topic of conversation and dispute; the lady Trifaldi and her duennas pretend to suffer the punishment of growing thick beards; the fabricated story's Princess Antonomasia becomes pregnant; Don Quixote's nose is mauled by the cats, just when he has begun to fear nocturnal threats to his virginity; extreme pathological descriptions distinguish the feigned story of the farmer of Miguel Turra (II.47); Sancho suffers hunger as never before; and so on. This diffuse symbolism of nature, corruption, and death is related to the fact, unique in this work, that figures such as the Duke and Duchess, whose social rank, according to the canonical system of genres, entitles them to appear in more idealized poetic regions, here are a central part of the sphere of comic realism. This metapoetic debasement contributes to the satire (while lending it a smiling and apparently innocuous air) of their existences, which not only are obviously to a large extent idle and vacuous, but also (as suggested more subtly) occasionally cruel and harmful. It is clear that these and other somber aspects constitute the background of the *Quixote,* not its sustained foreground. (And is it not relevant that several of these physical abnormalities and accidents appear only in "untruthful" reports by the characters?) The happy illusion covers the poetic universe of the work, but it is a semitransparent illusion. It can then be said that Cervantes *dissimulates* the depth of his image of life, and thus within the mode of the basic stylization—that is, within the imaginary region of comic realism—generates an incessant shifting between the poles of naturalism and beatific fantasy, though without actually reaching either one. We will return to this subject later.15

The Central Characters: Inexplicit Inwardness, Empirical Typicality, Literary Archetypicality

The Structure of Character. Our literary experience could not extend to such abstract and subliminal games as those that I have described in the preceding section, if it did not have a foundation of affective reactions. The reader's attention is held by a "human" interest in the protagonists: curiosity, laughter, sympathy, compassion, admiration. But for such sentiments to be generated in us, their object must first exist. The character has to be more than a name and a brief characterization, more than an aggregate of predicates or a multitude of sentences; in sum, more than a verbal entity. To be affecting, the character, or the imaginary person, has to be a live presence, consistent and unpredictable at the same time, familiar and yet endowed with inscrutable depth, something "human." How can we explain this power of the poetic imagination? How can we understand the moving, intense *reality* of Don Quixote in our minds? What follows adds to the considerations I presented in Chapter 2 about the constitution of the central characters.

An aesthetically efficacious personal presence exists only when the multiple actions of the subject go on repeating one unique character, maintaining an identity by the recurrence of recognizable traits. The most elemental literary forms of the constitution of personal identity are the proper name, the epic epithet, and the motif of characterization (the reiterated description of a gesture, a trait, a peculiar saying). But formal mnemonic devices of this sort do not suffice to beget a "live" person. The impression of character is generated when the varied conduct of the subject seems to emanate from a reduced number of dispositions or recurrent tendencies; or, stated another way, when his or her many actions can be understood as products of unchanging personal forces. Character is manifested only when the action to be taken implies *choosing* between different objective possibilities—that is, when none of them is universally unavoidable and therefore the action can be determined only by causes particular to the agent, thus revealing a "style of decision," as Aristotle says.[16] The character is the individualized combination of certain principles of conduct, the singular system that determines the open-ended series of a subject's actions.

The depth and vitality of a literary character is neither more nor less mysterious, I believe, than that of a real person, and seems to be at least partly founded on identical principles. The apparent *uniqueness,* the distinctness of a personality (literary or real) is the result of actions whose latent system is singular but simple and sustained. The impression of *profundity,* on the other hand, flows from manifestations *that are both systematic and improbable,* of "convincing surprises."[17] The crux of personality resides in the fact that, to be perceptible, it tends to be simple and flat, and, if profound, it tends to be confusing or lacking in a well-defined profile. A very complex personal organization will lead to forms of behavior that are highly varied in their stylistic determination, and even apparently contradictory. If the bases of such behavior do not become apparent, the person will seem literally unrecognizable, not only in the impression we gain in ordinary dealings but also in the reader's aesthetic contemplation. Paraphrasing Aristotle, we can say that such is the case of inconsistently inconsistent characters; they lack unity and efficacious presence. A real person of a similar constitution will impress us as *disconcerting,* disquieting (*unheimlich*), or simply chaotic; but real people will at least continuously preserve their physical identity, which forces upon us the conviction of an ultimate substantial unity existing behind each real character.

A literary character's identity is a phenomenon of the reader's imaginative intuition, not of a supposed intimate substance (transcending the reading consciousness) of the fictitious person. It makes no sense to say that a literary figure has unity and character, but that the unity and character are not accessible to the good reader. It does make sense to say (however implausibly) that a real person has a solid personal structure (detectable, say, in experimental tests), but that the structure is not perceptible to those who deal with him or her. There are radical differences, then, between the structure of a real person's personality and that of a literary character. Moreover, the character's fictitiousness permits his system of conduct to be (originally or conventionally) fantastic, and not only inverisimilar, but impossible a priori, for it can be based on a combination of systems that are logically irreconcilable and diverse.

Don Quixote's as well as Sancho's actions emanate not from a single character system but from a fantastic compound of various systems, some empirical, others strictly literary or conventional. We thus have a specifically literary complexity of character, remotely analogous to that of a split personality, but without pathological implications. This is very different from the fact that Don Quixote is, in addition, a madman, and as such behaves with consistent inconsistency. His madness is only one of the systems that determine his behavior.

In the *Quixote* the crucial conflict of identity versus complexity in the character's being is resolved in an astonishing way. The identity of Don Quixote's and Sancho's persons is continuous and at the same time radically changing. The artistic harmonization of the various systems that are combined in their complex personalities is as obvious in its results as it is indescribable in its marvelous execution.

A Mechanism Underlying Our Experience of Characters in Fiction. Of course, it is sensible to wonder whether the literary character is necessarily subjected to any laws, even the logical one of consistency which Aristotle indicates in the *Poetics.* But, at least in works of a traditional type, the character has to possess unity and continuity, identity of aesthetic presence, in order to produce the artistic effects that are its own potentials, to have the virtues that justify its imaginary existence, to interest and move the reader.

How does the literary character manage to reveal to readers the system (or the combination of systems) that defines its personality? How can it quickly establish itself as a discernible aesthetic entity, recognizable and efficacious? And supposing that the character's system is evident from the beginning, how can subsequent actions of the same subject surprise us as revelations of a personality's depth that has been hidden until then? The only answers that I find for these questions are (1) that the systems of the figure's personality are schemata already known to readers and immediately activated in their consciousness by the passages of the work that relate to the character; and (2) that the deep, complex character consists of more than one system, so that each time one of the systems enters into play, displacing the one that was determining the character's behavior, a surprising rupture is produced, which nevertheless can be interpreted immediately as consequential and systematic—that is, within the system that has been alternatively and newly activated. In Don Quixote's behavior the wise sententious man surprises us when we have been observing the actions of the hallucinating fool; the genteel hidalgo, when we were following the anachronistic knight. In Sancho's conduct, the sharp realist jolts us when we have been laughing at the silly rustic.

The air of familiarity, that recognizable configuration, that identical essence of the character in all its appearances cannot be based, it seems to me, on anything but a preestablished schema (or on a combination of such schemata) that the author activates in our imagination with the predicates that he initially attributes to his creature. The most conspicuous case of this procedure is that of the *types* of comedy, whose mere physical aspect suffices to open up a sphere of expectations that ought to be confirmed by their actions. Precisely because these basic, initial attributes of the character (explicitly stated or implicit in its attitudes), as well as the rest of its gestures and actions, are brought together naturally and congruently in a known organization, the totality of the character seems to us "convincing," which simply means that it corresponds to one of our available cognitive schemata. The imaginary individual that becomes consistent and recognizable soon after entering the scene is so because it obviously represents a universal stored in our passive knowledge.

With what universals are we dealing in the preestablished schemata of literary characters? What types are these that slumber in our imagination and can be awakened by the actualization of a few of the traits that constitute them? I believe it is useful to distinguish the empirical types (predominantly empirical) from the literary types (more remotely empirical). The empirical types are relatively direct products of our daily experience. The literary ones are part of an artistic tradition, whether very old or more recent. Among the empirical types, we can consider the characterological and the sociological ones. Among the literary ones are found those of comedy, those of "romance," those of the fairy tale, and so on.

Heterogeneous Composition and Intuitive Unity of Cervantes's Figures. The initial characterization of Don Quixote immediately evokes distinctive schemata of a sociological and characterological sort. Cervantes presents him as an hidalgo of a particular kind ("an hidalgo such as those who . . ."), thus fixing his social type, and as a man with a strong, lean physique and (before his madness) of somewhat solitary habits, rather punctilious and a little eccentric. Notwithstanding that it has always served to shape literary figures, this characterological type is empirical, and Kretschmer's classical work confirms it to the smallest detail. It is the type the German psychiatrist calls "schizothymic leptosome," with an initial "athletic" component.[18] With respect to the social determination, it seems unquestionable that we are also contemplating an empirical configuration, in this case historical: the relatively poor, idle Castilian hidalgo arising from the peace of the reconquered, imperial peninsula. It goes without saying that in sixteenth-century Spain, this empirical sociological type had already turned into a literary model, as the characterological type has done ever since antiquity. It suffices to mention the well-known figure served by Lazarillo de Tormes in one of his occupations.[19]

In Sancho we recognize the talkative fat man of variable, light humor; in Don Quixote, the thin introvert, grave and persevering. But how can we recognize the "hidalgo such as those who . . ." if this historical type is not part of our daily experience? Here we might have a case that illustrates the so-called fusion of historical horizons that, according to Gadamer, is an essential part of the hermeneutic process. The Spanish hidalgo to whom Cervantes alludes is not part of our historical horizon, so he cannot be a type we directly recognize from ordinary experience. On our daily horizon, however, there are similar figures that permit us to reconstruct that one: the idle gentleman living off the last remains of an inherited fortune, or the man enjoying a very modest early retirement. And on top of this basis of contemporary experience we project our literary experiences of the type, including those deriving from oral anecdotes, from the wit of the satirical entertainer, and so on. With a light touch Cervantes awakens in us an imaginary complex brimming with jesting potential, which overflows in laughter when we read that the hidalgo's spare time "was most of the year."

The activation of pertinent literary archetypes is analogous to that of the empirical types. The song of anticipated fame that Don Quixote bestows upon himself when he has just set out in search of adventures elicits the image of the man who brags of deeds not done, the archetypal and literary image of the *miles gloriosus* of comedy. The first references to Sancho (beyond typifying him, in the empirical registry, as a farmer, a common man, and later as a cyclothymic pyknic) place him as the simple rustic in the repertory of comedy, and immediately the clown (or joker or *gracioso*) appears.

The evocation of these literary systems at once creates specific comic expectations: the noisy collapse of the blusterer in the face of a real
challenge, the ridiculous stumbling of the credulous simpleton, the
sharp sallies of the jester. Certainly the *Quixote* satisfies these expectations; indeed, it far exceeds them. Later Cervantes introduces into
Don Quixote's configuration the archetypal system of the sententious
sage.

Given the typical and archetypal complexity of these two characters, it is understandable that they suggest highly varied and surprising
analogies, such as that (which I suppose must always have been perceived) between the duo of Don Quixote and Sancho, and the evangelical one of Christ and St. Peter. In such a partial archetypal community (that of the itinerant missionary sage and his rustic wavering
follower) lies the foundation of Unamuno's vision of Don Quixote as a
Spanish Christ. Indeed, even Don Quixote's phrasing is sometimes
similar to Jesus's.[20] But this same consideration of the plurality of
systems in Don Quixote's personality makes us see how aberrant it is
to read the work as a parody of the Gospel. In general, this is where
archetypal and analogical criticism can fail: to interpret a work in
accordance with a single archetypal system when it is in fact sustained
by the organization of several of them is to falsify it.

In Don Quixote the confluence of the archetypes of the *miles
gloriosus* and Jesus Christ(!), among others, demonstrates the immensity of this literary figure (and its unrealistic or metarealistic nature).
At the same time, this duality provides us with one more argument for
going beyond the interpretive antithesis of the funny book versus the
sublime book. This argument is analogous to the one I derived in
Chapter 2 from the paradigmatic and syntagmatic unities of action.
We laugh at the *miles gloriosus,* but never at Jesus Christ, who can call
forth only serious emotions in Cervantes's audience. But a Christ who
is at the same time a self-deceived, bragging hero of violence puts us in
such a disconcerting interpretive situation that "disconcerting" seems
an understatement. As a symbol of human life, this character is a
literary signifier of the most extraordinary ambiguity and multi-
valence, an endlessly, profoundly suggestive one. Therefore, to see
Don Quixote as a symbol of idealism and altruism (as opposed to
Sancho's materialism and egoism) or as a symbol of the active, heroic
life (in the face of Don Diego de Miranda's Christian Epicureanism) is
to glimpse vague partial truths, which become falsehoods when they
are asserted absolutely.

Nevertheless, the good readers of the *Quixote* find themselves not before an agglomeration of types and archetypes (these operate sub-consciously like transparent schemata) but before the images of live persons. We must try to explain how the mechanisms of these systems can come together in a personal entity that maintains a continuous and sensible identity despite the transformations that it suffers with the changes from one system to the other.

In Chapter 2 I proposed some ideas to explain the convincing pseudologic with which the inverisimilar changes in the *Quixote*'s central characters take place. I hinted at the effect of associations within the conceptual fields of our traditional culture. But on another plane (the most immediate one of the existential comprehension of the fictitious person) there is also a kind of pseudopsychology that authorizes the combination of irreconcilable figures. On this point it is useful to remember what Américo Castro teaches with respect to Don Quixote's structure as a character. In his prologue to the edition of the *Quixote* for Porrúa, Castro points out the internal dynamics of the protagonist: the tension between who he is and who he wants to be, between the given and the intended, a tension that anticipates an existentialist, not an essentialist, vision of the human subject's being.[21] As we read the novel, we witness the inception of the personality, its mobility, and its duality or intrinsic multiplicity. Here we flirt with anachronism only if we stretch this analogy with Ortega's idea of life too far.[22] We should not confuse the history of intuition and imagination with the history of conceptual systems. In any case, what we must retain of Castro's conception is the note of the fundamental instability of Don Quixote's personality (and, to the extent that he imitates his master, Sancho's): he struggles to be someone he is not, and so necessarily transforms himself. Thus, while the shifts of types and archetypes that are alternatively dominant in his conduct do not cease to appear inverisimilar when we reflect upon them, they become acceptable to our intuition when we are reading the novel, for they are produced within the framework of a consistent inconsistency.

In another sense, what happens with this figure is in a way similar to what occurs with the figure of Guzmán de Alfarache. The pica-resque hero, with epochal impudence, revives the Augustinian subjec-tive paradigm: the internal dimension of the subject who, in confess-ing his life, is divided into the confessing "I" and the confessed "I." So also Don Quixote, with his project of transformation, creates a ten-sion between his habitual self and his projected self. What emerges is interior space and the subject's intimate plurality.

The most profound device used to reconcile the systems' incongruities in the imaginary character's unity lies in the particular modality of Don Quixote's madness and its reflection in Sancho. This madness indissolubly mixes wanting to be with wanting to feign; it is at the same time straight imitation and mere pretending. Don Quixote wants to be a knight errant, but he is also satisfied with pretending that he is one. The incident of testing the helmet establishes this duplicity at the beginning of the story. Don Quixote wants a strong helmet, but after his pseudodextrous efforts fail, he settles for one that he knows very well only seems to be reliable. Dulcinea is like the helmet. Here also he is content with Aldonza, content to take her for the most exalted lady. Don Quixote believes that he is, yet he knows that he pretends to be; the intimate inconsistency is fundamental to his endeavor to be someone else. The submerged consciousness of the fact that he is pretending makes it natural for him to accept the obvious pretending of others when they try to make him believe that they share his views. Thus Don Quixote's and Sancho's excessive credulity becomes convincing. Also convincing are Don Quixote's reasonable remarks and wisdom, for his insanity's double consciousness (believing himself to be while knowing that he pretends) encompasses the half that knows, the part that realizes that he is pretending. In other words, it is a consciousness that is not hermetically sealed in madness, but is partially open to reality and sensibility. In a fundamental contradiction, Don Quixote deceives himself and he does not deceive himself. Upon this formal contradictory foundation are harmoniously erected all the other contradictions and incongruities: the insensate sage, the subtle simpleton, the man profoundly knowledgeable about his own epoch who lives like a naive anachronism; in sum, the oxymoron of hallucinating lucidity. The basically contradictory character makes possible, then, the apparent congruence of the incongruous in the protagonists' conduct, the richness of their systematic organization, the continuity and at the same time constant alteration of their identities.[23]

Finally, note that the impression of depth of personality also derives from essential inexplicit, hidden traits. Don Quixote's behavior has roots that the reader intuits obscurely (because the revealing signs are scarce and remain in the background), but they are like the shadow that lends relief to a figure. In a work like Cervantes's, nothing is less explicit than sexuality. The normative chastity that puts such limits on his mimesis prevents these intimate aspects from being represented directly, but the fundamental breadth of Cervantes's vision cannot help but reveal to us the remote traces and signs of the primary forces. Through these signs the reader projects virtual depths, perhaps without distinct awareness of doing so. The hidalgo's sexual impotence is a hidden but indirectly perceptible attribute of his being. We are told that he was in love with a girl from a neighboring town, but that she never knew it. The erotic timidity thus hinted at is added to other signs: his bachelorhood, his solitary habits, his living with a niece whose presence in his home cannot help but be an obstacle to a possible sexual relationship with the housekeeper. He is said to be chaste. (Chastity does not accord with his chivalric models.) In addition it is suggested that he is a virgin. Moreover, the hidalgo himself declares this to be the case in one of his interior monologues (II.48). The invention of Dulcinea, then, is Don Quixote's self-protection from the only chivalric adventure he fears: the erotic adventure (since victory in that arena is not a matter of willpower). In swearing fealty to an unattainable lady, he has a justification for fleeing from sexual encounters without losing the posture of the heroic gallant. In the Second Part there is a slight suggestion of a real search for the woman in the visit to El Toboso, but that too is neutralized and made impossible from the beginning, because of the distortions of the fantastic simulacrum: Don Quixote knows that Dulcinea is a country girl, but he looks for her in a palace, as a princess.[24]

Against such barely intimated backgrounds of the most penetrating, realistic psychology the complex and partly inverisimilar literary construction of the character is erected. We do not exhaust its secrets by analyzing it, but we learn to admire the power of Cervantes's imagination, which with boundless serenity exposes the forms of a culture in the work.

Chapter 4

Toward the Meanings

This is a strange work of literature, which, smilingly, pushes us to transcend the literary, and to see precisely in that transcendence the culmination of literature.

—Raimundo Lida, "Vértigo del *Quijote*" (1962)

Ideology and Rhetoric in the *Quixote*

Typicality and Exemplarity. Does the literary work embody a "conception of the world," a system of values, a persuasive force of a mythical, ethical, or cognitive nature? And if, as Wayne Booth has maintained, there is always a rhetoric in fiction, how can we methodically determine the "message" and the *will* of the *Quixote*?[1] We must bear in mind that we are searching not for Cervantes's conception of life (especially if we presume it to be one all-determining idea) but for the possibly multiple visions that may emerge in his works. This is a first (negative) methodological principle: it should not be presumed that an author's thought and all of his work necessarily express a single coherent world view.

When we speak of the ideology of a work of fiction, we are dealing fundamentally with edification or illustration by *example*. This has two dimensions: "so it is" and "so it should (should not) be," typicality and exemplarity (positive or negative). The two dimensions are mixed in varying proportions in the various styles of mimesis, but they are essentially different and obey different principles. Typicality lies in the adaptation of the literary image not to empirically verifiable reality (which cannot intervene once the aesthetic process of reading is initiated) but to readers' notions of reality. These notions include various collective prejudices, generalized empirical schemata, traditional clichés, types and archetypes of specifically artistic origin, and, in the supreme experiences of true art, the unearthed profound orders of life, which come to light as the recollection of a knowledge that has been forgotten for an immensely long time. Readers almost always see exemplarity, on the other hand, as an image not strictly representative of reality, but more or less utopian and exalted (or negatively exaggerated). While normally the typical elicits interest, the exemplary attracts admiring assent or aversion. Of course, a realistic exemplarity (that is, the coincidence of the typical and the exemplary) is possible. But realistic literature leans to the typical, romantic or romancesque to the exemplary. Exemplarity is most obviously linked to the work's rhetorical force, but there is already a *tendency,* a point of view, preferences, in the *selection* of the types that go into the image of the world in the work. Therefore, it is difficult to separate vision and tendency, cognition and will. The selection of types prepares a horizon that will frame the reader's evaluative impulses. The "so it is" sets limits to the possible field of action for the drive toward the "so it should be." (There are traces of this distinction in Aristotle's *Poetics,* but it is not clearly established. There the typical belongs to the sphere of verisimilitude, the exemplary to that of artistic idealization.)

Here, in relation to the theme of rhetorical force, as in other cases, it is useful first to consider primitive forms of literary experience. How is an indoctrinating effect, a reinforcement or alteration of readers' attitudes and values, produced in popular or children's literature? The essential mechanism is the division of the imaginary population into two bands, the good and the bad, headed by the hero and the villain. The behavior of the good is presented as desirable, the other's as odious. To defame a form of conduct or opinion, it is enough to locate it in the person of the villain; to recommend it, in that of the hero. But for heroes to lend prestige and attractiveness to certain kinds of behavior through their actions, and give them the force of an ethical model, the heroes themselves must be powerfully attractive, and to be so in a spontaneous and fundamental way. The Manichaean organization of the fictitious world cannot function without eliciting a basic polarization of affections, and this cannot be induced doctrinally or originate solely in a pure sensibility for moral values. The mechanism of sympathies and antipathies is based on reactions more radical than moral ones: the hero is young, handsome, strong, resolute, persevering, audacious, intelligent; not only that, but in these vital qualities he is superior to everyone about him. Though all of these attributes are "virtues" in a sense of the word traditional since Aristotle's *Ethics, morally* they are neutral. It is as possible to find them in the unjust as in the just. The hero attracts us, first of all, as a force of nature, awakening animal sympathy. Once the link of primitive emotion with the hero is created, his influence can radiate to the forms of conduct that one wishes to favor. In the work of fiction, the doctrines, in parasitical fashion, embrace the tree of life.

Human life is always at least partly subjected to this Manichaeism of totalitarian imagination. We are always susceptible to having our position determined by this ethical binarism. This is the basis of propaganda (religious and political no less than commercial). Enemies are not represented as radiantly joyful athletes, facing a herd of slobbering, slow, and unsightly positive heroes. (Christianity has not abolished these structures of the experience of the world and of art; it has only displaced them. Eternal health is promised, not an endless pious sickness. To be saintly is to be healthy.[2] Christian art does not present us with big-bellied or deformed sacred bodies; there ascetic thinness never lacks elegant musculature; the martyrdom of the flesh emphasizes the excellence of an energetic metabolism that makes the eyes look like flames. Let us grant that, as Hegel teaches, the life force is displaced from the self-contained pagan spiritualization of the body to the eyes and the interiority of the Christian creature, but it is always vitality that burns in the exemplary, and it is always animal magnetism that is captivating in its presence.)[3]

The question is whether the artistic vision ever manages to go completely beyond this pragmatic Manichaean articulation of the image of the world, or if it is limited to modifying it, refining it, transforming it. In other words, is art a form of imaginary experience radically different from myth, or does art only stylize myth's order of edification? Is the "tendency," the ideological rhetoric, an avoidable "pragmatic perversion of the image," or, on the contrary, is it universally and necessarily its motivator and its soul?

In any case, superior forms of literature, such as tragedy, exhibit an essential modification of the didactic mechanism. The people who perform the forbidden actions are the heroes, the superior men and women. Our sympathy and admiration go with them, at the same time that we consent to the cosmic justice of their fall. Their error, furthermore, is not an ugly, ignoble evil but a kind of vital transgressing excess that obeys principles that are also respectable. Tragedy unleashes contradictory sentiments; it does not predispose us to take an unequivocal attitude. Rather, it reveals the problematical nature of all normative orders, the abyss beneath human existence. As

Nietzsche says, what tragedy teaches is metaphysical sense, not the culturally relative prudence of doctrines.[4] Nevertheless, tragedy preserves the persuasion, central in the myths from which it derives, that a superhuman moral order exists, and that its violation is punished with the ineluctable force of a divine law. The tragic fall is the exemplary punishment of human hubris.

The Primary Site of Value in the Quixote. If we now turn to the *Quixote,* we note that the traditional mechanism of rhetorical polarization is not significantly operational there.[5] In the marginal stories, certainly, figures that have a great deal of the conventional hero predominate: beautiful, passionate young persons. But either they are very incidental (such as Don Luis and Doña Clara [I.42ff.]) or they soon betray imperfections that oblige the reader to stand at a temperate, smiling distance. As for Don Quixote and his regular companions, they constitute a gallery of battered and basically vulgar humanity. As I noted in Chapter 3, from the beginning of the work the attractiveness of the superior being has been displaced from the protagonist to the ironic narrator. Thus the rhetorical structure of the *Quixote* directs the reader's sympathies toward the intelligence that confronts the world of the literary figures. Here is life in its happiest mode: the freedom of the ironic spirit. Far from ingenuously submitting to the imaginary lives of the characters, the reader is called upon to identify with the sovereignty of the mind that creates them.[6]

I am not, then, being eccentric when I give the objectification of artistic *forms* a central place among the factors that determine the work's significance. When artistic forms are rendered visible (thus contravening the classicist injunction of Renaissance poetics, *celare artem*), the presence of the implied artificer is felt, and he is perceived as the ironic agent who manipulates them but remains free of their tyranny. Descartes's contemporary has unveiled an ideal interior universe, that of the preestablished schemata of the literary imagination, among which plays the flame of the thinking subject, more luminous than warm. Consequently, the work tends silently to encourage the subjective heroism of individuality. Therefore, the satire is initially directed against the objective heroism of individuality, incarnated in Don Quixote. Worldly engagement only leads to melancholy resignation, and life's plenitude is given exclusively to the consciousness that freely runs through the regions of the imagination and understanding. Narrowly, this rhetorical tendency can be seen as akin to an ideology of the literary profession, and as the expression of a will to spiritual introversion.

Obviously, that is only one aspect of the *Quixote*'s ethical suggestion. As I have said before, there is no doubt that the protagonist wins the reader's sympathy little by little, and his behavior soon takes on an ambiguous exemplarity. His entire enterprise is at once ridiculous and admirable, false and authentic, absurd and efficacious. Just as foolishness and wisdom are united in the character, ethical error and truth are united in his conduct. Perhaps we are to gather that the world does not accept heroic purity except in the guise of madness. This idea seems completely congruent with the tendency I just described: the apotheosis of the self-contained, sovereign subjectivity.

Christian enlightenment (a specific disenchantment with respect to the world) and resignation? A *baroque* vision of reality? The generality of these notions, though doubtless pertinent and even essential here, places them too far above the precise concepts needed to determine the particular meaning of the *Quixote*. Now, if those abstract quasi-persons of idealistic historiography are seen as historical individuals, as originating agents of spiritual life, among whose products we must count Cervantes and his works, our thoughts will be turned away from the particular work to a metaphysics of the subjects of cultural change. I believe it is imperative to keep our eyes on the particularities of the work we are studying, without letting it slip out of focus by prematurely attending to its spiritual circumstances.

As we know, at the same time that the poets and critics of German Romanticism emphasize Cervantes's irony, they are determined to make Don Quixote a hero. Thus an interpretive line is established that is often one-sided in the extreme, and it persists today. It emphasizes what is obviously noble in the human figure of Don Quixote, but in addition it converts into a virtue what the Enlightenment saw as his ridiculous defect. For the Romantic critics, Don Quixote's madness is a mystical vision. They present the work not as a satire of wandering imagination and anachronistic illusions but as a mythical manifestation of the freedom of the spirit in the poetic imagination. Don Quixote passes from comic figure to sublime prototype of a new humanity.

We know that the interpretation of eighteenth-century rationalism, equally one-sided, has persisted as well. An explicit synthesis of both lines emerges, perhaps for the first time, in Heinrich Heine's introduction to a German translation of the *Quixote*.[7] As I said before, a description of the work that focuses on structure and archetypes reveals its essential ambiguity and shows the inadequacy as well as the partial justification of those exclusive interpretations. The symbol, in absorbing them, surpasses them.[8]

Irony and the Unity of the Person. The ethical-metaphysical problem of irony occasioned intense discussion at the beginning of the nineteenth century. Hegel and Kierkegaard, each in his own way, condemned the spiritual attitude of "Romantic irony," especially as Friedrich Schlegel expressed it. Werner Brüggemann holds that Hegel misunderstood Schlegel.[9] His argument could be applied equally to Kierkegaard. Contrary to the judgment of these philosophers, ironic, artistic suspension of attitudes and doctrines does not deprive the writer of seriousness or of an ultimately affirmative position. To the young Schlegel, the horizon of the ironic Romantic artist was the infinitude of religious transcendence. One must, then, distinguish between crystallized dogmas (which are subject to irony like all other objective facts of the world) and the profundity of a faith that is joined seamlessly to the sense of midday reality.

This time in connection with the ironic attitude, let us again emphasize the complexity of the relationship between an individual (that is, his thought, his cognitive self) and his work. How can one properly differentiate among faith, belief, accepted doctrine, lived vision, and cognitive attitude, which may be more or less permanent or transitory? Ortega taught us to see these multiple manifestations of human existence when he distinguished between ideas and beliefs, the ideas that one *has* and the beliefs that are the basis on which one *stands*.[10] Influenced by Freud, structuralism, and analytical philosophy, we see today a much more complicated system at the root of human existence than the one described by the phenomenology of life in the first half of this century. As I have been suggesting, the question about that vital complex to which one alludes when one speaks of "the thought of Cervantes" has not yet been completely formulated. It is necessary to distinguish: the visions that have emerged in Cervantes's works; his conjecturable everyday view of things; the doctrines that, sincerely or insincerely, he would say that he accepted; the attitudes that he would adopt on particular occasions; his private reflections of a philosophical nature; his more or less unconscious assumptions, commonplaces of the time that he may have uncritically accepted; the doctrinal sentences and theorems stamped in his works (carried by the narrator's voice or by the voices of the characters); the rules that poetically govern the universe (never before glimpsed), which he must have beheld with wondering eyes in his own creative effort; the traditional world views that the literary forms he uses entail. . . .

The simplistic conception of human identity that I am criticizing presumes a linearity and a consistency in life which can be accepted only as a regulative idea, the basis of moral responsibility, and this only within proper limits. It will not be necessary to abandon the notion of the human subject (as some, anxiously avant-garde, suggest), but it is necessary to reconstruct it, and to reconstruct also the dimensions of the theme of the connection of artistic expression, theoretical vision, ethical will, ordinary knowledge, and habitual everyday leanings. That the experience of each single literary work, both for the reader and for the author, involves the transitory assumption of a unified transcendental subjectivity (which can be seen as illusionary, fictitious, or fantastic) may be grounded on this instability of the actual human subject, and on its need for wholeness (in all senses of the word).

Contradictory Exemplarities in the Quixote. Let us return to the typicality and exemplarity (that is, the "world view") in Cervantes's novel. Traditional types and exemplary figures appear at many points in his works. Noble blood is frequently a cause of superior conduct, of unusual beauty, or of gallant bearing. The common people are brutal and vile. The Christian is upright, the Muslim dubious. The Spaniard is the model of chivalry, and stands out in comparison with the foreigner. When beautiful young people fall in love, they do so at first sight and absolutely. Feminine loveliness is strictly anaesthetic. Erotic sensuality is associated with baseness of character and ugliness. However, all women are naturally corruptible, morally irresponsible. Fortune is providential; it carries out justice, finally punishing the villain and favoring the just (so-called poetic justice). The social/moral order is wise and natural. The Catholic church alone is the seat of truth and goodness.

Cervantes's reader easily remembers passages and plots of his works that convey these doctrines. Not only the didactic fragments spoken by positive characters but the very events of the fictitious world seem to confirm the thesis of a traditionalist and orthodox Cervantes. But whatever Cervantes's "thought" may have been, the fact is that these exemplary structures constitute a collection of irreconcilable doc-

trines, contradictory anthropologies. Above all, are these not just so
many commonplaces of the time that Cervantes uses to capture his
readers, taking advantage of their expectations and intellective habits
to domesticate them, reconfirming them in some of their ethical-cog-
nitive automatic responses and thus subjecting them, as in a hypnotic
trance, to the unforeseeable course of his imagination?[11]

As Cervantes's readers can also verify, various aspects of the stories
scattered through his works significantly contradict all these presumed theses. We see nobles of both good and vile conduct; generous
commoners and brutal ones; chivalrous bandits and unscrupulous
gentlemen; abject Christians and just Muslims; respectable Protes-
tants; treacherous and renegade Spaniards; beautiful youths who seek
marriages of convenience; sensually sensitive beauties, some corruptible, others not; undeserved misfortunes; institutionalized injustices;
alien beliefs that are not denigrated. One might even think that the
truth of Cervantes's work (but perhaps also that of literary works in
general, if truthful) consists in the invalidation of established doctrines
by means of a vision contrary to their implications. The work of art
thus emerges as a negative truth, as the falsification of the presumed
conceptual truths in the concrete manifestation of the image. The
image shows the falsity of the propositions of discursive reason insofar
as it goes beyond them in its inexhaustibility and its contradictory
ambiguity.

Don Quixote and his quest embody the maximum ambiguity: the
hero responds to an inauthentic call and sets out on a foolish adventure, from which he returns to a self-recognition that illuminates the
sensible truth of domestic wisdom. At the same time, however, his
sally generates an inexplicit revelation that the reader clearly sees but
that Don Quixote never quite grasps: mad and ridiculous as he is, he is
the bearer of the ideal in the midst of the world. Here again the
oxymoron reigns: ridiculous sublimity, unconscious lucidity, the triumph that is defeat, salvation that is the definitive fall of the hero, the
comedy that is tragedy, the dawning of the night of reason.[12] Certainly, these formulas do not exhaust the fount of meaning that is the
symbol.

Nevertheless, quantitatively, the traditional exemplary figures in the
Quixote are more than its nihilistic counterparts; so Cervantes's writing takes on a conciliatory tone. The air of conservatism that results is
as natural to a temperate radical skeptic as to a fervent supporter of
the established order, if not more so; indeed, it suggests the melan-

choly quietism of profound contemplation, not reactionary activism (still less, of course, the revolutionary).

As we have seen, this conciliatory and skeptical gesture constitutes the fundamental stylistic will of the *Quixote:* to go straight toward bitter and pitiless reality and then retreat into the unrealistic comfort of comedy with its happy levity, but all under the ironic and melancholy lucidity of the man who knows to which game of illusions he surrenders. We thus see that these brief considerations of the poetically objectified "thought" of Cervantes (that is, the assumptions exemplified in his characters and their destinies) can be confirmed by what, according to our methodological principle, is the only undeniable evidence of the character of his creative will: his style, the parameters of his imaginative stylization.

I grant that there are touches of doctrine, of formulable thought in the *Quixote* which are presented along the relatively univocal lines of parables. For example, there is the warning of the risks of the deluding, unrealistic power of literary imagination (risks that are obvious not only in Don Quixote but also in shepherds and shepherdesses). We are also advised of the dangers of being too curious about things that should be left unexplored and of exposing ourselves to the temptations of the animal forces in human nature (in "The Man of Ill-Advised Curiosity"). Cervantes's work is permeated by the ubiquitous suggestion of the wisdom of prudent moderation; with censure of the meanness and corruption that frequently hide beneath social dignity (the Duke and Duchess and principal persons of Barcelona); with references to the insensitivity and occasional brutality of the common people (Yanguesans, galley slaves, servants, spectators of the projected duel between Don Quixote and Tosilos, the public of Barcelona, etc.).

But these are not the depths of the work. The theme of literature and reality, for example, assumes a much more complex and inconclusive development than that of the mere satire of romancesque illusions, if we keep in mind everything that is pertinent here, such as the multiple regions of the imagination, the intersections of archetypes, and the ironization of the mimetic dimension.

Not only do we find in the *Quixote* stories that exemplify varied and mutually inconsistent ideals. The destinies that many of them project have an ambiguous meaning. Many critics celebrate Dorotea as a model of intelligence and ethical virtues, but Stephen Gilman found in her conduct signs of haughtiness and ambition, nurtured by bad literature.[13] The Curate is almost universally recognized as the image of sensibility and goodness, but Howard Mancing identifies some aspects of his conduct (besides those that Azorin pointed out) that permit another judgment of his personality.[14] Is Marcela in some sense a model of life? Is Zoraida a psychopathic "case" or the object of divine election? Does Anselmo have homosexual leanings or is he truly blinded by desire for certainty about the moral purity of his wife? Is Don Diego de Miranda exemplary or is he a figure that calls for a good deal of sarcasm and deprecation? Is Ricote a nice person? I mention these examples because the many debates they have aroused seem to demonstrate that what they exemplify is not unequivocal. But is it plausible to expect unequivocal exemplarity and poetic justice in a work that ironizes literature as such?

In general, unless literary stories exhibit clear didactic simplicity, in a novel the source of ethical orientation, if there is one—that is, the center of the rhetoric of the fiction—is normally the narrator, with his explicit or implicit commentaries and judgments, or those of some character of undeniable authority, provided that the novelistic irony does not render their judgments unreliable. The narrator of the *Quixote* is trustworthy in everything that has to do with narration and description of events. The inconsistencies that critics have noted in this respect are merely incidental and, in my judgment, do not constitute a system of mimetic signification, so that the reader perceives a well-determined and solid factual world.[15] But this narrator (whose personality and evaluative consciousness, from a merely formal point of view, is divided inscrutably among Cide Hamete, the translator, and "the second author") either does not make character judgments or does so equivocally. He is sharp and insistent (though occasionally inconsistent) in condemning Don Quixote's madness, but that condemnation is the most equivocal that may be conceived, because at the same time that he censures the knight, he manages to bring him closer to our sympathy and admiration. The Curate, the only major figure who can be considered a serious voice of authority in this novel, represents the traditional and common values in a discreet and likable form. Nonetheless, Cervantes does not refrain from showing his weaknesses—not, in my view, to make him a duplicitous and perfidious man, but to mark his good judgment as relative.

The facts of all these stories as they are presented are unencumbered by doctrine. Or, as in the exceptional case of "The Man of Ill-Advised Curiosity," they are accompanied by commentaries that are only partially adequate and do not go far enough. Moreover, as I suggested above, the stories frequently begin by evoking a conventional exemplarity: the dazzling youthful beauty who finds herself in trouble, like Dorotea, seems to have to be the totally innocent victim of injustice; the gallant and poetic youth Cardenio suffers, we believe at the beginning, from an undeserved blow of destiny; Zoraida's divine beauty seems to guarantee that her action, miraculously inspired, is the purest enterprise of virtue; the Duke and Duchess's disagreeable chaplain (condemned by the narrator with unusual and suspicious emphasis) seems to be wrong when he censures their behavior toward Don Quixote and Sancho; the elegant Duke, the fine and cultured Duchess, Don Antonio, and the Viceroy, all so eminent, even princely, do not seem the appropriate persons to be suspected of dubious businesses, collusion with bandits, or moral sordidness. (On the Duke and Duchess the narrator never pronounces a negative judgment. It is Doña Rodríguez who accuses them, without confirmation from the narrator. At the end, an ingenuous censure emerges in a quotation of Cide Hamete.) And *without these appearances simply turning into their exact opposites*—for that would only represent a case of elaborate and subtle but still univocal exemplarity—these perfections are more or less humbled and we are left with persons and actions of mixed quality, with whom we can sympathize or not, according to our particular inclinations, but who, if we understand them well, should lead us to reflect on the complexity of the ethical dimensions of life.

Dissimulation, Truth, and Style. This first appearance of innocuous conventionality cloaks the disquieting depth of the stories. We have here an essential trait of the Cervantine style, which we can call the (initial) *dissimulation of depth*. The masking of the paradoxical sense is an impulse of Cervantes's writing spirit that is manifested not only in macrotextual configurations (such as the double face of the stories and the repeated declaration that the *Quixote* is no more than an invective against books of chivalry) but also in minimal units, such as sentences in the Prologue that in a very precise sense are expressions of ironized and humorous false modesty, the transitory and ambiguous dissimulation of the author's consciousness of his greatness, soon almost imperceptibly transformed into sincere boasting, also ironized and smiling. "And so, what can my sterile and poorly cultivated creative faculty engender but the tale of a dry offspring, shriveled up and whimsical . . ." And now the revealing turn: ". . . and full of various thoughts never before imagined by anyone" (Prologue to Part

One). It is easy to overlook these reversions to the strange and unexpected, for at the beginning we let ourselves be carried along by the harmonic (and deceptive) rhythm of the prose, which at times *seems* even a little tumidly rhetorical and imprecise. (Even Unamuno and Borges, among others, have occasionally succumbed to this impression, and expressed disgust with the "style," the diction, of the author of the *Quixote*.) Cervantes, as we see, frequently starts from a familiar ground of commonplaces, sometimes from the traditional beginnings of the folktale. He seems to assure us that he is not going to perturb our tranquility or disappoint our habitual expectations. And for the superficial reader there is, in effect, a foreground parable that celebrates and consecrates the comforting certainties.

The impression of inflated vagueness that Cervantes's phrasing can sometimes give (I am referring, of course, not to the passages in which he parodies the hollow rhetoric of books of chivalry, but to his fundamental prose) derives, as I say, from the dissimulating tendency of his style. Cervantes tends to describe in very general categories, leaving the specification of the character to the reader's intuition (well oriented by the generalities). Therefore, certain characterizations, such as "discreet" or the conventional descriptions of feminine beauty, are repeated so often that if we attended only to the initial description and characterization, we could hardly distinguish Dorotea from Luscinda, or from Ana Félix, Camila, or Marcela. And they are all so different! What makes them singular are their actions and thoughts (almost always expressed, however, in fairly similar rhetoric). I will venture to say that Cervantes's style is dominated by the rhetorical figure that gives the name of the genre to one of its species: a form of the *totum pro parte*, that is, of synecdoche.[16]

Cervantes's "Message." A multifaceted vision, not a doctrine. An exposition in images of situations that evoke the great human issues, without anything like a handy solution; radical, individual heroism versus acceptance of traditional wisdom and order; the needed truth of literature (imagination of life, without which there is no *world* for the human subject) confronting literature as lie and disorientation; benevolent Christian epicureanism against the asceticism of the political struggle; humanitarian compassion against Machiavellian responsibility; skeptical and playful nihilism confronting faith in common ideals; a project of life that follows the ideal vocation at any cost versus a mode of humanity that is circumspect, warm, sensible, bent on concrete charity to one's neighbor. The *Quixote* does not tell us what we ought to do in the face of these disjunctives; it only invites us to see them clearly. It has, if one wants, a "message," but of quite a different sort from doctrinal messages. It is as if the contemporary of Galileo, Bacon, Descartes, and Shakespeare opened up the possibility of another order of thought.

If we agree to force the images of this novel a bit toward less immediate but less equivocal allegories, the result is suggestions of a veiled pessimism. Beauty conceals obsessed, lost minds (as in the cases of Marcela, Cardenio, Leandra, and, paradoxically, Zoraida). Chivalrous heroism is incarnated in a lunatic, Christian humanism in a somewhat vain and silly man, nobility in semi-irresponsible people, generous gentlemanliness in a bandit, political wisdom (briefly) in a simple rustic, and the ideal of woman in a mannish and vulgar farm girl. It is the collapse of Platonic heaven. In it we can see a diagnosis of a nation as much as of an epoch, but also, more radically, of the human condition. Isolated in this vast universe of baseness, unconsciousness, and madness, there remain only the pure appearances (however marginal and empty) of beauty, such as Ana Félix and Don Gregorio, minimal divinities cast into a brutal world, who nevertheless are the faint signs of nature's hope.

This vision reveals the abyss of every postreligious, enlightened age (or, more precisely, of all individual experiences of disenchantment) in which the subject's sense of freedom is paradoxically mixed with the sense of its natural determination, in the absurd environment of a life without meaning and without unquestioned norms. To this tragic vision the immensely lucid mind of Cervantes must have been receptive. But it may be conjectured that he fended it off with his religious faith, and he fends it off in many ways in his work, especially with the spirit of comedy. The skeptical, bitter image remains very much in the background, and neutralizing it is the fact that it is played out in the redemptive space of the archetypal fantasy of optimism. There we find no hopelessness or sadness that does not become transmuted into happy melancholy. The comic attenuation is absent only in the story of "Ill-Advised Curiosity," which for this and other good reasons is a formally alien text inserted into the basic one, and thus is marked as a radically different piece in its vision of the world. In my judgment, "The Man of Ill-Advised Curiosity" translates the deep pessimistic truth of the entire *Quixote* into the forms of tragedy, wholly appropriate but not sustainable over the long haul.

To imagine life and to be able to think about it, we have to make use of literary forms and their stylizations, which then distance us from reality. In order to live, we have to make use of moral codes, which then deprive us of absolute, concrete moral responsibility. Cervantes, as we see, relativizes the aesthetic codes by disrupting and ironizing their whole system, and the ethical codes by the complex and apparently self-contradictory moral allegory of his stories. Yes, there is a kind of rhetoric and persuasion in the *Quixote*. It persuades us not of a doctrine, however, but of our freedom to seek the truth. The *Quixote* does not move us to a determined agonic posture toward the world, nor does it impose upon us as readers a system of exemplary figures, positive and negative, in an effort to organize our sympathies and antipathies unequivocally and tendentiously. It awakens us to a stoic and tenaciously joyful liberty in the infinitude of imagination and intelligence.

The Construction of the Truth in the Work of Fiction

The Literary Work as "Discourse" and the "Language" of Literature. It is understandable that critics should tend to think (as so many still do, and as Roman Jakobson made paradigmatically explicit) that the literary work is a "message," a statement, or a complex act of language (a "speech act," in Austin's and Searle's sense), and that consequently they speak of the work's vision of the world, or of its "philosophy," as if these were semi-explicit theses, propositions of the author, or implications of a rhetorical discourse.[17] After all, the work is an arrangement of linguistic signs that are intentionally produced for communicative ends. Despite these appearances, however, there is a radical difference between literary communication and linguistic communication.[18] Likewise, the nature of literary "signification" differs from the signification of sentences and discourses. A sentence or a discourse has a well-constructed signification when it is consistent and unequivocal; besides, its signification is fundamentally conceptual. The signification of the literary work is certainly constructed with sentences (among other kinds of material) but it is not ultimately a conceptual offering. Rather, it is an experience, in part dreamlike, ambiguous, escaping formulation, just as the experience of the totality of our life escapes formulation. Literary experience is not a conceptual exchange but an event that entails living both this side of and beyond linguistic discourse, as well as in discourse itself.

Nevertheless, as a kind of experiment, until we clearly see its limits, let us consider the implications and potential of conceiving the work as a discourse and its signification as a quasipropositional assertion.

The text of the *Quixote* tells the story and circumstances of one Alonso Quijano. But what do this story and these circumstances "say"? What does the book mean? I have indicated time and again the enormous and rarely confronted methodological difficulties inherent in this question. To respond to it methodically and to determine if it really has a rigorous meaning we would have to know in what *language* the literary signification is expressed and what its forms of articulation and propositional reference are, its forms and acts of "discourse" (radically different from the acts of language in speech). The structuralist or semiotic program of describing the "language" (in the Saussurean sense of *langue*) of literature, a description that would be the natural basis of a theory and technique of literary interpretation, has not resulted in a consensus or in any developed system. We have no widely accepted theory of literary signification.[19]

The so-called *archetypes* constitute part of what can be called the language of literature. For example, the pure types of personality and destiny of comedy: the gallant, the maiden, the selfish old man, the faithful friend, the villain, the simpleton, the rustic, the clown, and so on, with their corresponding stories: love at first sight that overcomes great obstacles, the public shame and punishment of the villains, and the like. Or in tragedy: the almost totally admirable, overintense heroes, who commit excesses linked to their superior attributes, at times an excess of passion for justice, with their consequent destruction for the sake of the cosmic/moral order. This repertory of characters and destinies is like a vocabulary and a normative phraseology, proverbial words and sentences, reusable, whose intrinsic, unparticularized meanings are visions of the world and values.

Literary language consists, then, not only of words but also of ready-made sentences, not only of human types but also of typical destinies. And not only, certainly, of elements of strict literary origin, since it also includes the knowledge of common human experience, from which poetic typicality cannot be entirely separated. The discourse (in the Saussurean sense of *parole*) of literature is the singular concretization of archetypes in the characters and destinies presented in the work. As in speaking, the meaning of the discourse (in this case, of the work) is founded upon the general, habitual sense of the types of words and sentences that constitute it. Since literary language already includes ready-made sentences, the poetic *parole*, along with enunciating what has not yet been heard, ritually repeats an archetypal gesture; that is, it reedits a sentence's traditional meaning (a judgment or proposition).[20]

This ritual repetition is one of the significative functions of any work that represents an institutionalized genre. The inherited genre is a sentence, and it contains a repeatable meaning. (It is clear that there are analogous ritual redundancies and ready-made sentences in ordinary conversation and in other discursive practices.) Today "novel," for example, is already a traditional proposition about the world (a statement about its elements and its important processes, etc.), which can be reactualized, and twisted or invalidated, in the new work (as the authors of the *nouveau roman* have done in the second half of this century).

The preexisting literary words and sentences that the *Quixote* brings into play are doubtless more numerous than those I have indicated. I have mentioned the regions of the imagination, the archetypes of character, the comic and tragic curves of destiny, and some generic techniques of narrative literature. As we have seen, because the imaginative regions in the *Quixote* are diverse and articulated in a syntax of juxtaposition, they constitute an ironic enunciation, a self-denunciation of literature as mere literature. At the same time, they do not cease ritually to articulate their own straightforward meanings: the utopian (the pastoral region), the cynical-industrious and ambivalently repenting (the picaresque), the heroic-marvelous (the chivalric), intrigue and refinement (the courtly), quotidian atmosphere (the "realistic"), levity (the comic), and so on. These views of the world affirm the prevalence of a determined law in human life, and as affirmations they are all at least partly false. Their negation is one true meaning of the *Quixote*, but obviously this is only a critical insight, not a positive message.

Much the same can be said of Cervantes's use of character archetypes and curves of destiny. The truth that they seem to sustain is denied by the development of the work. The characters constantly go beyond the limits of the types (already contradictory in themselves) on which they are based, and they convince readers that they are in the presence of an irreducible and unforeseeable individuality. The wisdom of comedy and tragedy, too, is subverted in the *Quixote*. The protagonist's madness neither leads, like a winged passion, to the happy culmination of comedy nor impels him, like cosmic excess, to a tragic annihilation. Don Quixote's destiny does not conform to the expectations of traditional literary reason.

The critical act of the work (which is, let me emphasize again, only one of its dimensions of meaning), then, is radical. It is not limited to a satire on the (already receding) vogue of books of chivalry. With the sense of the words and ready-made sentences of the literary repertory dislocated, the work's discourse is constituted as the ironized being and perambulation of the pure individuality of the two original central characters in a world of inconstant and openly imaginary style, which is erected on the ground (evoked on the horizon of the novel) of the reader's lived (extra- or paraliterary) reality.

We can conclude that the hermeneutic model of the literary work as a message or discourse seems to dissolve when it is applied to a work such as the *Quixote.* There is more to literary meaning than the semantic complexity of all discourse.

Traditional Views of the Work's Meaning. When we read the *Quixote* our imagination submits to the discipline of a multiple effort, some of whose elements we have explored. The architecture of these many and varied images *tends,* as I suggested, to present a totalizing and final but not univocally defined vision of life. We read the work, which necessarily is *one,* with the intention of converting ourselves into subjectivities endowed with an absolute gaze. The work, in effect, gives us a light, however fragmented, and a universe, however discontinuous, without preventing us from enjoying the more mechanical pleasures of curiosity, comicality, dramatic tensions, the enchanting continuity of the discourse, and the ritual repetitions of the archetypal lines. Cervantes, as we have seen, does not allow us to doze off in these mechanical developments. He twists them; he disrupts them; he reconfigures them. He reactivates our reading at each step. He both entertains us and sharpens our minds. But we and he would have been weaving with sand if in the end we were left with no more than the memory of these comings and goings, the playing with the codes, the exercise of the functions of the linguistic-poetic network, the therapeutic agitation of the semiotic subconscious. On the contrary, to the extent that readers proceed to reweave the text (reconstruct the work), they erect a universe, and their attitudes shift to prepare them for that universe. At the least, the experience of the work is a joyful dream whose evanescent presence we retain for awhile. Now let us grant that the work creates a vision; it is a vision. But is it a vision of reality, of the world? Is the work a *truth*? What knowledge does the *Quixote* impart to us? In what respect does it modify or clarify our sense of things?

Various answers to these questions have emerged from this analysis, and I will soon summarize them. But first it helps to remember the traditional critical answers and the fictionalized suggestions that the text explicitly offers.

If we limited ourselves to the explicit, superficial indications in the text, the "lying books," the "badly constructed apparatus" of the chivalric stories would be the nontruth that the *Quixote* dispels. And this criticism of the nontruth would posit (so it would seem at first sight) the emergence of the image ("imitation") of reality in the work. Realism or verisimilitude ("truth") would be set against unrealism and fantasy. Basically, the procedure of this poetic criticism consists in presenting a character whose conduct is oriented by false images of the world in which he lives. The ruinous results of wrong conduct demonstrate the falsehood of the vision that determines it. The fall and the failure falsify (to use the modern positivist term) the erroneous theory.

But this commonplace description of realistic satire does not completely account for its procedure. As we saw earlier, it is easy to imagine fictive disasters of the opposite sense, that is, a literary work in which the erring theory is "realistic," while the established world obeys fantastic laws. In the romancesque, marvelous world, Amadis and his circumstances would overwhelmingly refute the realistic, cynical courtier who would cast doubt on the existence of giants, dragons, and enchanters, and the hero's capacity to triumph against great odds. The imaginative criticism of a naturalistic common sense (criticism in the Romantic tradition) has precisely this outlook. Kafka, Borges, Cortázar, Rulfo, García Márquez, and many others in our century produce antirealistic fictions. All fictional works impose their worlds as valid, whatever their degree of verisimilitude.

Poetically to invalidate a form of imagination as unrealistic, the world that the work imposes, within which unrealistic imagination fails, has to be perceived specifically as similar to our daily reality. The discordant imagination then seems like a dream, a delirium, or an absurdity. Cervantes *intimates* that a realistic world is the basic world of his novel (without ever giving concrete shape to a complete and sustained realism of the image), and to that end he immediately introduces the signs of daily life: "a place in La Mancha," "not long ago there lived," "an hidalgo of the kind that . . . ," and so on. And then the narrator refers to the romancesque imagination as unrealistic and foolish, so foolish that to confuse it with the reality of life is for him a sure sign of madness.

But plainly all of this is set forth and resolved even before the end of the first of the novel's 126 chapters. It does not seem reasonable to maintain (as some still do) that this certainty that the romancesque fantasy is unrealistic (a trivial certainty, although it became a very common literary motif, particularly in the nineteenth century) is the truth that the *Quixote* unfolds. The thesis that the nucleus of the work's meaning is a realistic satire of readers of books of chivalry attributes the dimensions of a multiple novelistic universe to an initial motif.

A second traditional interpretation sees the meaning of Don Quixote and Sancho in the allegory of the conflict and association of ethical idealism and materialism. (Perhaps it is more precise to say: the contrast between a slack will to power and wealth on the one hand and a strong will to be universally admired on the other.) This, too, is one of several sustained motifs, not an ultimate signification that predominates over all the elements of the work. The motif of heroic idealism doubtless is part of the *Quixote*'s substance (as of the chivalric genre's). What the novel does indirectly, however, is to set this motif in motion and expose it. The framework of traditional values evoked in the book (heroism, reasonableness, self-sacrifice, common sense, ideal passion, Christian resignation, etc.) is revealed to be less than stable, appearing under an ironic light.

We have, then, two principal themes in the traditional interpretations of the *Quixote*. The *epistemological-ontological* theme gives rise to the thesis that the work is realistic, and that realism represents truth and spiritual health; or, alternatively, to the romantic view, that the *Quixote* is a defense of visionary imagination, and that this imagination provides transcendent truth. The second theme is the *ethical* one, according to which one sees the book as a reincarnation of heroic idealism or, alternatively, its playful ironization.

A more recent epistemological variant insists on attributing *perspectivism* to the *Quixote*; that is, an implicit criticism of the assumption of a monolithic reality, a suggestion of the relativity of appearances and of being. Since the publication of studies by Américo Castro and Leo Spitzer, this variant constitutes a third (or fifth) in-

terpretive model.[21] This relativist model, if it is formally developed, is
not logically compatible with that of realism or with that of heroism.
If there is no absolute truth, there is no basis for realistically ironizing
the romancesque vision; if there are no absolute values, heroism cannot be exalted. If we assume that the work has an unequivocal, consistent meaning, the realistic model (akin to the neoclassical and rationalist points of view) is not compatible with the Romantic one of
the heroism of unlimited imagination, and the meanings of heroic
idealism and of its jesting satire are still less so. On the other hand,
ethical heroism and visionary imagination (which define the Romantic interpretation, and have been insuperably magnified in Unamuno's
Life of Don Quixote and Sancho), as well as realism and satire of
illusionary heroism (which correspond to the rationalistic approach),
are quite well matched.

Such is the traditional framework of the *Quixote*'s interpretations.
To advance somewhat in the bog of this complex thematics, it is
helpful here to clarify what is usually, and confusedly, called the *Quixote*'s "perspectivism." First of all, this work cannot be called perspectivist in the sense of the novelistic modality that characterizes Henry
James and his successors (a modality that, mutatis mutandis, is akin
to Ortega's philosophical perspectivism). James eludes the traditional
form that consists in erecting the fictitious world directly by means of
the narrative-descriptive assertions of an authorial narrator. In this
Jamesian technique, the logical privilege of the basic fictional speaker
is limited to presenting the characters' subjective experience.[22] The
world of the novel emerges before us only as far as they live it; the
narrator abstains from conclusively confirming or denying the validity
of his figures' vision. In the *Quixote,* where a technique like free
indirect style is not systematically used, the segments of the characters'
experience that do not receive authorial sanction (positive or negative)
are exceptional. Indeed, the only extensive example of a segment of
this nature is Don Quixote's vision in the Cave of Montesinos. The
basic narrator (the "second author") establishes the pertinent facts in
such a way that they necessarily imply that we are presented with a
dream of Don Quixote's. The stylistic law of the comic-realistic region
reinforces this interpretation by the reader. But the subsequent quotation (II.24) of Cide Hamete (formally, the most basic of the narrators
of this story) implicitly contradicts the initial categorical determinations by casting doubt (invoking the stylistic law) on the authenticity
of the facts narrated by Don Quixote. The truth of the vision (humor-

ously and jestingly, of course) remains unconfirmed and problematic until the end, contrasting radically with the rest of the work, thereby allowing the uncertainty of this Quixotic account to be playfully alluded to in later chapters.

What can be found in the *Quixote* are brief perspectivist moments in which the narrator, in a preliminary stroke, presents things as his characters see or hear them at a distance or confusedly. But soon the fundamental voice clarifies the nature of what they have observed.

We also have stories told by the characters, which the basic narrator does not certify. Here the authority and the narrative privileges are transferred to these secondary narrators, so that the stories that emerge have an authenticity and objectivity we do not question and therefore represent not merely one "perspective" but the truth of the case. Furthermore, Cervantes makes them conclude before our eyes, presented scenically by the fundamental narrator, and thus he consummates their accreditation. Because of all this, the deeds and objects of the world of the *Quixote* are solid, and, with respect to their raw identity, completely unequivocal. (The minimal inconsistencies pointed out by critics seem to me to be far from constituting an expressive system; they do not affect the structure of the world of the novel.) The characters do live through diverse and even shifting perspectives, but all of them confront the same world, which is entirely impervious to the cognitive accidents and peculiarities of their subjectivity. Because at the inn there is only a barber's basin, as the narrator has told us, and not a golden helmet, those present can make fun of Don Quixote and the poor barber. The barber's self-doubt and consternation demonstrate how much the judgment of the majority (especially of authority figures) weighs in our convictions. But this whole game could not occur without a presumption of the ontic stability and objective consistency of things. The very theme of deception by appearances, so essential in this novel, presumes an unequivocal reality. If reality were only what each subjectivity constructed, nobody could be self-deceived. In the world of Cervantes's characters, reality is totally independent of the interpretations they give it. The great, recurring theme is precisely how foolish these interpretations can be, and how inexorable the course of things is. Cervantes shows us a reality that is frequently enigmatic and largely misunderstood by human beings, but immovable in its cosmic order. What vary and change are our illusions and passionate falsifications of experience.[23]

In what sense could it be said that the *Quixote* presents a perspectivist vision? First, in the sense of the variety of interpretations of the facts and of life that its characters exhibit. But besides that, principally in the ironization and exposition of the various visions of the world associated with the traditional poetic regions. We have seen that the image of the world in the *Quixote* is in effect discontinuous, inconsistent *in its constitutive laws*. Discontinuities and ruptures affect even the internal consistency of each region.

But the characters of the work do not live in an inconsistent world. Even Don Quixote suffers only from the discontinuity between literary fantasy and reality, and is always confronting an unequivocal world, which he simply perceives or interprets badly. The *Quixote*'s readers are the ones who experience the discontinuity of the regions of the imagination and the intersections of style. It is precisely this that makes patent for them the fragility of fantasy, its arbitrary and volatile character, and its abysmal difference from reality. Thus the lesson that emanates from the epistemological parable of the alternatives of cognition that the characters live is the same one that animates the ironic experience in which the reader lives the unveiling of literature as mere literature. Reality is something other than the subjective imagination, something other than the institutionalized literary worlds, something other than the views of systematic doctrines. If there is a perspectivism here, it is an objectivist, not a relativist, perspectivism.[24] Cervantes's objectivity, which is a source of the variety of ways his stories are interpreted, is founded on the creation of unquestionable, solid (fictitious) facts, which are not further determined by an evaluating opinion, and even lack causal explanations sufficient to clarify all of the characters' motivations. The intelligibility of the stories' ultimate sense is often precarious, not because the facts themselves are "shifting" or equivocal, but because the totality of their actualized manifestations, naturally incomplete, refers us to unfathomed depths.

To summarize, the implicit doctrine, or meaning, of the stories does indeed involve a certain axiological ambivalence and ambiguity. The stylistic law according to which the fictional world is configured is unstable and discontinuous. The central characters exhibit incidental inconsistencies and undergo inverisimilar metamorphoses, and the world represented in the work occasionally suffers a suspension of the convincing force of fiction, as it is ironized as mere literature. Nevertheless, there is no instability or uncertainty when it comes to things, facts, and reality. Each of the various laws of style admits only certain types of facts and excludes others, but once a (fictional) fact stands, there it remains.

Uses of the Theory of the Levels of Meaning. As is well known, since antiquity there has been an exegetical tradition that presumes that a text has more than one mode and level of meaning. Many think, and Plato seems to have thought (according to his remarks on allegory in bk. II of the *Republic*), that this exegetical position originated in the desire to save the authority of canonical writings whose literal sense had become intellectually or morally unsustainable. Interpreters of Homer and ancient Jewish theologians postulated that canonical or sacred tales had an allegorical meaning as well as the literal one. God, who creates the beings or determines the course of events, can cause things (the facts of nature and of history), and not only words, to have meaning; that is, to contain philosophical, religious, and moral lessons. The development of these hermeneutic practices during the Middle Ages led to their theoretical formalization, the best known of which is offered by Aquinas in the *Summa Theologiae* (Ia. I, 10), with the four levels of meaning: (1) the literal or historical one, the meaning of the *words* (but which includes the immediate senses of the metaphorical expressions and of the parabolical passages, as far as these senses belong to the same level of what is primarily signified by the plain words of the text); and the three "spiritual" meanings, the meanings of the *things:* (2) allegorical (otherwise called typological), which in Aquinas's usage is limited to the correlation of the figures of the Old and New Testaments; (3) moral; and (4) anagogical.

Dante tried to apply this schema to the exegesis of a poem, his own. Reliance on the "allegorical" meaning (now in the sense of *spiritual* meaning, including the parabolic, moral, and even anagogical sense) soon became, as it had been in classical Greece, a weapon for the defense of poetry against attacks on its supposed frivolity and immorality: Also the poet, since he creates fictions, can make the "things" of his story have meaning. Today we often use these concepts indiscriminately. Their critical revival could well serve to clarify our interpretations. In fact, it is interesting to focus on the *Quixote* through the lens of the conception of a systematic multiplicity of meanings.

On the literal, "historical" level, the *Quixote* is a world of individuals and actions, the most characteristic of which are lunacies and foolish reflections, but some do constitute moments of wisdom and genuine moral elevation. On the most elemental allegorical level, the truth of the *Quixote* must be the possible mimetic truth of all fiction: do we recognize life in these images, and do we intuit it more profoundly because of them? Is this novel not only verisimilar but also revealing? This is the plane of the fictitious incarnation of the universal types of personality and conduct, which Aristotle saw as the philosophical virtue of poetry. To this level correspond the characterological and sociological (in general, anthropological) dimensions of literary meaning. Interpretations have not stopped there. In progressive abstraction, the work's figures and actions have been seen as more or less recondite parables, whose meaning is pondered in the name of symbol or vision.

It seems to me that the various critical stances correspond in some measure to preferences for levels of meaning. Can it be doubted that the literal level favors the understanding of the *Quixote* as a comic and satirical story? And that the level of allegory permits us to open up the novel to metaphysical intimations?

We have seen repeatedly that the *Quixote*'s parables contradict one another and are even themselves ambiguous. Is the negative space thus created a symbol sui generis? Cervantes himself suggested that readers of various levels of intelligence and education will attend to different aspects of a work, and that if the work is sufficiently varied, all of them can be pleased by what they read. (As the friend in the Prologue to the First Part says, an effort should be made so that "the melancholy man will be stirred to laughter, the merry be encouraged to laugh still louder, the simpleton be not worried, the wise admire your invention, the serious not despise it, nor the judicious reserve their praise.") Indeed, the *Quixote* can be read in several ways even on the most literal level of the stories. Superficial readers will allow themselves to be carried along by the conventional, romantic suggestion of the secondary stories, and by their apparent trivially edifying sense: beautiful young people, high passions, great obstacles, and at the end redemptive poetic justice. But more attentive readers will see how the ideality of these individuals and destinies is problematized. The simple audience will laugh without reservation at the very figure of Don Quixote. The discreet (who will laugh too) will also note his serious side. Simple readers will understand the lesson that one should not entertain unwarranted ambitions and should reject the illusions fostered by fantastic fictions. The prudent and discreet can capture the inexhaustible complexity of the work's moral. They will also understand the dimensions of Cervantes's irony, the supreme critical and metapoetic game.[25]

A Nondoctrinal Truth. The conclusion seems to be that the Cervantine "thesis," a specifically literary one, is *formally* of another order than those described by traditional interpretations, which are practically all of a doctrinal, exclusive type, and which seem to flow from a conception of the literary work as discourse. All of them can claim some basis in the work. It is this very fact that makes it impossible for these meanings to be consistently effective, for the work absorbs them all, and thus does not permit any one of them to claim exclusive validity. If the work has a unitary sense, it cannot be of a conceptualizable thesis in nature.

The work's epistemological aspect is very complex, as we have seen. The *Quixote* begins by scoring "realistic" notes. One could almost say that at the beginning it sounds historiographical and ethnographical. (So much so that such evocations of the daily environment, which is so historically changeable in its details, are at least in part dead for us. For today's reader, the "finest fleece," the "velvet shoes," and the dish of "griefs and great sorrows" are *thinkable* things, if only with erudite assistance, but they have no air of intimacy; they no longer produce the feeling that they are familiar and trusted, and they no longer have the flavor of what is known so thoroughly that it precisely defines everyday experience.) The fundamental complication of the *Quixote*'s stylistic law (which I believe it is excusable to reiterate) is that this dense immediacy of elements of daily life is promptly abandoned in favor of a comic buoyancy. The accumulation of familiar details in the first chapter of Part One is unique among all the chapters of both parts.[26] Nevertheless, the horizon of reality remains activated for the rest of the work. Occasional allusions to contemporary history and circumstances time and again poke holes in the comic veil, and allow us to perceive that extrapoetic horizon, beyond the absorbing novelistic universe.[27]

For that reason, and because of the successive variety of imaginative laws, the space of literature is broken. The artificial character of fiction, in contrast to the real solidity of life, is made patent within the work. We are led to experience this: Don Quixote and Sancho are phenomenally living beings (in a way they are more intensely alive for us than our neighbors are), but they are no more than literature. In the world of Don Quixote, the world of Amadís fades away as mere fiction; and at the same time, although much more subtly and reconditely, Don Quixote's world fades away, also as mere fiction, in the intellective field established and shared by the implied narrator and reader, and consequently by the real author and readers.

The comic-realistic negation of chivalric fantasy is only a transitory truth in the *Quixote*, a partial falsity, for it suggests momentarily the epistemological and ontological absolutization of comic realism. This apparent thesis is progressively devalued, since literary imagination proceeds to reveal itself as necessarily a falsification *in its entirety*, and therefore the difference in degree of verisimilitude among the poetic regions becomes less relevant.

In this dimension of its meaning, the truth of the *Quixote* is a progressive weakening of theoretical and literary dogmas. The book removes us from the protection of conceptual and generic-poetic habits to deposit us in a space beyond literature and discourse, in our real habitat, which cannot be more obvious or more unformulable. We are left standing in the fullness of the day, which is at the same time worn out and unlimited, comforting and anguishing. The book suggests that we never cease to be within true reality, which saturates us with its ungraspable presence. It is our conceptions and typical images that are "problematic," not reality. The *Quixote*'s narrative irony refers melancholically to this certainty. (Therefore, because the literary image of life thus turns out to be intrinsically deauthorized, the world of this novel cannot be hermetic. Only an imaginary world that is not ironized, and is imposed absolutely as *reality*, can enclose itself within the illusion of not having limits, which is what constitutes the hermeticity of the modern realistic novel.) But at the same time, Cervantes's imagination again persistently draws the veil over that transliterary presence (which ultimately is that of our mortality) with incidents, stories, destinies, characters, all of them, in different keys, fantastic. The amorphous true world is a negative presence in the work itself; it is evoked only by the ironization of the literary worlds. Such a kind of literary presence, that of real life, is consequently at once outside and inside the work. (We find another case of ambiguous positioning in the tale of "The Man of Ill-Advised Curiosity," whose text both is and in a sense is not a part of the text of the *Quixote*.)[28]

I suggest, then, that radically diverse, contradictory mental movements alternate in the *Quixote* and superimpose themselves on one another, thus constituting the "inconsistent," metarational experience that its reading affords us. This is a multiple fantasy, multiply undermined by a mature acceptance of human destiny.

An Attitude toward Values. Ortega does not explain the meaning of the quotation from Hermann Cohen's *Ethics* that provides an epigraph in his *Meditaciones del Quijote* ("Is *Don Quixote* by chance merely a farce?").[29] In the commentary to his edition of the *Meditaciones* Julián Marías cites a few additional words of Cohen's text.[30] They are suggestive. Cohen says that "the conflict of virtues among themselves" is "the tragedy of ethical thought." Cohen's book offers no further clarifications of this point, but having seen the many unresolved ethical dilemmas Cervantes presents, we can well understand the sense of this reference.

The validity of heroic values is not negated in the *Quixote,* but it is indirectly questioned (first of all by their being incarnated in a madman, who nevertheless, because of the values he chooses to assume, gradually acquires an air of pathetic sublimity). The validity of domestic values suffers a similar treatment. They are manifested in mediocre beings, such as the Housekeeper, the Niece, Sansón Carrasco, the Barber, but also in more respectable people, such as the Knight of the Green Cloak and especially the Curate. We do not find a new system of positive values in the *Quixote* (unless we count the subjective freedom of imagination and intelligence) or a radical negation of the traditional ones. Ingenuous idealism (which Cervantes embodies in characters in the marginal stories: Grisóstomo, Marcela, Don Luis and Doña Ana, Ana Félix and Don Gregorio) is suspended in an atmosphere of irony, as is nihilism (which the Duke and Duchess exemplify, as do, to a lesser degree, the gentlemen of Barcelona, Don Fernando, Ginés). What emerges as a nonironized positivity is the ironic, sovereign consciousness of the private individual, that of the reader (bourgeois? modern? Cartesian? Socratic? Augustinian?) whose absolute freedom of thought and fantasy Cervantes conjures with characteristic indirectness: in reference to a rather minor exercise of independence of judgment, in the Prologue of Part One (a passage I quoted in the Introduction). This sovereign consciousness is that of a man who melancholically encourages us to live in a world that does not follow beautiful lines of development and perfection but to whose being, ultimately incomprehensible and possibly meaningless, this man assents.

The System of Traditional Literary Regions. In the Introduction I rejected various hermeneutic procedures for determining what Cervantes's "thought" is, and I cast doubt on the notion that there is such a "thought" in his work, if we define "thought" as a conceptually articulated system that operates as the source or the architectural backbone of the novelistic image. I indicated that it is not legitimate to attempt to prove a thesis of this kind by what the characters say (because their statements are not consistent, and more important, they are ironized by the novelistic form) or by the narrator-author's ritual or ironic statements. Neither can the conjectured intended meaning of the *Quixote* be grasped through what happens to its characters, since their destinies are highly varied and ambiguous in respect to exemplarity. Only the artistic construction, I maintained, demonstrates a position with regard to the intellectual panorama of the time. And this position is ambivalent, for it is at once an affirmation and a subversion of literary tradition.

We have now reconsidered the somewhat broader theme of the ideology implicit in the *Quixote,* with results that differ only in details. We have seen that the rhetorical mobilization of sympathies and antipathies is not unequivocal in this work. Only intelligent subjectivity appears as a superior life. The vision of the world emerges tinged with fundamental negativity: denial of the cognitive validity of the pure imaginary regions, depreciation of assertive, dogmatic discourse, ironization of poetic justice. But we have also recognized as part of this work the relative positiveness of conventional exemplarity, and especially of symbol and allegory, which are metaconceptual elements of signification.

Now then, the traditional regions of the imagination are significantly manipulated in the *Quixote,* not only in their cognitive dimensions but also in their ethical claims. Let us agree that each of the genres—or better yet, the traditional imaginary regions—contains a particular vision of the world and an implicit scale of values. As I have suggested, these institutionalized visions constitute a system, and they are organized through binary oppositions. The golden, utopian age of the pastoral novel is opposed to the heroic, hierarchically conservative age of the epic and books of chivalry. At the same time, both archaic worlds are opposed to the contemporary world of comic realism. The contemporary world, as Don Quixote indicates in his discourse on the Age of Gold, harbors selfishness, hatred, and conflicts (which in this respect makes the present an "age of iron"). In contrast to the heroic

age (as he says when he criticizes the "courtly knights," especially in
II.1), the contemporary world is characterized by easy living, sensuality, luxury, and dissipation. In comparison with the heroic age,
then, the present is depraved and corrupt, not because of its hardness
but because of its softness. Thus it is obvious that the cosmological
and ethical postulates inherent in the traditional imaginary regions are
inconsistent among themselves, since it is not logical, for example, to
uphold the classical heroic ideal and that of utopian peace simultaneously.

The respective anthropological matrices and their images of life
differ in many ways, leading to varied series of binary oppositions.
The worth and the condition of chastity, for example, vary characteristically. In the *Byzantine* world, chastity is an absolute value of
religious significance, and it is constantly threatened by external violence, never by the heroine's bodily or spiritual weakness. In this
world, eroticism, neither tragic nor sensual but mystically sublimated,
dominates over the heroic. In the *pastoral* world there is less emphasis
on chastity, because there virtue appears as something natural, which
lacks internal and external enemies. Love, neither strictly tragic nor
comic, and beauty completely surpass the heroic as pastoral values.
Their connotations are not concretely religious, however, but philo-
sophical-contemplative, in the tradition of Renaissance Neo-
platonism. In the *courtly* sphere, chastity is important and is threatened (more by deception than by force), but it is not necessarily a
matter of life and death. Here the erotic is more a social than a
personal value, for it is attached to honor, matrimony, and civil well-
being. The heroic, on the other hand, is marginal in the courtly world.
In the *chivalric* world, which is heir to the medieval tradition of
courtly love, chastity is not an absolute value. Heroism is subordinated to erotic happiness, since the former is virtually a condition for
the attainment of the latter. The vision of the world of books of
chivalry correlates the values of physical beauty, rectitude, physical
strength, social power, divine grace (and even occasional demonic
assistance), and erotic passion as against ugliness or deformity of the
body, malice, meanness of passions, and social and religious margin-
ality.

As we can see, the pastoral, chivalric, courtly, Byzantine, and picaresque worlds, as well as the classical worlds of epic, tragedy, and
comedy, entail specific anthropologies and exemplarities, and have an
inspiring or comforting power that is also diverse and characteristic.

Heroism in battle, loyalty to one's lord, and other values of the nobility are transformed but persist through the passage from the classical epic (akin to tragedy) to the medieval epic and then to the chivalric romance, now quite removed from tragic severity, and in which
idealized eroticism is as exalted as military achievement, or more so.
Opposed to these heroic worlds are the picaresque (of ignoble existences, corrupt morals, sordid sexuality, and pessimism) as well as the
pastoral (optimistic with respect to human nature, alien to warlike
values, sublimatedly erotic and of pious sensibility).[31] Opposed to
both groups is the Byzantine world, in which the heroic is only a
marginal element, and the erotic ideal is encompassed and transformed by religious passion. Also the courtly world offers a different
example of life. The supreme value is erotic-social; morality is not
totally corrupt, but it is unstable and uncertain, a trait that is reconciled here with agents of extreme beauty (and of elevated social standing as well as a basically fair ethical stance). Finally, comedy admits
the mingling of the noble and ignoble, thematizes human weaknesses,
socializes the erotic in marriage, and redeems baseness in denoue-
ments of universal reconciliation. It purports to admit the reality of
life, but its image is that of a life that in the end is painless; it shows
our inferiority in the face of the ideal, and comforts us with the
wisdom of the social order.

By observing a few of its traits, we have been able to glimpse a rich
system of anthropological alternatives.[32] These arch-images still influence thought and life programs today. Their use, especially the particular turn they are given in a work, is an ideological and rhetorical
function. Each time these generic images are evoked, a vision of reality
and an ethical tendency are either recommended (or at least proposed)
or destabilized and broken.

Cervantes sets these great conceptions and doctrinal assertions of
literature in motion as if experimentally. The fortunes of these forms
vary from work to work. Despite its discontinuities of imaginary
region, *The Galatea* maintains the pastoral utopia. The *Quixote* (like
the *Dogs' Colloquy*) ends up destroying the bucolic image. On the
other hand, it marginalizes and even humorously ironizes the Byzantine peripeteias of pure loves, journeys, and religion which are displayed seriously in *The English Spanish Woman* and the *Persiles*. The
story of the Captive, in a serious tone, and that of Ana Félix and Don
Gregorio, humoristically, contain Byzantine elements.

As we can see, the styles and genres used by Cervantes also fail to give us an unequivocal ideological expression. But the meaning of his varied and intense stylistic search is fully revealed to us when we consider, as we have just done, that the regions of the imagination are not merely artifices of a world but programs for life.

Particularly in the *Quixote*, however, the insistent ironization of the chivalric imagination as well as of the pastoral and the prevalence of comic realism (which is not exempted from irony) suggest an ethical-political skepticism, as much in regard to individual chivalrous heroism as in regard to communal utopia. The ideological propensity of this work (as distinct from that of the *Persiles,* which is transmundane, and that of *The Galatea,* which is utopian) is conservative, as I indicated earlier. The pessimism about the qualities of the earth's human population is conservative. In the *Quixote,* human beings seem to be far inferior to the standards implicit in the reigning institutional system.[33]

Consequently the criticism of poetic reason in the *Quixote* is also an ethical-political search and an expression of resignation. The terms of the Cervantine life experience, if not their precise arrangement, are not far from those of our time. The present condition of existence does not escape the horizon of his alternatives.

The Created Consciousness. Who are we while we read the *Quixote?* Who is the subject, brought into existence by Cervantes, that produces this imaginary communication? What model of consciousness has been enduringly propounded in these pages? The *Quixote* does not offer us positive knowledge or a philosophy that can be expressed in conceptual discourse, but rather a way of enduring the world in imagination, of sustaining ourselves mentally in the world. In truth, it provides a refuge from madness, a salutary image of life. It is a book that produces an effect contrary to the one that books of chivalry, according to the novel's narrator, produced in Don Quixote. Laughter (the comic) is part of this quest for health. So is the candid admiration that makes us open our eyes wide. The best expression of the *Quixote*'s truth, however, is found not in these gestures but—as many have rightly indicated—in a smile (of knowledge and melancholy, of joy in life and resignation to the limitations of life, and to death). This truth blazes up as a complex epiphany as early as Chapter 18 of Part One, and is strengthened and purified right up to the end of the work.[34]

The interior form that produces that epiphany and brings about that smile is what I have tried to show. Because there are many ways of studying literature, the variety of interpretations of a work such as the *Quixote* certainly does not derive only from subjective accidents and a variety of prejudices but stems in large measure from the multiplicity of possible legitimate critical operations. These studies of mine are oriented by the conviction (which could be called broadly Kantian) that all experience is structured by a system of transcendental forms. The literary work is a highly organized experience, although, on living it properly as readers, we have to keep its architecture out of focus, assuming it indirectly, in order to attain the vision of life (stylized and apparently full of meaning) that it offers us. In critical reflection, after the plain reading, and opening the way to more attentive and perceptive readings, we can discern the constitutive frame of the work and describe its form. The lines that construct the work as a lived thing then become clear, and so does the direction its meanings take. Interpretation (that ever-precarious translation into concepts of an inexplicit experience of signification) finds a surer foundation in the description of form than in the mere impression of the aesthetic reading. As Aristotle teaches, the poem's form is subordinated to the production of the final poetic effect, and to some extent the latter can be explained as a function of the former.

In describing the *Quixote* I have used traditional poetological and rhetorical terms together with concepts derived from stylistics, structuralism, and archetypal criticism, as well as some that I have conceived ad hoc. But the method with which I have used that varied vocabulary is predominantly phenomenological. It is phenomenological because I have aimed at *describing* the essential traits of the work (taking the work as it is given in the felicitous experience of the reader); and because I regard the *Quixote* (like all literary works) as a singular form, not only of objectivity but also of objectifying consciousness, a transformation of the reading subject into a new transcendental subject (temporarily, of course, yet it does not disappear without a trace) who learns by reading to generate a universe different from the one of ordinary experience. That imaginary universe has constitutive laws, styles, design. The formal matrix of the *Quixote,* the transcendental position to which it moves us, the being that it asks of us: to describe that intersubjective structure is to describe a fundamental sense and truth of this imaginative effort, the model of a subject that it proposes, the momentary humanity that it constructs.

The Phenomenon of the Unrealistic Allegory of Realism

Unrealistic Aspects. Expressed in a variety of terms ("fantasy," "raving," "madness," etc.), the contrast between *illusion* (in the strong usage of the word, equivalent to hallucination or pathologically distorted experience) and *reality* is not only explicit but a central theme in the *Quixote*. Another contrast is the opposition of *appearance* and reality within normal experience, an opposition that is related to the first through the fact that it is also a possible source of deception. Both are linked to another explicit opposition, also repeated throughout the text: that of literary romancesque fantasies ("lying" or "fabulous" stories) and verisimilar fictions ("true" stories, "imitations"). The significative connection of these dichotomies is established by the fact that the protagonist is led into delusion through the repeated enjoyment of inverisimilar literature.

Authority figures in the book (the Curate, the Canon, the narrator) interpret Don Quixote's insanity as an exemplary consequence, if indeed extreme and unique, of the consumption of literary fantasies unfettered by good sense (which is to a large extent the sense of reality). The inverisimilitude of fictions, they assure us with somewhat Platonic echoes, is harmful to the republic, and at the same time artistically inferior and less pleasurable than poetic creations that are kept within sensible limits and subjected to neo-Aristotelian precepts. Within the fiction that is the *Quixote,* the protagonist's illusions, based on fabulous stories, are shown to be false views of "reality"— spectacularly, by his repeated failures. Even his successes are products of mistakes and misinterpretations. Thus it *seems* at first glance that this Cervantine fiction is intended to be exemplarily verisimilar or realistic. Its imaginary world seems to reproduce the general characteristics and fundamental laws of reality, so that behavior that does not comply with them invites the consequences, in Don Quixote's world as in our own.

It is thus understandable that many critics have defined the *Quixote* as a realistic work and as a *novel,* in the narrow sense of the word that opposes it to *romance* (the latter being a narrative of idealized and somewhat fantastic adventures). We frequently read that the introduction of formally realistic imagination into the development of literature dates from the *Quixote,* and that it is the first modern novel, the prototype of the genre that becomes prevalent in the nineteenth century. (Some pages ago I cited Marcelino Menéndez y Pelayo as a representative advocate of this thesis. His followers can be found in great numbers even in the most recent publications.) Consequently, the intertextual dimension of the *Quixote* is generally defined as a satire or parody of books of chivalry, criticized in the name of realism. At the same time, however, it is conceded that this work is a compendium or "anatomy" of all the literary genres of Cervantes's time, which, as I have shown, does not accord with the other opinions just noted.

A virtual refutation of the thesis that the *Quixote* is realistic appeared only a few years after it was published: a commentator denied verisimilitude to many of the novel's actions, and to the very madness of the protagonist.[35] The German Romantics also assumed a stance in opposition to the philo-realistic interpretation, but positive toward Cervantes's imaginative game. In my opinion, this surprisingly extreme critical divergence persists today because the stylizing dimension of the work has not been examined with concepts adequate to its complexity, and because insufficient attention has been paid to what our immediate sensitivity as readers tell us. Attentive readers know from the beginning, for example, that an hidalgo who goes mad *from* reading many books of chivalry is offered with a smile, as a fancy satirical joke, and certainly not as a "realistic" case that could seriously attract the attention of a psychiatrist. For Cervantes to endow his figure even with clinical verisimilitudes manifests precisely the complexity of the type of imagination with which he confronts us, whose fundamental "impurity" I have emphasized throughout this study. As we all know, clinical interpretations of Don Quixote's personality abound. In one of the more recent, Carroll Johnson shows that many elements in the text seem to point to a realistic origin and development of this insanity.[36] The image of Don Quixote that Cervantes presents seems to indicate that even before he read the books that so strongly affected him he did not enjoy ordinary mental health. Johnson's psychological diagnosis of the origin of Don Quixote's madness (a "midlife crisis" combined with sexual impotence and an incestuous erotic fixation) has a certain plausibility and contributes to the enrichment of the reading of several passages. But its absolutization as the one essential key to the character's behavior turns this diagnosis into a falsehood. Johnson's thesis does not sit well, for example, with the fact that Alonso Quijano has been deservingly known as "the Good," not a fitting reputation for a more or less misanthropic psychopath. Nor does it seem that Don Quixote's love is really directed toward his niece, as Johnson holds, when we hear the hidalgo say in reference to Aldonza Lorenzo, "I would venture to swear that really, in the twelve years that I have loved her more than the light of these eyes that will one day consume the earth . . ." (I.25), for if Aldonza were only a disguised surrogate for or "displacement" of the Niece, we would have to assume that Don Quixote fell in love with her when she was not yet eight years old. (It must be conceded that these "facts" about Don Quixote's life are not attested to by the basic narrator. They are pronounced by the character. But the narrator does not deny them, and they sound highly credible in the circumstances and in the way they are uttered.) There are many other points concerning the figure and his actions that do not obey psychoanalytic etiology, simply because they proceed from determinations that are not psychological-realistic but mythic-archetypal or satirical-caricaturesque. The character Don Quixote, as we have seen, is a fictitious composite of many ingredients of which realistic typology is only one. Because psychological verisimilitude is only one element of the character's structure, we should not force the exegesis in that direction, as if it were the only explanation for his conduct. We have to respect the difficult game of harmonization of the realistic and the fantastic in which the work unfolds in all its complexity. Beyond a point, psychological precision becomes impertinent in the *Quixote;* then a tactful reading requires vagueness in this regard. As Horace pointed out, one can look at a poem, as at a painting, too closely.

In any case, the surprising psychological profundity of the character, a measure of whose revelation we owe to Johnson, is another of the objects of the Cervantine operation that I have designated as dissimulation of depth. The psychological depth of the characters and the background realism in the vision of human life that the stories exhibit are initially disguised. But their symbolic and allegorical meaning, their nonimmediate ethical implications are also partly hidden. Also left unexpressed on the surface of the work is the astounding metapoetical range of the ironic game, which recalls the relationship and the antagonism between imagination and reality. Isn't the greatest of these dissimulations the suggestion that "all" of such a book "is an invective against the books of chivalry" and that its writing "does not look beyond debunking the authority and influence that the books of chivalry have in the world and in the rabble" (Prologue to Part One)?

As in other cases of notable inverisimilitude, Cervantes humorously declares the fanciful nature of the Quixotic madness. The intelligence of the author-reader usurps Cardenio's voice when the latter, in a lucid moment, confirms the Curate's assertion that Don Quixote's madness is a "strange thing": " 'It is,' said Cardenio, 'and so strange and never before seen that I don't know whether, if one wanted to invent and make a fiction of such a madness, a genius so acute could be found as to produce it' " (I.30). In earlier chapters we met other statements that also have meanings on two radically different levels, the intra- and the metapoetic.

The Suggestion of Realism. Critics of romantic fantasies, daydreams, or illusions, whether within or outside of literature, usually contrast them with "hard reality." The illusions thus prove to be far weaker than the natural order of things. In other words, the course of events does not obey the illusory expectations; it belies them; it reveals another law. To discredit unrealistic imaginings in the field of literature, however, as we have seen, it is not enough to contrast illusion and reality (that is, images that normally would be illusory and images that conform to the laws of ordinary experience). In fiction, the realistic image does *not* impose itself automatically (simply by its own force) as the truth of the imaginary universe. (It does do so in our ordinary experience, since our lives depend on our ability to see and know what is really going on and what is mere imagination, daydream, obfuscation.) In fiction, the true course of events can well be fantastic and "demonstrate" the validity of a dreamed vision of the world; this is the case with fantastic literature, in the broadest sense of the word. The author of fictions can give effective proof of any conception of the world; that is, he can make his created entities conform to that conception.[37]

Now then, the writer's fundamental instrument to determine the course of events in the work of fiction is the privilege accorded in narrative logic to the basic speaker of the narration. Except when specific modifications of his function intervene (ad hoc indications that he is not to be trusted as a narrator), the events he affirms as having occurred are simply the facts of the case. To suspend this faith in his narrative-descriptive word is equivalent to refusing to receive the narrative discourse, to withdraw from the game of literature.[38] This universal logic of literary narration encompasses the possibility not only of establishing varied worlds of fantasy solidly, without irony, but also of ironizing the ordinary, "realistic" vision of things and making it seem an illusion before the greater force of laws ordinarily peculiar to the reverie or the nightmare. To that end, in the confrontation of the two cosmologies, it is enough for the basic narrator to assert that the events of the unnatural realm prevail. A good example is Kafka's *Metamorphosis,* in which a nightmarish event is solidified as part of the dailiness of the vigil. Gregor Samsa, ordinary inhabitant of a European city at the beginning of the century, awakens one morning to find himself changed into a monstrous insect. Many of the anti-realistic creations of Cortázar, Robbe-Grillet, and numerous others have a similar structure, the fantastic converted into an ineradicable part of reality. Thus, as I suggested in Chapter 1, today we find an inversion of Cervantes's purported satire on the magical world of romance.

It is both significant and ironic that the eminence of "magical realism" in our time has led the *Quixote* to be reinterpreted in ways that are similar to those of the German Romantics and that resist seeing it as a realistic satire on the imagination of the marvelous. In my view, these interpretations can be supported not by the adventures of the hero but only by the paradoxes of time and narrators in the book.[39] Indeed, Cervantes also performs some "magical realism," although he limits it to the plane of the narrative situation and the fictional origin of the text. Cide Hamete's "old" manuscript relates the story of a contemporary of Cervantes in Arabic, and its Castilian version is published at the same time that the events that are narrated occur. This fanciful liberation and growth of the narrative source emblematizes developments of the narrative genre in advance. As we have seen, in the *realistic* novel of the nineteenth century, the fantastic character of the narrative act becomes, paradoxically, the precise complement of the realism of what is narrated. The unrealism of the narrative mode does not contradict the realism of the narrated story. Hence this aspect of the *Quixote,* fantastic but marginal, is no reason to deny realism to the world he presents to us.

Whatever the character of its narrator may be (realistic or fantastic), he exercises his logical privilege in establishing a fictitious world, the one inhabited by Don Quixote and Sancho, which, in contrast to that of books of chivalry, at first seems to be a straight imitation of our lived reality. (As we have seen, this confrontation of created worlds, others as well as the chivalric one, is a fundamental cause of the [false] impression of realism that the basic plane of the work gives.)

Consequently, it is not just this contrast between the world of Don Quixote and Sancho and a much more idealized world that gives the impression that the first is completely realistic. The force of the logical privilege of the narrator also supports this impression, for the semi-realistic world of Don Quixote and Sancho is firmly established in this novel, authenticated by the narrator; not so that of the books of chivalry. This magical world is only the object of the descriptions voiced by Don Quixote (I.21, I.50, II.22), never confirmed by the basic narrator. (It is also noteworthy that, in general, the stories that exclude the protagonists are told, largely if not completely, by secondary narrators, and though they assume the logical privilege of the basic narrator, they are always subject to his greater structural authority.) In addition, Cervantes throws the central figures and their actions into relief by consistently applying only to them a narrative technique that is almost completely scenic.

The factors that contribute to the superficial appearance of realism, then, are (1) the contrast between "comic realism" and imaginary regions of greater inverisimilitude, (2) the convincing force of the narrative logic that establishes such "realism" as the basic world of the work, and (3) the suggestion of the immediate presence of this world owing to the scenic method that is applied solely to it. Once these factors are recognized, we can see whether Don Quixote and Sancho's world is truly realistic. And it is not difficult to prove, as we saw in the Introduction and in Chapter 1, that the *Quixote*, even if we consider only the parts in which Don Quixote and Sancho figure, cannot be said to present a realistic image of the world. In light of the preceding discussion, however, it is easy to understand how one might fall into such an error.

There is still another reason, I believe, for the lack of consensus on this matter. The false impression of realism also derives from a more subtle and more important confusion, which perhaps can finally be cleared up. The *Quixote* does not constitute a realistic image, but it is an allegory of realism. In the basic sense of presenting the *image* of a world determined by the laws of ordinary experience, the *Quixote* is not a realistic work. But its intrinsically unrealistic figures and events make symbolic or allegorical reference to the sense of reality and to the realistic imagination. Its unrealism signifies and denotes realism allegorically. And that is the most basic reason for the incessant recurrence of the idea that the *Quixote* is a realistic work with a realistic message.

Let us add up the evidence. The *Quixote*'s image of the world is not even consistently verisimilar. Nevertheless, the work strongly evokes and thematizes the sense of reality and the virtues of realism of the imagination (in practical life as in art). This signification is produced by the creation of the pseudo-realistic image (not in itself verisimilar, but strewn with realistic features) of a madness that consists precisely in losing one's sense of reality and pursuing illusory fantasies based on romancesque literature. The pseudo-realistic character of this image is strengthened by contrast with more obviously unrealistic images, the privilege that distinguishes it as the basic narrative plane of the work (authorized by the narrator), and the force of immediacy and presence to the senses that derives from the scenic narrative mode. But superimposed upon this pseudo-realistic image is the radical ironization of this entire literary structure by the undermining of the mimetic illusion and its hermeticity, an effect achieved by allusions to contemporary historical reality, obvious inverisimilitudes, and discontinuities of the style of imagination. Thus we are made to remember that *all* literature is illusion, and all its imaginative forms are falsifications of the real order of life. Finally, this complex, comprehensive objectivization of the theme of the difference between truth and deception is summarized and condensed, as in an emblem, in the figures and actions of Don Quixote and Sancho. They, as "real" beings, suffer because of the fantastic illusions of their imaginations. Thus the central figures and actions of the book, themselves not always verisimilar, are constituted in an allegory of reality, and of the conflict between realism and unrealism in ordinary imagination, thought, and literature.

We can see this allegory in any of Don Quixote's "adventures." The windmills are "real" windmills, not fantastic giants. Don Quixote crashes to the earth. This is the most elemental allegory: reality, solid and unequivocal, does not cede to illusions. It is indifferent to them and imposes a harsh limit on the deluded. The novelistic image thus approaches realism. But Don Quixote suffers only temporary contusions from the fall. Time and again he recovers, with the ideal invulnerability of the comic hero. Such an image of life constitutes an unreal world. Therefore, its truth is not mimetic, but allegorical and symbolic. (Sancho is, among many other things, the allegorical figure of the sense of reality, which is perverted by ambition and by respect for the social and spiritual authority embodied in his master, with his talk of myths and ideals.)

The basic, comic-realistic sphere of the *Quixote* thus represents and evokes true reality without being realistic. It does so only indirectly,

and in two simultaneous, counterposed ways. The first is the allegorical one just described. The relationship between the solid "real"
world in which Don Quixote acts and his insubstantial, illusory world
of chivalry and portents is an allegory of the relationship between the
real world, ours, and (all) the worlds of literary fantasy. In this sense,
the central imaginary stability and solidity of the "real" world of Don
Quixote (that is, the internal consistency of the comic-realistic sphere)
is an emblem of the solidity of the universe of which the author and
reader form a part. The second way in which the comic-realistic
sphere evokes reality is the opposite of the first. Impulses of de-
stabilization go from the edges of the comic-realistic world to its
center. In other words, an intensified consciousness that the fictional
world is mere literature is generated by the marginal undermining,
ironization, and rupture of comic-realism, due, in turn, to the humorous exaggerations or partial inconsistencies of its development
(Camacho's wedding, Sancho's transfigurations, etc.) and also to the
occasional insertion of historical features that can be recognized as
part of the contemporary world of the implied reader, although they
become fictionalized within the work.[40]

What is not found in the *Quixote* is the direct transparent illusion
of reality that makes one temporarily forget the difference between
literature and life—that is, modern realism, the immediate fictional
condensation of the sense of reality into characters and actions. "Realism," as the truth of the *Quixote*, is not an attribute of its *image* of life.
It is not a style of its fictitious world, not a mimetic possibility of its
types of literature, but a knowledge that is evoked as an allegorical
and symbolic meaning of its unrealistic configuration. The *Quixote* is,
in this dimension of its being, an allusion to reality, as much thematic
(allegorical) as indirect and diffuse (symbolic). It is an intense activation of the sense of the real. The realism here is outside the work, like
an aura.

Now then, don't several other significations we have encountered in
this novel revolve around this one? The evoked reality is precisely
what overwhelms all literature and all doctrine. Their ironization has
its basis there, in that infinity beyond the grasp of the image or the
concept, which nevertheless can and should be wisely meditated. The
relativization of the traditional forms of imagining the world (poetic
regions, styles, archetypes) and of the corresponding ethical-political
programs, as well as the ironization of the discursive doctrines, all of
that points toward that horizon which is beyond the domain of the

letter. At the same time, the ironic and syncretistic use of these systems signals the necessity of rethinking and applying them as figurative and conceptual models. It seems that we can sharpen the sense of reality only by a progression of images and constructions that are false and vain, and that nonetheless contain a half-hidden truth.

Chapter 5

Verisimilitude, Realism,
and Literariness

Already in the Homeric poems we find the mythical world in retreat. Progressive enlightenment expanded ever more the sphere of natural explanation and made the presumption of supernatural interventions less and less credible.

—Wilhelm Dilthey, *Einleitung in die Geisteswissenschaften* (1883)

If art was progressive we should have had Michelangelos and Raphaels to succeed and to improve upon each other. But it is not so. Genius dies with its possessor and comes not again till another is born with it.

—William Blake, *Annotations to Reynolds' "Discourses"* (ca. 1808)

Does the *Quixote* Suggest a *Defense* of Books of Chivalry?

Parody or Indirect Satire? To say that the *Quixote* is a *parody* of books of chivalry seems misleading to me.[1] The work never assumes the modalities of such books. In its basic diction and image of the world, the work is rooted from the beginning in the world contemporary to Cervantes, then stylized toward the comic. Vladimir Nabokov's classification of the *Quixote* as *picaresque* is surely in error, but, as I have noted, it is telling in this respect.[2] Events characteristic of the chivalric world do not take place in the world of Don Quixote. They are merely evoked, especially by the protagonist's mistaken interpretations of his surroundings and by the well- or ill-intentioned lies and fabrications of friends and strangers. The chivalric world is present only in the imagination of the characters and in the memory of readers. To call it forth Cervantes uses a variety of characteristic motifs (besides the narrator's direct references to the protagonist's reading and Don Quixote's own use of the language and concepts of his books). There are the delicate voices of complaint as the knight passes through the forest, the bifurcation of the road seen as destiny's choice, the fearsome giants, the arrival at the castle and magnificent reception of the hero, the tournaments and battles of honor, the solitary small boat or the mysterious lake that invites the daring to venture into the unknown, the enemy magicians. And above all the horseman, the arms, the personalized mount, the squire, the occasionally antiquated speech, the sally with no fixed destination, and so on. Within the fiction that is the *Quixote,* the chivalric world is only a fantasy, constantly present but nothing more than imagined and bookish, an ideal cloud over the "real" world. It is a literary region that is not part of the basic worldly stratum of the work (that is, on the plane of the facts established by the authority of the basic narrator). And this is interesting, since all the other regions of the era's literary imagination are embodied, either in Don Quixote's adventures or in the secondary stories. Obviously they are closer to the fictionalized contemporary world than the fantasized Middle Ages of chivalry. The ironization and satire of books of chivalry, then, is particularly indirect. It especially contrasts with that of the pastoral, Byzantine, courtly, and picaresque novels, whose typical stories the narrator tells us, or authorizes with confirming details if characters tell them. Thus these are established in the book's basic world, where they are at the same time erected and broken down, disfigured, so that a paradigmatic form of satirical parody is carried out with them. Thus I believe the *Quixote* should be seen not as a parody of books of chivalry but as a satire on all literary forms, or better still, as a satire on those readers who do not know how to take the imaginary worlds of art, humoristically emblematized in a mad reader who takes fantasies to be historical truths.

This interpretation does more justice, I believe, to Cervantes's (conjecturable) ambivalence toward the chivalric genre. Certainly the *Quixote* is a satire on the lack of a sense of reality, but this defect is a twin of the inability to understand fiction as fiction, imagination as art. Hence the book is also, indirectly and subtly, a criticism of the doctrinal condemnations of inverisimilar imagination. Is it, finally, and with the characteristic Cervantine twist, a *defense* of books of chivalry, of all literary imagination, of the freedom of fantasy?

A Place for Chivalric Romance. This thesis may seem overstated and paradoxical, but it does not seem unreasonably extravagant to me. In the critical thought and the high literature of the sixteenth century, as I noted in Chapter 1, strict neo-Aristotelian classicism ran parallel to the taste for stories of romancesque adventures among readers of all levels of refinement. Our examination of the form of the *Quixote* shows creative operations that in a fascinatingly complex way correspond to this pregnant antagonism of styles. What is distinctive about Cervantes's attitude toward books of chivalry (the attitude manifested in his work, that is) can be explained only uncertainly and secondarily by what is said and what occurs in the novel, and better, by the very design of the work as a whole, which, as we have seen, repeatedly ironizes all the generic forms, and in doing so reduces them to their limits and redeems them all.[3]

Neither does an unequivocal condemnation flow from the passages of the *Quixote* that argue against these books. Instead of burning them all, the Curate saves those books of chivalry that he thinks have some literary merit (I.6). The Canon censures the maladroitness of many he has had in his hands, but he praises the literary space opened up by the genre (I.47–48). The most explicit condemnations of these books are made not by the narrator but by others; not by the "author" of the Prologue to the First Part but by his anonymous friend; at the end of the work, by Cide Hamete; in the theoretical passages, by the Curate and the Canon. Here, then, there is a formal distance between the implied author and the condemnatory judgment. (It is also consistent with Cervantes's literary career to see him as defending all the generic forms of the imagination.)

But have I not said often and emphatically that the *Quixote* presents a radical criticism of all literary imagination? Precisely. This universal ironization of literature goes hand in hand with the enthusiastic representation of its multiple forms. Cervantes's "criticism" of literature points to the necessary artificiality of its imaginary worlds, to the difference between it and the real experience of life. It is a call to the sense of reality, a warning not to confuse the archetypal figures of daydreams with the order of existence. Without contradiction, it is possible then to extol the beauty of literature, the educated enjoyment of artificiality, its *indirect* truths, perceptible with a conscious effort of sensibility and intelligence. To indicate the limits of literature is at the same time to underline its autonomy. The relationship between literature and reality, as Cervantes's work suggests, is not so simple as Don Quixote and many of our contemporaries believe. *In their proper place,* books of chivalry are inoffensive and if indeed all or almost all have amounted to much less than superlative art, the *form* of the genre does not exclude the possibility of an admirable specimen. Thus in Chapter 48 of Part One the Curate says to the Canon, at the end of his argument for the institution of a royal censor of *comedias:*

> and if the same official, or someone else, were entrusted with the task of examining the books of chivalry that are to be published in the future, no doubt some would appear with the perfection you have spoken about, thus enriching our language with the gracious and precious treasure of eloquence and leading to the eclipse of the old ones by the radiant presence of the new. They would furnish honest entertainment not only for the idle, but also for the busiest of men, for the bow cannot remain forever bent nor can our frail human nature bear up without its moments of lawful recreation.

With this consideration, the long poetological colloquium in Chapters 47 and 48 of Part One concludes.

It can also be recalled here that in the satchel that the author of "The Man of Ill-Advised Curiosity" has left behind at Juan Palomeque's inn (I.32) there are found, together with other books and the manuscript of the novella, two books of chivalry.[4]

Verisimilitude and Realism: The Classical Tradition

Modified Veracity and Aristotle's Poetics. The generic forms and imaginary regions that Cervantes handles, or those to which he alludes, were literary institutions of his time. Realism was not among them. There was a literary (and theoretical) tradition of verisimilitude around 1600, but not one of realism, though elements in Mateo Alemán's picaresque novel obviously anticipated it. The *comic* realism that is the basis of the *Quixote*'s universe certainly has a long tradition, that of comedy and that of the humorous or satiric story. The comic universe always contains a hint of realism because it deflates the heroic and tragic idealizations by taking the most ordinary human weaknesses as its themes: the common passions, the tyranny of bodily needs, the daily minutiae, moral baseness, torpidity, and foolishness.

But at the same time the comic outlook is happy and optimistic; it springs from a fundamental illusion of invulnerability and immortality, and of a benevolent justice that operates in human events. Despite suggestions to the contrary, comedy is much less realistic than tragedy, and it idealizes the image of the world—so thoroughly that the comic plot can be identified by the fact that its denouement signifies the restoration of happiness as the normal state of human affairs. When we speak of "comic realism," we refer, then, to a very relative "realism."

The *Quixote* doubtless contains much that is part of a realistic image of the world. Such elements corrode the comic beatitudes, but in turn they are suspended by the force of stylization that is inherent in those beatitudes. Thus, if the *Quixote* never embodies the world of books of chivalry, it never establishes a realistic imagination either. Is this, then, a "verisimilar" work, in the traditional sense, the one prevailing in Cervantes's time? To answer this question we must first specify the Horacian and neo-Aristotelian concept of verisimilitude. I will now supplement the considerations on verisimilitude and realism of Chapter 1.

It seems to me that "realism" can be defined basically, though somewhat vaguely, in the terms Aristotle uses in his *Poetics* to define correct imitation. Aristotle's concept can be explained this way: A correct imitation presents a succession of fictitious events that, *to the immediate sensibility and understanding of the spectators,* and seen according to their generic nature, are at least always possible, and preferably probable or necessary.[5] This formula, however, is vague enough to cover realism as well as verisimilitude, so it served traditionally, as it did in Cervantes's times, to define the classical ideal of verisimilitude. The problem for us is to determine what we are to take as the immediate sensibility and understanding of the spectators.

The receptive apparatus of the spectators is undeniably tied to the sense of reality they have formed in their ordinary experience. As the briefest reflection shows, without reference to common extraliterary experience even the most fantastic work would be unintelligible. On the other hand, it is equally reasonable to admit that the sense of the possible, probable, and necessary that the spectator exercises *qua* educated consumer of fictions (one who recognizes fictions as such) has undergone specific modifications that differentiate it from the mere empirical sense of reality. Here we encounter that "willing suspension of disbelief" which allows the spectator to accept represented events that in reality are improbable and even impossible.[6] In several of his brief observations, Aristotle explicitly and implicitly accepts, as a fact and as a norm, poetry's transformation of the sense of what is possible. There are two reasons for this relativization of the mimetic norm. One is that spectators occasionally take as possible things that really are not, and conversely, they are unaware of the reality of other things, and tend to disbelieve them if they are presented onstage.[7] In these cases, the poet ought to yield to the predispositions of the spectators, for their assent, according to Aristotle, is essential to the ends of art. The other reason is merely historical. The great literature that Aristotle knew is not imaginatively confined within the strict probability of the natural order. A considerable part of the poetic worlds of Homer, Aeschylus, Sophocles, Euripides, and Aristophanes is irreconcilable with ordinary experience. Those worlds contain supernatural and fantastically monstrous elements, the prodigy, the miracle, the marvelous; they confirm the power of destiny, the truth of prophecy, and the intervention of the gods in human life. Clearly Aristotle recognizes the fundamental part that myth plays in poetry.

But the *Poetics* is not merely a description of the great literature of those times. In large measure, I suggest, it is a theoretical exploration of poetic possibilities that until then had been imperfectly realized or unknown. As he describes the works of the past, Aristotle proposes artistic ideals. In my view, this dual role explains many points of his theory.

Plato had placed artistic imitation under the imperative of truth, with considerable intolerance toward the traditional myths and ultimately without much faith in the cognitive possibilities of poetry.[8] Aristotle continues but relativizes this aesthetics of cognitive orientation. For him art does have a cognitive function, though its value is not supreme. Along with this function there exists another, more affective than intellectual, which Aristotle seems to consider primordial, and which we can call psychotherapeutic, in a sense that includes the education of the sensibility and the edification of the spirit. (This concept of the *edifying* function of art is not foreign to Platonic philosophy, but Plato reduces its scope and virtues to an elemental pedagogy.) Despite these qualifications, Aristotle concedes importance to the cognitive dimension of art. Several of the normative principles expounded in the *Poetics* are a consequence of the Aristotelian ideal of a true, "philosophical" art. And they are precisely those norms and propositions that go beyond the empirical description of the literature of the time to sketch an unrealized desideratum incompatible with the designs of mythological poetry. Thus it is understandable that although Aristotle accepts the traditional stories (suffused with mythology), he wants to eliminate or downplay their "irrational" aspects and convert them into natural sequences of events; that is, into imitations or fictions that closely correspond to the universals of human experience, to the possible, probable, and necessary.

For reasons I just indicated, however, Aristotle does not consistently insist on this "realistic" ideal. The preeminence of the emotional and ethical effects of the tragic spectacle determines the undesirability of a radical veracity. At the same time, this therapeutic effect requires at least minimal veracity. It is not possible to move the spectator if the spectacle lacks poetic *credibility*, which requires a measure of truthful imitation. Although modified by artistic convention, the educated spectator's sense of reality has limits that it is not possible to breach without spoiling the emotional effect. The spectators know that they are contemplating a fiction and playing an imaginative game, but they want to be able to play it seriously, with that (also modified) form of festive seriousness with which one follows a tragedy, for example. This credibility or modified veracity is what constitutes the traditional norm of *verisimilitude*. The term is not strictly Aristotelian, but it accords with the conception we find in the *Poetics*.[9]

Verisimilitude, then, is a kind of compromise between the sense of reality and the dreaming imagination of the marvelous, the portent, the supernatural (including the supernatural character of the comic reign of modest but universal and enduring happiness). Only this modified sense of the imitation of reality makes some of the Aristotelian norms understandable. To condescension toward the erroneous prejudices of the spectators must be added the imperative not only to choose men "better" than we as tragic heroes but to embellish them. There is also the norm of an elevated and uncommon language, subjected to the measure of the verse (whose rhythm, Aristotle says, should nevertheless come as close as possible to the rhythm of ordinary speech; this norm reproduces, in respect to ficticious discourse, the compromise between veracity and exalting fantasy). The principle of verisimilitude requires, then, careful manipulation of the supernatural and the fantastic. Aristotle recommends displacing the supernatural (as well as, for other reasons, the cruel) from the events actually presented on stage to the characters' narrations, because much of what is accepted in accounts and descriptions is not tolerable before

one's eyes. Consequently, more unrealism can be granted in epic poetry than in drama. This observation is repeated in Renaissance and
neoclassical poetics.[10] (With this distinction between the virtues of the
narrative mode and those of dramatization before one's eyes, Aristotle
opens up a complex thematics whose application to *narrative art* has
been a familiar theme of twentieth-century criticism ever since Henry
James's theoretical writings. I mean the conceptual pairs "telling" and
"showing," "panoramic method" and "scenic method," "narration"
and "presentation," and so on.)[11] Also part of the compromise of
verisimilitude are the conventional character types that Aristotle prescribes for the dramatist. The old man, the woman, the child, the slave
are fixed figures who should not be destabilized by their individuation
in the play.

But equally important are the Aristotelian norms that derive wholly
or in part from cognitive ideals. The central norm of unity of action is
justified by aesthetic principles of formal perfection and emotional
effectiveness, but also and essentially by the cognitive function of
poetry. Aristotle wants the events that make up the action of tragedy
to occur in a causal chain, one following another either out of necessity or with a high degree of probability. (Unity is thus an internal or
structural property of well-constructed action, and although Aristotle
does not make this distinction, it is clear that he is not speaking
primarily of unity in the numerical sense—he is not saying that there
should be only one action, not two or more parallel actions in the
same work. The numerical unity of the dramatic action seems rather a
corollary of the imperative of structural unity, for it is obvious that if
more than a single action is presented in a work, the work will contain
some events that are not linked by causal connections, because they
are parts of different chains of action.) Now then, the causal cohesion
of the events stimulates the sense of reality and the cognitive faculty,
because causality will be perceived when the actions and reactions of
the dramatic agents become intelligible as manifestations of the natural course of things. This perception of natural determination presumes the intellectual operation of recognizing the fictitious agents
and their actions as examples of certain classes of beings and behav-
iors. Because we recognize Achilles as a proud hero, we understand his
reaction to Agamemnon's offense as natural and necessary or very
probable. Our perception of stories presumes a consciousness (normally inexplicit) of general patterns of human conduct, types of personalities and psychological laws, universal characteristics of reality.

Since the poet configures artificial events, he can ensure that the typical and universal motives of human action stand out in them more purely and clearly than in ordinary experience and, a fortiori, more clearly than in the nonfictional records of historical events. We thus see that the ideal of unity of action (the natural chain of plotted events) is intimately linked to the cognitive, "philosophical" ideal, under which Aristotle places poetry. Artistic imitation is imitation not of concrete individuals (though Aristotle's repeated and unfortunate example of portraits suggests that) but of the universals embodied by the individuals, real as well as fictitious. It is logical that, insofar as it is imitation, the value of art depends directly on the fidelity and distinctness with which the fictitious individual embodies the universals of reality.

As I have indicated, however, Aristotle's text does not permit us to infer that art is absolutely subjected to the finality of discovery and faithful reproduction of the universals of our experience. To paint a hind, or female deer, with horns is not, according to Aristotle, a significant artistic error. What, then, would be an artistic error in this order of things? Though it seems improbable that Horace knew the *Poetics* or its doctrine, and I do not mean to suggest that the *Epistula ad Pisones* is wholly consistent with the *Poetics*, I believe that the question can be answered with the first lines of Horace's didactic and satiric poem:

> Say that a painter's caprice joins the neck of a horse to a human
> Head, and adds plumage of multiple hues to the random-assembled
> Bodily parts, till the woman of beautiful features above ends
> Up as a fish and disgustingly ugly below: on admission
> Into the studio, friends, could you manage to stifle your laughter?[12]

What is the relevant difference between these two aberrations of imaginary nature, the horned hind and the multiple monster? It is not simply the fact that perhaps the majority of spectators do not realize that a hind has no horns, while all recognize that a monster like the one Horace describes is a natural impossibility. Rather, the horned hind, even if one knows it to be unreal, is closer to ordinary experience than the fantastic monster. It is easier to grant fictional assent to it. With the horned hind poetic credulity is not abused. The horned hind is not a true image, but it *resembles* the truth. It is "verisimilar."

Nevertheless, it is possible to interpret this and other passages of the

Poetics as referring not exclusively to the verisimilitude of the *object* represented but also to that of the *manner* of the imitation. Whether the hind one painted had horns or not, it would be an artistic error to violate the general forms of perception (for example, the separation of figure and background) or the prevailing conventions in regard to the consistency of figure, space, light, and color. The manner itself is a factor in credibility. We recall that Aristotle counts it as an error to present gods and their actions onstage, but they are acceptable in a narrative. There are some objects that withstand our direct gaze; if "illogical," unreal objects are inevitable in the work, they ought to be presented at a distance, under a veil of artistic dissimulation. Thus the pertinence of the manner of the imitation to the phenomenon of verisimilitude is succinctly indicated in the *Poetics,* and it is a theme that Cervantes makes explicit in more than one poetological conversation in his works.[13] We will reexamine this point later.

Whatever the causes attributable to its historical origins (its relation to mythology and other sources), the describable fact is that the earliest forms of the poetry of the West decisively bypass straight realism and exercise various modalities of verisimilitude, in which the proportion of partial realism varies. The synchronic reason for this fundamental inclination toward the fantastic appears clear enough in Aristotle's observations: mimetic truth is not the only end of art. Its function is also to induce the experience of the marvelous, to give form to moral exemplars, to embellish and elevate the image of life, and to develop the imaginary satisfaction of desire. The desire for justice, for example, and for the relentless succession of human travails to be revealed as ultimately meaningful, is satisfied by the process and denouement of the mythological fables, including the enigma of destiny (which presumes a horizon of meaning), the realization of prophecy, and active divine providence. All of this compels poetry imaginatively to go beyond observable reality.[14]

For Aristotle, then, poetry should go beyond its limited philosophical function, but not so far as to impede the game of serious ironic credulity. A pure realism, an exclusive, strict imitation of the universals of experience, makes it impossible to attain the psychotherapeutic and edifying objectives. But an unrestricted, marvelous unrealism not only would eliminate the cognitive value of art but would also lose the potential of greater emotional effects, which require a basis of partial realism. The artistic image ought to come close enough to ordinary experience to arouse the spectator's sympathy for the fictitious agonists. ("Sympathy" must be understood here in a basic sense, as the condition that makes possible sympathy and antipathy, in the acceptations of current usage.) The fictitious agents must be experienced (with ludic seriousness) as human beings. More concretely: they and their fortunes and misfortunes have to be able to arouse in the spectator such emotions as horror and commiseration or mocking laughter.

A commonplace of sixteenth-century Italian criticism is the correlation of verisimilitude and the capacity to move people emotionally. Filippo Sassetti, for example, asserts that only what is credible can move spectators. Francesco Robortello, Francesco Buonamici, Antonio Sebastiano Minturno make essentially the same observation. The influence of generalized opinions, religious beliefs, and the public's historical knowledge (all elements that change over the course of time) upon the body of what is credible were then also widely discussed. Also recognized as factors in verisimilitude were the habits of reception, the accepted and agreed-upon usages, the correspondence of fiction to the expectations and precast types of the literary tradition (Antonio Riccoboni); that is, to classical "decorum" (which Alessandro Piccolomini sees as a convincing force). This is what I have designated as modification of the sense of reality by the education of the spectator in the game of verisimilitude.[15]

For Aristotle the spectator's activities and impressions are essential factors in poetry's being.[16] Spectators discern the universals inherent in the similarities of the imitation, and, assenting to their poetic credibility, give themselves over to the emotions whose resolution constitutes the generic *telos* of the work. Therefore, the measure of mimetic appropriateness in poetry is not primarily the reality of nature but what the spectators hold to be true, and especially what traditional habituation permits them to expect as plausible within the fiction. Hence Aristotle's preference for what is verisimilar but impossible over what is possible but not verisimilar. This explains why a hind with horns is preferable to, say, a sudden and inexplicable change of personality in a character.

The expectations and predispositions of the spectators *qua* spectators, as I indicated, constitute a modified sense of the possible, probable, and necessary, but we cannot rightly hold that this is entirely different from the ordinary sense of reality. Verisimilitude is not merely the product of traditional artistic conventions. There are limits, though apparently they cannot be specified, to poetic transformations of the sense of the possible. The more "serious" the poetic genre under consideration, the narrower the limits. The poet's mastery must determine to what extent and to what effect empirical credibility can and should be exceeded while poetic credibility is maintained. This decision and others, according to Aristotle, Horace, and the whole classicist tradition, cannot be totally rationalized. Ultimately they depend on the "natural" talent of the poet; they cannot be taught.

Seen as a supreme poetic norm, the concept of verisimilitude is an essential part of the classical tradition of criticism up through Boileau, Alexander Pope, Ignacio de Luzán, Samuel Johnson. It dominates the poetics of Cervantes's time, and it is formulated in dialogues in the *Quixote*. I venture to say that this concept truly accords with what was in fact the mimetic law of that extensive era of literature. One of the great paradoxes of the *Quixote* seems to be that the question of the relationship between the sense of reality and literature and consequently the prospect of realism as a novelistic possibility are made to enter violently into the literary space, and that nonetheless these issues are brought to light wholly under the law not of realism (which is still far in the future) but of verisimilitude.

Nonmimetic Meanings. Realistic literature of the nineteenth and twentieth centuries does not lack conventions, but the events it presents fall under the same inexplicit laws that determine our daily expectations of what is possible, probable, and necessary. Now novelistic stylization is applied not to the objects represented (as in verisimilar literature) but exclusively to the mode of their presentation. Realistic literature obeys the imperative of strict mimetic truth. The question whether a certain figure or a certain event in a realistic novel or drama is possible in our life is not only legitimate and pertinent but a criterion of the work's stylistic consistency and cognitive value. Here it is not proper to compromise this mimetic truth in favor of other artistic objectives.

This does not mean that realistic literature does not submit to ends other than mimetic truth, or that mimesis is the only form of literary truth. Mimetic truth is the relatively *direct* imitation or discovery of the universals of experience through their fictitious incarnation. Other kinds of poetic truth have been pointed out since antiquity. These truths are more hidden, analogical or allegorical. As early as Greece's classical period the defenses of poetry against philosophical or religious criticism turned to allegorical interpretations of the mythological stories (as witness Plato's critical reference to such interpretations in the *Republic*). Later Dante and Boccaccio, Henry Reynolds, and many others used the same procedure. These ideas found support in the hermeneutic doctrine of the theologians (among others, Porphyry, Philo, and the Christian Origen in antiquity, St. Augustine and Aquinas in the Christian era) about the various levels of meaning of a text. It is true that such thinkers as Plato, Aristotle, and Bacon downgraded or cast doubt on the validity of many allegorical interpretations, and with good reason. But the idea of a variety of meanings and of forms of "truth" in a literary work seems inevitable to us today, especially if we consider the various exegetical methods that can legitimately be brought to bear on the texts.

Thus to point out the most important of the nonmimetic (in the down-to-earth, Aristotelian sense of "mimesis") meanings and truths that have been attributed to poetry, let us recall their sources: the enduring Platonic conception of beauty (a sensuous presence of the divine idea); the Aristotelian doctrine of catharsis; the notion of transport or ecstasy as the effect of great writing, in Longinus's influential treatise on the sublime; the renewed association of beauty and mystical contemplation in the philosophy of Plotinus; and the development of the thematics of the beautiful and the sublime in the eighteenth century. Accruing elements of a persistent Platonic tradition, which in part runs parallel to Aristotelian neoclassicism, the Romantic concept of the *symbol* as the essence of the work of art finally imposed the idea that superior art offers a visionary and mystical truth. Since Kant and especially Schelling, German Idealism has metaphysically nourished this concept, shared by Goethe and in a limited form by Hegel, and continued by Coleridge, Schopenhauer, Carlyle, Baudelaire, Emerson, Bergson, and, in our century, by Heidegger.

Mimesis, allegory, symbol, transport, edifying effect, vicarious satisfaction of desire, "delight." The literary work appears to be endowed with a multiplicity (possibly systematic or structured) of simultaneous functions and meanings, some rhetorical-emotional, others cognitive. The persistent analogical conception of the literary work as an act of discourse (an idea still widely held today) is therefore fundamentally inadequate. It suggests that the work has *one* meaning (reference, thesis) and *one* purpose (rhetorical or ideological). It is far more accurate to say that literary works not only usually have various simultaneous functions and references but also can be true and false in various senses at the same time. This implies no relativity or instability of meaning; I am speaking of an unequivocal and determined polysemy.

As we have seen, the basic comic realism of the *Quixote* constitutes a marked idealization of the image of life, so as a kind of mimesis it is not completely truthful or realistic. But its typological truth and its internal imaginative richness and consistency do give it admirable verisimilitude. This poetic credibility makes possible its satirical, pathetic, and in general dramatic effects. In the marginal stories and in some parts of the central one, Cervantes even passes beyond the limits of verisimilitude. Thus in the description of Camacho's wedding, in several parts of the pastoral passages, and in the story of Ana Félix and Don Gregorio we find humorous exaggerations or unconvincing and weightless adventures. These moments of straightforward inverisimilitude are few, and their function in the book's global ironization of literature is like a discreet emphasis, analogous in this respect to Sancho's inverisimilar transformations, which the narrator (or the "translator") ironically judges to be apocryphal. Far from being realistic, Cervantes's game easily settles into the terrain of traditional verisimilitude, transforming it, extending it, ironizing it. His novelistic image determinedly moves away from the reality of life to things that "elicit admiration," "amazement," and "awe," thus achieving an entertainment value, offering a "delight" that neither Cervantes nor the classical traditional disdains. Thus the *Quixote* submits to the characteristic tension of traditional poetry, often expressed by the critics and poets of the time: the strain of linking objective imitation and fascination, philosophy and edification, intelligence and emotional transport, wanting to present something marvelous (which frequently means something truly impossible) without thereby failing to capture the reader's ludic assent, voluntary-involuntary credence, and emotional surrender. This game can take us to the limits of the verisimilar, and occasionally beyond, in "lies" "made with art."[17]

The truths of the *Quixote* emanate more than from its characterological and satirical verisimilitude, from its allegorical and symbolic dimensions, and from its peculiar evocation of the sense of reality, which I examined in Chapter 4. This truth of the *Quixote* is (paradoxically) the distance of all literature from the truth of life. It shows us that literary imagination is all a dream, an illusion, a gentle insanity. The *Quixote* puts an end to the tradition of verisimilitude and reveals the dawn of realism on the horizon. The imaginary laby-rinths of the book (unlike those of many works of our century) suggest not that the consistency and solidity of reality are questionable but, on the contrary, that literary imagination is light and fragile and the power of nature irresistible.

The vision of the world in the literature of verisimilitude is religious, theological, not naturalistic. Naturalism was certainly a possible way of understanding reality since antiquity, as we see in Thucydides, Democritus, Aristotle, Epicurus, Lucretius, and, obliquely, in Eccle-siastes. But it does not become an established form of narrative and dramatic imagination until the age of modern science, though even now it does not completely dominate the literary world, and in mod-ern works it is counterbalanced by the idealisms of the symbol and the projection of eschatological sense on the secular. Characteristics of the religious vision in literature are the force of destiny, divine providence, the transcendent sense of life, the teleology inherent in the course of events. Poetic verisimilitude links human actions to supernatural in-tentions and consequences, which appear as more powerful than nat-ural determinism and random, meaningless chance.

Thus Cervantes's subliminal critique of the literary tradition, pre-sumably without his awareness, contains elements of criticism of the religious vision of life. This signifying dimension is not incongruous with the air of intellectual liberalism and secularization that so many have perceived in the *Quixote*. That certainly does not authorize us to draw conclusions about Cervantes's religious faith, especially when we realize that the faith of the Spanish Baroque (already structured in Cervantes's time), with its axiological and ontological degradation of earthly existence, is not incompatible with disenchantment of the image of ordinary life; that is, its secularization. Such religious con-sciousness favors a pessimistic realism with respect to life this side of death, and has a recognized connection with the spirit and the forms of picaresque literature. Lack of illusion regarding worldly vanities is akin to seeing activities, occupations, and social roles as meaningless. The traditional literary idealizations can thus seem to be holdovers from the pagan mythification of nature, deserving of the irony of a disenchanted observer.

This, however, is only one of the faces of the internally contradicto-ry spirit of the age, and of Cervantes's work, which with equal passion glorifies beauty in the world and exalts the beneficent power of liter-ature.

The Transfigurative Course of the Stylistic Matrices

Realistic Backgrounds, Comedy's Veils.[18] As there was no realistic literary tradition in Cervantes's time, the sources of a possible narrative realism are found in historiography, in private correspondence, and in ordinary speech, with its accounts of noteworthy events and odd circumstances in ordinary life. Biography, parodied humorlessly in books of chivalry, functions in the *Quixote* as the paratext of an openly funny game. Here historiographic form is a sign not of realism but of fictionality. (Yet in passing references to contemporary history we catch brief glimpses of the political reality of the era.) Private correspondence had already been fictionalized as a literary genre in the *Epístolas familiares* of Antonio de Guevara, whose influence on Cervantes has frequently been noted.[19] In fact, not only are there echoes of Guevara's diction in Cervantes's; the two writers are also united in their interest in the extravagant and amusing in obscure provincial people. Thus they raise to the status of literature (as in the picaresque) the sphere of minor, trivial life, as distant from epic and tragic grandeur as from the winged mobility of comedy. Such are the connotations of "a place of La Mancha," "not long ago there lived," "an hidalgo of the kind that . . . ," and the like.

Now then, as commentators have indicated, "In a place of La Mancha" is a line of a ballad, a literary quotation, which is not presented as such but ought to be recognized by the reader of the time; "whose name I do not wish to recall," besides being a traditional literary motif, is a gesture of either sovereign subjectivity or unconcerned imprecision, according to whether we read the "I do not wish" ("*no quiero*") as "I do not desire," "it does not suit me," or "I cannot," a meaning that was also current in the period. These are signs of literariness, of playfulness, that establish not only a tone of discourse but a norm for reception, indicating to the reader that the work is fictional. They do not suspend the realistic connotations of the initial sentences; they merely ensure that readers will read the book appropriately.[20]

The basic world of the *Quixote* is full of common folk. The protagonists are originally common people, and in their wanderings they frequently encounter other common people in common circumstances. Ordinary human beings—innkeepers, merchants, servants, peasants, various folk, even gentlemen and a duke and duchess—are presented ultimately (that is, beyond the literary types they embody) with cold objectivity. Moral baseness, folly, and depraved insensitivity predominate (as Bruno Frank rightly suggests in his 1934 historical novel *Cervantes*). The human horizon and background of the *Quixote* consists of a population that does not live up to its duties to God, secular master, or neighbor. This is not "criticism of the social order," of the institutions; quite the contrary, it is criticism of contingent humanity, inferior to the roles and functions the social order prescribes. The realistic pessimism of this vision is the ethical-sociological background of the entire work. But this realism, which is serene, does not appear in the foreground, and rarely appears without comic stylization. This background image tends to disappear from the fictitious scene and blend with the transparent sense of reality that lurks in the *Quixote*'s implied reader.

The personalities of Don Quixote's familiars (the Niece, the Housekeeper, the Curate, the Barber, and Sansón Carrasco, all of them mediocre but of sound judgment and generally of goodwill) also have realistic elements. In addition to their virtues, each shows some moral imperfection. The Curate, who with the Canon enjoys the bloody spectacle of the fight between Don Quixote and the goatherd Eugenio (an attitude so shocking that Azorín, perhaps spurred by a passage on the *Quixote* in Nietzsche's *Genealogy of Morals,* found it necessary to postulate the historicity of moral sensibility in order to explain it);[21] the Niece and the Housekeeper, their sorrow over Don Quixote's imminent death mingled with the pleasure of knowing they will receive an inheritance; the Barber, trying to amuse himself by humiliating the hidalgo with jokes about his insanity; Sansón, allowing his unjustified vengeful resentment to supplant his good intentions in his endeavor to defeat and subdue Don Quixote. The scenic projection of these persons, however, turns them into figures of comedy and conventionalizes their images, softening them. What is sordid and bitter in human existence is there in the *Quixote,* but out of focus. Its own joyful transformation is superimposed upon it. Similarly, criminal vileness is elevated to flamboyant ingenuity in the comic turn that Cervantes gives to the picaresque figures, making clowns of picaros. (Examples can be seen in the first innkeeper, Ginés, and to a lesser degree in the Duchess's maid, Altisidora, and the Duke's majordomo, who represent the comic transformation of their masters' cruelty.) Naturalistic objectivity is veiled with recognizable and tranquilizing literary types.

The Complex Dynamism of Style. The first imaginative operation in this work, then, is the suggestion of realism imparted by elements of trivial experience, ordinary circumstances akin to curious incidents in the neighborhood and in the family. The second operation is the comic idealization of these elements, which generates the basic imaginary sphere of the *Quixote*: comic realism, an idealized and "denaturalized" realism. The third is the evocation of the world of books of chivalry within the sphere of comic realism. Fourth is the indirect effect of a (false) appearance of strict realism, lent to the basic sphere by its contrast with the chivalric region. Fifth, the picaresque-comic stylization of potentially realistic types (carried out for the first time with the innkeeper in Chapters 2 and 3 of Part One). Until Chapter 12, only one imaginary region, the comic-realistic one, has been fully embodied.

But the expansion of the metaliterary game is foreshadowed by the introduction of the motif of the manuscript source and the reappearance of the various "authors" at the end of Chapter 8. A sixth operation is the gradual transition to the traditional pastoral region of Grisóstomo and Marcela, a region rendered in an almost canonical manner, and one that Don Quixote and Sancho, characters of another poetic biosphere, can enter only marginally. When Don Quixote wants to follow Marcela, as I noted in Chapter 1, he does not find her, for although they are in the same geographical place, they are in worlds of different style. The touches that Cervantes gives to the episode which are alien to the pastoral region (the Christian "abbots" of the town, the fact that one of the protagonists is a university student who *has become* a shepherd, the "rich" peasant, Marcela's father, and other details) constitute a seventh operation, designed to ironize the traditional archetype. In an eighth stylistic transition, we see the brusque return to the comic-realistic region represented by the adventure of the Yanguesans.

There is no need to go on enumerating transitions; I have counted them thus far only to make evident the instability of the law of the work's figuration. The series of these transformations and adulterations of the stylistic matrix proceeds, with changing rhythm, throughout the book, and, as we have seen, is one of the most fundamental principles of the creation of the *Quixote*.

The destiny of the pastoral evocation in the *Quixote* is intimated from the beginning. The stylistic tainting of this region by comic-realistic elements progressively increases, and leads to a satirical breakdown of the pastoral vision. The pastoral world reappears for the first time (if we leave aside the shepherds who surround Cardenio in the sierra) toward the end of the First Part, in the story of the goatherd Eugenio. The impurities of this pastoral universe are multiple and openly humorous. In the figure of Vicente, comedy's *miles gloriosus* (converted into an industrious picaro) seduces the "shepherdess," flees with her from the town, and, robbing her of her jewels, abandons her without sexual consummation. Although Leandra, the victim (who, like Marcela, is the daughter of a rich peasant), is immediately cloistered in a convent, she is projected in the memory of her suitors as a shepherdess, thus drawing to the hills a dense and growing multitude of lyrical lovers dressed as shepherds, many of whom have never even set eyes on her, and who bump into one another with their comings and goings, as they are unable to find an unoccupied tree under which to settle and sing their amorous complaints. In the midst of this ludicrous swarming the story ends, without a final denouement (as if the author were suggesting that it is not worth the effort to continue the tale). In the Second Part (II.20–22) there are pastoral echoes in the episode of Camacho's wedding, mixed here with another traditional region, the folkloric country of Cockaigne (which recalls the carnivalesque imagination studied by Bakhtin in his book on Rabelais),[22] and also with the picaresque motif of bold deception. Here the decomposition of the pastoral region is already definitive. Its next evocation is not a fictitious fact but a fictitious fiction: a group of noble maidens in costume as shepherdesses entertain themselves in the forest reciting eclogues. Finally, on Don Quixote's homeward journey, after his defeat and his promise that he will cease to be a knight errant for a year, he and Sancho converse about the possibility of passing that time as poetic shepherds, an alternative insanity that places pastoral novels and books of chivalry on an equal footing as artificial fantasies. These five mutations of the pastoral, distributed between the beginning and the end of the book, lead from the almost fully incarnated and serious form to its ironic contamination, decomposition, and desubstantiation, finally ending with its reduction to an infantile game and a fantasy of crazy people. The intermittent evocation of the pastoral region parallels the allusion, more sustained but never concretized in a story, to the chivalric region. Both regions, by contrast, confer a spurious confirmation of unrestricted realism on the basic region of comic realism.

Added to these interregional games is the parody of classical myths and epic (and especially Ajax's madness) in Chapter 18 of Part One. Here Don Quixote assumes the tone and role of the epic bard, and from the heights of unlimited vision, and from a slight elevation of the terrain, he gives an account of the forces that march to battle, the latter of historic-universal proportions. More than the Homeric catalog of ships, it is the Virgilian description of Turnus's armies that is the paratext of the parody. (The humorous detail of the hero whose arm is exposed by a turned-up sleeve alludes, I believe, to Virgil's curious batallion of those who march resolutely with one foot shod and the other bare [*Aeneid,* bk. VII, ll. 678–90].)

The adventure of the galley slaves condenses the picaresque climate, a genre to which Ginés explicitly alludes in his self-presentation as both hero and author of the story of his life. The criminal element, as I indicated, is drolly stylized here in ironic characters who make fun of themselves, who indict themselves insincerely and take pride in their own audacities.

These stylistic discontinuities are magnified in the First Part as they take the form of long interpolated stories that have little or nothing to do with the activities of Don Quixote and Sancho and are of widely divergent imaginative regions. Like Lucius in Apuleius's *Golden Ass* (also a work of notable stylistic discontinuities and of known influence on the *Quixote*), Don Quixote is an avid listener to stories told by the people he encounters in his wanderings. The Curate and other guests at the inn, not to mention the innkeeper himself and his family, also relish listening to stories. A variety of secondary narratives thus emerges with some naturalness, and two of them extend over several chapters. The stories of Dorotea and Cardenio, as well as that of the Captive, pass from the secondary narration into the primary one, and come into play alongside Don Quixote and Sancho, or briefly involve them. Another long secondary narrative is inserted with conspicuous abruptness and as a genuine literary work into Don Quixote's world. It is a novella in manuscript, forgotten at the inn by the fictionalized Cervantes himself. The appearance of this manuscript violates the fictitious frame of the book, alluding to the author and his real existence. On the other hand, and in the contrary sense (thus repeating the double operation we noted earlier), this manuscript reinforces the pseudo-realistic illusion of the basic imaginary region, since, by virtue of the fact that the Curate and others are reading a fiction, they themselves seem not to constitute one.

The reading of this novel at the inn also represents an explicit thematization of literature, as do the scrutiny of Don Quixote's books, the poems by Grisóstomo and Don Diego's son, the critical conversations between the Curate and the Canon, and quite a few other longer and shorter passages. As we have seen repeatedly, the secondary stories themselves, because of their stylistic variety, also indirectly thematize the literary institution. We can see them as a great exhibition of the power and amplitude of the imaginary palette of the craft or as a playful demonstration of the artificiality of its images of life.

The double story of Cardenio, Dorotea, Luscinda, and Don Fernando departs from comic realism toward a different style of idealization. The social rank of the protagonists is more or less elevated. The romancesque attributes of youth, gallantry, beauty, and intense, absorbing passions are dominant. The conflict is extreme: the forces of love and honor can lead to insanity and death. But ultimately they do not. The double story is resolved in one of comedy's "happy endings," which seems forced and lacks verisimilitude. Cervantes indirectly declares the accidental and "providential" nature of the meeting of the protagonists (as he does in other cases of crass inverisimilitudes, ironizing them, and as if he were humorously soliciting the reader's complicity in a little game that is beneath the intelligence of both). Those present there say to Don Fernando that "he should consider that, not by accident, as it seemed, but with heaven's particular providence, all had joined together in a place where anyone would least have expected" (I.36). (Here, of course, we have another example of double signification, at the same time intra- and metapoetic.) This story is resolved not by the effect of its internal causality but by a kind of deus ex machina. In this as in other respects it contrasts intensely with "The Man of Ill-Advised Curiosity," which shares its basic idealities with the story of Dorotea and company, but is consistently verisimilar and tragic. Both stories represent a clear generic-stylistic alternative, a metapoetic counterpoint. So it is not strange that Dorotea's story has a coda that is both comic and farcical, in which she and Don Fernando take part, before the surprised gaze of Sancho, and that makes this intra- and metapoetically corrupt ideality flow finally back into comic realism, when the latter again takes over the course of the book.

The Captive's story differs from the others in its historical ambience. Here the protagonists' destiny is not merely a private drama but part of the great political-religious conflicts of the era. Rui and Zoraida never speak of love, nor do they seem to experience any erotic agitation. In the distance we can recognize Mary and Joseph in the figures of Zoraida-María and Rui.[23] The imaginative type of this story does not have stylistic purity. (None of the stories of the *Quixote* does, except "The Man of Ill-Advised Curiosity.") From the point of view of the style of imagining, it is an oxymoronic confluence of contemporary history and miracle legend, with a fairy-tale beginning in which a father divides his fortune among his three sons. In no other part of the *Quixote* do we find the serious historical and geographical specifications of this narrative; or, as here, a supernatural intervention in the life of the protagonists (which certainly, in very Aristotelian manner, is not shown in a scene but narrated, and even this narration is secondhand, so that the miracle remains very distant from the events taking place before the reader's eyes). The narration moves powerfully, notwithstanding these violations of the imaginative law. But Cervantes signals the literary artificiality even of this story, which in theme and tone is the most serious of all the stories of the *Quixote*. When the Captive ends his account, Don Fernando addresses to him those words of recognition and approval that I quoted in Chapter 1 and that do not, as might be expected, allude to the suffering, heroism, and miraculous salvation of Don Rui Pérez de Viedma and Zoraida-María. Far from it, the trapped seducer formulates a literary judgment, as if the Captive's account (a real and truthful account in Don Fernando's world) were a poetic fiction, a "story," full of accidents that "marvel and amaze," giving great "pleasure" to those who listen to it (I.42). Although not unique of its kind in the *Quixote*, as we saw, this is one of the work's most surprising passages (but explicable when one considers the metapoetic Cervantine game).

As I indicated in Chapter 1, the secondary narratives of Part Two of the *Quixote*, although brief, also configure imaginary regions other than the comic-realistic one. Don Quixote's own account of his descent into the Cave of Montesinos (II.22) can be seen both as a comic-realistic dream and as a display of a Gothic-chivalric sphere tainted by grotesque humor. This parody of the long classical series of descents into hell (those of the *Odyssey*, the myths of Hercules, Perseus, and Orpheus, Aristophanes's *Frogs*, the Platonic myth of Er in the *Republic*, the *Aeneid*, the Gospel story, "Cupid and Psyche" in Apuleius's *Golden Ass*, Dante's *Divine Comedy*, etc.) is one of the three plastic evocations of the chivalric region made by Don Quixote. (The other two are in I.21 and I.50.) Of these three, it is the only one that represents a singular action, not a typical one.

Also, the more or less romancesque character of these brief interludes in the comic realism of Part Two (Camacho's wedding, the Cave adventure, and the episodes of Roque Guinart, Claudia

Jerónima, and Ana Félix) tends to reinforce the basic region's air of solid reality. The numerous and prolonged deceptions have the same effect. In the First Part we find Sancho's lies about his supposed encounter with Dulcinea and the well-intentioned schemes of the Curate (the "magical" disappearance of Don Quixote's library, Princess Micomicona, etc.), and, in Part Two, the pseudo-enchantment of the pseudo Dulcinea, Sansón's tricks, the practical jokes of the Duke and Duchess and of the gentlemen in Barcelona. Therefore, "The Man of Ill-Advised Curiosity" is not the only piece of fiction within the fiction that indirectly serves as apparent authentification of the fundamental line of the *Quixote*'s events.

At the same time, however, Cervantes distorts the borders of the comic-realistic region to underline its artificiality. The story of Ricote, with its references to the political conditions of the time, as well as other allusions to contemporary circumstances, pokes holes in the comic-realistic region through which we glimpse the reality surrounding the book. In the opposite direction, Cervantes transforms Sancho in such a way that occasionally Sancho departs from the comic-realistic region and assumes openly inverisimilar attitudes, as in his "apocryphal" conversation with Teresa (II.5) and in his Solomonic moments as governor. Here Cervantes invites us to the pleasure of utopia, melancholically ironized, in which goodwill overcomes limitations of education and nature.

Thus the theme of reality and illusion proliferates more subliminally than explicitly in the *Quixote*. The imaginary regions, either evoked or incarnated, signal by their contrasts and their internal inconsistencies that they are artificial. The genuine image of reality is thus projected outside fiction, as a region that is not imaginary and not stylized. The work exhibits the fact that its entire universe is confined within the regions of art, both verisimilar and inverisimilar. The book ends, appropriately, with the ironized proclamation of Cide Hamete, who, obviously serving here as the author's metaphorical representative, affirms the originality of his creation and his exclusive domination of it. Indirectly he thus declares Don Quixote to be a literary invention, not a historical figure.

Beneath all of this there seems to breathe a mimetic-epistemological yearning for a novel that is not bound by any stylistic constraints. The institutionalized styles of the time (chivalric, pastoral, picaresque, sentimental, Byzantine, courtly, epic-heroic, tragic, comic) define closed worlds, with their respective unequivocal, well-defined anthropologies. This literary system has to appear tainted with negativity when one aspires to a comprehensive image of the world, open to contradictions.

"The Man of Ill-Advised Curiosity" as a Key to Meaning

Aristotelian Unity of Action. Among the *Quixote*'s stories "The Man of Ill-Advised Curiosity" is unique for several reasons. It is the only fiction that is amply developed as such within the fiction. Its insertion in the book is openly casual and has a very weak supplementary motivation. (That the tired travelers, shortly after arriving at the inn, would wish to read and listen to a rather lengthy story that has been incidentally found there is not very probable, though possible.) That distinguishes it markedly from the rest of the work. In addition, this is the only story in the *Quixote* that has complete stylistic purity. No elements foreign to its imaginary region shake its monolithic consistency. Finally, it is the only major story of a tragic nature, and the only one that thoroughly satisfies the prime principles of classical poetics, especially those of verisimilitude and unity of action. What I am most interested in demonstrating here is that this tale complies with the letter and the spirit of Aristotle's precept of the unity of action in a way more radically appropriate than the very classical stories he mentions. In this respect, it achieves the Aristotelian ideal of an absolute sequence of actions that are verisimilar and tragically conclusive.

The most interesting example that Aristotle gives of unity of action is not a tragedy; it is the *Iliad.* Homer, according to the philosopher, demonstrates his mastery in what he excludes from his poem (the greater part of the story of the Trojan War) in order to isolate a partial action, a relatively brief incident that can be treated as an absolute action (with a beginning, middle, and end) and that can be seen to have unbroken continuity of causal connections.[24]

It is possible, I think, to interpret this brief Aristotelian reference in detail. The chain of the *Iliad*'s argument begins when Agamemnon refuses to return the daughter of Apollo's priest, whom he has taken as a prize of war. Enslaving the vanquished is nothing out of the ordinary, but to affront the priest of a powerful god is itself a momentous gesture, a culpable transgression, a beginning with consequences. Naturally the priest seeks revenge of his god. Also plausible, for Homer's audience, is Apollo's punitive act, which follows swiftly: he afflicts the Achaian encampment with pestilence. This disaster of course provokes the alarm of the expedition's leaders; an assembly is convened to find the cause and seek redress for it. The diviner cannot help but identify the guilty one. With the chief humiliated before his followers, it is an almost necessary consequence that he would want to reaffirm his supreme authority. To do so, in a surprising but nevertheless understandable decision, he appropriates the young woman who has been the trophy of Achilles, the greatest hero of the expedition, who to take part in it has subordinated himself to the monarch of Argos. Achilles being the kind of person he is, his pride takes enormous offense, and he vacillates between killing Agamemnon and refusing to fight at his side from then on. It is understandable, in view of the loyalties of the heroic code, that he chooses the second course. It is readily believable that Achilles's absence from the field emboldens the Trojans, just as it dispirits his comrades, and it is a very probable consequence of that lowering of morale that many deaths occur among the Achaians, who make a disastrous retreat. It is also convincing that the offended Achilles maintains his stubborn refusal to return to battle, despite his friends' entreaties. One can well believe that, moved by the pain of injured companions and the danger of a definitive defeat, the sensible Patroklos wants to wear Achilles's armor, to deceive and thus demoralize the Trojans. Their initial withdrawal before the apparent Achilles is a highly probable event. It is not unforeseeable that an excess of confidence and daring will take possession of the triumphant Patroklos, who ventures to fight beyond the limits of prudence. It is almost inevitable that his trick will be discovered, and it is to be expected, then, that Hector will confront him and, being stronger, kill him. A necessary consequence is Achilles's grief and anger, his decision to avenge Patroklos, his return to combat, his pursuit and defeat of Hektor. The temporary insanity and the excesses of violence and cruelty of his soul, twice injured (by Agamemnon's offense and by the death of his beloved friend, for which he is partly responsible), are understandable. The succeeding recovery of his humanity and his momentary compassion toward Priamus also are probable.

This series of actions obeys the pertinent circumstances, the heroic types and principles, and the general laws of the human psyche. I conjecture that, thus remembering the argument of the *Iliad,* Aristotle could perceive a strict causality as the unifying structure of its actions; and we can, too.

The Conflict of Naturalism and Myth in Classic Poetry. But the fact is that Homer does not tell the story that way. More precisely, that is not the story that Homer tells. In the Homeric poems the connections joining one action to the next are not unilinear determinations or links in a chain consisting only of natural human actions and reactions. Divine intervention shapes almost all the heroes' movements. (Achilles, for example, refrains from killing Agamemnon because Athena, invisible to the rest, takes him by the hair and persuades him not to do it.) Only when we reinterpret the supernatural causality in terms of human psychology can we (re)constitute a univocal, unilinear causal course in these epic stories. In the Homeric poems there is double causality. They frequently present what can well be understood as a natural process that follows determinations intrinsic to the heroes' souls as a consequence of divine action. We find a similar duality in the parallelism of human (or divine) freedom and the unquestioned predetermination of destiny. In this respect, the Homeric world is fundamentally ambiguous. Mythic vision and naturalist lucidity have equal parts in it. This confluence of antagonistic interpretations of life still persists in Greek tragedy centuries later, giving rise to specific paradoxes of moral responsibility, so apparent in *Oedipus the King* and explicit in *Oedipus at Colonus.*

Aristotle is also an heir to the Greek enlightenment of the previous century and to Plato's abstract and antimythological theology. He would look with reserve, perhaps even with some disgust, at this partially archaic and irrational poetic vision (just as Thucydides expressly disliked the historical works of Herodotus, tainted with superstitions). So we can understand Aristotle's precept that "the irrational" of the traditional myths should be confined to the margins of the tragic action, that is, that gods and destiny should not determine the action. The issue here is not only the elimination of the grossest cases of deus ex machina. The Aristotelian ideal is a rationally intelligible action, in unequivocal terms of enlightened knowledge; a transparent action that makes visible the universal forces operating in the concrete fact. It is the ideal of a "philosophical" imagination. It is clear that Aristotle does not consequently maintain this imperative in the *Poetics,* and, as we have seen, he yields before the evidence that art is not purely a cognitive undertaking. But this ideal, which is not realized in the art Aristotle knew—nor was it those authors' aim—assumes a special value in the more secularized intellectual atmosphere of the Renaissance. Verisimilitude and (causal) unity of action are now imperatives that can be strictly carried out. (All indications are that these epochal transformations of the content and the law of the credible have been perceived since their beginnings, for there are already signs of it in Renaissance criticism. In the same sphere is the distinction made in the eighteenth century, and a commonplace among Romantic aesthetes: Greek tragedies are tragedies *of destiny;* Shakespeare's are tragedies *of character.*)

An Aristotelian "Beginning." On concluding his reading of "The Man of Ill-Advised Curiosity," the Curate praises the novella, but he censures as "impossible" (that is, highly inverisimilar) Anselmo's decision to test the honesty of his wife, and especially by such a test as the one he devises. If it were unconditionally valid, this critical objection would be devastating, for the entire action of the tale moves in a straight line from this initial decision. (The last sentence of the novella's text is, in fact: "This was the end of them all, born of such a misguided beginning.")

Francisco Ayala has suggested a psychological interpretation that makes Anselmo's obsession a possible, if indeed not a common, manifestation of subconscious homoeroticism.[25] It must be added that Anselmo's behavior does not lack precedents, either classical or canonical.[26] In Herodotus's *Histories,* in the part referring to the origins and antecedents of Persian power, we find the account of the curse that falls upon the royal house of Lydia, and the celebrated passage about Candaules and Gyges. The king, Candaules, so greatly admires and adores his wife's beauty that he has to share this vision. He forces Gyges, his young lieutenant, to hide himself and observe the queen when she undresses for bed. The consequences of this "madness" are fatal for Candaules, and after several generations, also for King Croesus and the entire nation. Genesis has a similar story. We are given the disturbing account of an action by Abraham (at that time called Abram), who, arguing that he fears he will be murdered because of his wife's beauty, forces Sarah to pretend that she is his sister, and thus to expose herself to the sexual solicitations of third parties. As a result, she eventually becomes Pharaoh's concubine. In the next generation the motif is repeated in the story of Isaac and Rebecca. In neither case are the consequences ultimately negative. The unconscious desire to provoke the sexual union of one's wife with a friend or a worthy stranger seems to be manifested in these actions.[27] In Candaules as in Anselmo, the obsessive and finally irresistible urge to open the intimate sphere of the married couple to a young and attractive friend is a tragic error. For both, the real and profound desire, which of course is socially and consciously unacceptable, has to manifest itself in a disguise (in one case as an act of sharing a vision of beauty, in the other as a test of marital fidelity). So the naturally hidden meaning of the behavior can never be revealed by the evidence, and the behavior itself is incomprehensible and strange. And what actions are strange if not those whose cause and ends escape us? Strange behavior is the kind that does not allow the workings of causality to be seen. Strange, incomprehensible actions are undesirable in the course of a tragic plot, as prescribed by Aristotle, because the plot ought to exhibit the universal logic of its process.

Not all the parts of the tragic action are subject to this norm of causal intelligibility, however. The actions that constitute the *middle* of the fable ("that which follows something by causal necessity and is followed by something necessarily") and the *end* of it ("what follows something necessarily, but is not in its turn followed by something") are subject to it. On the other hand, the *beginning* of the fable is "what is followed by something necessarily, but does not follow anything" (*Poetics*, VII, 1450b). The beginning, therefore, is what seems like an absolute action, with no cause, pure spontaneity. And is not the optimal realization of a pure beginning precisely the action whose cause we do not see, the inexplicable and strange deed? Cervantes gives a supreme solution to this Aristotelian norm of the absolute beginning, problematic in itself. The cause of the beginning of Anselmo's tragedy necessarily must remain invisible, nonexistent to consciousness. His tragic error is unmotivated; nevertheless, to a penetrating intuition it is part of the unfathomable order of nature.

The Tragic Novella's Unity of Action. After this absolute beginning of the story of "ill-advised curiosity," the norm of unity of action is equally perfectly realized. When Anselmo asks his friend Lotario to try to seduce his wife as a test of her honesty, it is natural for Lotario to refuse with alarm, until Anselmo threatens to ask someone else, surely less worthy of his trust. Lotario thus feels forced to feign acceptance of the experiment. He assures Anselmo that he is going to pretend to approach Camila amorously, but naturally, at first he does not even begin to carry out the ruse. Nevertheless, he is obligated to visit her and spend hours in her company. These inevitable periods of shared solitude, idleness, and silence naturally lead to mutual contemplation of their respective beauties. The rest of the world is shut out, and this is the most propitious condition for that kind of pathological contraction of the faculty of attention in which, according to Ortega, lies the psychic mechanism of falling in love.[28] It is highly probable, then, if not necessary, that the feigned siege should become real and the adultery be consummated. Then of course they must hide what has happened. The dissimulation is fragile. Camila's servant, Leonela, cannot help but be aware of the situation, and with plebeian forwardness she takes advantage of her power of extortion to enjoy her own erotic recreations under the same roof more comfortably and without fear of reprimand. Leonela's liberties are likely to create the risk that Anselmo will note that all is not well in his house. Finally he finds himself impelled to force a confession from the servant. The imminence of the revelation makes the adulterers flee, and anagnorisis and peripeteia fall with implacable logic upon Anselmo. Neither gods nor miracles, fate nor fortuitous, improbable accidents intervene in this action (here greatly condensed and simplified). This story fulfills Aristotle's ideal prefiguration of what a tragic action should be. Its internal coherence is, with one minimal exception, perfect; its beginning and its end are absolute; its naturalistic intelligibility is unrestricted.

The rigor of the causal logic of the tale of "ill-advised curiosity" is demonstrated by the fact that we can detect its one, very minor illogical moment; in a story of looser texture it would attract no attention. When Lotario declares (falsely) that he has already tried Camila's virtue more than enough and that she has responded with unshakable honesty, Anselmo calls himself satisfied and happy, but he asks his friend to continue to court her, now as a game for pleasure. This does not fit the *apparent* logic of the matter, and should have provoked a (feigned) scandalized protest on the part of Lotario. Thus it is inverisimilar that Lotario, easily and without serious discussion or at least pseudorational justification, accepts this prolongation of the test, which he has repeatedly declared to be so painful for himself and so unworthy of Anselmo and Camila. It is verisimilar that both desire to continue it, but not that these desires are permitted to run their course without encountering an obstacle in the (culturally and psychologically inescapable) conscious and discursive rationalization of their relationship. But the fact that such fine points of psychological and ethical motivation are relevant here shows to what high tensions of consistency and verisimilitude Cervantes has carried us in this story.

(Furthermore, Cervantes's technique at this juncture accords with the solution Aristotle prescribes for "irrational" passages: summary narration, very brief and conceptual, instead of fully illuminated dramatization. As the Canon recommends in I.47, the author's craft here serves to "facilitate what is impossible.")

Cervantes has provided subtle metapoetic signs to emphasize the strictness of the plot's logic. It is significant that this text exhibits such marked and even pedantic rationality in its dialogues, dominated by arguments and counterarguments of almost scholastic formality.[29] In one of them Lotario goes so far as to invoke the persuasive force of the "mathematical demonstrations that cannot be negated, as when they say 'If from two equal parts we take away equal parts, those which remain also are equal'" (I.33). Is it not surprising to find a formal analytical principle seriously and literally quoted in a novella? And how emblematically appropriate it is in the Aristotelian climate of this exemplary tragedy! Besides formal logic, there are also allusions to the semialchemical experimental techniques of nascent modern science (prevalent then in the Italy in which the story is set), for Anselmo is seeking to prove his wife's virtue by an experiment: "I cannot be sure of this truth, if not by testing it in such a way that the test makes clear the carats of her goodness, just as fire shows those of gold" (I.33).

"The Man of Ill-Advised Curiosity" is a fundamental piece in the *Quixote*'s design because, on the one hand, it joins with the tragic vision, the genre of systematic pessimism, to complete the structure of the poetic visions of life. On the other hand, it is the only unit of classical style in the book. And it is the only embodiment of an imaginary region that renders it pure, neither ironized nor breached. Stylistically, then, it is of one piece, unlike all the rest of the book.[30] It is no accident, therefore, that it is presented as an interpolated text, the only one. If we accept the hypothesis that a fundamental part of the project of this Cervantine work is to reproduce all the generic forms of the literary universe, a classically tragic piece has to appear in the *Quixote*. And since the context, although varied, is almost entirely *comic,* and the other imaginary regions all emerge as stylistically contaminated, impure (because that is the law of Cervantes's ironized universe), the classical, tragic, and stylistically pure piece must be inserted in the book as something from another world. *It has to be* a literary manuscript incidentally found by the characters of comic-realistic impurity. I do not believe it is possible to imagine a solution of greater aesthetic rigor. This novella is a flower from the classical slope of the Renaissance, placed in the midst of the Baroque fermentation and syncretism of types, genres, and regions. It is easy to imagine that Cervantes might have put this novella in the middle of the book because it is a unique literary jewel, worthy of the most opulent setting. But as we have seen, there are powerful formal reasons that make such an explanation unnecessary, and that do not permit us to continue to believe that the pertinence of the novella in the book is arbitrary or superficial.

Neither, however, is this story a "realistic" work, in the modern sense of the word. First of all, its formal habit is very abstract and it exhibits a strong stylization. Concrete details are absent, as are transitory atmospheres, indifferent circumstances—anything that is irrelevant to the logic of the action. But even the action itself requires extreme isolation of the protagonists. There are no other occupations or encounters that could shake Anselmo's design. The surrounding world seems to withdraw to make room, as in a void, for the purity of the experiment. The figures are drawn with sharp lines in the center of a hierarchically ordered space. On the other hand, Anselmo's madness is too prolonged and persistent to be reconcilable with the parallel persistence of his discursive reasonableness and lucidity. His is also, like Don Quixote's, a "strange madness." The causal logic, as we saw, is almost impeccable, but the premises of character and circumstance depart somewhat from real possibility, which Cervantes suggests by the Curate's commentary (excessively critical, we noted). Strictly speaking, the story is an admirable example of demythified verisimilitude, of what could be called "abstract realism."

The ideology of this story also accords with the tragic spirit. At first sight, it seems to convey traditional edification, and to some extent it does. The "honor" of husband and wife ought to be protected as an essential element of the moral order. The holiness of matrimony and the virtue of true friendship are affirmed, as is the need for particular *prudence* in this delicate sphere; equally sustained is the wisdom of distrusting the moral stability of women, who should not be submitted to temptations, because "woman is an imperfect animal" (I.33).[31] And the course of the actions seems to corroborate this pessimistic vision of feminine nature. Yet the first to succumb to temptation and violate his own honor and that of his friend is the highly noble Lotario. "Camila surrendered; she surrendered; but what wonder, if Lotario's friendship could not endure intact?" (I.34). So the "imperfect animal" is the human being. Anselmo's curiosity and scheme are themselves transgressions of his wife's honor, his own, and Lotario's. Now then, this strange "curiosity" seems at first glance, as we observed, to be the purest contingency, absolutely unmotivated and capricious, and it introduces chaos into the moral order. But the word "animal"—which, like all of Cervantes's words, does not appear by accident in the text—signals that rather than chance or chaos, it is the order of nature that is manifested in this course of events. Nature is the force that disrupts and destroys the perfection of these rational, beautiful, and noble characters. Is there a eugenic law behind the alienation of Anselmo, his predecessors, and other kindred souls? However that may be, it is the repressed forces of animality that originate the destructive, centrifugal movement of this story, which ends in the dispersion of the characters to the countryside, leaving behind a city that seems to be emptying out. Disorder and death strike the final note of the melody of this story and close it with the most accomplished logic: the artistic perfection of its form restores to us the Apollonian illusion that has been destroyed in its characters.

The Cervantine conception of tragedy is, in essence, the same one that Nietzsche presented centuries later, developing ideas of Schopenhauer's, to the surprise and incredulity of philological Europe.

Conjectures beyond Literary Meaning. We have seen that dissimulation of depth is an objective trait of the Cervantine style and ways of fabling. It is manifest in his ironized expressions of false modesty, in the conciliatory temper of his measured, calm, rhetorically traditionalist prose, in his stories of conventional and romancesque appearance. It is also apparent (let us now realize) in the seemingly casual and unjustified way in which "The Man of Ill-Advised Curiosity" is inserted in the novel.

We also have observed repeatedly that there is a double constitutive gesture in Cervantes's creation. Often his narrative seems to move toward the evocation of reality in its daily dullness or baseness, and immediately it retreats toward a protective illusion, an illusion that consists in the stylization of the image of life according to the traditional literary orders. Cervantes distorts and ironizes these orders, but to some extent allows them to exercise their tranquilizing power. Thus the sustained foreground of his stories sometimes has the conventional, inoffensive appearance of canonical daydreams, in which a providential destiny rules. Only in the background does an attentive reader catch fleeting glimpses of distressing vistas. We have seen that this double movement of the imagination characterizes both the macrotextual units (the comedies of disguised corruption) and the microtextual ones (sentences of ambiguous direction, which sound precise realistic notes and immediately suspend them with connotations of literariness and idealness). The ironization of literature in the *Quixote* is therefore in part a subliminal, concealed operation, as is the evocation of the sense of reality. Certainly, on a basic plane, chivalric literature is ironized head on in the *Quixote,* and so the "reality" of Don Quixote's world is evoked. But this confrontation is only an emblem or allegory of a more radical one: that of all literature (including the "realistic" comedy that is Don Quixote's world) before the sense of true reality.[32]

As we saw, "The Man of Ill-Advised Curiosity" also displays this double plane. The appearance of a story of strangely idiosyncratic tragic insanity (which includes a timeless lesson of prudence) conceals and reveals a depth of enigmatic but determinant animality. Evidence of the natural law emerges from a formal experiment, nurtured by logic and protoscientific empiricism. The comic attenuation found in the rest of the *Quixote* is absent here. The rigorously tragic form itself does not hide the pessimistic depth of the story; rather, it underlines it. Therefore, the novella is the key to one of the most recondite meanings of the work. It points to the *Quixote*'s hidden side, the other face, whose contemplation cannot be sustained for long. As much from the point of view of the content as stylistically and formally, it is the *other* text of the work, the one that completes the signifying unity and embodies one of its deepest dimensions.[33]

Presumably the duplicities and dissimulations of Cervantes's writing are more or less vaguely intuited by most readers. Critics have frequently pointed to these phenomena of "ambiguity," which have even been seen as forms of understandable hypocrisy, forced by the repressive climate of post-Tridentine Spain. But what does Cervantes want to cover up? Or, better, what does he want to suggest to us in a dissembling way? Of the many hypotheses that have been offered, the most widely accepted is that it is convictions of the underground Erasmian tradition that move Cervantes to resort to distancing and precautions. It is not difficult, in fact, to conceive that a man of the sensibility, intelligence, and worldliness of Cervantes would dislike superstitions that the Tridentine church decided to consecrate (with a populist instinct, by the way, considerably more appropriate to the reality of the Mediterranean peoples than the illusions of the aristocratic and frustrated Spanish humanist reformers). A crypto-Erasmist, however, would probably be more cautious. We should not forget that our author does not repress striking satirical derisions of popular religious practices, but elaborates them (among others, those of the disproportionate rosaries in Don Quixote's penitence and in the Cave of Montesinos). In many places there are elements of unembarrassed and light anticlerical humor, fitting indeed for a believer very sure of his faith. The allusions to the Inquisition, in the book-burning scene and in relation to Don Antonio's magic bronze head, seem obvious enough. Someone who makes his mad protagonist speak in Christlike phrases, allows a change of asses' harness to be called "mutatio caparum" (I.21), and makes a pretended descent to hell one of the Duke's and Duchess's practical jokes (II.69–70), not to mention other innocent blasphemies and heresies (in II.34, II.41, for example), does not seem to fear suspicions about his orthodoxy.[34] Cervantes's dissimulation is not the dissimulation of a heretic.

It is rather the dissimulation of a believer who, wanting to be orthodox, has glimpsed, in intermittent instants in which his spiritual dwelling is torn away, an abyss of senselessness and inhumanity in the profound order of things, and who has had a vision of the unredeemable animality of the human being and the radical hopelessness of existence. This is more than heresy. It is a state of absolutely irreligious consciousness, a simultaneously decisive and intolerable experience that Cervantes tries to hide from himself and (like Unamuno's San Manuel Bueno) from his own, his readers, but that he cannot help but reveal, cloaking it in the truthful allegory of his image of life. (In this biographical conjecture I go beyond the limits that I have set for myself: those of describing only the thought objectified in the work. The plausibility of this conjecture rests in its being consistent with what Cervantes has *done* in his book, including the irreverent jokes to which I have alluded, as well as with what we know of his life and of his time.) This double thread of the Cervantine work (uncovering and veiling, despair and consolation) motivates its characteristics of style and structure. Insofar as it is an operation of veiling and happy semblance, the movement is expressed in the gesture of the enchanting, humoristic, and amiable captivation of the reader's will. It is shown also in the fables of comedy, in orchestrating all the instruments of the literary tradition (with its verisimilar intelligibility, its redemptive providence, its comforting exemplarity, its guarantee or intimation of a meaning behind the ups and downs of life), and in hiding baseness and corruption in the background. On the other hand, we have the movement toward the real, beyond the mythic bounds of literature; the ironization and satire of the idealizations of style, the erosion and subversion of the regions of the poetic faculty, the metapoetic game, the multiple evocation of the sense of reality, the recognition of the falsity of the comforting illusions generated by the imagination.

This double gesture is affirmative but ironic, joyous but melancholy. The transcendental form of the work, its poetic design, thus finally shows its connection with the complex system of its meanings. The poetological description formally demonstrates the intuitable sense of the creation.

Are there not anachronisms in this interpretation that attributes a naturalistic pessimism to the spirit objectified in the *Quixote*? One generally tends to think that in Cervantes's time the Spanish mind shielded itself against the skeptical, experimental, and rationalist winds that agitated the Italy of Galileo, the Europe of Descartes, the England of Shakespeare and Bacon. But it is not difficult to imagine the young Cervantes, avid for world and knowledge, absorbing, in five long Italian years, the scientific spirit of the age, with its radical questioning of all presumed truths of tradition and its mathematical-experimental determination of the order of nature. Besides, it seems beyond doubt that Cervantes was familiar with the work of his contemporary and countryman Juan Huarte de San Juan. Huarte's *Examen de ingenios para las ciencias* was published in 1575 and reissued several times before the end of the century. And it is obvious (it did not escape the vigilant eyes of the Inquisition) that Huarte, with his physical-physiological explanations of psychic phenomena, implicitly proposes a materialistic anthropology.

In the historical-political realm, has not Cervantes lived through the age of the apparently definitive failure of the ancient, venerable plan of the Christian empire of universal peace, with all its bitter consequences? Is not the next step to doubt that the course of history is providential and has meaning (some of Shakespeare's characters express this thought), and to think that one stands before the absurdity of an axiological void? I believe that to suppose that these experiences were part of Cervantes's life, and that we are not mistaken when we sense them in his work, is no more strange than to verify moments of religiousness, mythical irrationalism, and metaphysical idealism in writers who are our contemporaries, who profess themselves to be materialists, and who mock traditional beliefs. A lucid mind cannot avoid perceiving the senselessness of nature, its indifference to human desires and ideals; neither can an intense sensibility abandon hope for a justification of being. Perhaps it is a sensible heuristic principle to suppose that at any time during the history of civilization, individuals can end up conceiving any of the fundamental visions of life, and that their minds (our minds) will always be an inconsistent composite of experience and myth. What the spirit of the age can determine is which of the conceptions becomes habitual and which are repressed.

Literariness and Metapoetic Signs

Two Kinds of Metapoetic Signs. Is a metapoetic dimension peculiar to the *Quixote?* Does not all literature give signs of its being literature? Subtitles, circumstances of recitation, verse, poetic diction, fictional narrative modes, stylization, absence of precise, consistent references to contemporary reality, and so on are indices of literariness. Is not the recognition of literary discourse as linguistic fiction the necessary condition of an appropriately literary reading? And has the poetic institution ever claimed that its images are images of real facts? What, then, does Cervantes's thematization of literariness have that is, if not unique, specific to its kind?

Let us distinguish between two phenomena. One, the general one, consists of the signs and traits with which the literary work is offered to us as a representation of persons, actions, and circumstances that are at once singular and fictitious. The other phenomenon is the ironization of the *universals* incarnated by the fictitious individuals. This is not a characteristic of all literature. It is completely absent from works of serious realism or of sustained verisimilitude. Such pieces do not ironize the imaginary region that they display; they do not question the laws that rule in their fictitious worlds. On the contrary, they tacitly claim that the universal implications of their fictitious stories are true, adapted to the known general determinations of empirical reality, or at least that they are verisimilar, that is, in part congruent with these determinations.

Certainly *comedy* archetypally tends to expose, by a sort of self-reflexive intimation, the lightness and unreality of its images of life, at the same time that it strives for a typological and satirical wisdom. We know that the *Quixote* shares this comic trait. But in the *Quixote,* the ironization of the types of imagination is universal. This ironization is carried out, as we have seen, with touches of internal inconsistency, stylistic contaminations, and abrupt contrasts of configurative law. The typological and satirical wisdom of the various systems of poetic imagination and the allegorical and symbolic truths of fictitious stories are not lacking in this work, but at the same time the distance that separates the stories from lived reality is positively marked. All the forms of the imagination are used and their visionary potential is realized, but in a parallel action they are discredited. The more believable and alive Don Quixote and Sancho become, the more paradoxical becomes Cervantes's criticism of the literary imagination. Literature, the *Quixote* suggests, is the only instrument we have for projecting the secular truth of our life into an image, and it can seem to do that with great force, but it is a seductively deceptive medium. The *vision* of reality is a labor of Sisyphus, a fleeting glimpse (a kind of mirage?) between the enthusiastic perception of the poetic symbol and the disenchantment brought about by the sense of reality.

But the sense of reality, as we have seen, could not be activated without the habit of realism that the domestic region of Don Quixote and Sancho assumes. This sphere emphasizes the idealizations of the other imaginary regions, thus generating the movement that is critical of poetic reason. Therefore it is important to recall once again that the internal ironization of the basic region is only incidental (Sancho's transformations and some minor hyperbolic passages) or marginal (the paradoxes of the narrative source and of calendar time). For the most part, the comic-realistic region is solid and consistent. Don Quixote's hallucinations are always hallucinations, and are presented against a background of unequivocal facts, established by the narrator and well perceived by the figures of good sense. In this central, decisive sphere, there are no magic games in the manner of twentieth-century antirealistic literature. That the laws of nature can be inconstant and in some recondite space invalid is a modernist motif dear to many of our contemporaries, among them Borges and Unamuno. It is a postnaturalist hope to find reality's somber determinism disrupted somewhere. One looks for encouraging inconsistencies of logic itself, insuperable paradoxes in mathematics, marvelous fissures in the natural order, for in the light of science and reason, the universe is seen to be indifferent to human desires and suffering and void of supernatural agents of redemption. Cervantes does not live within such a historical consciousness. Conjecturably, he has approached this abyss only at moments. His work loses subtlety and complexity if it is interpreted in a manner akin to the imagination of a Borges or an Unamuno.

Verisimilitude of the "Object" and of the "Manner." I have asserted axiomatically that all literature signals its character as a game and alludes to the purely imaginary nature of its singular world. Such characteristics are not an obstacle to its serious intent to present mimetic, allegorical, or symbolic truths. But does this determination not preclude, a priori, the possibility of thoroughly realistic fiction?

The idea of strict realism implies the exclusion of systematic idealizations and stylizations of the objects of the fictitious world, for these idealizations are always, at least subliminally, in conflict with the sense of reality. (The complex formal game of the *Quixote,* as we saw, objectifies and exposes precisely that conflict.) Has there ever been realistic literature in this sense of the word—that is, art not merely believable by reason of a modified sense of reality in the tradition of verisimilitude but rigorously truthful with respect to the universal implications of its fictitious individuals? Is the realistic and naturalistic novel of the nineteenth and twentieth centuries that kind of art? And if it is, how does this novel then indicate its fictionality?

In the realistic novel the signs of fictionality have been transferred from the represented fictitious world to the agent, also fictitious, who presents it; that is, from the characters, actions, and places to the narrative source, to the descriptive power of the narrator.

Up to this point, I have considered verisimilitude and realism only as they apply to the fictitious or fictionalized persons, actions, and circumstances that constitute the literary work's imaginary world. In Aristotelian terms, I have considered the mimetic virtue only of the represented *object,* and not that of the *manner* of the representation. As I indicated earlier, Aristotle observed that the manner of presenting the fictitious objects has implications for the verisimilitude of the spectacle, so that certain objects that are believable in a narration would not be believable if they were staged. Aristotle's analysis of verisimilitude nevertheless deals primarily with the character of the objects. In the neo-Aristotelian poetics of the Renaissance and of classicism, on the other hand, the question of the verisimilitude of the manner of presentation acquires greater importance. That explains the attention that, at least since Castelvetro, has been paid to the dramatic unities of place and time (the latter barely and ambiguously mentioned by Aristotle, the former not mentioned at all). While unity of action refers to the structure of the object represented, the unities of place and time principally concern the manner of arranging the story for the stage. Castelvetro, Maggi, Bonciani, Sidney, Corneille, Dryden prescribe the unities of place and time for the sake of the verisimilitude that they grant to the staged event.[35] According to these critics of the sixteenth and seventeenth centuries, the illusion of real life would be more solid if the spectator perceived the action as occurring in a single imaginary place, because that way the imaginary place would be easily confused with the real site of the stage, and seeing would coincide completely with imagining. On the other hand, a change of imaginary place during a single representation would make the spectators aware of the real presence of the stage and its machinery, and would immediately activate the consciousness, dormant before, of the artificiality of the spectacle. Analogously, the time represented, according to the neoclassical critics, ought in general to be regular and continuous, without noticeable accelerations or lapses; that is, it ought to tend to be coextensive and isochronically coordinated with the real time of the representation. If one sensed a rupture of the synchronic parallelism, the fictionality of the represented action would be detached from the real event of the staging, and the illusion of attending a real occurrence would thus be disturbed.

These classicist arguments were never completely convincing. Dr. Johnson criticizes them, and much earlier Italian theoreticians of the cinquecento (for example, Alessandro Piccolomini) had done so. They argue that there is no evidence that it is not possible for the spectator to submit easily to the illusion of two or more imaginary places on the same real stage, and that if there is a difficulty, it is already given in imagining one place, for to imagine it implies consciousness of the illusionistic game.[36]

It is interesting to note that the classicist critics' analyses, no less than their adversaries', deal with topics that today are part of a phenomenological psychology of literary reception, and that they have affinities to my description of the anti-illusionistic function of the discontinuities of style in Cervantes's exposition of the artificiality of literature. In both cases we are dealing with the illusion-breaking, ironizing effect of changes of the representation's basic forms in the course of its development.

We see, then, that the question of the fictional representation of reality involves two issues: (1) the truth or the credibility of the laws implied by the actions of the fictitious beings (intrinsically, that is, independently of their mode of appearance before the reader or spectator); and (2) the similarity that the mode in which they appear before the imagination may have with the mode of the real perception of objects. The new technical problem of the classicist dramatists and critics, then, was that of the spatial and temporal forms in which the imaginary object ought to be presented, and the relation of the manner of presentation to the illusion of reality, that is, the value of the manner of presentation as a factor of verisimilitude.

Ultimately this is the problem of novelistic technique that writers and critics from the end of the nineteenth century till the middle of the twentieth discussed under the rubrics of the function of the narrator and the narrative "point of view," and currently is involved in issues related to the mode of presentation. Flaubert, James, Lubbock, Ortega, and Kayser took part in this discussion, whose ramifications and systematic treatment continue today in the narratological studies of Wayne Booth, Dorrit Cohn, Franz Stanzel, Gérard Genette, and various others.[37] The classicist preoccupation with the unities, as well as the reflections of Flaubert, James, and their successors on the figure of the narrator, have a side that is formally artistic: they express the will to achieve an absolute work, of strict internal cohesion, homogeneous and absorbing. But they also have in common an epistemological, perceptual aspect that is related to the illusion of reality. The illusion of reality! We find expressions of this ideal in the writers and neo-Aristotelian critics of the sixteenth and seventeenth centuries and in such writers as Henry James. In the former, it means accomplished verisimilitude of the scenes presented; in the latter, the efficacious "dramatization" of a rigorous realism in the novel.

I noted in the Introduction that the conversation between the Curate and the Canon (I.47–48) refers to the unities of time and place in the context of the principle of verisimilitude. The *Quixote* lacks unity of action, but it approaches an epic or novelistic version of the unities of place and time. Admittedly there are paradoxes of calendar time in the overly long summer of the three sallies. On the other hand, the adventures of Don Quixote and Sancho, as we know, play themselves out with a regular tempo and are sometimes linked by very brief summaries of a few days with no incidents. This treatment of time seems to be the nearest narrative equivalent to the theatrical synchrony of the representation and what is represented (if we set aside the rare totally scenic novelistic forms). Cervantes avoids precise chronological information. (Often we do not even know the approximate hour of the day or night, and never or rarely the day of the week; on two or three occasions the month is named, or a commemorative holiday, or the date including the month and year. These few precise pieces of information usually are, as we saw, paradoxical.) Thus the reader's consciousness of the time frame is nebulous, and we perceive the series of adventures and conversations as if they were presented with uninterrupted, homogeneous continuity (which is perhaps a necessary condition for the impression we get that the pair's wanderings extend not over a summer or a period of years but eternally).

There is also considerable continuity in the places represented. We are not subjected to brusque leaps from one locale to another. Therefore, it is possible to trace Don Quixote's approximate route on a map of central and northeastern Spain. The movement of the protagonists is presented with a fairly regular narrative rhythm, but the geographical specifications, like the chronological ones, are often imprecise, so that, with the exception of the sojourns with the Duke and Duchess and in Barcelona, the actions seem to unfold in a single location: the road and its surroundings (inns, hills, villages).

Thus, in the extensive narrative form, Cervantes anticipates the use of technical devices that were theoretically formulated and applied in the theater several decades later by Pierre Corneille. It seems to me that the classicist side of the *Quixote* is manifested in this treatment of time and space. This aspect is more noticeable in Part Two, owing to the absence of long secondary stories. I can thus understand, although I do not accept, the thesis of Knud Togeby, who defines the Second Part of the *Quixote* as a work of classical style.[38]

In these characteristics one can also grasp the *Quixote*'s *theatricality*. Direct dialogue is the most sustained modality of the book. Notwithstanding its "scenic" manner of presentation, the *Quixote* is quite the opposite of a *dramatic* work, for its main story lacks any tension driving toward a resolution. It has no unifying conflict that could speed the course of events. In a word, it lacks unity of action. It is an eminently "epic" work in Schiller's and Goethe's sense, a concept that Giovan Battista Pigna anticipated in 1554 in his description of the non-Aristotelian (*romanzesca*) law of the Ariosto-style poem: multidirectional ambulation that often stops and is diverted toward discontinuous, varied activity.[39] The "theatricality" of the *Quixote*, then, does not find its raison d'être in dramatic force. As I said earlier, I think the use of the scenic modality is another aspect of Cervantes's suggestion of the sense of reality. This novelistic technique induces the negative presence of the ordinary world, its "tempo lento," its resistance to the winged stirrings of longing and impatience, its stability. Joined with this theatricality is an element that is opposite to it but of equal "realistic" effect: the company provided us by the narrator, whose sensibility and good humor let the tone of daily experience keep vibrating. The "scenic method" (in Lubbock's term)[40] in the novel promotes the nearness of the objects. They can be shown and seen in detail, spatially and temporally. Their imaginary presence can thus acquire a quasi-perceptual quality. We "hear" the voices of the protagonists, for their statements are reproduced verbatim. This imaginary proximity is more apt for producing an illusion of reality (and, as Aristotle teaches, less apt for dissimulating inverisimilitudes) than the distancing of the facts through the conceptualizing medium of the summary account.

The "scenes" of the *Quixote,* however, are not yet as exactly perceptual as those of the realistic and naturalistic novels of later centuries, just as the "realism" of the *Quixote* does not have the rigor of their realism. What is lacking, in this sense, is the precision of situation and gesture, the minor detail (an occasional hesitation, incidental pauses, activities not obviously related to the theme of the conversation, unintentional imperfections of speech), and especially the pulsation of time, the direct, not merely evoked sensation of the ordinary passing of life. Cervantes's description of physical circumstances is also synthetic and frequently vague. And all of it demonstrates, certainly, that the *Quixote*'s law of stylization (even with respect to this basic region, the most "concrete" of the novel) is considerably abstract, and reduces situations and dialogue to an ideal essentialness. After all, the central characters (and all of those of the book, to a greater or lesser degree) are close to being archetypal figures, a fact that excludes a *realistic* individuation of the type. (Hence the possibility of conceiving of Don Quixote, as the Romantics and Unamuno do, as a *mythical* creation.)

As, in general, the movement of the book in the direction of realism is reversed by that of comic idealism, so the inclination toward the concretely scenic image and individual psychology is restricted by the typification of landscapes and locales, and by the high stylization of the characters and their discourses.

The Fantastic Figure of the Narrator and the Realistic Novel. The narrator of the *Quixote,* I observed, also helps to induce a sense of the real. In its simplest form, this effect proceeds from the humorous irony. The persistent ironic suggestion is that the story being told is nothing but a literary invention. This indirect reference to real experience is reinforced by the personality of this narrator. Nominally there are three basic narrators in the *Quixote:* Cide Hamete, the not totally faithful translator, and the rewriter of the translation or "second author." The latter is also, phenomenally and by order of appearance, the first narrator, the only one in the first eight chapters, though at the end of the eighth he mentions a first author and calls himself "the second." Additionally, he has already spoken at the beginning of the work of various "authors" of the history of the wanderings of Don Quixote. Nevertheless, the continuity of tone and manner, systematically much more determinant than the merely incidental allusions to the text of Cide Hamete, makes the "second author" the narrative authority, the source of the narrative thought and voice of the book. This narrator appears and speaks as if he were the same person that has introduced himself as the (fictionalized) author of the Prologue. Thus the figure that is the dominant narrator of the book is manifestly an author of fiction. This connotation of fictionality never disappears completely from the basic discourse, and it is the foundation of the humorous irony projected over the events of the story. Besides, the author-narrator explicitly characterizes himself as a neighbor of unexceptional position, with his burden of common afflictions. The self-mocking attitude alternating with the proud gesture complete the image of this narrator. He is an equal of his undistinguished reader, a human being of fairly domestic existence, unexceptional tribulations, good humor, and sensible resignation. The story is told and heard, then, in the midst of ordinary life.

Because of his constant ironization of the truth of his narrative, this figure of the narrator differs from the narrator of the realistic novel, who seriously relates his story. Nevertheless, the two have some things in common. In the first place, both are personal presences that are perceived as autonomous entities, held apart from the narrated world. Then, both have unrestricted access to this world. Cervantes uses the narrator's logical privilege to approach the interior of the characters (their solitary actions, their thoughts) from the outside, describing their actions as an invisible, clairvoyant witness would do. Certainly, this is what the third-person narrators of (for example) Homer and Virgil do. Those narrators are not ordinary neighbors, however, but seers of divine inspiration, distant from all systematic self-ironization. In consequence, the narrative mode of the *Quixote* constitutes the paradox of the supernatural epistemological privilege of an ordinary man, who tells us a story that is not sacred or part of universal history but profane and private, with gestures of visionary omniscience.

This paradoxical personality has become the classical narrative source of the modern novelistic genre. Undeniably and amazingly, this personality is not only not realistic but even inverisimilar. Like the *Quixote,* the modern realistic novel is narrated systematically by a speaker who is not only fictitious but fantastic. Cervantes was well aware of the inverisimilitude of this structurally necessary component of the fiction that obeys the design of the (modified or radical) illusion of reality. Sancho tells Don Quixote (II.2):

> ". . . last night Bartolomé Carrasco's son arrived from studying at Salamanca, where he was made a bachelor. And when I went up to welcome him, he told me that the history of your worship is already told in a book by the name of *The Ingenious Gentleman Don Quixote of La Mancha.* And he says that they also mention me in it by my own very name of Sancho Panza, and Lady Dulcinea of El Toboso, too, and many a thing that happened to us in private, which made me cross myself in amazement to think how the history writer could have got wind of what he wrote."
>
> "You may be sure, Sancho"—said Don Quixote—"that the author of our history is some wise enchanter, for nothing of what they want to write can be hidden from them."

And at this point we find the answer, briefly anticipated above, to our question about the possibility and existence of an intrinsic signalization of *realistic* literature as literature. What proclaims the fictionality of the realistic novel and its discourse is the fantastic character of the narrative source and of the whole basic communicative situation. The novelistic world emerges as opposite to the narrative discourse. Therefore, if the latter is fantastic and thus openly fictional, the former can be completely realistic and the work will still be classified as fiction. Here the narrative *manner,* the medium of presentation (not the stylization of the narrated object), is the feature that indicates the fictionality of the fiction. The epistemological fantasy of unlimited perception leads to literary realism in two senses. First, it opens up the possibility of a quasi-perceptual, detailed, omnimodal presentation of the objects, including the objectification of the immediate subjectivity of experience, thus favoring the "illusion of reality," that of direct evidence. Second, it frees the characters, places, and actions from the necessity of carrying signs of fictionality, that is, from the necessity of a stylizing configuration. The fictitious individuals can thus embody universals that correspond completely to our sense of reality. They can lack marked idealizations or stylizations. The consciousness of play, the voluntary suspension of disbelief, is not disturbed by this realism, because the fictionalizing attitude is confirmed by the fantastic narrative clairvoyance, by the unreal nature of the novelistic discourse.

It is only consistent that the *Quixote*, lacking a strict realistic image of the world, should present us with a narrator whose clairvoyance and "omniscience" are considerably limited in comparison with those of the modern novel (a point obvious if we consider that the *Quixote*'s narrator does not exhibit certain knowledge of the past and the future of his characters or any detailed perception of their subjective processes). There is an element of stylistic truth in the narrator's pretending to be a "historian."

Misdirections from a History of Forms. As we see, the *Quixote* is a technically transitional work in more than one sense. From a historical viewpoint, it can be seen as a step toward realism, toward a fully scenic novelistic method, toward the secularized narrator of unlimited cognitive authority. By contrast, in its encyclopedic and hyperbolic stylistic discontinuity it also anticipates, negatively this time, the homogeneity of style, the continuity of imaginary region, characteristic of the modern novel.

The false implication of such a historical perspective, however, is that it makes the work seem like a limited artistic achievement, as if later creations had "surpassed" the *Quixote* and realized perfectly what Cervantes tried but did not quite manage to do. This kind of critical approach is frequent (although I do not remember having seen it explicitly applied to the *Quixote*) and, in my view, quite wrong. I believe that a determination of a literary work's position in the historical evolution of forms (innovative, intermediate, or mature) should be entirely irrelevant to our appreciation of its value and significance. (At times, for example, I have the impression that so far as certain aspects of temporal continuity are concerned, the scenes of Avellaneda's *Quixote* are technically more "advanced" than those of Cervantes.) A common tendency in criticism is to praise the "maturity" or perfection in the use of a technique, or its novelty, its "revolutionary" character. It is not strange, then, that we hear it said so often, as a kind of high encomium, that the *Quixote* is the first modern novel, despite the many facts that speak against such an assertion. Or it is extolled as the sum and culmination of all the traditional genres, including books of chivalry, which also is untrue, for it displays them not to consummate them but to twist them and erode them.

Undoubtedly Cervantes's innovations are of considerable magnitude, and they place the *Quixote* among the predecessors of the modern novel. But the most radical of the work's formal traits (its universal collection, ironization, and reconfiguration of the forms of verisimilitude), although they influenced the literary consciousness of its own age and the ones that followed it, have not endured in the history of the novel.

Even those technical innovations that had lasting effects, however, were innovations at a time that is long past; they have been repeated and surpassed by many successors, so that it is no longer possible (if it ever was) to marvel before these "revolutions" of form, which today are old commonplaces. If the work is alive, it cannot be because of its contribution to the history of literary forms. We can concede that technical innovation, for historical-psychological reasons, as the Russian Formalists believed, is a fundamental necessity of the life of art, and also that works that convey new creative possibilities often represent great literary achievements. But the *telos* of the work and the aesthetic operations of the recipient are not directed toward the execution of a formal dialectic that would thematize the historical course of the genre. A work cannot be enjoyed as a phase of formal development between this and that period, or as an anticipation of this thematics or that technique. The work and the reading are *now*, and if they are felicitous, they are self-sufficient and final. The critic can discern Cervantes's contributions to the history of letters, but the function of such forms in Cervantes's work is not to contribute to future works but to be part of an immediate and undeferrable imaginary experience. In this respect, either they are appropriate and efficacious or they are not.

It is certainly reasonable to wonder whether it is always justified to give a positive interpretation to the *Quixote*'s discontinuities, its ruptures of style, and the impurities introduced into the canonical forms of imagination of its time—to see them as necessary elements in an artistic design and achievement rather than as errors, failures, lapses, and weaknesses. I have attempted to show that it is. The *Quixote*'s formal characteristics manifest the profound questioning of the literary imagination that is part of the essence of the Cervantine creation: the sense of reality passes like a gale through the framework of art. The structure trembles and, transformed, resists and sustains a great and conciliating configuration.

In the mimetic dimension, any average realistic narration of the last two centuries is more truthful than the *Quixote*. But for Cervantes's ends, verisimilitude is a perfectly appropriate norm, and even inverisimilitude is incidentally necessary. With respect to the multiple allegorical and symbolic dimensions, few works of any time seem comparable to this novel. Its dismantling of the traditional institutions of literature should ultimately be understood not only as a critical act, although it is that also, and as such I introduced it in Chapter 1, but as part of the highly complex creation of an ambiguous symbol. This symbol consists of the whole work, including its metafictional layers. It is not limited to the figures of Don Quixote, Sancho, and their adventures.

Conclusion. We can conclude that the truth of the *Quixote* is realized in the confluence of the two dimensions of the poetic organism, each one multiple in itself:

1. The mimesis of a variedly stylized world whose foreground is conciliatory, consoling, and even celebratory. It is a world of amiable mediocrities, inoffensive comicality, worthy gentlemen, a natural and just social order, with insertions of winged presences, virtuous beauties, free souls (free, that is, paradoxically, as in the Kantian ethic: totally subjected to absolute ideals), and poetic justice. This foreground almost completely hides a boundless depth, disquieting, pessimistic, and tragic, where the ultimate reality of the body creeps in, with its inevitable corruption of all happy dreams. The naturalism, suggested but absent (subtly manifest only in that piece placed, in a sense, outside the text, "The Man of Ill-Advised Curiosity," which incarnates the rationalistic abstraction of tragedy), is concealed by the enchanting figures of the stylizing, traditional literary imagination. The various romancesque idealizations as well as the negative delineations of the picaresque share a common comic ground. (These positive or negative idealizing styles are what the *Quixote* has of its own time, and they are the elements that bear a date, for Cervantes could not help but include the institutionalized illusions of his cultural medium to offer a consoling image of life to his readers.)

2. A multiple metafictional game that deauthorizes the image of life offered by all literature, including this novel.

A truth that suggests itself is that these two signifying dimensions point to the same experience of undeception, which is exaggerated, simplified, and emblematized in the enterprise and disillusionment of

Don Quixote. But the spiritual movement of the work goes in both directions. It is not merely critical of the illusions, but melancholy and wise in its acknowledgment of their vital necessity and their beneficial effect on imperfect humanity. Hence the essential ambiguity of Don Quixote's peripeteia, the tragicomic character of his end. Hence, when the extrapolation of the literary dream has failed him, he turns to God, while Sancho, who is younger, still wants to continue with the romancesque illusion. This complex, ambivalent, and ironized parable presents a view of the human condition that, in its moral aspect, exposes the alternatives of an ethics of freedom and absolute ideals and one of necessity and pragmatic compromise. On the cognitive side, it shifts between a pessimistic sense of reality and stimulating illusion.[41]

Today we tend to express these dualities in the terms with which the European spirit tries to react against the triumphant naturalism of the nineteenth century, terms well known from the formulations of Schopenhauer, Nietzsche, Ibsen, and others. They give an anachronistic appearance to an interpretation of the *Quixote*. But this is a superficial impression induced by the proximity of the linguistic formation. It should be observed that, after all, Nietzsche chooses mythological wisdom of classical antiquity for the anthropology of his study of tragedy. With respect to Cervantes's times, we do not lack explicit manifestations of the same truths. And furthermore, the connection of Schopenhauer, Gracian's translator, with the Spanish Baroque is well known. In his *Praise of Folly* Erasmus considers the possibility that human happiness depends on a pinch of deception, and that it is natural for the human spirit to incline more toward fiction than toward truth. And "if something can be known, this knowing is not rarely harmful to the joy of living" (XLV.216). Today we can read meditations on this theme in the works of Robert Nozick and other contemporaries.

But I have already insisted enough on these antirelativist arguments.

Epilogue

> . . . Laws eternally
> Preserve the living treasures
> With which the universe has adorned itself.
>   —J. W. Goethe, "Bequest" (1829)

The polysemy that can and should be experienced in the reading of every literary work is not the consequence of the relativities and indeterminacies of the reception, but, on the contrary, an objective, determined function of the work's traditional generic structures. By writing a fictional narration, the author inevitably sets in motion a preestablished apparatus of multiple effects. Some of the significations that his work assumes and particularizes as it progresses may not have figured in his first, deliberate intention, but in general we must presume that he accepts them consciously when they emerge in the course of his creation. In any event, they arise and remain as objective attributes of the work. The ancient, medieval, and Renaissance poetological ideas, as we know, clearly acknowledge that the literary work has a (systematic) multiplicity of meanings.

Cervantes had doctrinal terms at his disposal, topics of discussion common in his time, that reflect the constitutive complexity and multidirectionality of the literary function. Literature is (1) "a perfect imitation" and "a mirror of customs," but at the same time (2) "a model of virtue." The function of the poet is (3) "to delight," to give "pleasure," "contentment," and "honest diversion," and also (4) to provide "teaching" and moral "benefit." Finally, (5) he should "marvel" and "astound" with his invention. The effect of the poetic work thus being multiple, it should not surprise us that a work may show various faces to readers who are not ideal, and even that it may be possible to satisfy each of them separately (as Cervantes's Prologue to the First Part suggests), according to their particular temperament, talents, and degree of cultivation, and each time by virtue of different qualities found in the work.

Because this "feigning" that "entertains" us is an image of life, life's most radical questions can enter the sphere opened up by distraction and contemplative distance. Every literary work must be read simultaneously as an intranscendent game and as a possible revelation of great visions, as vain and insubstantial fiction and a manifestation of wisdom. Since Aristophanes and Plato this polarity has been repeated in the misery and the grandeur of the figure and the self-consciousness of the poet.[1] And it seems to be that precisely what is intranscendent in the pastime, its playful distraction and contemplative freedom, is what makes it possible for the transcendent to enter the mind of the "unoccupied" reader. We see in Cervantes's prologues how this consciousness of being a modest entertainer and at the same time a sovereign and supreme imaginer of the course of life stirs beneath his sinuous personal expression. But we also have seen that his entire work is touched by this ambiguity of values. Distance is a basic element of the vision objectified in the Cervantine work: what you are contemplating, it hints, is no more than literature, invention, dream. Reality is something else. But that something else, the seriousness of life, its abysses and heights, is strongly hinted to the reader. The artistic forms of the *Quixote* correspond to the objectified metaphysical, ethical, and religious concerns of Cervantes, as well as to his complex and problematic feeling about literature, which we perceive in multiple manifestations. These questions agitate and determine the artistic construction, and give a perennial sense to the figures of the pastime.

The "infinite" meaning of the symbol, of the work of art as a symbol, is the horizon of life and the world. The artistic, symbolic image gives us a heightened sense of this horizon, which we ordinarily sustain only in a sort of latent mode, as an atrophied spiritual dimension. That totality without limits, however, does not become thematic, for it is a horizon that surges like an aura around the figures of the fiction and gives them the specific splendor of art. The artistic potency of the images, then, is their capacity to gather around themselves the virtual totality of experience, and thus to give the spectator the illusion of being beyond particularity and suffering (as, with other implications, Schopenhauer teaches). Are the symbolic meanings of *all* works, then, the same actualization of the world's horizon? Yes, in a sense, ultimately. But each one places a singular aspect of this totality

in the foreground, coloring it with its own affective tonality and inject-
ing into it, so to speak, tensions of the will that are also unique.

In saying that a particular meaning of the *Quixote* is the intense
actualization of the *sense of reality*, I have meant that this is one of the
most notable aspects that the semipresence of the real world (that is,
the horizon, the aura of the figures) assumes in the work. The *Quixote*
evokes the world insistently as the opposite of literature, as what
resists the domination of illusions, of stylizations, of the institutionalized and archetypal comforts. This is not to deny that the *Quixote* also thematizes the cognitive and ethical dilemmas of existence. It
presents them principally through allegory but integrates them in this
complex image. An image, then (in a direct as well as in an indirect
sense), of *life*.

Readers and interpreters may sometimes project their own metaphysical and ethical tendencies over that image of the world. But even
such a reception does not cease to be objectively determined by the
work, and the reception will be the more enriching the more it is
openly exposed to the influx of the text and its figurations. Thus we
can gain an experience that is profound and is not limited to repeating
our own. And this is what is meant by a "correct" or "proper" reading
of the text. The infinity of meaning is released only when we exactly
recreate the original symbol. That the signification of the symbol is
unlimited, as are the responses of good readers, is only superficially
contrary to the normative necessity of a single and original composition of meanings.

I have shown some formal projections of the conjecturable themes
of Cervantine thought, which I think can bring these themes into
sharper focus. I have denied that Cervantes's work, in its most essential traits, can be understood deductively from a supposed system of
thought or doctrinal conception of the author's. Furthermore, I suggested that it is a dubious hermeneutic principle to presume, as an
absolute axiom, the spiritual unity and coherence of the person, and
even those of the person objectified in the work. We cannot exclude
the possibility that the vision embodied in a great work may be formally inconsistent, internally contradictory or discontinuous; and
that its unity may lie ultimately in the mere fact that one objectified
consciousness, very broad, comprehensive, and lucid, momentarily
unites such polarities and conflicts. Such a consciousness is also an
objectified meaning (actually, the basic one) of the work, which thus
translates an experience of life and a vision of the world.

Despite the necessary simplifications that expository discourse requires, I have intended to keep in mind the complexity of our object, its problematic entity, and its ontic dependence on the (re)constitutive operations of the reader. But I have assumed from the beginning that we who write on the *Quixote* are referring to the same imaginary entity, which is accessible to all its readers and which in a sense is a stable part of our common intersubjective world. When we examine writings on this book, including those that seem misguided, we recognize a common object and subject matter, and we assume that those readers' experience of the work has been, after all, very similar to ours. This is justified, since there we find multiple references to a novelistic world that is also the one revealed through our reading, and we also can verify that the readers' reactions, however different from ours, have been motivated by the same fictional figures and circumstances. As with the perception of any object, real or imaginary, obviously there are those who look more attentively and persistently and those who impatiently project inappropriate expectations. Besides, in a thing as complex as this novel, the reader has preferences for certain incidents and passages and fails to be equally interested by others, remembers this well and forgets that. We may conclude that no matter how widely two competent readers may diverge in their experience of the work, these differences do not justify us in abandoning a belief in the objectivity of this imaginary object. The text can be reread, examined, and discussed. And given much time and goodwill, it should be possible to reach agreement by confronting irrefutable evidence.

Certainly, however, the ideal of a common, unhurried reading, undisturbed by a desire to stick to a stated opinion or by partisan passions, is rarely achieved. To these difficulties must be added the personal limits of our intelligence and sensitivity. From our own experience of rereadings we know that a text can be read well or badly, and that sometimes we go wrong by reading superficially and inattentively, by being emotionally out of tune, by following the wrong rhythm and tempo. And we also know when we are right in our reading, for on such occasions we are confirmed and reassured by the fact that we sense the necessity of the work's elements and order, and the object assumes the splendor of signification, if not always of beauty or grace. This aura is given only to an exact, deep carrying out of the artist's design. In what may seem a parody of *Anna Karenina*'s opening sentence, we can say that there is only one felicitous way to take in a given work of art (or better, one fruitful path of reading, of various degrees of intensity and extent) and countless wrong and unfortunate ways.

Although this supposition in fact guides the critical labor of the majority of scholars, it does not represent the ideas most explicitly held today. The thesis of the radical subjectivity of the literary experience has many partisans; that of its historical, social, and sexual relativity has still more. The present intellectual climate, with its confusedly antiauthoritarian and antirational preferences, favors these relativisms. That may help to explain the success of relativist philosophies of science and knowledge, such as those of Thomas Kuhn and Richard Rorty. In the influential field of English criticism, such authors as Frank Kermode and Stanley Fish have done a great deal to spread the belief (which, as we have seen, is ambiguous) that the meaning of the great works is constantly evolving, that it depends on the hermeneutic will of the "interpretive communities" (as Fish says, following Kuhn's idea of the scientific paradigm) and changes substantially over time, without ceasing to live forcefully.[2]

As I have suggested, these relativistic arguments do not clearly distinguish between the reading of a work and a critical examination of it.[3] It is obvious, for example, that my descriptions and interpretations of the *Quixote* are relative to certain intellectual interests and conditions of our time; they could not have been produced in this form centuries earlier. Besides, they deal with only certain aspects of the work, which attract particular attention today. But the reading on which they are based, and to which they reflexively lead back, has always been possible. Moreover, if my theses are valid, that reading is the original reading, that of an educated contemporary of Cervantes. At the same time it is the best reading, forever prescribed by the text and its pertinent circumstances.

Though it seems boastful, this is a modest claim. For my theses concern aspects of the reading of the *Quixote* that, although essential, are secondary. As for most of the reading of this novel, my study presumes its conformity with the diffuse traditional consensus that underlies almost all critical disputes and interpretive differences. And indeed, it would be an inauspicious sign if one claimed to offer a radically new basic reading of a work that has been read and discussed so often by so many for so long.

Descriptive and interpretive theses are true or false (and central or marginal) statements, verifiable by the objective measure of the felicitous reading. And, as suggested above, the regulative ideal of literary life is that the text permits only one aesthetically successful way of reading it, the one that gathers up all its elements into a unified, coherent experience of multiple signification. It goes without saying that critics may be satisfied with too little pleasure and substance in their reading, and thus obtain a weaker novelistic image of the world, thereby reducing their sense of its extent and signification. They can also fail in their methodical reflection (like any scholar of any subject) out of conceptual vagueness, inconsistency, and the like. None of this calls into question the objectivity of the literary experience. It is not surprising that critical ideas vary so widely. Given the difficulty of the task, the surprising thing would be unanimity.

The relativist propensities of our time have led to the thesis that Cervantes's work has a similarly relativistic design. I have already commented that a relativistic perspectivism (rather than the objectivist one it indeed displays) has been attributed to it. What Cervantes in fact suggests in passages such as those of the basin-helmet (relativistic interpretation's favorite example) is that unless the interpreter is a fool or mad or confused, the objective characteristics of the basin do not permit it to be interpreted as a helmet. When Don Quixote takes possession of "Mambrino's helmet" (I.21), he says: "Doubtless the pagan whose measure was first taken for this famous morion must have had a huge head; and the worst of it is that half of it is missing." The knight errant immediately decides that he will have the unrecognizable helmet fixed "in the first place where I can find a blacksmith."

Thus even Don Quixote sees (though he then manages to forget) that if he is to go on interpreting and using the basin as a helmet, it will have to be reshaped. The functional nature of the parts of such a simple implement as a basin is fixed and precise, and it excludes other satisfactory uses. Is the functional interdetermination of the parts of a sentence not much more precise and delicate? And what can be said about the whole of an extensive text, created with a particular design? Will such an immense machine, constructed of very finely specified parts, admit a multitude of independent and diverse aesthetic uses as a work of literary art?

The school of thought I criticize, in postulating that literary works are undetermined texts open to a multiplicity of structurally diverse and equally valid readings, inadvertently holds that the poetic creation is less well organized than the simplest artifacts; that its elements are not reciprocally functional; that they have no necessary arrangement; and consequently that any of them can be eliminated without any effect on the signification and value of the whole. It is clear that these principles can shape an artistic *program* (whether such a program would be consistent and practicable need not concern us here). But as a project for the reception of works of the traditional literary enterprise they are nonsense. These absurdities derive from a confusion between the subdetermination or indetermination of the amorphous and the superdetermination of the plurivalent. The ambiguities of great works are "intentional"; they constitute a *design,* not the product of indetermination. They are *unequivocal* ambiguities—so much so that not to perceive them is to misunderstand the sense of the corresponding part of the text. The sense (single, multidimensional, and superdetermined) of the classical work is realized when we recover, in the correct reading, the image of life that it offers us, and with it the prospect of the unlimited series of possible appraisals and interpretations (secondary, reflexive, critical, doctrinal, idiosyncratic, historical) of represented life. It is on this plane that the endless game of discrepancies and variations functionally begins—not on the plane of the representation itself, which is unequivocal, and which is the work. Certainly time's erosion of life forms and of historical memory may make the text's meanings fade and finally disappear, and the laws that preserve them may move beyond our grasp; but then we do not have a different historical version of the same work but no work at all.[4]

What consequences derive from my study for the *reading* of the *Quixote*? They concern mainly the manner in which the reader ought to construct an *ironized* novelistic world, a world ironized through the recurrent self-reflection of the narrative, in which the mimetic transparency is suspended by the game of metapoetic opacities.

The image of the world given by a narration (as by ordinary perception and experience) is always incomplete; it selects certain aspects and rejects countless others. A virtual background has to be furnished by the reader to complete the fictional world.[5] Among the most important implications of Aristotelian poetics, we find that the intellection of the fictitious event, and consequently the filling of the gaps of its textual representation, must be guided by the idea of natural causality (though this principle must be combined with the supernatural aspects of traditional myths and with the stock types of dramatic convention). The idea of natural causality is the basic norm of verisimilar and realistic imagining.

It is also basic in the *Quixote*. But it is important to understand that, as we have seen, Cervantes repeatedly suspends the causal continuities in an ironic and metapoetic game. And at those moments it is *inappropriate* to force the construction of the image toward a psychological verisimilitude, or even toward any serious continuity on the plane of what is represented. The usurpations of the voice, the abrupt alternation of opposing archetypes within the same character, the metamorphoses of the principle of stylization (the transitions of imaginary region), the purely associative continuities of the shared culture's symbolic field—all of these forms oblige us to construct an image that at such points is remote from verisimilar possibilities.

Consequently, it is not always possible to interpret the (inconsistent and reversible) evolution of Sancho's figure, for example, as if it were seriously a psychological and physical development of Sancho's fictitious *personality*. For that would imply supernatural, miraculous transformations on the objective mimetic plane, which all evidence indicates are not in the game of this novel, nor would they match its general ironic and humorous tone. On the abstract symbolic plane of metafigural reflection, on the other hand, we can ironically play with continuities that differ in nature from verisimilar transformations. In Sancho's case, such conceptual continuities relate to the qualities of simplicity, humility, and sensible candor, associated with goodness, and finally, justice and wisdom. We also have seen similar symbolic sequences in the figure of Don Quixote.

Our imagination has to round off the character, to give it its inexplicit depth, but in these cases it cannot do so with consistent verisimilitude. Other dimensions of the literary figure must be incorporated into these characters. The Curate also comes across as having some psychologically inconsistent features. (He is simply inconsistent, not consistently inconsistent, because this latter kind of inconsistency, as Aristotle indicates, is a form of verisimilitude.) If we force the data of the text toward a verisimilar and transparently mimetic construction, to the exclusion of other planes, this person becomes perversely enigmatic. On the other hand, if we accept that the unity of his various interventions is a sort of collage, his occasional cruelties and insensitivities do not detract from the radical bonhomie and the uprightness of his more habitual and characteristic attitudes. His being a good man is as "authentic" and "sincere" as his being, incongruously, a bit of an insensitive prankster.

Howard Mancing, like E. C. Riley, upon whose interpretation I commented earlier, overextends the verisimilar construction of the *Quixote*. He does so when he diagnoses the Curate's personality as perverse, and again when he deals with Don Quixote's second arrival at the (second) inn, upon his return from his penitence in the Sierra Morena. Observing the seemingly unjustified fact that, having arrived at the inn, Don Quixote immediately goes to sleep, broken and exhausted, since nothing has occurred in the preceding days to explain this prostration, Mancing attempts to find an explanation within the purely mimetic and verisimilar realm: "Perhaps, however, there has been a cumulative effect produced by his several physical misfortunes, and perhaps his spiritual and intellectual humiliations and sufferings have also taken their toll."[6] Such hypothetical constructions are out of place here, for this work does not always follow a design of consistent verisimilitude, and this is one of the passages governed by a different law. What occurs at this juncture is that Don Quixote has to disappear temporarily or pale as a character for metapoetic reasons, for if he were present, active, and in his habitual role, he would be an unmanageable obstacle to the conclusion of the stories that belong to other regions of the imagination, and that now converge at the inn. This marginalization of Don Quixote is neither a psychological nor an intranarrative necessity, but an artistic, reflexive, ironic requirement.

Of course these mimetic inconsistencies are the sort of thing that critics object to in unsuccessful and inferior works. And censure is wholly justified when the books in question are works of serious realism, for then such infractions of natural determinism go against the artistic purpose. But the *Quixote*'s design, as I have shown repeatedly, is constitutively discontinuous and ironic, and gradual or abrupt transitions of the configurative modality are part of the game it offers us. Among these transitions is the passage from the normal thematization of the represented facts to the metapoetic thematization of the representative medium and its forms. The reduction and neutralization of Don Quixote at the inn are not part of the logic of the represented facts but an expression of the forces of style and composition converging there. They constitute one of the forms of the thematization of literature in this novel.

I believe that this critical perspective, which thematizes metamimetic phenomena, ought to be added to the growing descriptive and even interpretive consensus of contemporary Cervantes scholarship, which owes a great deal to both Riley and Mancing.[7]

Notes

Prologue

1. Northrop Frye, *Anatomy of Criticism* (Princeton, 1957), p. 72.

2. Américo Castro, "Prólogo" to Cervantes, *El ingenioso hidalgo don Quijote de la Mancha* (Mexico City, 1963).

3. See José Ortega y Gasset, *The Dehumanization of Art and Notes on the Novel*, trans. Helene Weyl (Princeton, 1948).

4. Miguel de Unamuno, *Our Lord Don Quixote: The Life of Don Quixote and Sancho, with Sixteen Essays*, trans. Anthony Kerrigan (Princeton, 1967).

5. Jorge Luis Borges, "Pierre Menard, Author of *Don Quixote*," trans. Anthony Bonner, in Borges, *Ficciones*, ed. Anthony Kerrigan (New York, 1963). It should be noted that the idea of the stable self-identity of literary works does not exclude the possibility of works that are basically ambiguous with respect to the meaning of their symbols, and even with respect to the nature of their figures and actions. Such works are *unequivocally* ambiguous, and a reader who missed the ambiguity would miss the meaning.

6. Although the fragility of relativist theories such as Michel Foucault's and Hans-Georg Gadamer's has been shown in various studies, they are still very influential. The idea of a radical discontinuity of history can be said to culminate in Foucault's willfully catachrestic dictum that "man is a recent invention," not earlier than the nineteenth century: *The Order of Things* (New York, 1973), final paragraphs. Arguing from neo-historicist suppositions, Gadamer maintains that it is not possible, for essential reasons, to recover the original meaning of texts from another era, and that understanding is always understanding differently. This thesis pervades his *Wahrheit und Methode,* published in English as *Truth and Method*, trans. G. Barden and J. Cumming (New York, 1975). The attentive reader finds insurmountable contradictions in this book. On the one hand, Gadamer insists on the existence of a valid "truth," a proper meaning, a genuine sense in texts of the past; and he considers it imperative to strive to grasp that meaning. Those works "speak to us." On the other hand, he postulates radical

historical limitations to our understanding, because we cannot escape the prejudices of our time. He thus presents the most problematic and incompatible commonplaces about the hermeneutic experience as if they were the answer to the questions that they themselves raise. For some lucid criticisms of Gadamer's views, see E. D. Hirsch, *Validity in Interpretation* (New Haven, 1967), especially pp. 245–64; Dieter Freundlieb, *Zur Wissenschaftstheorie der Literaturwissenschaft* (Munich, 1978); and Charles Larmore, "Tradition, Objectivity, and Hermeneutics," in *Hermeneutics and Modern Philosophy,* ed. R. Wachterhauser (Albany, N.Y., 1986), pp. 147–67. Regarding Foucault's relativistic inconsistencies, see Jacques Derrida, "Cogito and the History of Madness," in his *Writing and Difference,* trans. Alan Bass (Chicago, 1978), pp. 31–63; and Jürgen Habermas, *Der philosophische Diskurs der Moderne* (Frankfurt/Main, 1985), chaps. 9 and 10. In the United States these relativist positions have become popular in recent years. Stanley Fish presents them with conviction and wit in *Is There a Text in This Class?* (Cambridge, Mass., 1980). With respect to the principles of interpretation, broadly speaking, I find myself close to the positions taken by E. D. Hirsch in his book just mentioned and by P. D. Juhl in his *Interpretation: An Essay in the Philosophy of Literary Criticism* (Princeton, 1980), although many points of contention would have to be discussed, if the occasion allowed, for a full examination of such a complex matter. At appropriate places throughout this book, however, methodological reflections will suggest my hermeneutic outlook.

In a study undertaken according to a method inspired in part by Wolfgang Iser's reception theory, Theo In der Smitten examines the variations found in German translations of the *Quixote,* and relates the "readings" embedded in them to the ideological and stylistic-doctrinal horizons of the various periods when they were written. Nevertheless, he expressly presumes an ideal reading, the one corresponding to the "implied reader." I will add in passing that Smitten's study is based on what he considers an "unprejudiced" attention to the entire text, including all the graphic aspects of the first editions, and including Avellaneda's *Quixote* as an integral part of the work, set between Cervantes's Parts One and Two. The study's radical methodology brings together phenomenological and historical presuppositions with a concept of textuality that goes beyond its traditional limits. It also goes beyond the codes that govern literary production and reception in Cervantes's time, and that in general still govern them today. See Theo In der Smitten, *Don Quixote (der "richtige" und der "falsche") und sieben deutsche Leser* (Bern, 1986).

7. This subject continues to interest critics. Both positions can be found in two studies by distinguished Cervantists, published in 1985 and 1986. Jean Canavaggio refers to the *Quixote* unequivocally as "the first modern novel," although he indicates that its "realism" is not identical to that of the nineteenth century: *Cervantès* (Paris, 1986), pp. 10, 231, 343. P. E. Russell disagrees with this common opinion, because it seems to him that the parodic and, in general, comic modality of the *Quixote* is not the norm of the modern novel: *Cervantes* (Oxford, 1985), p. 106.

Doubtless one can say, as José Antonio Maravall does, that the *Quixote* is "the first great novel of the modern world" (though that is certainly not to declare it the first modern realistic novel): *Utopía y contrautopía en el "Quijote"* (Santiago de Compostela, 1976), p. 11. Maravall adds (p. 18) that Cervantes's work "in large measure anticipates the literary form of the modern novel." That also seems to me, with the necessary qualifications, to be (roughly) true. John J. Allen deals with aspects of this topic in *"Don Quixote* and the Origins of the Novel," in *Cervantes and the Renaissance,* ed. Michael D. McGaha (Easton, Pa., 1980), pp. 125–40.

8. See my "Hermeneutic Criticism and the Description of Form," in *Interpretation of Narrative,* ed. Mario J. Valdés and Owen J. Miller (Toronto, 1978), pp. 78–99; "El sistema del discurso y la evolución de las formas narrativas," *Dispositio* 5–6 (1980–1981): 1–18; "Towards a Formal Ontology of Fictional Worlds," *Philosophy and Literature* 7 (1983): 182–95; "The Stability of Literary Meaning," in *Identity of the Literary Text,* ed. Mario J. Valdés and Owen J. Miller (Toronto, 1985), pp. 231–45; "Forms of Mimesis and Ideological Rhetoric in Cervantes's *La gitanilla,"* in *Textual Analysis: Some Readers Reading,* ed. Mary Ann Caws (New York, 1986), pp. 64–73; and "El *Quijote* y el debate hermenéutico," in *Actas del Segundo Congreso de la Asociación Internacional Siglo de Oro* (forthcoming).

Introduction: Questions and Points of Confusion

1. The following paragraphs contain some well-known generalities of Cervantes scholarship, whose repetition seems to me nevertheless pertinent. Readers interested in examining some of the traditional themes will find the titles of references, well organized by subject, in the chapter on Cervantes in J. L. Alborg, *Historia de la literatura española,* vol. 2 (Madrid, 1970); in José Simón Díaz, *Bibliografía de la literatura hispánica,* vol. 8 (Madrid, 1970); in J. B. Avalle-Arce and E. C. Riley, eds., *Suma cervantina* (London, 1973); in the bibliography of Luis Andrés Murillo's edition of the *Quijote,* vol. 3 (Madrid, 1978); also in *Cervantes, a Bibliography: Books, Essays, Articles and Other Studies on the Life of Cervantes, His Works, and His Imitators* (vol. 1, New York, 1946; vol. 2, Minneapolis, 1962), by Raymond L. Grismer; in *"Don Quixote" (1894–1970): A Selective, Annotated Bibliography,* 4 vols. (1, Chapel Hill, 1974; 2, Miami, 1978; 3, New York, 1980; 4, Lincoln, Nebr., 1984), by Dana B. Drake; in *An Analytical and Bibliographical Guide to Criticism on "Don Quijote" (1790–1893),* by Dana B. Drake and Dominick L. Finello (Newark, Del., 1987); in *Approaches to Teaching Cervantes' "Don Quixote,"* ed. Richard Bjornson (New York, 1984); in E. C. Riley's *"Don Quixote"* (London, 1986); and in Teresa Malo de Molina y Martín-Montalvo's "Aproximación a la bibliografía básica cervantina," *Anthropos,* suppl. 17 (Barcelona, 1989), pp. 275–83. The *Anales Cervantinos* (Madrid, 1951–), the annual MLA bibliography, and the journal *Cervantes* (Bulletin of the Cervantes Society of America, 1981–) supplement these guides.

2. In asking this question, I am thinking primarily not of a unique, outstand-

ing critical work but rather of a consensus that can be derived from multiple and scattered efforts. Certainly, the case of a unique study that assumes dominant status is not rare; Dámaso Alonso's work on Góngora is such a study. His interpretations of the *Soledades* or of the *Polifemo* are of course not beyond dispute, but they have conveyed truths so fundamental and of such scope that they must be acknowledged as the cornerstone of all later investigation. The position of Amado Alonso's work on the poetry of *Residencia en la tierra* is similar. Justified corrections and new points of view have enriched the exegesis, but *Poesía y estilo de Pablo Neruda* (Buenos Aires, 1940) has become established as the indispensable book for the critical reader of the *Residencias*. There has never been an interpretation of the *Quixote* which could claim such a prerogative. It goes without saying that these pages do not claim to fill that void. Rather, they may point to some of its causes.

If I am told that to ask for a basic consensus on a subject of such complexity as the *Quixote* is to yield to illusions about the potential of literary studies, and even implies an authoritarian restriction of free hermeneutic florescence, I can only respond that the ideal of a shared objectivity is inherent in all critical effort, even in the most ordinary speech, and that those who formulate a subjectivist skepticism contradict themselves in the act.

3. In regard to editorial matters one must mention Robert M. Flores's work on the textual effect of the practices of the publishers of the *Quixote*'s first editions. See *The Compositors of the First and Second Madrid Editions of "Don Quixote,"* Part I (London, 1975), and "The Compositors of the First Edition of *Don Quixote*, Part II," *Journal of Hispanic Philology* 6 (1981): 3–44; also Flores's recent edition, *"Don Quixote de la Mancha": An Old-Spelling Control Edition Based on the First Editions of Parts I and II* (Vancouver, 1988). See also Daniel Eisenberg, "On Editing *Don Quixote*," *Cervantes* 3 (1983): 3–34. Editions of the *Quixote* by Celina Sabor de Cortazar and Isaías Lerner (Buenos Aires, 1969), Luis Andrés Murillo (Madrid, 1978), and Vicente Gaos (Madrid, 1987) deserve special mention. Together with those by Martín de Riquer (Barcelona, 1962), Alberto Sánchez (Barcelona, 1976), and John J. Allen (Madrid, 1989), these editions have been widely used in the academic community.

4. Helmut Hatzfeld, *El "Quijote" como obra de arte del lenguaje* (Madrid, 1949); Leo Spitzer, "Linguistic Perspectivism in the *Don Quijote*," in *Linguistics and Literary History* (Princeton, 1948), pp. 41–85; Enrique Moreno Báez, *Reflexiones sobre el "Quijote"* (Madrid, 1968); Dámaso Alonso, "Sintagmas no progresivos y pluralidades: Tres calillas en la prosa castellana," in Dámaso Alonso and Carlos Bousoño, *Seis calas en la expresión literaria española*, 4th ed. (Madrid, 1970), pp. 23–41; Angel Rosenblat, *La lengua del "Quijote"* (Madrid, 1971) and "La lengua de Cervantes," in Avalle-Arce and Riley, *Suma Cervantina*, pp. 323–55; Howard Mancing, *The Chivalric World of "Don Quixote": Style, Structure, and Narrative Technique* (Columbia, Mo., 1982). On the theme of language in Cervantes's work, see Elias Rivers, "Cervantes and the Question of Language," in *Cervantes and the Renaissance*, ed. Michael D. McGaha (Easton, Pa., 1980), pp. 23–33.

5. Enrique Moreno Báez, "Arquitectura del *Quijote*," *Revista de Filología Española* 32 (1948): 269–85; Knud Togeby, *La composition du roman "Don Quijote"* (Copenhagen, 1957); Edmund de Chasca, "Algunos aspectos del ritmo y del movimiento narrativo del *Quijote*," *Revista de Filología Española* 47 (1964): 287–307; Joaquín Casalduero, *Sentido y forma del "Quijote"* (Madrid, 1970); Edward Dudley, "Don Quijote as Magus: The Rhetoric of Interpolation," *Bulletin of Hispanic Studies* 49 (1972): 355–68; J. B. Avalle-Arce and E. C. Riley, "Don Quijote," in *Suma Cervantina*, pp. 47–79; Cesare Segre, "Costruzioni rettilinee e costruzioni a spirale nel *Don Chisciotte*," in *Le strutture e il tempo* (Turin, 1974), pp. 183–219; John J. Allen, *Don Quixote: Hero or Fool?*, 2 vols. (Gainesville, Fla., 1969, 1979); Mancing, *Chivalric World of "Don Quixote."* Also worth consulting on this matter are Alexander Parker, "Fielding and the Structure of *Don Quixote*," *Bulletin of Hispanic Studies* 33 (1956): 1–16; Raymond Immerwahr, "Structural Symmetry in the Episodic Narratives of *Don Quijote*, Part One," *Comparative Literature* 10 (1958): 121–35; Colbert I. Nepaulsingh, "Cervantes, *Don Quijote*: The Unity of the Action," *Revista Canadiense de Estudios Hispánicos* 2 (1978): 239–57; and Celina Sabor de Cortazar, "Para una relectura del *Quijote*: El género. La composición. La estructura. Los protagonistas," in *Para una relectura de los clásicos españoles* (Buenos Aires, 1987), pp. 25–60.

6. Casalduero's *Sentido y forma del "Quijote"* (first published in 1949) is a thorough commentary on the text in its totality, and as such constitutes a standard of reading that in my opinion should be attentively considered by scholars, though it should not be unconditionally accepted as basic truth about this novel. With respect to the question of consensus to which I have alluded, it is revealing that Casalduero mentions no other study on the *Quixote*, only common views "of the nineteenth century," "of Romanticism," and the like. Casalduero's interpretation is directed principally toward a symbolic translation of the elements of the work's world in terms of the historical consciousness of the era—designated as "the Baroque." He portrays Cervantes's work as a rejection of the Gothic and Renaissance literary past and an introduction to the modern world (the 1605 *Quixote*) and as a foundation of the Baroque vision of the historic present (the 1615 *Quixote*). These historico-cultural perspectives frequently lead to labored symbolic exegesis that wanders far from the immediate sense of the text. At times the eminent critic reads the *Quixote* as a kind of allegory of part of the history of Western culture. Casalduero's exegesis, however, is not like Unamuno's *Vida de don Quijote y Sancho*, which, if read as an interpretation of Cervantes's *Quixote*, turns out to be absurd and greatly diminishes the significance of the masterwork. (It follows that this is not the best reading of Unamuno's book.) See Miguel de Unamuno, *Our Lord Don Quixote: The Life of Don Quixote and Sancho, with Sixteen Essays*, trans. Anthony Kerrigan (Princeton, 1967). But the fact that one cannot reject Casalduero's most remote symbolic connections by well-grounded argument demonstrates the lack of hermeneutic principles by which literary studies could be validated. For these reasons, a work such as R. L. Predmore's *The World of Don Quixote* (Cambridge, Mass., 1967), which describes the imaginary

objectivities that the work fundamentally projects in a way that is both sensitive and exact, is an essential step.

In these remarks I am referring to the state of the discipline rather than to individual achievements. Also, I do not mean to suggest that an acute awareness of the methodological problem is lacking. See, for example, the circumspection with which Antonio Vilanova proceeds to elucidate Erasmist elements in the text of the *Quixote,* in his "Erasmo, Sancho Panza y su amigo don Quijote," *Cervantes,* special issue, Winter 1988, pp. 43–92, and in his *Erasmo y Cervantes* (Barcelona, 1989).

7. Ludwig Pfandl, *Geschichte der spanischen Nationalliteratur in ihrer Blütezeit* (Freiburg, 1929); Jean Cassou, *Cervantès* (Paris, 1936); Stephen Gilman, *Cervantes y Avellaneda: Estudio de una imitación* (Mexico City, 1951).

8. See José Camón Aznar, "*Don Quijote* en la teoría de los estilos," *Revista de Filología Española* 32 (1948): 429–65. Arnold Hauser also places Cervantes fully in the Mannerist movement, whose second phase coincides, he says, with the first stages of the Counterreformation: *Sozialgeschichte der Kunst und Literatur* (Munich, 1953), chap. 5; *Der Ursprung der modernen Kunst und Literatur* (Munich, 1973).

9. Emilio Orozco, "Características generales del siglo XVII," in *Historia de la literatura española,* ed. J. M. Díez Borque (Madrid, 1975), vol. 2, pp. 15–125, considers the first part of the *Quixote* to be Mannerist, the second Baroque. Harri Meier, "Zur Entwicklung der europäischen *Quijote*-Deutung," *Romanische Forschungen* 54 (1940): 227–64, summarized the positions, stating that the point of contention is whether "the *Quixote* should be ascribed to the Middle Ages or to the Renaissance (Castro), to the Reformation (see Unamuno, Ortega), or to the Counterreformation (Lollis, Toffanin, Hatzfeld), to Classicism (Hazard), to the Baroque or Antibaroque (Pfandl)." My purpose is neither to discredit the efforts toward periodization nor to pass judgment here on the dilemmas they entail. It seems to me that it is necessary to refine the description of the individual works, not only to comprehend them better but also to develop the conceptualization of periods. I believe that this is also the thrust of Rosenblat's observations on this matter: *Lengua del "Quijote,"* pp. 351–52.

10. Cesare de Lollis, *Cervantes reazionario e altri scritti d'ispanistica* (Florence, 1947); Paul Descouzis, *Cervantes, a nueva luz,* vol. 1, *El "Quijote" y el Concilio de Trento* (Frankfurt/Main, 1966) and vol. 2, *Con la Iglesia hemos dado, Sancho* (Madrid, 1973).

11. Unamuno, *Our Lord Don Quixote.* Heine's characterization appears in the introduction that he wrote for an anonymous German translation of the *Quixote:* Cervantes, *Der sinnreiche Junker Don Quixote von La Mancha* (Stuttgart, 1837). See Heinrich Heine, *Sämtliche Schriften,* ed. Klaus Briegleb (Munich, 1978), vol. 4, pp. 151–70.

12. On the issue of the irreconcilable interpretations, see Harri Meier's study (n. 9) as well as Anthony Close, *The Romantic Approach to "Don Quixote"* (Cambridge, 1977). Since Oscar Mandel's proposal of picturesque and William Jamesian terminology in "The Function of the Norm in Don Quixote," *Modern*

Philology 55 (1958): 154–63, the tendency is to classify interpretations of the work in two groups: the "hard" interpretations (typically those of the Baroque and the Rationalist-Neoclassical periods) that consider the *Quixote* to be a funny and satirical book, and the "soft" interpretations, of which the Romantic heroizations of Don Quixote (which reached their epitome in Unamuno's *Our Lord Don Quixote*) are paradigmatic. Among the "hard" ones, Erich Auerbach's figures prominently: "The Enchanted Dulcinea," in *Mimesis: The Representation of Reality in Western Literature,* trans. Willard R. Trask (Princeton, 1968), chap. 14; so does that of P. E. Russell: "*Don Quixote* as a Funny Book," *Modern Language Review* 64 (1969): 312–26, and his *Cervantes* (Oxford, 1985). Daniel Eisenberg, "Teaching *Don Quixote* as a Funny Book," in Bjornson, *Approaches to Teaching Cervantes' "Don Quixote,"* pp. 62–68, also belongs in this group, although in his recent *Study of "Don Quixote"* (Newark, Del., 1987) he seems to be moving beyond this alternative. Anthony Close not only characterizes this polarity in *Romantic Approach* but also takes sides (against the Romantic position). In relation to these disputes, Javier Herrero's study of the figure of Dulcinea in "Dulcinea and her Critics," *Cervantes* 2 (1982): 23–42, should be consulted. James A. Parr's "*Don Quixote*": An Anatomy of Subversive Discourse (Newark, Del., 1988) can be seen as a culmination of the hard approach.

In this book I am trying basically to describe the novel's form rather than to interpret the work. Yet some of the aspects highlighted by my examination make evident, I think, that the alternatives of satiric comicality and heroic sublimity not only cannot but should not be resolved one way or the other, if the work is to offer all its potential play of signification. On this point my views coincide with those expressed in the criticism of John J. Allen (n. 5), which clearly shows that this and other hermeneutic dilemmas can be overcome by a detailed description of the work. I will return to this issue later. See also A. G. Lo Ré, "The Three Deaths of Don Quixote: Comments in Favor of the Romantic Critical Approach," *Cervantes* 9 (1989): 21–24. Though he disagrees with Allen on specific points, Lo Ré does not question the double meaning of the figure and story of Don Quixote or the pattern of inversion of emphasis in the course of the novel (from the predominance of ridicule to that of the sympathetic or admirable).

13. The endeavor to appropriate the classics is universal, and today many examples of it can be observed. The ethnocentric or the political will is not the only source of narrow, preposterous, or partially illuminating and partially distorting interpretations. The German Romantic critics, to give an eminent example, used their version of Cervantes, as well as those of other authors of the Romantic canon that they created, to illustrate and lend authority to their own programmatic intentions—in many ways, naturally, different from the sense of the works of those "precursors"—yet they nevertheless illuminated aspects of the Cervantine work (as of others) that had escaped critical understanding until then. Readers of Nietzsche have learned that interpretation is an act of "the will to power," although this does not exclude the possibility of objectivity. Presumably the degree of objectivity and the nature of the aspects emphasized in the description of the work depend in good measure on the nature of the critical will. I

suppose that the intention, somewhat ascetic and unworldly, of favoring the growth of inner life is one of the motivations most akin to the traditional and fundamental impulse of literature, and therefore is among those most capable of objectivity with respect to its being and potentialities. That intention, I think, is what most forcefully governs the present study. Expanding and refining the experience of felicitous reading, by means of conceptualizing and descriptive reflection, is the principal aim of my undertaking.

But there is another side to the epistemology of interpretation (which, although not absent from Nietzsche's pages, is not one of his favorite or characteristic themes): logic and method, which have very much to do with the objectivity and validity of interpretive theses. Whatever the appropriative impulse may be, it can be either hasty and blind or lucid. Decisive here are the clarity of purpose, the formal consistency of the assertions, the breadth and accuracy of the descriptive base, the definition and stability of the terminology, the reflection on the more general assumptions and their occasional specification, and finally, the abundance and representativeness of textual confirmations for the hypotheses.

Obviously, the richness and depth of the primary reading (which indirectly may be helped, of course, by methodical efforts and which is subjected to the restricting or liberating influence of the assimilating will that motivates it) formally precedes all systematic cognitive enterprise, and is the basis of all objectivity. This point was well emphasized some time ago by Dámaso Alonso, *Poesía española* (Madrid, 1950), pp. 37–45, and by Alfonso Reyes, "Aristarco o Anatomía de la crítica," in *La experiencia literaria* (Buenos Aires, 1952), pp. 83–93.

14. Helena Percas de Ponseti's initial considerations in *Cervantes y su concepto del arte,* 2 vols. (Madrid, 1975), where she reviews the state of Cervantes studies, are similar to mine. It can be said that we have a consensus with respect to the fact that there is no consensus on any of the principal themes.

15. Américo Castro, *El pensamiento de Cervantes* (Barcelona, 1972, first published 1925), p. 30; Giuseppe Toffanin, *La fine dell' Umanesimo* (Turin, 1920, chaps. 13, 14, and especially 15 ("Il Cervantes"); Angel Sánchez Rivero, "Contestación," *Revista de Occidente* 17 (1927): 291–315.

16. See Garci Rodríguez de Montalvo, *Amadís de Gaula,* ed. E. B. Place (Madrid, 1959), vol. 1. Also Mateo Alemán, "Declaración para el entendimiento de este libro," in his *Guzmán de Alfarache* (1599). I have used Samuel Gili Gaya's edition for Clásicos Castellanos (Madrid, 1972 [1926]).

Proper names are an important detail in Aristotelian poetology, attentive as it is to the interweaving of fiction and reality, precisely because of the radical nature of its distinction between "imitation" and "history." The issue of historical names, not uncommon in classicist poetics, is already found in Aristotle, in reference to myths and traditional legends; in Lodovico Castelvetro's commentary to Aristotle's *Poetics;* and in Pinciano's *Philosophía antigua poética* (see n. 17), among other places.

17. For the work of Alonso López, el Pinciano, see the edition of Alfredo Carballo Picazo, 3 vols. (Madrid, 1973). The book was originally published in 1596. Many expressions of the elemental distinction between history and fiction

are found in the extensive review of criticism and literary theory of the Italian Renaissance offered by Bernard Weinberg in *A History of Literary Criticism in the Italian Renaissance,* 2 vols. (Chicago, 1961). It would be superfluous even to mention the endurance of these fundamental concepts if extravagant historical relativism were not one of the intellectual whims of our time.

18. The matter becomes only marginally complicated if we take into account Bruce Wardropper's propositions in his article (indispensable, in any case, for the consideration of this theme) "*Don Quixote:* Story or History," *Modern Philology* 63 (1965): 1–11. Wardropper notes the fictionalizing degeneration of the historiography of the period, and he suggests that Cervantes made use of this generic confusion in the *Quixote* to enhance effects of illusion of reality. My reading of the book fails to corroborate this last point, but obviously such a design would be possible only on the basis of the radical distinction between history and novel.

19. Northrop Frye has made limited use of these distinctions in "Historical Criticism: Theory of Modes," in his *Anatomy of Criticism* (Princeton, 1957). So have the Neo-Aristotelian critics from Chicago (see Ronald Crane, ed., *Critics and Criticism* [Chicago, 1952]) and Robert Scholes, in his *Structuralism in Literature: An Introduction* (New Haven, 1974). Additional references and significant observations on this subject can be found in the Introduction to Robert C. Spires, *Beyond the Metafictional Mode: Directions in the Modern Spanish Novel* (Lexington, Ky., 1984).

20. Unless otherwise indicated, the English for all quotations from *Don Quixote* is based on Walter Starkie's translation for Signet (New York, 1964), with revision for literalness when the point requires it.

21. I cite the edition and translation of G. M. A. Grube (Indianapolis, 1958).

22. There are other interesting aspects to the poetological disputes about history and poetry in Cervantes's day; for example, problems regarding what we would now call the fictionalization of historical figures and facts—that is, their use as part of the poetic fable, especially in respect to historical facts well known by the public. As I remarked earlier, Aristotle already considered this matter when he referred to poets' use of traditional myths. The public's knowledge and expectations impose limits on the plausible transformations of the myths. The Renaissance epic renews this preoccupation, which is central to the poetic work and criticism of Tasso. Here the "particular truth of History" is indeed pertinent to poetry. First, because, as Aristotle says, what has happened is possible, and therefore verisimilar; consequently, historical material can serve to obtain the public's assent, its ludic belief in the "reality" of the story being presented. Second, because the poet has to avoid contradicting what the audience knows, since such a discrepancy would necessarily destroy the seamless credibility of the representation. But is is clear that this is not a crucial issue for the creations of Cervantes. Historical facts (the expulsion of the Moors, the wars of the sixteenth century, etc.) constitute, at the most, an incidental part of the remote horizon of the *Quixote*'s world. None of its characters (except the incidentally mentioned "friend" of the Priest and companion in misfortunes of the Captive: "that Saavedra fellow," Cervantes) has to be recognized as historical for the correct

understanding of the work. And Cervantes is quite careful, with the one exception of Roque Guinart, to hide the identity of those persons whom, as scholars have shown, he has used as models for the free elaboration of his figures.

It is another matter that the beings invented by the poet may have *typical* characteristics of their time and thus may be incarnations of a historical mode of life. This, clearly, is related not to the *particular* truth of History but rather to its *general* truths, to the period's universals. Also in this regard, the *Quixote* is not, as I will show later, dedicated to the truthful representation of historical reality, or of the society and ways of its time, although it is obvious that some of that does enter into the book's imaginary world.

23. It can also be conjectured, I acknowledge, that there is a subtler irony in those passages. In them we can perceive the author's sly boasts about the richness and magnitude of his character, who is capable of extreme but nevertheless convincing transformations (here the undiscerning "translator" would be the butt of the irony). This figure wears a general trait of the Cervantine style, and later I will furnish several examples of what can be called "the concealment of depth." All in all, that the character continues to be *convincing*, despite the partial inverisimilitude in it, does not mean that there is no inverisimilitude in it. That is precisely what is attempted in certain essential aspects of the Cervantine art: to extend the force of the believable beyond what is strictly verisimilar. I will return to this theme.

24. See Francisco Márquez Villanueva's commentary in his *Personajes y temas del "Quijote"* (Madrid, 1975), pp. 229–31, on an observation of Paul Hazard's in *"Don Quichotte" de Cervantès* (Paris, 1949), p. 131. Erich Auerbach's discussion of the *Quixote* is found in chap. 14 of his *Mimesis*. The view of the *Quixote* as a picture of historical society is represented in Alberto Sánchez, "La sociedad española en el *Quijote*," *Anthropos,* suppl. 17 (Barcelona, 1989), pp. 267–74.

25. Américo Castro, *Cervantes y los casticismos españoles* (Madrid, 1966) and *Hacia Cervantes*, 3d ed. (Madrid, 1967).

26. See Wolfgang Kayser, *Das sprachliche Kunstwerk: Eine Einführung in die Literaturwissenschaft* (Bern, 1948), chap. 10, for the notions of narratives "of action," "of space," and "of character." Kayser's typology is indebted to Edwin Muir, *The Structure of the Novel* (London, 1928).

27. I do not mean to suggest that literature and reality are or ever have been entirely disengaged spheres. The figures of art are transformations of the images of real experience and in turn exercise their influence on these images. (This influence is at times deceptive, as we are cautioned by the longstanding critical-didactic tradition from Plato, Tertullian, and Saint Augustine to the humanists and moralists of the sixteenth and seventeenth centuries, and no less by the constant pronouncements of our own times against the illusions generated by the cinema, the popular novel, and television. With humorous ambiguity, the *Quixote*'s censure of books of chivalry is set in this context.) But the fact is that literature and art do not have merely a mimetic function, as Cervantes rightly indicates. Even in naturalistic works written centuries later we find an illusionary exaltation of the image of life that, if it does not falsify, at least transfigures and surpasses the givens of our

real experience. Now, the extent to which literary styles transform the image of life is variable, as I noted in reference to the Aristotelian distinctions. In Cervantes's art there is always a considerable degree of stylization, and therefore the foreground of his imaginary world has a marked look of artifice and play. It always evokes, deliberately and with pleasure, the traditional institutionality of literature. Yet the more remote background, which one sometimes has difficulty getting at, is hard truth, apparently not amenable to formulation. Therefore I believe it is legitimate to say, as I have done, that sociohistorical particularity is not *shown* in the *Quixote*, although it and transhistorical human reality all emerge silently on the horizon half-concealed by fantasy's figures. A plain example of these more or less recondite references is the implication of the corruption of the Spanish court, suggested in the very brief mention of the schemes of Don Antonio Moreno (II.65). He decides to go to the court to solicit an exemption from expulsion for the rich Moor Ricote. The dubious advocate, a principal gentleman of Barcelona, is a good friend of the viceroy there—and of the bandit Roque Guinart. Cervantes advances not the slightest condemnatory characterization of the figure of Don Antonio. Even in this case, however, the complex social and political phenomenon of Catalan bandit gangs in Cervantes's time is not given anything approaching a thorough representation in the novel, as one can verify by reading John Elliott's studies on the subject, such as chap. 4 of *Spain and Its World, 1500–1700* (New Haven, 1989). We could also say, certainly, that the society of the period *is* shown in the *Quixote*, if not in its own image, then transfigured into traditional literary types, and Cervantes's new ones. Don Quixote himself is "one of those gentlemen who . . . ," a member of a historical social class, but molded into such archetypes as the *miles gloriosus*, the sententious wise man, and even the evangelical Christ. Additional evidence, if indirect, can be seen in the fact that when precise satirical and sociological notes are given in the work, they stand out because of their infrequency (as, for example, in chap. 24 of the Second Part). With these remarks I am anticipating a dominant theme of this study: the relationship between stylization and truth, between imaginary regions and the sense of reality. It is a recurrent and explicit theme of the *Quixote*, but there it also assumes less obvious and, one might say, subterranean dimensions, which I will endeavor to bring to light.

28. Juan Huarte de San Juan, *Examen de ingenios para las ciencias*, a book first published in 1575 that Cervantes supposedly knew. There is a recent edition by Esteban Torre (Madrid, 1976).

29. To prove this assertion, it suffices to indicate the enormous inconsistencies, from a realistic point of view, that the central characters present, in both their psychic and their physical aspects. (I elaborate on this theme in chaps. 2 and 3.) These inconsistencies do not rule out the possibility that among the dimensions of the main characters, as well as of many others in the *Quixote*, may be an abstract psychological one of profound observation. This has been shown by, for example, Salvador de Madariaga in his analysis of Cardenio and Dorotea in *Guía del lector del "Quijote"* (Buenos Aires, 1943) and by Francisco Ayala in his study of "The Man of Ill-Advised Curiosity": "Los dos amigos," in his *Ensayos: Teoría y crítica*

literaria (Madrid, 1971), pp. 695–714. In contrasting the archetypes of traditional imagination with scientific typologies, I am not dealing, as I indicated earlier, with two universes of totally irreconcilable notions. The methodical development of the traditional psychophysical types recast by Cervantes in his greatest figures (initiated by Ernst Kretschmer in his celebrated *Körperbau und Charakter* [Berlin, 1931]) is good evidence of the kinship of literary imagination and reality. On the contemporary sources of Cervantine characterology, a work worth consulting is Harald Weinrich, *Das Ingenium Don Quijotes* (Münster, 1956), subtitled "A Contribution to Literary Characterology," as well as Carroll B. Johnson, *Madness and Lust: A Psychoanalytical Approach to "Don Quixote"* (Berkeley, 1983).

30. Percy Lubbock, *The Craft of Fiction* (London, 1921).

31. Certain restrictive qualifications to this assertion can be inferred from Martín de Riquer's argument in "Cervantes y la caballeresca," in Avalle-Arce and Riley, *Suma cervantina,* p. 286, as well as from Daniel Eisenberg's *Study of "Don Quixote,"* especially chap. 1.

32. The classic study of the theme of literature in the *Quixote* is Mia I. Gerhardt, "Don Quijote: La vie et les livres," *Mededelingen der Koninklijke Nederlandse Akademie van Wetenschappen* 18 (Amsterdam, 1955): 17–57. On a related topic, see Michel Moner, "La problemática del libro en el *Quijote,*" *Anthropos* 98–99 (1989): 90–93.

33. See René Wellek, *A History of Modern Criticism (1750–1950),* vol. 1 (New Haven, 1955), Introduction, ii. Cesare Segre (n. 5) affirms that few works are more distant than the *Quixote* from the poetic doctrine that is formulated in them.

34. Benedetto Croce, *Aesthetic as Science of Expression and General Linguistic,* trans. Douglas Ainslie (London, 1909), chap. 1; José Ortega y Gasset, *Ideas sobre la novela,* in *Obras completas,* vol. 3 (Madrid, 1966).

35. Ciriaco Morón Arroyo independently makes the same observation in *Nuevas meditaciones del "Quijote"* (Madrid, 1976), p. 120, which makes me think that, in effect, Cervantine art *tends* toward this modern conception of unity. Nevertheless, I now believe that to attribute to the *Quixote* a complete integration of the theoretical material in its novelistic world is going too far, beyond a certain historic boundary in the evolution of literary forms. But of course my argument should not proceed extrinsically, as if one were dealing with an anachronism; rather, it should arise from the examination of the text.

36. I examine the problem of the unity, limits, and relative closure of the universe of the *Quixote* in chap. 2.

37. E. C. Riley, *Cervantes's Theory of the Novel* (Oxford, 1962) and "Teoría literaria," in his and Avalle-Arce's *Suma cervantina,* pp. 293–322; Alban K. Forcione, *Cervantes, Aristotle, and the "Persiles"* (Princeton, 1970).

38. Forcione, *Cervantes, Aristotle, and the "Persiles,"* p. 94n.

39. On this topic see Bernard Weinberg, *A History of Literary Criticism in the Italian Renaissance* (Chicago, 1961); Corneille, "Des trois unités," in his *Discours* (1660); and Dr. Johnson's "Preface to Shakespeare," in *Samuel Johnson on*

Shakespeare, ed. H. R. Woudhuysen (London, 1989), pp. 129–65, published originally in Johnson's edition of Shakespeare's dramatic works in 1765.

40. Riley, "Teoría literaria," in *Suma cervantina*, p. 312, sees no more in this inconsistency than the expression of Cervantes's ambivalence before the two ideals (the classicist and the romancesque) of literary creation. Precisely this ambivalence, which I think we can take as a fact, must lead to the rejection of exclusionist poetic doctrines and to indifference toward the incoherence of their conjunction.

41. Martín de Riquer, *Aproximación al "Quijote,"* 3d ed. (Barcelona, 1970), p. 155.

42. According to Paul Hazard, "without giving us any lesson, he teaches us everything, both wisdom and folly. He does not dogmatize on the conflict between appearances and reality, but he places it at the heart of our life": *"Don Quichotte" de Cervantès* (Paris, 1931), p. 7.

43. Marcelino Menéndez y Pelayo, *Historia de las ideas estéticas en España,* vol. 2 (Buenos Aires, 1943), and "La cultura literaria de Miguel de Cervantes y la elaboración del *Quijote,*" in *Estudios y discursos de crítica histórica y literaria,* vol. 1 (Buenos Aires, 1944), pp. 323–56; Marcel Bataillon, *Erasmo y España* (Mexico City, 1966); Castro, *Pensamiento de Cervantes;* Riquer, *Aproximación al "Quijote";* Jean-François Canavaggio, "Alonso López Pinciano y la estética literaria de Cervantes en el *Quijote,*" *Anales Cervantinos* 7 (1958): 15–107; Enrique Moreno Báez, "Perfil ideológico de Cervantes," in Avalle-Arce and Riley, *Suma cervantina,* pp. 233–72; Riley, *Cervantes's Theory of the Novel;* Francisco Márquez Villanueva, *Personajes y temas del "Quijote"* (Madrid, 1975); Morón Arroyo, *Nuevas meditaciones del "Quijote."*

44. Hatzfeld, *"Quijote" como obra de arte del lenguage,* p. 180.

45. Today these ideas have spread with the work of Bakhtin and his theory of the novel as a "polyglot" (transhistoric) genre. According to this theory, the novel not only contravenes all preexisting orthodoxy but does not formulate any proposal for a new one, since it exhibits plural visions on an equal footing. See Mikhail Mikhailovich Bakhtin, *The Dialogic Imagination,* trans. Caryl Emerson and Michael Holquist (Austin, Tex., 1981). Let me indicate in passing that in essence this view is none other than the Schlegelian theory of irony, and of the novel as the "romantic" genre par excellence.

46. Castro, *Pensamiento de Cervantes,* pp. 280–91; Bataillon, *Erasmo y España,* pp. 796–97. I cite only two authors who may be taken as paradigms from among the great number of those who have defended one or the other side in this debate. On this subject, see the analysis and review of the discussions by Márquez Villanueva in his *Personajes y temas del "Quijote,"* pp. 229–335.

Rafael Osuna, who has studied the internal and external chronology of Cervantes's works, suggests that it is possible to infer exactly, from a chronological ordering of the pertinent *loci*, the character and evolution of Cervantes's position regarding the expulsion of the Moors. Reasonable conjectures, of course, can be made about this and similar questions, but that will not do away with the extravagant and characteristically Cervantine ambiguity of passages such as those on

Ricote. See Osuna's articles in *Boletín de la Real Academia Española* 48 (1968), *Thesaurus* 25 (1970), and especially "La expulsión de los moriscos en el *Persiles*," *Nueva Revista de Filología Hispánica* 19 (1970): 388–93.

47. Hatzfeld, *"Quijote" como obra de arte del lenguaje*, pp. 179–204 (doctrinal pronouncements, some from the lips of Don Quijote, others from Sancho's), 249 (on the irony that permeates the work).

48. To be sure, quite a few people have read the work that way, and the worthy Francisco Rodríguez Marín seems to sympathize with that anti-Romantic interpretation. See his edition of the *Quixote* for Clásicos Castellanos, vol. 7, p. 317n (chap. 73 of the Second Part). But Castro's studies are antagonistic to such radically antiheroic interpretations. Predmore's examination in chap. 2 of his *World of Don Quixote* is sufficient, in my view, to invalidate the thesis of an unequivocal moral exemplarity in the configuration of the actions of the novel.

Eisenberg bases his study of the *Quixote* on a critically examined and yet excessive generalization. According to the literary understanding and conventions of Cervantes's time, he asserts, every doctrinal statement by a serious, respectable character will be an expression of the author's didactic intention, and unless the text gives indications to the contrary, the character's views will correspond to the author's (*Study of "Don Quixote,"* p. xvii). In that case, external evidence will help us decide whether a work's explicitly didactic passages are "sincere" or merely conventional. Eisenberg would not deny, I think, that internal evidence may complicate the matter considerably. A literary work's doctrinal passages can be inconsistent with each other and a mere composite of assorted commonplaces. They can be inconsistent also with the theoretical implications of the fictional course of events. Most important, they can be inconsistent with the artistic design of the work. I intend to show that all of these complications abound in the *Quixote*. Therefore, I maintain that the doctrinal speeches of its characters ("authors" and narrators included) cannot be taken as direct expressions of Cervantes's ideology or of the rhetorical-didactic meaning of his work.

Further, Eisenberg's hypothesis implies that, as a rule, one mind and thought speak through all the respectable voices in any work of literature written before, say, the Romantic revolution. Until then, no dialectic tension would inhere in the spirit of the fictional genres or necessarily in great creations of literary art. Cervantes's characters would possess no thought of their own, hence no full aesthetic autonomy. The liberating potential of literary imagination would have been constrained by a didacticism of direct address to the public. Can we read Sophocles's *Antigone*, Euripides's *Bacchae*, Shakespeare's plays in this way?

49. Angel del Río, "El equívoco del *Quijote*," *Hispanic Review* 27 (1959): 200–221; Manuel Durán, *La ambigüedad del Quijote* (Xalapa, Mexico, 1960). Also see J. B. Avalle-Arce's analysis of insuperable interpretive dualities in the section "Grisóstomo y Marcela" of his *Deslindes cervantinos* (Madrid, 1961). It is interesting to remember that many critics have attributed to Shakespeare that same spirit of ideological and even ethical indifference for which Dr. Johnson censures him in the "Preface." A problem, however, derives from the fact that the New Critics tend to find this ambiguity in all (great) works, and not just in

novelistic forms, as Bakhtin does. Rather than doubt the genuineness of these findings, I am inclined to suspect that two kindred forms, one constitutive of art and the other peculiar to some writers, are still confused in our critical thought.

50. Alberto Porqueras Mayo, *El Prólogo en el manierismo y barroco españoles* (Madrid, 1968).

51. There is a sort of subliterature in which authors use nondidactic genres to let us know their opinions. In my discussion I am referring to works of the vast order to which the *Quixote* belongs, in whose archgeneric design the imagination is at the same time the instrument of knowledge and the horizon of communicated vision, and within which the doctrinal-didactic intent would be a structural contradiction. The archetypically didactic literature that uses imaginative devices, such as the philosophical dialogue, the epistle, the didactic poem, and the apologue, is something else. Works of the *Quixote*'s kind are written not to illustrate a satirical or didactic preconception but to set in motion an imaginary world that has multiple relations of meaning with reality and with literature, some of which are unforeseeable and possibly unheard of.

52. Wolfgang Kayser's thesis in *Entstehung und Krise des modernen Romans* (Stuttgart, 1954) can be related to the (broader) conceptions that I have already mentioned, of Romantic irony and also the category of the novelistic in the critical work of Bakhtin. The plurality of voices, the dialoguism, the nonmonolithic vision of the world are for Bakhtin essential traits of the spirit of the genre. But certainly for the Russian critic this literary phenomenon does not begin with the modern novel or with Cervantes, although it is fully displayed there; rather, it belongs to all forms of critical literature, to all discourses that escape mythical, univocal dogma. See Bakhtin, *Dialogic Imagination*. A very fine elaboration of the theme of interior distances in the novelistic space of the *Quixote,* and of the conflicts between the imagining control and the automony of the imagined persons, will be found in Ruth El Saffar, *Distance and Control in "Don Quixote": A Study in Narrative Technique* (Chapel Hill, N.C., 1975).

53. Márquez Villanueva, *Personajes y temas del "Quijote."* Gerald L. Gingras, "Diego de Miranda, 'Bufón' or Spanish Gentleman? The Social Background of His Attire," *Cervantes* 5 (1985): 129–40, has debated the historical interpretation that Márquez offers of the Knight of the Green Cloak's garb. This is an element of Márquez's understanding of the episode, which we will consider shortly. For a suggestive view of the complex meaning of the encounter of Don Quixote with Don Diego de Miranda, see Randolph D. Pope, "El Caballero del Verde Gabán y su encuentro con Don Quijote," *Hispanic Review* 47 (1979): 207–18.

54. Percas de Ponseti, *Cervantes y su concepto del arte*, pp. 24–25.

55. Mandel, "Function of the Norm in *Don Quixote*."

56. This dilemma is explored, with noticeable Cervantine echoes, by José de Cadalso in his *Cartas marruecas.* See letters 69 and 70. I have used Juan Tamayo y Rubio's edition for Clásicos Castellanos (Madrid, 1935, 1967).

57. José Ortega y Gasset, *Meditaciones del "Quijote"* (Madrid, 1914), pp. 128, 55.

58. These dislocations may call to mind Bertolt Brecht's techniques of "Ver-

fremdung," also designed to break the verisimilar illusion and the pathetic effect, so that the way is opened for reflection on the social functions emblematized in the character. With the difference that Brecht, in the end, does not want to leave us free to judge and meditate on the political dilemmas. If we are to do so, we have to begin by rejecting his persuasive suggestion. Even if we had less information about Brecht's life than we have about Cervantes's, and if all of Brecht's program-matic writings and doctrinaire declarations had been lost, we would have no difficulty recognizing his ideology in his literary works, and his interpreters would not go on debating about it interminably. In Brecht's case the work indeed alle-gorizes a thought that we can readily identify with this man's most characteristic conception of the world, even if it must be granted that Brecht's work admirably surpasses its ideological limitations in many respects. His ideology, shared by many people, can be internalized and carried along constantly either as an instru-ment of action or as a utopia of subjective edification. It preexists as a constructed system, and it places no particularly perplexing problem before the spectator. It is not necessary to go so far as Peter Handke does and say that Brecht is a trivial writer to recognize that this incidental comparison suggests a categorical dif-ference in both the function and the rank of Brecht's and Cervantes's works. And it is not a difference that we can explain by saying that Cervantes, having no way to escape the Inquisition's terror, had to hide his own thought, while such writers as Brecht could, in the end, express themselves freely. What we find in the deeper sense of Cervantes's work goes far beyond what was illicit in his time; the hidden *skandalon* is not the relatively simple phenomenon of heretical doctrines.

59. I am aware of the burden I take on with this assertion, opposite as it is to Thomas Mann's reaction to the (translated) episode. See his "Meerfahrt mit *Don Quijote*," first published in the *Neue Zürcher Zeitung* in November 1934.

60. In saying this I presume that Machiavelli's thought is well understood, not only from the text of *The Prince* but also from the *Discorsi*, and that clearly it is not an expression of diabolical perversity.

61. Paul de Man, "The Epistemology of Metaphor," *Critical Inquiry* 5 (1978): 13–30.

62. Bertrand Russell, *An Inquiry into Meaning and Truth* (London, 1940), chap. 14.

63. Here Jean-Paul Sartre's concept of writing as an appeal to the reader's freedom comes immediately to mind. See *What Is Literature?* (New York, 1966), pp. 32, 36.

64. Friedrich Schiller, *On the Aesthetic Education of Man, in a Series of Let-ters*, ed. and trans. E. M. Wilkinson and L. A. Willoughby (Oxford, 1967), letter 22.

65. I have preferred the word "romancesque" to avoid the ambiguity of "ro-mantic," which, although it is used in the general to denote "idealistic" works of imagination, is applied especially to a historical current of the nineteenth century. In Spanish, the use of *romance* in a sense that corresponds to the English "ro-mance" (which has been understood since the late eighteenth century as opposed to "novel" and its type of realistic fiction) is quite rare. But I have noted that

Amador de los Ríos, in his *Historia crítica de la literatura española* (Madrid, 1861–65), for example, uses *romancesca* to qualify the medieval novel. We also have, then, a transhistoric Spanish term for this poetic archetype. The dictionary of the Real Academia Española (Madrid, 1956) accepts it, although, in declaring it a synonym of *novelesco* (justifiably, since ordinarily this word is used in that way), it deprives it of the specificity that interests me here.

66. Marcelino Menéndez y Pelayo, "El *Quijote* y sus interpretaciones" (1904); "La elaboración del *Quijote* y la cultura literaria de su autor" (1905). In the first of these discourses, Menéndez Pelayo says that the *Quixote* is "the last of the books of chivalry" and "the first and unsurpassed model of the modern realistic novel" (p. 315), ideas that he repeats in the other one. See his *Estudios de crítica histórica y literaria* (Buenos Aires, 1944), vol. 1, pp. 303–22 and 323–56. Perhaps the truth lies just beyond the incompatibility of these two affirmations.

1. Cervantes and the Regions of the Imagination

1. Shakespearean criticism has had a similar history, as one can surmise by reading Coleridge's defense of the Elizabethan dramatist's artistic consciousness. See Samuel Taylor Coleridge, "Shakespeare's Judgment Equal to His Genius" (ca. 1808), in *The Critical Tradition*, ed. David H. Richter (New York, 1989), pp. 303–5. Romantic criticism is the beginning of a more fitting interpretation of the authors of the nonclassicist tradition. But the idea that the *Quixote* is largely a product of "improvisation" endured until the beginning of our century, as J. B. Avalle-Arce and E. C. Riley recall in "Don Quijote," in their *Suma cervantina* (London, 1973), p. 60. From a contemporary critical point of view José Manuel Martín Morán revives and transforms the study of Cervantes's presumed or real inconsistencies: *El "Quijote" en ciernes: Los descuidos de Cervantes y las fases de la elaboración textual* (Turin, 1990).

2. Critical consecration of the *Quixote*'s *form*—as well as elevation of the genre of the novel to a position equal or superior to classical epic, tragedy, and comedy—is not a very recent development. Although there are precursors for the apologia of the novelistic form among the "moderns" of the Italian Renaissance, who defended the "romanzo" (exemplified mainly, of course, by Ariosto's verse epic) as a new and non-Aristotelian genre, the dignity of novelistic prose was not fully recognized till the second half of the eighteenth century, and then extolled in the aesthetics of German Romanticism. But note that the early Romantics' concept of the novel does not strictly apply to the modern novel; their ideal corresponds to the type of novel realized in the *Quixote*. The mixture of genres and subjects, of the tragic and the comic, of idealization and realism, of seriousness and jest, of enthusiasm and irony, the "ordered confusion," the creation of mythic characters, the "allegorical" meaning (which, bowing to the terminological preference of Goethe, Schelling, Hegel, Coleridge, Carlyle, and other authors of this tradition, we would do better to call "symbolic," since the reference is to the infinite and

unspecifiable, not to a predetermined conceptual frame)—all these traits are declared to be exemplary expressions of "Romantic" art. For Schelling, the Schlegel brothers, and Ludwig Tieck, as well as in Hegel's aesthetics, this concept includes the entire nonclassicist tradition of Christian Europe, whose pinnacles are Dante, Shakespeare, Cervantes, Calderón, Goethe. In relation to a number of these points, see Werner Brüggemann, *Cervantes und die Figur des Don Quijote in Kunstanschauung und Dichtung der deutschen Romantik* (Münster, 1958).

3. René Girard, *Mensonge romantique et vérité romanesque* (Paris, 1961).

4. I use this Kantian term to refer to one of the fundamental forms of the singular literary work, the form that we are examining here in the *Quixote*, and thus I distinguish it from other essential structures, such as those called "syntagmatic" (whose prototype is perhaps found in Vladimir Propp's morphology of the folktale) and "paradigmatic" (whose relevance to the fabric of myths has been revealed by Lévi-Strauss and whose function in the lyrical organism has been brought to light by Roman Jakobson). In chap. 2 I shall examine some aspects of the *Quixote* from the point of view of its syntagmatic and paradigmatic structures.

This transcendental structure of the singular work should not be confused with the universal transcendental structure of literature, which I have described in *Fictive Discourse and the Structures of Literature: A Phenomenological Approach,* trans. Philip W. Silver (Ithaca, N.Y., 1981).

5. Cervantes declares this structural principle of his work through Cide Hamete, at the beginning of chap. 24 of the Second Part; that is, immediately after the chapter in which Don Quixote has related his descent into the Cave of Montesinos. The Arab historian says that he cannot convince himself of the truth of this account: "the reason is that all the adventures which have happened until now have been possible and verisimilar." The title of the preceding chapter hints that "this adventure" is taken "for apocryphal."

6. The strong presence of comedy in the *Quixote* and in some of the *novelas* must have been perceived in Cervantes's own time, as we can conjecture from the Prologue of Alonso Fernández de Avellaneda's second (or fifth) apocryphal part. José Ortega y Gasset cites this reference in his *Meditaciones del "Quijote"* (Madrid, 1914), "Meditación Primera," but, contrary to what I maintain in this study, he grants the dimension of realism to comedy.

7. Marcelino Menéndez y Pelayo, "La cultura literaria de Miguel de Cervantes y la elaboración del *Quijote,*" in *Estudios y discursos de crítica histórica y literaria* (Buenos Aires, 1944), vol. 1, pp. 323–56.

8. We owe to Ruth El Saffar a decisive study about the variety of genres in these Cervantine works. See her *Novel to Romance: A Study of Cervantes's "Novelas ejemplares"* (Baltimore, 1974). I will only observe here what I have already suggested, that the dichotomy novel/romance is not sufficient to explain the stylistic varieties of these works.

9. Francisco Ayala indicated the principle of this transition from one generic sphere to another in "La invención del *Quijote,*" in *Los ensayos: Teoría y crítica literaria* (Madrid, 1972), pp. 619–59. On this point see also Celina Sabor de

Cortazar, "Historia y poesía en el episodio de Marcela y Grisóstomo," in *Para una relectura de los clásicos españoles* (Buenos Aires, 1987), pp. 61–75. For other aspects of the passage, see J. B. Avalle-Arce's "Grisóstomo y Marcela," in *Deslindes cervantinos* (Madrid, 1961). John J. Allen has shown that transitions of imaginary region, which Ayala and I have pointed out are a fundamental part of the *Quixote*'s design, extend to the details of diction that an attentive stylistic analysis can determine. See Allen's "Style and Genre in *Don Quixote*: The Pastoral," in *Cervantes* 6 (Spring 1986): 51–56.

10. On other aspects of Cervantes's use of anticipations as a literary device, see Avalle-Arce's and Riley's "El *Quijote*," in *Suma cervantina*, pp. 47–79. These authors deal with thematic and plot anticipations, however, not with those examined here, which are less tangible, as they relate to styles and ways of imagining.

11. The land of Cucaña is often confused with Jauja, as in the Second Part, bk. III, chap. 6, of *Guzmán de Alfarache*, Clásicos Castellanos 114, V, p. 89.

12. We must keep clearly in mind what should be understood by the "usurpation of a character's voice." One could argue that in traditional literature and even in all literature, the author's style, or conventional literary language, takes possession of the characters' discourses and gives them a form alien to the one such discourses would take in real life. The author's style thus usurps the characters' voices. But that argument would assimilate and conceal a relevant difference. What we are looking at here is an *internal* diversity in the character's discourse, whose speech (doubtless always somehow stylized by the author's literary language) has a basic verisimilar or conventional connection with the speaker's personal traits and with the situation in which he finds himself. This link is already prescribed in Aristotle's *Poetics*, as a principle of consistency and propriety, and is expressed in the classical tradition by the term "decorum." What we have observed is just the opposite, a disruption of this classical norm in the dialogues of Cervantes. Verisimilar discourse is suddenly displaced by expressions incompatible with the premises of character and situation already established, but with no interruption in the continuity of voice and discourse.

13. Salvador de Madariaga, *Guía del lector del "Quijote"* (Madrid, 1926), chaps. 3 and 4.

14. Perhaps this is an oversimplification. Francisco Márquez Villanueva, in his *Personajes y temas del "Quijote"* (Madrid, 1975), pp. 22–24, indicates that these figures too, especially Dorotea, involve some complexity and embody intersections of archetypes. In Dorotea the "damsel in distress" of books of chivalry is fused with the Renaissance heroine dressed like a man.

15. A different view of this setting and its implications is found in Javier Herrero, "Sierra Morena as Labyrinth: From Wildness to Christian Knighthood," in *Critical Essays on Cervantes*, ed. Ruth El Saffar (Boston, 1986), pp. 67–80.

16. On the elemental mimetic level, these actions of Dorotea and Don Fernando strike a note of indiscreet "realism." On the level of the idealizing style appropriate to their story, the actions are an ungrammaticality, a rupture of "decorum" (in the technical sense of what is conventionally appropriate to a type). In the metapoetic context, they constitute a play of borderline transgression of the laws

of the canonical regions. This multiple level of meaning is representative of the essence of Cervantes's ironic, self-reflexive art.

In his *Gespräch über die Poesie* (1800) Friedrich Schlegel incidentally touches on what today we would call the metapoetic dimension of the *Quixote,* which he conceives as autoreflexive. Considering how the First Part is reflected in the Second, Schlegel says that the work contemplates itself ("gleichsam in sich selbst zurückkehrt"). See Schlegel, "Dialogue on Poetry," trans. Ernst Behler and Roman Struc, in *German Romantic Criticism,* ed. Leslie Willson (New York, 1982), pp. 84–133, esp. 92. What we should understand here is not merely that the First Part is discussed in the Second, or just that because the protagonists are already known, the nature of their encounters with other subjects changes. There is more to it than that. The kind of adventure that is characteristic of the First Part occurs only once in the Second Part (with the enchanted boat). The madman has become more reflective. Something like an undercurrent of revision of the first two sallies can be perceived in the last one. And this is true not only with respect to the protagonist, who seems to reconsider his undertaking; it can be sensed also in the leading spirit that inhabits the work. This phantom of the authorial mind seems to have a keen awareness of what was done earlier, and he seems to observe the artistic rule of variety. This is one of various dimensions of the *Quixote*'s metapoetic irony.

17. E. C. Riley, *"Don Quixote"* (London, 1986), p. 84.

18. Ibid., p. 121.

19. The fact that the jesting author of this subtle travesty is the same one who uses the Byzantine form most seriously and with marked religious significance in his "novella" *La española inglesa,* as well as in the lengthy *Persiles,* permits us to glimpse the dimensions of Cervantes's spiritual personality.

20. Heliodorus of Emesa, *Aethiopian History Written in Greek by Heliodorus,* ed. Charles Whibley, trans. Thomas Underdowne (New York, 1967).

21. See Karl-Ludwig Selig, "The Battle of the Sheep (*Don Quixote* I, xviii)," *Revista Hispánica Moderna* 38 (1974–75): 64–72.

22. It is tempting to explore other aspects of the *Quixote* and the literature of its time for structures analogous to the ones I have described as the heterogeneous conjunction of styles of the imagination. Thus the syncretistic pantheon of contemporary literature, so noticeable in Góngora, is somewhat similar to the impure mixture of imaginary regions. Also Don Quixote, in a rhetorical lament (I.25), names pagan mythic figures ("rustic gods") as witnesses to his penitence in imitation of Amadís. Here Christian asceticism, its secularization in chivalric courtly love, and the pagan pastoral topos are intermingled. Do these rhetorical games have no effect whatever on the religious consciousness of the period?

In this conceptual frame, George Haley's and Herbert Lindenberger's observations about Maese Pedro's puppet show are relevant. Haley points out another of the profound Cervantine transitions in this episode: "The story of the donkey-like aldermen and the demonstration of the man-like ape together constitute a carefully graduated introduction to Maese Pedro's puppet show. These complementary cases of mimicry mark successive stages in a process of dehumanization that culminates in the representation of the legend of Gaiferos and Melisendra by inanimate dolls made of paste": "The Narrator in *Don Quixote: Maese Pedro's Puppet Show,*" *Modern Language Notes* 80 (1965): 145–65. For Lindenberger, the scenes of the episode are structurally analogous to the composition of an opera, because in both cases there is a polyphony or variety of alternating or simultaneous types of expression. See his *Opera: The Extravagant Art* (Ithaca, N.Y., 1984), pp. 151–56. Indeed, the styles of popular ballads, popular rhapsodic epic, the puppet scene, and the comic-realistic commentary of Don Quixote and Maese Pedro are intermingled in that chapter. The creation (as if ex nihilo and by theoretical fiat) of the genre of the opera by Florentine humanist musicians between the last decade of the sixteenth century and the first decade of the seventeenth suggests a temporal parallelism that perhaps it would not be prudent to exploit.

23. See Riley, "*Don Quixote,*" p. 118. On this theme in general, see Mikhail Bakhtin, *Rabelais and His World,* trans. Helene Iswolsky (Bloomington, Ind., 1984); and especially Manuel Durán, "El *Quijote* a través del prisma de Mikhail Bakhtin: Carnaval, disfraces, escatología y locura," in *Cervantes and the Renaissance,* ed. M. D. McGaha (Easton, Pa., 1980), pp. 71–86, and James A. Parr, "*Don Quixote*": An Anatomy of Subversive Discourse (Newark, Del., 1988), chap. 8.

24. Julián Marías, "La pertinencia de 'El curioso impertinente'" (1953), in *Obras completas,* vol. 3 (Madrid, 1959); Raymond S. Willis, *The Phantom Chapters of the "Quixote"* (New York, 1953); Bruce W. Wardropper, "*Don Quixote:* Story or History?" *Modern Philology* 63 (1965): 1–11; Richard L. Predmore, *The World of Don Quixote* (Cambridge, Mass., 1967).

25. A valuable study of the effect of reality and the autonomy of the characters, achieved by the contrast between their actions and the literature that forms part of their world of experience, is presented by Predmore in *World of Don Quixote,* especially in chap. 1.

26. By "modern novel" I do not mean postmedieval novel, for this would also include the pastoral novel of the Renaissance and the picaresque, which predate the *Quixote.* Nor do I mean what Bakhtin understands by "novel," since for him this is any work that is open, ironic, and perspectivist, and presents a reality that is problematic and not cut according to official doctrine—in sum, any "heteroglot" or "polyglot" and dialogic work, such as have been produced since antiquity, as the Russian critic says. The modern novel is generally understood to be that form which reached maturity in the nineteenth century. Many critics relate that form to the *Quixote,* postulating that Cervantes's work is the prototype, a paradigmatic prefiguration of what became generalized only much later. This is precisely the thesis I consider questionable.

27. Emile Zola, *Les Romanciers naturalistes* (Paris, 1891), p. 128. A few passages earlier Zola wrote: "*Madame Bovary* had a purity and a perfection that made it the typical novel, the definitive model of the genre." And "the primary characteristic of the naturalist novel, of which *Madame Bovary* is the type, is the exact reproduction of life, the absence of any novelesque element." Mario Vargas

Llosa says in "Updating Karl Popper," trans. Jonathan Tittler, *PMLA* 105 (October 1990): 1024: "What we call the genius of Tolstoy, of Henry James, of Proust, of Faulkner has to do not only with the lingering vigor of their characters, the subtle or labyrinthine prose, the powerful imagination these authors command but also, most outstandingly, with the architectonic coherence of their fictitious worlds, with the solidity and seamlessness of those worlds." Obviously the aesthetic ideal expressed here is the classical one of Aristotelian and Horacian unity and consistency. For example: "If you stage something never before attempted, and dare to build a new character, let it be until the end such as it was at the beginning, and consistent with itself" (*De arte poetica*, 125–27). As is widely known, several passages in Aristotle's *Poetics* and in the *Epistula ad Pisones* prescribe unity and consistency categorically.

28. See Dámaso Alonso, "La novela española y su contribución a la novela realista moderna," *Cuadernos del idioma* 1, no. 1 (1965): 17–43; and Aldo Ruffinato, "Efectos de lo real," in *Sobre textos y mundos: Ensayos de filología y semiótica hispánicas*, trans. José Muñoz Rivas (Murcia, 1989), pp. 127–45. See also Bernardo Subercaseaux, "Conciencia estética y novela moderna en una obra de Cervantes," *Neophilologus* 61 (1977): 541–50.

29. Just as interpretations can range from hard to soft, they can range from apprehending the characters as thoroughly realistic, at one extreme, to denying that they possess any imaginary consistency, at the other. Carroll Johnson, who approaches Don Quixote as if he were a real person and proceeds to psychoanalyze him, represents the first extreme; James A. Parr, who deconstructs the mimetic dimension of the book, can be said to represent the other. As I shall show in chaps. 2 and 3, this interpretive polarity, too, must be surmounted.

30. Robert Alter, among others, has studied it, in *Partial Magic: The Novel as a Selfconscious Genre* (Berkeley, 1975); so has Lucien Dällenbach, in *Le Récit spéculaire* (Paris, 1977).

31. Note that the *theme* of reality and the realism of the imagination and even that of the aesthetic and moral desirability of a realistic literature are posed from the beginning in the *Quixote*, without any necessity for the *Quixote* itself to be realistic. What is thematized is at bottom the conflict between illusion (madness or idealistic imagination) and the customary or natural *sense* of reality. Thus "realism" in life is evoked, and, more remotely, realism as a possibility of art, but artistic realism is not embodied as a form of the image presented in the work. This duplicity of the theme of reality in the *Quixote* will occupy us more extensively in chap. 4.

32. See Francisco Rodríguez Marín's edition of *Don Quixote* for Clásicos Castellanos (Madrid, 1913), II.65.

33. The usurpation of Don Quixote's voice and discourse by the discourse of reason is, as I indicated earlier, one of the most complicated and subtle of Cervantes's operations. There is also a "genuine" rationality to Don Quixote, corresponding to his facet of sententious wise man (more will be said about this in chaps. 2 and 3). In such cases it cannot be said that Don Quixote is dispossessed of his voice so that it may be used to express the correct vision of things, contrary

to his own. For example, it is *he* who holds the prudent and learned opinions about the education of children and about literature which he expresses to Don Diego de Miranda. The case of ruptures such as those I have cited is different; there, parts of a discourse contradict its meaning and conditions, and inject ironic lucidity into feverish nonsense. But there are also macrotextual variations of this ironic rupture which *resemble* passages of genuine quixotic lucidity. An example is the most critical and realistic vision of himself that Don Quixote produces (just at the moment when he prepares to perform his mad acts of penitence in the mountains) by confessing to Sancho that Dulcinea is both Aldonza Lorenzo and a product of his illusionistic imagination (I.25). This passage subverts the entire demented quixotic undertaking. Don Quixote is possessed here, as when he comments on this subject to the Duchess (II.32), by a critical spirit that is not part of the character's fundamental structure. (Let us observe, incidentally, how often the play of Cervantes's imagination illuminates the theme of personal identity and its possible inconsistency, to which I referred in the Introduction, with respect to Cervantes himself and "his thought.")

In Don Quixote's speech to Sancho about Aldonza-Dulcinea (I.25) we find that proposition of a paradoxical logical form which struck Alfred Schutz (and, according to Schutz, also Hermann Weyl), who compares it with the celebrated paradoxes of the philosophers: "And to conclude, *I imagine that everything I say is as I say*, without lack or excess, and I paint her in my imagination as I wish her to be . . .": "Don Quixote and the Problem of Reality," in his *Collected Papers,* vol. 2 (The Hague, 1964), p. 146; emphasis mine. I believe that the paradox can be explained as a result of the usurpation of Don Quixote's voice by the intelligence of the work. This intrusive spirit is the one that maintains that Don Quixote imagines that everything he says is the truth, a proposition that is not at all paradoxical.

34. My translation and italics.

35. The anomalousness of this passage, of course, has not escaped the observation of Cervantists. See, for example, Avalle-Arce, *Deslindes cervantinos,* p. 154.

36. Also in this category of dislocated literary commentary is what Don Quixote says when, having had his meal, he prepares to listen to the goatherd Eugenio: "[All] I need now is refreshment for the mind, and this I shall give it by listening to this good man's story" (I.50).

37. See K. L. Selig, "Battle of the Sheep" (cited in n. 21) and "*Don Quijote* and the Exploration of (Literary) Geography," *Revista Canadiense de Estudios Hispánicos* 6 (1982): 341–57.

38. E. C. Riley, "Teoría literaria," in Avalle-Arce and Riley, *Suma cervantina,* pp. 293–322.

39. E. C. Riley, "Cervantes: A Question of Genre," in *Medieval and Renaissance Studies on Spain and Portugal in Honor of P. E. Russell* (Oxford, 1981), pp. 69–85. Similar to Riley's view is Edwin Williamson's in his "Romance and Realism in the Interpolated Stories of the *Quixote*," *Cervantes* 2 (1982): 43–68.

40. Joaquín Casalduero, *Sentido y forma del "Quijote"* (Madrid, 1970).

41. A. W. Schlegel, *Sämtliche Werke,* ed. Eduard Böking (Leipzig, 1847), vol.

11, pp. 408 ff.; G. W. F. Hegel, *The Philosophy of Fine Art,* trans. F. P. B. Osmaston (London, 1920), pt. 2, sec. 3, chap. 3, 2.b.

42. Rosalie Colie, *The Resources of Kind: Genre-Theory in the Renaissance* (Berkeley, 1973).

43. Concepts pertinent to this subject, such as that of "countergenre," can be found in Claudio Guillén, "Genre and Countergenre: The Discovery of the Picaresque," in his *Literature as System* (Princeton, 1971), pp. 135–58.

44. Arturo Marasso, *Cervantes: La invención del "Quijote"* (Buenos Aires, n.d.). As Michael McGaha notes in "Cervantes and Virgil," in *Cervantes and the Renaissance* (Easton, Pa., 1980), pp. 34–50, the relationship between the *Quixote* and the *Aeneid* had been pointed out by Vicente de los Ríos in the prologue to his 1780 edition of the *Quixote,* and by a series of other commentators, including Diego Clemencín. Since authors such as Sir James Frazer, Carl Gustav Jung, Vladimir Propp, Joseph Campbell, and Northrop Frye revealed the universal patterns of archetypical stories, we know that similarities between two narratives are not necessarily the result of influence or cases of parody.

45. Gérard Genette, *Palimpsestes* (Paris, 1982).

46. Vladimir Nabokov, *Lectures on "Don Quixote"* (New York, 1984), pp. 11, 41.

2. The Unity of the *Quixote*

1. Sigmund Freud, *An Outline of Psychoanalysis,* trans. James Strachey (New York, 1963; first published in German in 1940).

2. Barbara Herrnstein Smith has dealt with the forms of closure of the lyric poem in *Poetic Closure* (Chicago, 1968). With respect to the novel, a classic text is José Ortega y Gasset, *Ideas sobre la novela,* in *Obras completas,* vol. 3 (Madrid, 1966), which also touches on this aesthetic phenomenon as a universal of art.

3. Wolfgang Kayser, *Das sprachliche Kunstwerk: Eine Einführung in die Literaturwissenschaft* (Bern, 1948), chap. 10, 4, c.

4. My outline of narrative temporality is somewhat different from that presented by Gérard Genette in his "Discours du récit," in *Figures III* (Paris, 1972), published in English as *Narrative Discourse: An Essay in Method,* trans. Jane E. Lewin (Ithaca, N.Y., 1979). Generally speaking, various narratological distinctions that I formulate in this chapter are related to the Russian Formalists' terms *fable* and *sujet.* I prefer to avoid these terms, however, for they are used rather imprecisely today. *Sujet,* for example, designates both (*a*) the order and modality of appearance of the events of the story or "fable" and (*b*) the fictionalized narrative process that is an intrinsic part of the work (the situation and acts of the fictive narrator). One tends to overlook the fact that this process is itself potentially a "fable," and that in that case it also has an order and modality of appearance. Thus this conceptual pair is not a satisfactory analytical tool.

5. See Rodríguez Marín's note at the end of chap. 60 of the Second Part, in his Clásicos Castellanos edition, vol. 8, p. 122.

6. See Murillo's edition of the *Quixote* (Madrid, 1978), vol. 2, n. 2 to chap. 1, n. 9 to chap. 4, and n. 9 to chap. 11 of the Second Part. On the theme of time in the *Quixote,* also see Luis Andrés Murillo, *The Golden Dial: Temporal Configurations in "Don Quijote"* (Oxford, 1975). Other relevant details are found in E. C. Riley, *"Don Quixote"* (London, 1986), p. 78; and in Alfred Rodríguez and Karl Roland Rowe, "Midsummer Eve and the Disenchantment of Dulcinea," *Cervantes* 4 (1984): 79–83, and "Cervantes's Redundant Midsummer in Part II of the *Quixote," Cervantes* 5 (1985): 163–68.

Murillo interprets this return to spring, however, not as part of the labyrinthine design I have described but as if the spring were that of the following year, as if the narrator had skipped the autumn and winter months. I find no textual basis for this interpretation. I believe that, like Hartzenbusch's and Rodríguez Marín's interpretations mentioned earlier, it obeys the desire to salvage the *Quixote'*s supposed verisimilitude, if not its "realism," despite ample evidence that it is not subject to such stylistic laws.

7. Leo Spitzer, "Linguistic Perspectivism in the *Don Quijote,"* in *Linguistics and Literary History: Essays in Stylistics* (Princeton, 1948), pp. 41–85. According to Spitzer, the point of view from which things in the *Quixote'*s world are presented is changing and unstable. I believe there is much stronger evidence than the onomastic inconsistency to support the contention that the Cervantine design eludes a monolithic consolidation of the *aspect* of the image. See also Maurice Molho, *Cervantes: Raíces folklóricas* (Madrid, 1974).

8. I find no basis for Américo Castro's assertion that an uncertain or "problematic" sense of reality is projected *on this plane* of the *Quixote,* and I believe that Hans-Jörg Neuschäfer has rightly protested against the repetition of this judgment in Cervantes criticism: *Der Sinn der Parodie im "Don Quijote"* (Heidelberg, 1963), p. 57n. In chap. 4 I examine the sense of reality in the *Quixote,* and there I will have more to say about this point. For now it is enough to remember that there is a strong critical tradition against the proposition that reality in the *Quixote* is problematic or "shifting." Erich Auerbach believes that reality appears well founded and solid in this novel: "The Enchanted Dulcinea," in his *Mimesis: The Representation of Reality in Western Literature* (Garden City, N.Y., 1957). Also unequivocal and eloquent is Alexander Parker, "El concepto de la verdad en el *Quijote," Revista de Filología Española* 32 (1948): 287–305. Richard L. Predmore, too, does not agree that the reality fictionalized in the work is ambiguous: *The World of Don Quixote* (Cambridge, Mass., 1967). John J. Allen concurs: *Don Quixote: Hero or Fool?* (Gainesville, Fla., 1969), pp. 21–22. J. B. Avalle-Arce says: "Of course there is 'shifting reality' in the *Quixote.* But I would like to specify that it is not so in connection with *Don Quixote* as a book, and applicable to it as a whole, but that it does hold with respect to Don Quixote de la Mancha, character and protagonist of this book whose imagination and fantasy are impaired": *Don Quijote como forma de vida* (Valencia, 1976), pp. 111–12.

9. Various authors have tried to explain this error as the consequence of transposed chapters. See Luis Andrés Murillo's edition, vol. 1, p. 278 and n. 5, and p. 380 and n. 26.

10. Ernst Kretschmer, *Körperbau und Charakter* (Berlin, 1931); William H. Sheldon, *The Varieties of Human Physique* (New York and London, 1940).

11. Anyone who insists on a "realistic" understanding of the *Quixote* should expect that uninterrupted wanderings under the summer sun would make the protagonist look fairly healthy; at least his face would be tanned. The subconscious pressure of habitual expectations, fed by novelistic traditions of a later age, makes even a reader such as Vladimir Nabokov repeatedly want to see Don Quixote acquiring a "brown" or "sun-tanned" face: *Lectures on "Don Quixote"* (New York, 1984), pp. 16, 20, 27. Cervantes never paints him that way, however, although once, inconsistently, he is called "dark" (*moreno* [II.31]). On the contrary, Cervantes repeatedly tells us—the longer Don Quixote is on the road, the more frequently—that the hidalgo's face is pale and "yellow" (*amarillo* [e.g., I.29, 37; II.7, 16, 62]). Even Don Quixote himself remarks on "the yellowness of my face" (II.16)—another instance of the usurpation of his voice.

12. The characterological inconsistency indicated by Ramón Menéndez Pidal in *Un aspecto en la elaboración del "Quijote"* (Madrid, 1920), is really not so pronounced. There Don Ramón deals with the very transitory deviation of Don Quixote's character, under the influence of the anonymous "Entremés de los romances," in chap. 5 of the First Part, toward the heroic models of the ballad tradition, not of books of chivalry. But this deviation does not affect the more profound structures of the character, as do the transformations I have indicated.

13. Marcelino Menéndez y Pelayo, "La cultura literaria de Miguel de Cervantes y la elaboración del *Quijote*," in *Estudios de crítica histórica y literaria* (Buenos Aires, 1944), vol. 1, pp. 323–56.

14. E. M. Forster, *Aspects of the Novel* (London, 1949; first published 1927), pp. 65–75. Forster contrasts "flat" characters (who have one trait) with "round" (complex ones).

15. This is one more case of the usurpation of a character's voice by the point of view of the author-reader, and thus also a break in verisimilar consistency.

16. See Salvador de Madariaga, *Guía del lector del "Quijote"* (Buenos Aires, 1943), chaps. 7 and 8.

17. Mark van Doren, *Don Quixote's Profession* (New York, 1958).

18. Claude Lévi-Strauss, *Structural Anthropology*, trans. Claire Jakobson and Brooke Schoepf (New York, 1963); *The Savage Mind*, trans. George Weidenfeld (Chicago, 1966).

19. It is true that the *Quixote* does not lack instances of near or complete textual collage. For example, there is the use of traditional stories in various episodes; insertions of folkloric motifs; the inclusion of lines from well-known ballads (in the original edition they are not distinguished typographically, since readers are expected to recognize them) and of legal phrases (such as the repeated "donde más largamente se contiene"). The doctrinal discourses that Don Quixote

and other characters pronounce as their own also have something of the collage in them. This enumeration is not exhaustive.

20. Certainly the hybridization of archetypes is not unique to Cervantes. It can be considered a root of the baroque or a permanent possibility of literature. The comedy or tragicomedy of Calisto and Melibea, *The Celestina* (which, from the point of view of the main action, is a work of tragic form), gives us a notable example of the discordant intersection of types in the figures of Calisto's obnoxious and philosophical servants.

21. On the concepts of the comic and tragic myths, see Northrop Frye, *Anatomy of Criticism* (Princeton, 1957), first and third essays.

22. Copies of the so-called Porras manuscript have preserved a primitive version of this novella in which the adultery is sexually consummated, as opposed to the version published by Cervantes, which ends with a frustrated union. Possibly moral reasons dictated the change. In any case, the story as originally printed inhibits a thorough execution of the comic archetype, although it does not diminish the rigor of its tragic side. The text of Francisco Porras de la Cámara's manuscript was published in Rodolfo Schevill and Adolfo Bonilla's edition of the *Novelas ejemplares* (Madrid, 1922–1925).

23. On the figure of Sancho, from other points of view, Francisco Márquez Villanueva, "La génesis literaria de Sancho Panza," in his *Fuentes literarias cervantinas* (Madrid, 1973), pp. 20–94, is very instructive.

24. Howard Mancing, *The Chivalric World of "Don Quixote": Style, Structure, and Narrative Technique* (Columbia, Mo., 1982), pp. 93–110.

25. After the preceding description of the *Quixote*'s narrative situation, read the following passage from chap. 20 of the First Part:

"And so, my dear master," Sancho continued, "as I've said, this shepherd fell in love with Torralba, the shepherdess, who was a buxom, rollicking wench, a bit mannish, for she had a slight moustache; I fancy I'm looking at her this moment."

"Did you know her, then?" inquired Don Quixote.

"No, I didn't know her," replied Sancho, "but the fellow who told me this story said it was so certain and genuine that when I told it to anyone else, I might affirm and swear that I had seen it all. . . ."

26. On the question of the narrator in *Don Quixote*, see José María Paz Gago, "*El Quijote:* Narratología," *Anthropos* 100 (Barcelona, 1989): 43–48.

27. Also in this category is the logical paradox that attracted the attention of Alfred Schutz ("*Don Quixote* and the Problem of Reality," in his *Collected Papers,* vol. 2 [The Hague, 1964], p. 146). See chap. 1, n. 33.

28. Riley, "*Don Quixote,*" p. 156.

29. On these subjects, see also Félix Martínez-Bonati, "The Act of Writing Fiction," *New Literary History* 11 (Spring 1980): 425–34, and "El sistema del discurso y la evolución de las formas narrativas," *Dispositio* 5–6 (1980–1981): 1–18.

30. Knud Togeby, *La Composition du roman "Don Quijote"* (Copenhagen,

1957); Joaquín Casalduero, *Sentido y forma del "Quijote": 1605–1615* (Madrid, 1970). Schelling says that "it would not be entirely inadequate or entirely false to call the two parts the *Iliad* and the *Odyssey* of the novel" ("die beiden Hälften könnte man weder ganz unschicklich noch ganz unwahr die Ilias und die Odyssee des Romans nennen"): Friedrich Wilhelm Joseph Schelling, *Philosophie der Kunst* (Darmstadt, 1966; first published 1859), p. 323. Behind this affirmation is Schelling's conception that the theme of the *Quixote* (like that of all superior art, as he says) is the struggle between the ideal and the real, terms that should be understood here in a metaphysical sense. In the First Part, the ideal confronts the ordinary real; in the Second, because of the mystification of which Don Quixote is a victim, the world deceptively seems to be ideal; and the hidalgo is again defeated. The Duchess is the Circe of this Odyssey. But in the work as a whole, according to Schelling, the ideal, personified in the hero, triumphs, for it obviously emerges as the superior principle.

31. Ferdinand de Saussure, *Course in General Linguistics,* ed. Charles Bally and Albert Reidlinger, trans. Wade Baskin (New York, 1959), chap. 5, sec. 3. Roman Jakobson's and Jacques Lacan's assimilation of the paradigm/syntagm distinction to the old rhetorical opposition of metaphor and metonymy has been widely adopted. Both terms have since undergone an enormous semantic expansion. I doubt that this metaphoric and catachrestic use of "metaphor" and "metonymy" is a felicitous conceptual step. In the acceptation I would criticize, "metaphor" applies to all relations of identity, similarity, community of essence, permanence, and timelessness; while "metonymy" designates relations of difference, contiguity, sequence, external connection, temporality, linearity. Even this cursory enumeration makes it obvious that the terms in question are far less precise than more common words. The ancient rhetorical treatises present much finer distinctions. There, metaphor is strictly defined as a trope of similarity among others, and likewise metonymy as one of contiguity. Also, the eighteenth century's formulations of the mental "laws of association" appear less vague than the current all-inclusive use of the rhetorical terms. Present usage does not seem to represent a cognitive gain, and it is often a confusing affectation. Behind Jakobson's and Lacan's terminological choice is the Romantic view of language as transcendental form of all human experience, a view that has been extremely powerful in our century.

There is more to current usage of the word "metaphor." The fundamental phenomenon of art that Goethe and most Romantics termed "symbol," in opposition to "allegory," and that some Romantics called "Christian allegory," in opposition to pagan symbolism, often has been called "metaphor" in the twentieth century. See, for example, Philip Wheelwright, *Metaphor and Reality* (Bloomington, Ind., 1962), and Paul Ricoeur, *The Rule of Metaphor* (Chicago, 1977). A metaphor (in the usual rhetorical microtextual sense, as a figure of speech) can illuminate the hidden nature of a thing by applying to it a word and a concept that are alien to the thing, but have a revealing similarity to it. Analogously, novels, poems, and plays are "metaphors" of reality because, in "imitating" life, in modeling its image, they reveal nature's hidden forces through similarities. Any literary work is a limited picture of particular fictitious events, but its ultimate referent is reality as a whole. On the basis of these insights, the Romantics defined a symbol as a finite representation of the infinite. Certainly systematic differences motivate this variety of terms, but we should not overlook the fact that their ultimate referent is the same. Intellectual order is served sometimes by terminological discrimination, sometimes by conflation.

32. Genette, *Narrative Discourse*.

33. José Ortega y Gasset, *Notes on the Novel*, in *The Dehumanization of Art and Notes on the Novel*, trans. Helene Weyl (Princeton, 1948).

34. Ruth El Saffar has pointed out the artistic functionality of this linguistic detail in her *Distance and Control in "Don Quijote": A Study in Narrative Technique* (Chapel Hill, N.C., 1975), p. 48. Maurice Molho and Dominique Reyre have undertaken very interesting studies of Cervantes's fictional onomastics, combining linguistic and folkloric erudition with bold anagrammatic exegeses. See Molho, *Cervantes: Raíces folklóricas* (Madrid, 1974); and Reyre, *Dictionnaire des noms des personnages du "Quichotte"* (Paris, 1980).

35. Dámaso Alonso sees it similarly in "Sancho-Quijote; Sancho-Sancho," in *Del siglo de oro a este siglo de siglas* (Madrid, 1968).

36. Unamuno-style hyperboles that proclaim Don Quixote's reality, that he is not merely a fictional entity, are presumably based on such experiences. These passionate affirmations betray the ontological confusion between the unreal, nonexistent object, not to be found in our practical life, which is the fictitious *person* Don Quixote, and the literary reality of the *character* given in our imaginative experience as readers. I have written on this matter in "Representation and Fiction," *Dispositio* 5 (1980): 19–33.

37. As I have indicated, it was Wolfgang Kayser in his *Entstehung und Krise des modernen Romans* (Stuttgart, 1954) who called attention to the epochal significance of this Cervantine creation of the personal, ironic narrator.

38. Spitzer, "Linguistic Perspectivism in the *Don Quijote*."

39. Helmut Hatzfeld has studied Don Quixote's expressions of his chivalric mission in El *"Quijote" como obra de arte del lenguaje* (Madrid, 1949), pp. 18–21.

40. A fine study of this allegorical dimension is José Echeverría, El *"Quijote" como figura de la vida humana* (Santiago de Chile, 1965).

41. On the other hand, the *comedia* (which, as I said, so far as its principal action is concerned is not comedy or tragicomedy but tragedy) of Calisto and Melibea has a dramatic structure that does not admit a continuation. Thus an obvious artistic conflict results when additional parts are interpolated into it, a conflict on which Julio Cejador insisted in the Introduction to his edition of the work: Fernando de Rojas, *La Celestina*, ed. Julio Cejador y Frauca (Madrid, 1913). The *figure* of Celestina, however, does allow for a continuation, since, like the knight errant and the picaro, she is defined by her profession or way of life, that is, by an activity that repeats itself in a series of cases of the same kind, intrinsically unlimited in number.

42. The "moderns" of the Italian cinquecento who defended Ariosto and the

romanzi sometimes tried to extend Aristotelian principles to genres that developed after Aristotle's time. Others resolutely attacked Aristotle's *Poetics,* and even the classical poetic tradition as a whole. Cervantes's texts seem to indicate that he was aware of these debates, but we will never know how familiar he was with them or how much he approved of the strict neo-Aristotelian classicism of his countryman El Pinciano. It is reasonable to speculate that Cervantes clearly saw the artistic grandeur of the classical ideal and occasionally (as I shall show in chap. 5) tried to represent it in a way that was formally impeccable and at the same time contemporary. On the other hand, he lived within the sensibility and the creative impulses of an era at once inharmonious, rich, and confused, in which an emphasized tradition did not manage to conceal the crisis of its forms and contents. Consciously and ironically, then, he affirmed both the classical ideal and the literary forms derived from medieval and popular sources as worthy artistic possibilities, surely well aware of the incompatibility of the doctrines that supported these types of art. The Canon's speech, in fact, incoherently unites both aesthetics, naively and at a theoretical level much inferior to what Cervantes's idea of literary art must have been. Here, as elsewhere, the vitality of his spirit is expressed as ambivalence. To this extent I agree with Riley's interpretation of the Canon's discourse: Edward Riley, "Teoría literaria," in J. B. Avalle-Arce and E. C. Riley, *Suma cervantina* (London, 1973), p. 312.

43. It could even be said (if one accepts a brief descent into a more playful hermeneutics of allegorical apercus) that the anxiety generated by the possible inconclusiveness of the story is symptomatically indicated in the First Part through the repeated motif of interrupted narratives—that of the basic narrator about the battle between Don Quixote and the Basque (I.8) and the one Cardenio presents to Don Quixote about his own past (I.25). There are also the unfinished ones, Sancho's about the crossing of the river with the sheep (I.20) and the shepherd Eugenio's (I.51–52), which includes all of the events up to the moment of the account but leaves us in the dark as to how Leandra's destiny and the extravagances of her admirers will turn out (although this curiosity does not torment us, as Cervantes well understands and suggests). On the motif of interruptions, see Stephen Gilman, *The Novel According to Cervantes* (Berkeley, Calif., 1989), chap. 2.

44. Georg Lukács touches this theme when he terms "abstract idealism" the position supposedly criticized in the *Quixote.* See his *Theory of the Novel: A Historico-Philosophical Essay on the Forms of Great Epic Literature,* trans. Anna Bostock (Cambridge, Mass., 1971), II, 1.

45. Mancing, *Chivalric World of "Don Quixote."*

46. Donald W. Bleznick, "An Archetypal Approach to *Don Quixote,*" and Morgan Desmond, "'Quixotiz y Pancino': *Don Quixote* at an Ag and Tech," both in *Approaches to Teaching Cervantes' "Don Quixote,"* ed. Richard Bjornson (New York, 1984), pp. 96–103 and 136–42.

47. John J. Allen, *Don Quixote: Hero or Fool?* vol. 2 (Gainesville, Fla., 1979), p. 78 and "Conclusion."

48. Certainly the structure of imaginary regions is a central part of what is

traditionally called the work's genre, and the paradigmatic and syntagmatic unities are aspects of what is called the plot or the fable. Literary studies of the past
were perhaps too insistent on determining the plots and genres of works. But there
are good reasons for that critical and pedagogical practice. Genre (connoting a
manner of stylization) and plot are, together with the characters, the greatest
signifiers of literature. It is a common error to overlook their internal complexities
and to forget that since they are connected to all the other elements of the text,
their precise meaning is determined only through the work's whole system.

3. The *Quixote:* Its Game, Its Genre, and Its Characters

1. Torrente Ballester employs a different notion in *El "Quijote" como juego*
(Madrid, 1975), at least in the greater part of his essay. Being a game is not taken
by Torrente as a characteristic of literature, whose specification in the *Quixote* has
yet to be determined, but as a distinctive quality of this particular work, or of a
certain reading of it. His notion of game approaches that of an ironic and jesting
exercise, of hermeneutic subtlety, so he deals with only some kinds of what I call
games—and he does succeed in indicating some notable aspects of this novel.

2. Marcelino Menéndez y Pelayo, "La elaboración del *Quijote* y la cultura
literaria de su autor" (1905), in *Estudios de crítica histórica y literaria,* vol. 1
(Buenos Aires, 1944), p. 326, says that "in the opinion of many, the *Quixote*
constitutes a new aesthetic category, original and distinct from any fable that
human ingenuity has created; a new breed of narrative poetry never seen before or
since." (Later in the same study he declares, inconsistently, that the *Quixote*
"provided the first and unsurpassed model for the modern realistic novel.") Schelling, like Friedrich Schlegel, Ludwig Tieck, and other Romantic critics, sees the
Quixote as the prototype of the genre of the *novel (Roman);* on the other hand, it
does seem to him that Dante's poem is formally a unique entity that is outside of
any grouping of works of a common design. See F. W. J. Schelling, *Philosophie der
Kunst* (Darmstadt, 1959), pp. 323, 330; published in English as *The Philosophy
of Art,* trans. Douglas W. Stott (Minneapolis, 1989).

3. On this work, today generally considered anonymous but attributed to
Cervantes by Adolfo de Castro and by Marcelino Menéndez y Pelayo, see the
latter's "Obras inéditas de Cervantes" (1874), in *Estudios de crítica histórica y
literaria,* vol. 1; and Ramón Menéndez Pidal, "Un aspecto en la elaboración del
Quijote" (1920), in *De Cervantes y Lope de Vega* (Madrid, 1964).

4. The formal principle of the juxtaposition of the heterogeneous has also
been indicated by Arthur Efron, *Don Quixote and the Dulcineated World* (Austin, Tex., 1971), and Cesare Segre, "Costruzioni rettilinee e costruzioni a spirale
nel *Don Chisciotte,*" in *Le strutture e il tempo* (Turin, 1974), pp. 183–219.

5. Concurring with various authors cited in chap. 2, I maintained that there is
an evolutionary line in the character of the central figure, and that this gives
syntagmatic (although not Aristotelian) unity to the action of the *Quixote.* But I

also indicated that the paradigmatic or repetitive unity of the work is stronger than the syntagmatic one. This is the reason why the evolutionary line is not quite consistent and the characters of the protagonists remain essentially unchanged to the end: chivalric madness and pedestrian good sense. One can therefore justifiably say that the game resides in the progressive revelation of the figure's static complexity rather than in its dynamism.

6. On the logic of Don Quixote's private "subuniverse" and its progressive conflict with the world of intersubjective experience, see Alfred Schutz, "Don Quixote and the Problem of Reality," in *Collected Papers,* vol. 2 (The Hague, 1964), pp. 135–58.

7. The book about Don Quixote's life that Sansón Carrasco and other inhabitants of Cervantes's novelistic world have read is the same one we have read. Thus the *Quixote* is part of the world that it itself constitutes. The whole is a part of itself. We also can describe the phenomenon by saying that a part mirrors exactly and completely the whole of which it is a part. Moreover, since the replica of itself contained in the book is identical with the containing whole, the replica also must contain a perfect replica of itself within itself, and this new replica another, and so on endlessly. An abyss thus opens in a spot of this image of life. André Gide called this imaginative operation *mise en abyme.* In the *Quixote* this operation adds to the various ironic disruptions of hermeticity and verisimilar illusion. On the general topic of these reflections, see Lucien Dallenbach, *The Mirror in the Text,* trans. Jeremy Whiteley with Emma Hughes (Chicago, 1989).

8. Salvador de Madariaga, *Guía del lector del "Quijote"* (Buenos Aires, 1943), p. 144, says that in general Sancho is a replica of Don Quixote "in a different key." And for Joaquín Casalduero he is "the same melody in another key": *Sentido y forma del "Quijote"* (Madrid, 1970), p. 70. But I am more interested here in the temporary assimilations that imply a marked transference of functions or attributes.

9. Francisco Márquez Villanueva, *Personajes y temas del "Quijote"* (Madrid, 1975), pp. 21–24.

10. No doubt the intellectual inclinations of an era can distort the interpreters' perception of works produced in other times. The critical interest that the *Quixote* generates in some periods (the Romantic and the present, for example) has some spurious motivations. Thus the Romantics presented the *Quixote,* with some justification but one-sidedly, as an expression of their own aesthetic ideals. Today the vogue of metafiction and cryptic texts intended to be deciphered by professionals and the initiated tends to overvalue the self-reflexive games of Cervantes's writing and to overburden its enigmatic aspects with multiple meanings. In the present study, certainly, I am concerned with the metapoetic and allegorical-symbolic dimensions of the novel. I still insist, however, that the work's greatness, as has been seen throughout the pertinent critical tradition, lies essentially in the verisimilar (and even inverisimilar) vitality of its characters. A would-be Borgian way to *read* the *Quixote* does not provide a comparable experience.

11. This is the sentiment that Pablo Neruda expresses, though with a note of

anxiety, in "Walking Around," in *Residence on Earth,* trans. Donald D. Walsh (New York, 1973).

12. Wolfgang Kayser, *Das sprachliche Kunstwerk: Eine Einführung in die Literaturwissenschaft* (Bern, 1948), chap. 10.

13. This could be called the ambiguity of basic Cervantine *écriture* in the *Quixote,* in the sense given the word by the early Roland Barthes in *Le Degré zéro de l'écriture* (Paris, 1953). But this term has been so abused that it is nearly useless for a critical vocabulary.

14. Friedrich Schiller, *On the Aesthetic Education of Man, in a Series of Letters,* ed. and trans. E. M. Wilkinson and L. A. Willoughby (Oxford, 1967), letter 22.

15. On the subject of the body in the *Quixote,* Arthur Efron has made suggestive observations, working from premises other than mine, in *Don Quixote and the Dulcineated World* and in two articles, "Sexual Boundary Shifts in *Don Quixote,* Part II" and "On Some Central Issues in *Quixote* Criticism," *Cervantes* 2 (1982): 155–64 and 171–80. In the same issue of that journal Cesáreo Bandera eloquently discusses Efron's theses in "Healthy Bodies in Not So Healthy Minds," pp. 165–70.

In *Novel to Romance: A Study of Cervantes's "Novelas ejemplares"* (Baltimore, 1974) Ruth El Saffar has proposed that Cervantes's work as a whole (and the *Exemplary Novels* in particular) shows an evolution from "novelistic" forms (more realistic and perspectivistic, and with autonomous characters) toward "romancesque" forms, in which an absolute vision idealistically homogenizes the created world and suppresses interior ironies. The plausibility of the chronological thesis has been debated, but what seems more important to me is El Saffar's thematization of the generic matrices. As I indicated earlier, the analysis I have been developing seems to suggest that the polarity of novel and romance is not sufficient to capture Cervantes's game with the forms of stylization. On the other hand, a work such as the *Quixote,* we have just seen, contains these displacements in multiple ways and in both directions.

16. Aristotle, *Poetics,* 1454a.

17. So says E. M. Forster in defining his "round" characters, as opposed to those that are "flat" or of one piece: *Aspects of the Novel* (London, 1949), p. 75. That is a paraphrase, I believe, of a passage from Aristotle's *Poetics* (IX.11), in which Aristotle explains the possibility of combining surprise and causal consequence, marvel and verisimilitude. The unexpected makes us marvel, and our amazement is heightened when we realize that it could have been expected, given all the premises.

18. Ernst Kretschmer, *Körperbau und Charakter* (Berlin, 1931). In "Don Quixote: From Text to Icon," *Cervantes,* special issue, Winter 1988, pp. 103–16, E. C. Riley considers the sources, mostly historical, of the continuous and very lively *visual* image of Don Quixote and Sancho that is ubiquitous in our culture. Riley does not deal with the contribution that *natural* typology, inherent in ordinary human experience, must have made to this memorable plasticity of the pair

consisting of a talkative, voluble obese man and a persistent, solemn thin man. We can go even further in the search for nonhistorical causes of this phenomenon of imagination and memory. It is plausible to speculate that there is a kind of geometrical, if not logical, basis to this duality of opposite and connected forms: the straight line and the curve, the angular and the circular, the high and the low, the vertical and the horizontal. All of this is a transhistoric factor of the universal figurative tendencies of the species, and explains the easy assimilation and retention of the most salient traits of the Cervantine pair, as of other similar pairs in literature and the cinema.

19. If there are no human literary types without an empirical basis, neither are there traditional sociological or psychological ones without some literary element. I am aware that the scientific effort, in sociology as in psychology, tends to eliminate these intuitive figurations from its concepts and models by formalizing and mathematizing its language. But even today in presumably scientific texts we find types of such an irreducible intuitive-artistic lineage as "the bourgeois," "the common man," and "the intellectual."

20. Miguel de Unamuno, *Our Lord Don Quixote: The Life of Don Quixote and Sancho with Sixteen Essays*, trans. Anthony Kerrigan (Princeton, 1967). I believe that the evangelical phrases in Don Quixote's speech would have been intolerable in Cervantes's time if readers had not perceived in the mad hidalgo something of the pathetic grandeur that Unamuno exaggerates and that is an essential part of the Romantic interpretation of the *Quixote*. It is most improbable that we will ever collect enough documents to reconstruct the work's reception by Cervantes's contemporaries in all its richness and variety. Nevertheless, to suppose that no one read the *Quixote* as more than a comic satire until the Romantics began to stress its elegiac and heroic aspects seems to me a highly problematic hypothesis. In this respect I quite agree with Francisco Fernández Turienzo's observations in "La visión cervantina del *Quijote*," *Anales Cervantinos* 20 (1982): 3–27.

21. Américo Castro, "Prólogo," in Miguel de Cervantes, *El ingenioso hidalgo don Quijote de la Mancha* (Mexico City, 1963). See also Castro, "La estructura del *Quijote*," in *Hacia Cervantes* (Madrid, 1967).

22. J. B. Avalle-Arce carefully ponders this issue in *"Don Quijote" como forma de vida* (Valencia, 1976).

23. The fact that the inconsistencies in Sancho's character, as we have seen, are not limited to the alternation of simple rustic and witty jester deserves greater elaboration. This habitual duplicity is in turn counterposed to the Solomonic governor (which itself constitutes a development of the archetype of the wise and astute common man, embryonic in the basic figure) and to the modified incarnation of Don Quixote which he exhibits to his wife. I have indicated that even as governor, Sancho is not a consistent character. At times he acts as a self-confident and authoritarian wise man, at others as a clumsy and timid rustic. Upon returning from his few days as governor, and to readers' momentary puzzlement, he tells the Duke and Duchess that he did not make any laws (II.55), while we have been told that he made many (II.51). Here Sancho's double constitution as governor

prepares us to accept a double version of the facts. We have no great difficulty in following the game of these occasional instabilities, which is neither realistic nor verisimilar, though now the game affects not merely the character but the events of the story themselves. But this game is exceptional and does not determine the nature of the world in which Don Quixote and Sancho live.

24. Don Quixote's personality has undergone many psychological examinations, and methodical work of this sort continues to appear. See Carroll B. Johnson, *Madness and Lust: A Psychoanalytic Approach to "Don Quixote"* (Berkeley, 1983). My reservations about this kind of analysis derive from what I have been explaining in the preceding pages. Verisimilar psychology that permits us to look deep into the human soul is only one of the many systems that compose the substance of this literary figure and determine the laws of his behavior. Don Quixote is a character, not a person. Moreover, he is a character that, if predominantly verisimilar, is decidedly not realistic. To try to explain all of his actions in accordance with principles of a scientific psychology (according to a program like Johnson's: "to consider Don Quixote as though he were a real person," p. 2) is a tour de force that distances us from the work.

Although it is easy to turn this assertion around and speculate on the function of literary archetypes in the makeup of our own personalities, that should not erase the differences. Don Quixote is not a natural psychic organism making use of archetypes to construct itself as a personality, but an artificial composite of archetypes, *one* of which (fundamental only in an aesthetic sense) is the fictionalized, semirealistic natural and social subject. This one system cannot explain all of his behavior because in Don Quixote, unlike a real being, it is not functionally more basic than the others. To represent an exact psychology, and one that is consistent even at the unconscious level, is not Cervantes's design. The *Quixote* is literature. Moreover, it is unrealistic literature.

4. Toward the Meanings

1. Wayne Booth, *The Rhetoric of Fiction* (Chicago, 1961).

2. The similarity of *sanctus* and *sanus,* which persists in their Romance-language derivations, as well as that of *heilig* and *heil, holy* and *whole, hale, healthy,* etc., suggests an etymological and conceptual link. Nevertheless, an etymological relationship is not enough to ensure that the words share semantic elements. This can be determined only by the use of the words in actual speech, not by a display of one of those etymological and anagrammatic superstitions that run through today's critical prose and perpetuate, often inadvertently, a nostalgic and romantic reverence for a dreamed archaic clarity.

3. W. G. F. Hegel, *The Philosophy of Fine Art,* trans. F. P. B. Osmaston (London, 1920), pt. 2, sec. 3, Introduction.

4. Friedrich Nietzsche, *The Birth of Tragedy from the Spirit of Music,* trans. Francis Golffing (New York, 1956).

5. Diana de Armas Wilson has called my attention to the sentence with which the narrator commences chap. 12 of bk. 4 of the *Persiles:* "It seems that good and bad are so little distant from each other that they are like two concurrent lines that, although they set out from different beginnings, end in one point."

6. Leo Spitzer sees this phenomenon as making the figure of the author god-like. He calls it the "glorification of the artist": "Linguistic Perspectivism in the *Don Quijote,*" in *Linguistics and Literary History: Essays in Stylistics* (Princeton, 1948), pp. 41–85.

7. See Heinrich Heine, *Sämtliche Schriften,* ed. Klaus Briegleb (Munich, 1978), vol. 4, pp. 151–70.

8. Anthony Close, *The Romantic Approach to "Don Quijote"* (Cambridge, 1978), as well as other partisans of a "hard" understanding of this novel, continue to represent these one-sided interpretations. The reduction of the work to a "funny" book is no less inadequate than its idealistic beatification. On this subject, see Lowry Nelson's lucid commentary in "Chaos and Parody: Reflections on Anthony Close's *The Romantic Approach to 'Don Quijote,'" Cervantes* 2 (1982): 89–95.

9. Werner Brüggemann, *Cervantes und die Figur des don Quijote in Kunstanschauung und Dichtung der deutschen Romantik* (Münster, 1958), p. 242. René Wellek holds the same opinion: *A History of Modern Criticism: 1750–1950* (New Haven, 1955), vol. 2, pp. 16, 301.

10. José Ortega y Gasset, *Ideas y creencias* (1940), in *Obras completas,* vol. 5 (Madrid, 1947).

11. This strategy, to which I think Cervantes's imagination is always inclined, can be compared with Aristotle's idea of the persuasive operation in his *Rhetoric.* As we saw in the Introduction, however, doctrinal persuasion is not Cervantes's aim.

12. Pardon this oracular phrase. It can also be cast as the sunset of individual heroism in the modern world of bureaucratic rationalism. I believe that Márquez Villanueva sees the same thing in the eclipse of chivalry (*Personajes y temas del "Quijote"* [Madrid, 1975], p. 189). The moral antinomies incarnated by Don Quixote and his village (the Priest, Housekeeper, etc.) in their opposition are also embodied, as I have indicated, in some passages of Cadalso's *Cartas marruecas* that clearly evoke Cervantes's work. Letter 69 approvingly presents a kind of Knight of the Green Cloak, epicurean, noble, Azorinesque *avant la lettre.* Letter 70 criticizes that private and withdrawn happiness in the name of a heroic public virtue. I see this double figure as a central element in Cadalso's reading of the *Quixote,* an element that also figures in my understanding of the work. See José de Cadalso, *Cartas marruecas,* ed. Juan Tamayo y Rubio (Madrid, 1935, 1967).

13. Stephen Gilman, "Los inquisidores literarios de Cervantes," in *Actas del Tercer Congreso Internacional de Hispanistas* (Mexico City, 1970), pp. 3–25.

14. Howard Mancing, *The Chivalric World of "Don Quixote": Style, Structure, and Narrative Technique* (Columbia, Mo., 1982); Azorín, "La evolución de la sensibilidad," in *Clásicos y modernos* (Buenos Aires, 1939), pp. 33–36.

15. On this topic, see chap. 13 of E. C. Riley, *"Don Quixote"* (London, 1986).

16. Indirect confirmation of this point of what could be called a generative stylistics can be seen in Theo In der Smitten's criticism of Caesar's German translation of the *Quixote*. The phrasing of this translation, he complains, is "too complete," with explicative additions and specifications of what Cervantes merely hints. They damage the text's economy of expressive resources, and the style loses its *Prägnanz*. See Theo In der Smitten, *Don Quixote (der "richtige" und der "falsche") und sieben deutsche Leser* (Bern, 1986), p. 694. Joachim Caesar's German translation of the *Quixote* was published in Coethen in 1648 and in Hamburg in 1928.

17. Roman Jakobson, "Linguistics and Poetics," in *Style in Language,* ed. Thomas A. Sebeok (Cambridge, Mass., 1960), pp. 350–77; J. L. Austin, *How to Do Things with Words* (Oxford, 1962); J. R. Searle, *Speech Acts* (Cambridge, 1969).

18. I have dealt with this subject before, especially in "Mensajes y literatura," in *Teoría semiótica: Lenguajes y textos hispánicos* (Madrid, 1985), pp. 187–97; rpt. in *La crisis de la literariedad,* ed. Miguel Angel Garrido Gallardo (Madrid, 1987), pp. 65–78.

19. The closest thing we have to a grammar and vocabulary of literature still seems to me to be Northrop Frye, *Anatomy of Criticism* (Princeton, 1957), despite its imprecisions. In my view, the hermeneutics of A. J. Greimas in *Structural Semantics: An Attempt at a Method,* trans. Daniele McDowell, Ronald Schleifer, and Alan Velie (Lincoln, Neb., 1983), *Du Sens* (Paris, 1970), etc. is marred by a radical reductionism.

20. Strictly, sentences should be considered instances of discourse (*parole*), not elements of the *langue,* but there is a tendency to count ready-made, stereotypical sentences as part of the systematic repertory of the language. Michael Riffaterre does so in his critical works.

21. Américo Castro, *El pensamiento de Cervantes* (Barcelona, 1972), chap. 2; Spitzer, "Linguistic Perspectivism in the *Don Quijote.*" In a new development of this line of interpretation, Anthony Cascardi has shown that the *Quixote* contains epistemological parables of unsuspected complexity. See his "Cervantes and Descartes on the Dream Argument," *Cervantes* 4 (1984): 109–22, and *The Bounds of Reason: Cervantes, Dostoevsky, Flaubert* (New York, 1986).

22. I have written about these fundamental forms of narration in *Fictive Discourse and the Structures of Literature: A Phenomenological Approach* (Ithaca, N.Y., 1981) and in "El sistema del discurso y la evolución de las formas narrativas," *Dispositio* 5–6 (1980–1981): 1–18.

23. Carroll Johnson has renewed the perspectivist position in a modality of radical relativism, stating that there are no essences or natures of things, just signs, and signs are only arbitrary expressions of the *character* of the interpreter: "Beyond Metaphysics: Semiotics and Character in *Don Quijote* I," *Cervantes* 5 (1985): 3–18. But, like all relativisms, this one invalidates itself; for obviously the *character* itself cannot be a mere arbitrary sign, and it is not one in this theory, for it is a substantial reality that creates the interpretations of the signs. Consequently, there *is* in this theory a nature of things, and there *are* essences, but they are pure

subjectivities, with which we return to old philosophical positions of known questionableness. Johnson also inflicts on us Michel Foucault's aperçus on Cervantes, but to criticize that would be the subject of a longer digression.

24. This objectivist perspectivism consists in relating all narrated events to their being objects of the experience of individuals. See John J. Allen's distinction between the mere unfocused "event" of then-traditional narrative and the "experience" of the modern novel, in this respect anticipated by Cervantes: "*Don Quixote* and the Origins of the Novel," in *Cervantes and the Renaissance,* ed. Michael D. McGaha (Easton, Pa., 1980), pp. 125–40.

25. Related to these issues is E. Michael Gerli, "Romance and Novel: Idealism and Irony in *La gitanilla,*" *Cervantes* 6 (1986): 29–38, where he shows the duplicity of superficial romancesque appearance and problematic novelistic background in *The Little Gypsy Girl.* I believe the structure is common to many of Cervantes's stories: he takes up traditional forms and appears to be treating them in the traditional way, while he is slyly subverting them by transforming their archetypal identity and sense. It seems to me that Bruce Wardropper has described this phenomenon very exactly in "Ambiguity in *El viejo celoso,*" *Cervantes* 1 (1981): 19–28.

26. This stylistic determination is even declared incidentally by the narrator (II.18):

> Here the author describes in detail Don Diego's home, whose contents were those of a wealthy farmer's house, but the translator of this history thought fit to pass over in silence these and similar particulars, seeing that they have little to do with the main purpose of the history, which draws its strength rather from truth than from dull digressions.

The contrary principle, certainly, is asserted elsewhere, in *ironic* praise of Cide Hamete (I.16) as a "very punctilious" historian who does not skip over any of the history's details, no matter how "minimal" and "vile" they may be. This ambivalence corresponds exactly to the shifts we have found at the source of Cervantes's imaginative style: an approach to ordinary reality with its trivial details, then a reversion to the more idealized sphere of comedy. The work thus comes across as much more *detailed* than books of chivalry or pastoral novels, for example, but at the same time much less trivial and more synthetically "true" than daily discourse, since it projects a universal image.

Here I am referring, of course, to the stylizing reduction of *ordinary* details. There are other accumulations of details in the *Quixote,* such as the ornamental profusion of them that Don Quixote injects into his romancesque descriptions of the typical adventures of knights errant, and also in the account of his stay in the Cave of Montesinos. But they do not belong to the basic comic-realistic region whose development throughout the work I want to indicate.

27. The allusions to contemporary social reality are frequently indirect and veiled in the *Quixote.* The figure, relations, and concerns of Don Antonio Moreno, a gentleman from Barcelona, have satirical undertones of great range, even extending to the royal court; nevertheless, Cervantes dares to be explicit enough in this criticism. The allusions to the much more disquieting power of the church are

very clear but unbiased. On this subject there has been much unfounded and extravagant speculation. One interesting aspect of this occasional dimension of the meaning of the novel is examined with textual precision by Antonio Gómez-Moriana, "La evocación como procedimiento en el *Quijote*," *Revista Canadiense de Estudios Hispánicos* 6 (1982): 191–223, and *La subversion du discours rituel* (Quebec, 1985), where he discusses not only the *Quixote* but especially the subversive intertextuality of the *Lazarillo*.

Certainly there is no shortage of interpretive hypotheses based on solid historical research which nevertheless magnify allusions supposedly disguised in the work to a degree incongruous with its literary nature and with its universal appeal, which of course extends to peoples who lack any knowledge of the special circumstances of Spain around 1600. The best known of these theses is Américo Castro's with respect to Hispanic castes: *Hacia Cervantes* (Madrid, 1967) and *Cervantes y los casticismos españoles* (Madrid, 1974). Another is presented by José Antonio Maravall in *Utopía y contrautopía en el "Quijote"* (Santiago de Compostela, 1976). Maravall writes: ". . . if we see it as a revelation of the contrast between humanist utopia and acceptance of the modern world, searching for the latter's possibilities of correcting itself, then the *Quixote* will acquire a transparent and total sense" (p. 21). Maravall himself restricts the scope of his thesis on the following page, noting that this is only one of the lines of the vision objectified in the *Quixote*.

28. Perhaps we must recognize in this Cervantine two-step (advancing toward reality and realism, pushing aside traditional literary forms to do so, then stepping back into a happy stylization) the essential movement of the artistic imagination, which first iconoclastically destroys the inherited illusions, then feels forced again to pull the veil over the amorphous horror with a new form of stylization. The self-critical task of literary imagination (a central topic of Russian Formalism), that of proceeding constantly to reconstruct the type, the law, the transcendental quality of the artistic image of the world, never ends. What Cervantes does in the face of the narrative forms of the sixteenth century Jane Austen does, for example, in the face of the sentimental and Gothic novels of the eighteenth century. Both are readjustments oriented in the direction of the realistic. In our century, on the other hand, we have seen naturalism supplanted by a fantasy of mythic and neoreligious symbols.

29. "Ist etwa der *Don Quijote* nur eine Posse?": Hermann Cohen, *Ethik des reinen Willens* (Berlin, 1907), p. 487.

30. José Ortega y Gasset, *Meditaciones del "Quijote,"* ed. Julián Marías (Madrid, 1957), p. 281.

31. Fernando de Herrera noted in 1580, in his *Anotaciones a Garcilaso* ("Egloga" section), that the pure pastoral region does not admit violence; see my epigraph to chap. 1.

32. The inconsistency of Don Quixote's "discourses" (on the Age of Gold, arms and letters, and so on) is similar to the systematic inconsistency of the varied wisdoms implicit in the traditional regions of the imagination. I have indicated that his discourses cannot be seen as a pure expression of the personality of the

one who pronounces them, but must be seen, to a point, as prefabricated pieces inserted into the novel in the manner of a collage. They are topical discourses, sustaining doctrines that cannot be reconciled. In the hidalgo's voice, the utopia of spontaneous and natural peace joins with the doctrine of peace obtained by arms, heroic haughtiness with Christian humility, and so on. This juxtaposition of doctrines, too, indirectly ironizes inherited wisdom.

33. The pastoral utopia, on the other hand, with its faith in a benevolent nature, tends to interpret evils as the products of institutions, private property, the power of money, the artificiality of technology and customs, social hierarchies, and so on. Obviously many moments of our intellectual tradition accord with this type of political imagination; among others, certain facets of Montaigne's thought (his essay on cannibals, for example), Rousseau's early works, many of the ideas of Marx and Engels, and even the occasional illusions of Claude Lévi-Strauss about the natural goodness of the primitive Nambikwara, in his *Tristes Tropiques* (Paris, 1955). Such illusions demonstrate the astonishingly persistent power of archetypal dreams.

34. Alan S. Trueblood has done a suggestive study on laughter in the *Quixote:* "La risa en el *Quijote* y la risa de don Quijote," *Cervantes* 4 (1984): 3–24. Is there a study on the smile in this work? Interestingly, while Cervantes often mentions laughter, he mentions smiling very rarely, though references to minor facial expressions (tears, blushing, and the like) are not lacking. As Gonzalo Sobejano indicated to me, we can hypothesize that the semantic field in question had a slightly different structure in Cervantes's Spanish, and therefore some of the expressions we call today "smiling" (*sonreír*) were then called "laughing" (*reír*). On the other hand, since smiling and laughing are not only natural reactions but also part of the signs and manners of a culture, one could speculate that the scarcity of smiling in *Don Quixote* reflects a fact of a past age's forms of behavior.

35. See the 1633 commentary of the French novelist Charles Sorel, quoted extensively in an appendix to Ciriaco Morón Arroyo, *Nuevas meditaciones del "Quijote"* (Madrid, 1976). Sorel's observations on the inverisimilitude of actions in the *Quixote* are doubtless correct. Where he errs is in assessing it as an artistic weakness. To understand such things as part of a design is a more complicated critical task, as we have seen.

36. Carroll Johnson, *Madness and Lust: A Psychoanalytic Approach to "Don Quixote"* (Berkeley, 1983).

37. Therefore, Émile Zola's idea of the "experimental novel" is basically misleading. See Zola, *The Experimental Novel and Other Essays,* trans. B. M. Sherman (New York, 1894). It is interesting to reflect on the partial truth embodied in Zola's theory: that of the iron necessity with which the sense of reality, once admitted into the creation, imposes itself on the freest imagination, if the imagination is truthful and sensitive.

38. On these theoretical questions, see chap. 1 of my *Fictive Discourse and the Structures of Literature.*

39. See Dian Fox's suggestive article "The Apocryphal Part One of *Don Quixote*," *Modern Language Notes* 100 (1985): 406–16. Here I am using the term

"magic realism" in one of the vague senses it currently has. For a precise determination of the concept see Michael Scheffel, *Magischer Realismus: Die Geschichte eines Begriffes und ein Versuch seiner Bestimmung* (Tübingen, 1990).

40. As I have suggested, the barber's basin, which Sancho once calls "basinhelmet," is not part of this game of marginal inconsistencies; on the contrary, it is part of the central solid "reality" with which Don Quixote's mad imagination collides.

5. Verisimilitude, Realism, and Literariness

1. In *Cervantes* (Oxford, 1985), p. 24, P. E. Russell describes the *Quixote* as a parody of books of chivalry, but clearly indicates Cervantes's ambivalence in regard to these books. E. C. Riley, *"Don Quixote"* (London, 1986), p. 36, questions the work's parodic character. A critical tradition does raise doubts about the range and relative weight to be accorded the condemnation of these books expressed in the text. Francisco Fernández Turienzo denies that we are dealing with a parody of books of chivalry, and recalls that Francisco A. de Icaza saw it in the same way, in *El "Quijote" durante tres siglos* (Madrid, 1918). See Fernández Turienzo, "La visión cervantina en el *Quijote*," *Anales Cervantinos* 20 (1982): 3–27. From the perspective of my first chapter, which sees the *Quixote* as an ironization of the literary faculty as a whole, the criticism of the chivalric genre is radically displaced and relativized. Certainly the question whether the *Quixote* is a parody of these books should not be confused with another: whether the condemnation of them pronounced by the "friend" of the Prologue and by various characters is an unequivocal part of the work's meaning.

2. Vladimir Nabokov, *Lectures on "Don Quixote"* (New York, 1984).

3. To repeat: the most faithful expression of the signifying will of a work is its constitutive form, the stylistic matrix of the imaginative act that creates it. That is why my methodology is based on a description of the form. It is a poetics of the singular configuration.

4. My opinion on this question is not the prevalent one even today. Daniel Eisenberg has presented a well-argued statement in support of the view that the *Quixote* is "an attack on *libros de caballerías*" in "Cervantes and the *Libros de caballerías*," *Anthropos*, suppl. 17 (Barcelona, 1989), pp. 249–55, and in *A Study of "Don Quixote"* (Newark, Del., 1987). In this book, however, Eisenberg argues in favor of the hypothesis that Cervantes did write a book of chivalry: the *Bernardo*.

5. In this sentence (not a paraphrase of the Aristotelian text) I summarize a few of Aristotle's points that subordinate the art of poetry to the emotional and intellectual tendencies that can be presumed to be present in the (educated) spectator.

6. According to Coleridge's celebrated phrase. See S. T. Coleridge, *Biographia Literaria*, ed. George Watson (London, 1987), p. 169. The idea is not foreign to

Renaissance critics. Alessandro Piccolomini, for example, lucidly examines the spectator's fictionalizing consciousness. See Bernard Weinberg, *A History of Literary Criticism in the Italian Renaissance* (Chicago, 1961), pp. 547–53.

7. Examples of such paradoxes can be seen in the long commentary on the *Poetics* that is the *Philosophía antigua poética* of Cervantes's contemporary Alonso López, el Pinciano, ed. Alfredo Carballo Picazo, 3 vols. (Madrid, 1973), letter 5, vol. 2, pp. 67–70.

8. See *Ion; Republic*, bks. 2, 3, 10; *Laws*, bk. 2.

9. The Greek *eikós*, applied to a figured event, signifies "likely," "probable," and is translated by the Renaissance humanists with the Latin *verisimilis*.

10. Like other classicist authors, Boileau resolutely confines the marvelous within the range of the epic: *L'Art poétique*, canto 3.

11. See Percy Lubbock, *The Craft of Fiction* (London, 1921); José Ortega y Gasset, *The Dehumanization of Art and Notes on the Novel*, trans. Helene Weyl (Princeton, 1948).

12. *The Complete Works of Horace (Quintus Horatius Flaccus)*, trans. Charles E. Passage (New York, 1983), pp. 359–60.

13. Within this poetological tradition, the Canon says (I.47): "Works of fiction must match the understanding of those who read them, and they must be written in such a way that, by toning down the impossibilities, moderating the excesses, and keeping their readers in suspense, they may astonish, stimulate, and entertain so that admiration and pleasure go hand in hand. But no writer will achieve this who shuns verisimilitude and imitation of nature, in which lie the highest qualities of literature."

14. I am presuming that the capacity to distinguish between poetic (and mythic) vision and the sense of reality is fundamental to human experience. Certainly awareness of the difference between them does not always reach the stage of conceptualization and explicit acknowledgment. By Aristotle's time, this awareness had already been made explicit, as we can read in Thucydides and in Plato, and it was part of the tradition of philosophical criticism of poetry and mythology since Xenophanes and Heraclitus.

Among the prejudices in fashion today is that what we call *reality* is nothing but another fiction, a "cultural fiction," used (casually?) in daily life. Another hypothesis (logically inconsistent with the first, but its frequent companion in sophisticated talk) is that artistic *realism* has no special relationship with lived reality, but is just one of the "conventions" of literary style. That realism is a style, an artistic and idealizing way to shape an image of the world, is shown by the historical evidence of the variety of realisms and naturalisms, the persistence of archetypal and even mythical structures in realistic stories, and the obvious existence of "conventions" (figures, techniques, and traditional or deliberate manners) in the realistic representation of the world. But none of this logically invalidates the distinction between fantastic dream and sober perception, insensate illusions and practicable prefigurations, unverifiable and verifiable ideas; or the distinction between fantasies subjected and fantasies not subjected to the regularities and probabilities we know from constantly repeated daily experience.

15. For the Italian references, see Weinberg, *History of Literary Criticism,* pp. 391, 531, 549, 550, 603, 650, 697, 737, 844.

16. This (re)creative participation of the spectator is not, certainly, a discovery of the "aesthetics of reception" of our day. In Lessing's *Laokoon* the reader finds extensive analyses of this dimension of art.

17. That in the *Quixote* and some other works Cervantes tends not only to evoke the sense of reality but truly to go in the direction of realistic imagination (never, I insist, extensively configured) can be seen in his preference for phenomena that are at once astonishing (strange events that amaze and fascinate) and natural: those of mental dysfunction. The gallery of madmen in his work is conspicuous. Nevertheless, they are invented, literary figures of madness, not clinical pictures. Here again the *Quixote*'s general law of imagination is demonstrated: a step first toward ordinary and extraordinary reality, then a step backward toward comforting fantasy.

18. In the previous chapters one of my aims has been to show how Cervantes constructs his ironic exposition of literature, with his own comic realism included, and how he simultaneously activates the sense of reality in the reader. Here I will take up this theme again, with a somewhat different emphasis. The following description represents my version of those transcendental movements involving reality, heroic ideality, tragedy, comedy, and the novel, which Ortega examines in the concluding sections of *Meditaciones del Quijote.* It may be possible, but in any case very difficult, to reconcile views that differ as much as these two. Ultimately the subject of such discussions is the relation between reality, style, and truth. The particular angle from which I have chosen to approach this subject can be found in the Aristotelian passages I have repeatedly referred to, and also, among many others, in the following statements by Coleridge and Goethe. In chap. 14 of his *Biographia Literaria,* ed. George Watson (London, 1987), pp. 168–69, Coleridge writes:

> In this idea originated the plan of the *Lyrical Ballads;* in which it was agreed that my endeavors should be directed to persons and characters supernatural, or at least romantic; yet so as to transfer from our inward nature a human interest and a semblance of truth sufficient to procure for these shadows of imagination that willing suspension of disbelief for the moment, which constitutes poetic faith. Mr Wordsworth, on the other hand, was to propose to himself as his object to give the charm of novelty to things of every day, and to excite a feeling analogous to the supernatural, by awakening the mind's attention from the lethargy of custom and directing it to the loveliness and the wonders of the world before us; an inexhaustible treasure, but for which, in consequence of the film of familiarity and selfish solicitude, we have eyes yet see not, ears that hear not, and hearts that neither feel nor understand.

In a conversation with Eckermann on the French painter Claude Lorrain, April 19, 1829 (Johann Peter Eckermann, *Gespräche mit Goethe,* ed. Ernst Beutler [Zurich, 1949], p. 355), Goethe says: "The landscapes have the highest truth, but no trace of reality. Claude Lorrain knew the real world to the last detail, and he used it as a means to express the world of his fair soul. This is genuine ideality, which makes use of real means in such a way that the true appearance produces an illusion, as if it were real."

19. On various aspects of this influence, see Francisco Márquez Villanueva, "Fray Antonio de Guevara y la invención de Cide Hamete," in *Fuentes literarias cervantinas* (Madrid, 1973), pp. 183–257.

20. In such passages we see how the great swerves of Cervantes's imagination (the forms of stylization and other major structures) which determine the course taken by the stories and the connections between them are also condensed in minimal emblems or signs, brief versions of the same figure of the imagination. In chap. 1, for example, I examined the many details that signal transitions of imaginary region, prefiguring them. We have also seen that the shifting of Cervantes's imaginative style (which heads first toward reality and then moves away from it toward idealization, only to return surreptitiously to a disguised depth of reality) is manifested microtextually in characteristic phrases, such as those I have cited from the *Quixote*'s first chapter.

Another of the work's constitutive principles that becomes ubiquitous in minor units of the design is double ironic objectification, where one can distinguish (1) the mimetic plane of what is referentially represented (the characters, circumstances, and actions, whose emergence is made possible when the narrative discourse becomes transparent), and (2) the metanarrative plane, whose activation draws the reader's gaze back and redirects it toward the representation itself and its lines of style, and even toward the narrative discourse as a linguistic entity. Thus these linguistic forms, whose primary function lends them the imperceptibility of a crystalline medium, become opaque and visible. The first syntagm of the extensive work ("In a place of La Mancha . . .") is already a sign of that duality (on the one hand of reference, and on the other of a reflection on the expressive medium), for at the same time that it is part of a narrative-mimetic sentence, it is an undeclared quotation. Literariness emerges sharply next to the narrated world, although readers may not tell themselves so. Thus we appreciate the macro- and microtextual insistence of the fundamental vectors of the Cervantine design. (In regard to the traditional motif, see María Rosa Lida, "De cuyo nombre no quiero acordarme . . . ," *Revista de Filología Hispánica* 1 [1939]: 167–71.)

21. Azorín, "La evolución de la sensibilidad," in *Clásicos y modernos* (Buenos Aires, 1939), pp. 33–36.

22. Mikhail Bakhtin, *Rabelais and His World,* trans. Helene Iswolsky (Cambridge, Mass. 1968). Also relevant here are Manuel Durán, "El *Quijote* a través del prisma de Mikhail Bakhtin: Carnaval, disfraces, escatología y locura," in *Cervantes and the Renaissance,* ed. Michael D. McGaha (Easton, Pa., 1980), pp. 71–86, and James A. Parr, *"Don Quixote": An Anatomy of Subversive Discourse* (Newark, Del., 1988), chap. 8.

23. Joaquín Casalduero noted this: *Sentido y forma del "Quijote"* (Madrid, 1970), p. 176. Incidentally, he understands Zoraida's story as a monolithically didactic example of conversion and Catholic faith.

24. This passage from Aristotle is echoed in chap. 44 of Part Two of the *Quixote*, where Cide Hamete asks "that he be praised, not for what he writes, but for what he has refrained from writing."

25. Francisco Ayala, "Los dos amigos," in *Los ensayos: Teoría y crítica literaria* (Madrid, 1972), pp. 695–714. Georges Güntert also underlines the significance of the story of "ill-advised curiosity" for the *Quixote* as a whole: "El 'Curioso impertinente': Novela clave del *Quijote*," in *Cervantes: Su obra y su mundo*, ed. Manuel Criado de Val (Madrid, 1981), pp. 783–88.

26. See Diana de Armas Wilson's " 'Passing the Love of Women': The Intertextuality of *El curioso impertinente*," *Cervantes* 7 (1987): 9–28. This feminist study illuminates the sociocultural and ethical dimension of the story.

27. In his analysis of "The Man of Ill-Advised Curiosity," Cesáreo Bandera calls attention to the similarity between Anselmo's conduct toward Lotario and Cardenio's toward Don Fernando: see his *Mimesis conflictiva* (Madrid, 1975), esp. chaps. 4 and 8. His interpretation of their behavior, which follows René Girard's theory of triangular desire in *Mensonge romantique et vérité romanesque* (Paris, 1961), is very different from the one I propose. For Bandera, as for Girard, desire, rivalry, and conflict between men are the consequence of a straying of the imagination, of a "mimetic fiction," in which the aura of divinity is transferred to human beings, making them idols. Desire is always the other's desire, and therefore it is always triangular and conflictive. An ordinary expression of this alienation is romancesque literature; its best expression as well as its cure is the novel at its great moments. The novel's truth is the revelation of this tragic insubstantiality of desire and of conflict, and of the demonic effect of fiction and literature on human life. That, in brief, is Girard's and Bandera's striking idea. Although I have insistently described aspects of the Cervantine creation that represent a criticism of literary imagination (especially but not exclusively of its romancesque forms), my understanding of Cervantes's anthropological depth is quite the opposite of Girard's. To see human passion as a consequence of an error of a heretical mind is to see it as something essentially correctable. This optimistic anthropology has little in common with the melancholy irony manifested by the *Quixote*.

28. José Ortega y Gasset, *Estudios sobre el amor* (1941), in *Obras completas*, vol. 5 (Madrid, 1947).

29. Carroll Johnson makes an interesting observation: that Anselmo's name can be associated with that of St. Anselm, the author of the ontological proof of God's existence, a seeker of rational certainty when only faith is possible. See Carroll B. Johnson, *Madness and Lust: A Psychoanalytic Approach to "Don Quixote"* (Berkeley, 1983), p. 215n.

30. We could say, in Bakhtin's terms, that "The Man of Ill-Advised Curiosity" is the only "monoglot" story in the *Quixote*. For this reason, and also because it is a "tragic" work, it cannot be "novelistic." See Mikhail Bakhtin, *The Dialogic Imagination*, trans. Caryl Emerson and Michael Holquist (Austin, Tex., 1981).

31. Ciriaco Morón Arroyo, *Nuevas meditaciones del "Quijote"* (Madrid, 1976), p. 324, recalls that this is an Aristotelian and scholastic definition, a fact that accords well with the rationalistic tenor of the narrative.

32. In reference to this poetic vision, we can speak of a cognitive process in which discovery and concealment unite and alternate.

33. Actually, without "The Man of Ill-Advised Curiosity" and its naturalistic element, the *Quixote* would seem stylistically determined by the desire to bypass and elude the despairing naturalism of Mateo Alemán's *Guzmán de Alfarache*, published in 1599, when Cervantes presumably was conceiving and elaborating the First Part.

34. Pp. 309 and 346 of vol. 2 of Luis Andrés Murillo's edition (Madrid, 1978).

35. Lodovico Castelvetro, *Poetica d'Aristotele volgarizzata e sposta* (1570), ed. Werther Romani (Bari, 1978); Sir Philip Sidney, *The Defense of Poesie* (1583); Pierre Corneille, "Des trois unités," in his *Discours* (1660); John Dryden, *Essay on Dramatic Poesie* (1668). For Vincenzo Maggi and Francesco Bonciani, see Weinberg, *History of Literary Criticism*, pp. 415 and 540. Sidney's and Dryden's texts, as well as a translation of Corneille's, can be found in Hazard Adams, *Critical Theory since Plato* (New York, 1971).

36. *Samuel Johnson on Shakespeare*, ed. H. R. Woudhuysen (London, 1989), p. 134. Cervantes reduces the classicist theory of theatrical illusion to absurdity in the scene of Don Quixote's reaction to Maese Pedro's puppet show. This will be confirmed by the discourse of Comedy in the second act of *The Fortunate Ruffian:*

> It little matters to the spectator
> That in an instant I pass
> From Germany to Guinea
> Without moving from the theater.
> Thought is swift,
> They can well accompany me.

37. Wayne Booth, *The Rhetoric of Fiction* (Chicago, 1961); Dorrit Cohn, *Transparent Minds* (Princeton, 1978); Franz Stanzel, *Theorie des Erzählens* (Göttingen, 1979); Gérard Genette, *Narrative Discourse*, trans. Jane E. Lewin (Ithaca, N.Y., 1980), and *Narrative Discourse Revisited*, trans. Jane E. Lewin (Ithaca, N.Y., 1988).

38. Knud Togeby, *La composition du roman "Don Quijote"* (Copenhagen, 1957).

39. Giovan Battista Pigna, *I romanzi: Terzo libro*, ed. Neuro Bonifazi (Urbino, 1975).

40. Lubbock, *Craft of Fiction*.

41. I have spoken repeatedly of the "dissimulated" or "semihidden" depth of the *Quixote*, and of the symbols, allegories, and parables that lead to significations that are not immediately apparent. But the horizon of meaning to which these concepts refer is always that of the potentially *conscious* human experience, with its enigmas and its epistemological, aesthetic, ethical, characterological, political perplexities. This implies that I have explored the field encompassed by traditional culture, which author and readers are immediately free to examine, however strenuous this may turn out to be. Although I know that the difference is problematic and imprecise, it seems to me that a Freudian interpretation of this work, as of all works, is radically different. For there the reader's spontaneous

thinking (even if it is persistent) cannot lead to the postulated *hidden* sense of the symbols. Freudian methodology needs the mediation of a theoretical, hypothetical construction of interpretive codes. Its result is not a deepening of the current sense of things but its total invalidation and surprising replacement by a hitherto unknown system of intrapsychic dynamisms, which civilized life has repressed automatically and relegated to an absolute, inaccessible unconscious. Is this methodological difference as radical as I sketch it here? Is the hypothetical psychoanalytical truth inherently deprived of phenomenological-intuitive verification? I only suggest the difficulty of these questions. This note is occasioned by an interesting series of Cervantist publications of varied, heterodox, original psychoanalytical orientation: Carroll Johnson's *Madness and Lust;* Eduardo González, "Del *Persiles* y la Isla Bárbara: Fábulas y reconocimientos," *MLN* 94, no. 2 (1979): 222–57; Louis Combet, *Cervantès, ou les incertitudes du désir* (Lyon, 1980); Ruth El Saffar, *Beyond Fiction: The Recovery of the Feminine in the Novels of Cervantes* (Berkeley, 1984); Diana de Armas Wilson, " 'Passing the Love of Women': The Intertextuality of *El curioso impertinente*," *Cervantes* 7 (1987): 9–28.

Epilogue

1. See Aristophanes's *Frogs* and Plato's *Ion* and *Republic* (bks. 2, 3, 10).

2. Frank Kermode, *The Classic* (London, 1975); Stanley Fish, *Is There a Text in This Class?* (Cambridge, Mass., 1980).

3. This distinction is *not* identical to E. D. Hirsch's well-known distinction between "meaning" and "significance" (*Validity in Interpretation* [New Haven, 1967]). In both theoretical stances, however, a stable object is postulated (the "reading" as well as the "meaning"), along with an open series of varying actualizations or reactions (that of the critical conceptions as well as that of the subjective, historical, relative "significances"). I cannot enter into an analysis of these concepts here. I will only suggest that my notion of a satisfactory plain reading includes part of what Hirsch calls the "significance" of the work, and therefore it assumes that not everything in this "significance" is relative.

4. I realize that the hermeneutic problem I have touched upon here is too complex for cursory treatment. Elsewhere I have tried to clarify these and other points of methodology. The interested reader can refer to my articles "Lectura y crítica," *Revista Canadiense de Estudios Hispánicos* 1 (1977): 209–16; "Hermeneutic Criticism and the Description of Form," in *Interpretation of Narrative,* ed. Mario J. Valdés and Owen J. Miller (Toronto, 1978), pp. 78–99; "Fenomenología y crítica: Notas para una discusión," *Dispositio* 9 (1984): 91–106; and "The Stability of Literary Meaning," in *Identity of the Literary Text,* ed. Mario J. Valdés and Owen J. Miller (Toronto, 1985), pp. 231–45.

5. This is a principal theme of Wolfgang Iser's theory of literary reception. See Iser, *The Act of Reading: A Theory of Aesthetic Response* (Baltimore, 1978). See

also my essay "Erzählungsstruktur und ontologische Schichtenlehre," in *Erzählforschung 1*, ed. Wolfgang Haubrichs (Göttingen, 1976), pp. 175–83. For a perspective on the *Quixote* related to Ingarden's and Iser's theories of reading, see Darío Fernández-Morera, "Cervantes and the Aesthetics of Reception," *Comparative Literature Studies* 18 (1981): 405–19.

6. Howard Mancing, *The Chivalric World of "Don Quixote": Style, Structure, and Narrative Technique* (Columbia, Mo., 1982), p. 97. I referred to the pertinent passage of E. C. Riley's *"Don Quixote"* (London, 1986) in chap. 1, n. 17.

7. References to my epigraphs are: Miguel de Cervantes, *Viaje del Parnaso*, ed. Francisco Rodríguez Marín (Madrid, 1935), p. 19. Sir Philip Sidney, *An Apology for Poetry*, in Charles Kaplan and William Anderson, *Criticism: Major Statements* (New York, 1991), p. 132. Dr. Johnson, "Preface to Shakespeare," in *Samuel Johnson on Shakespeare*, ed. H. R. Woudhuysen (London, 1989), pp. 130–31. Fernando de Herrera, *Obras de Garcilaso de la Vega con anotaciones de Fernando de Herrera*, ed. Antonio Gallego Morell (Madrid, 1973), p. 507. Giovambattista Strozzi, *Dell'unitá della favola*, cited by B. Weinberg, *A History of Literary Criticism in the Italian Renaissance* (Chicago, 1961), vol. 2, p. 705 (my translation). Plotinus's passage is cited in William K. Wimsatt and Cleanth Brooks, *Literary Criticism: A Short History*, vol. 1: *Classical and Neoclassical Criticism* (Chicago, 1978), p. 114 (their translation, slightly modified). S. T. Coleridge, "Shakespeare's Judgment Equal to His Genius," in Hazard Adams, *Critical Theory since Plato* (New York, 1971), p. 462. Raimundo Lida, "Vértigo del Quijote," *Asomante* 18 (1962), p. 7. Wilhelm Dilthey, *Einleitung in die Geisteswissenschaften: Versuch einer Grundlegung für das Studium der Gesellschaft und der Geschichte* (Stuttgart, 1959), vol. 1, p. 143. William Blake, *Annotations to Sir Joshua Reynolds's "Discourses,"* in *Poetry and Prose of William Blake*, ed. Geoffrey Keynes (London, 1939), p. 801. J. W. Goethe's lines from the poem "Vermächtnis" are cited by Wolfgang Kayser on the closing page of his *Das literarische Kunstwerk: Eine Einführung in die Literaturwissenschaft* (Bern, 1948).

Index of Authors

(This index includes editors but not translators)

Library of Congress Cataloging-in-Publication Data

Martínez-Bonati, Félix.
  "Don Quixote" and the poetics of the novel / Félix Martínez-Bonati;
  Translated by Dian Fox in collaboration with the author.
      p. cm.
  Translated from the author's unpublished Spanish manuscript.
  Includes bibliographical references and index.
  ISBN 0-8014-2359-7
    1. Cervantes Saavedra, Miguel de, 1547–1616. Don
  Quixote. 2. Cervantes Saavedra, Miguel de, 1547–1616—
  Technique. 3. Fiction—History and criticism. I. Title.
  PQ6353.M369 1992
  863'.3—dc20   92-5913